"I took the Swedish team Malmo to I   tournament Derek had organised. Wall   everybody seemed to say hello to 'Jesus'. I took the Switzerland national team there in the mid '90s and it was the same again. I never saw him play, but he has some story to tell!"

— *Roy Hodgson CBE*
Manager, England national football team, 2012-2016

"I first met Derek when I came out to Hong Kong for the Sevens in 1990 just after Scotland had won the Grand Slam. We thought we were the heroes but the real Hong Kong heroes were 'Jesus' and his great pal Walter Gerrard, aka the Water Buffalo, who we enjoyed so many happy times with over the years. What a pair of Scots they were together."

— *Gavin Hastings OBE*
Former captain, Scotland national rugby team

"Derek Currie is one of the friendliest and smartest people I have ever known. He is not only an extremely talented football player, but also shows outstanding sportsmanship – I don't think I have ever seen him lose his temper, on or off the pitch. Even before retiring from football, he was a great businessman and developed numerous partnerships with people from all walks of life. Due to his iconic long-haired, bearded look, we, the Hong Kong media, nicknamed him 'Jesus'.

Derek was one of the first foreign footballers to play in Hong Kong and played a pivotal role in bringing quality to the Hong Kong game. His skills and performance brought us to new heights, kickstarting a 10-year breakthrough period in local football – the most remarkable period post-WWII. Derek truly is an icon for Hong Kong football."

— *Lai Yu-ching*
Sports television producer, Hong Kong

"Like Derek Currie, I was a youngster when I first went to Hong Kong, only 18 when I first met him; by then he was already a local football legend. But our joint love of racing led us to becoming great friends.

Derek went on to become champion tipster in the racing sections of the *Hong Kong Standard* and *South China Morning Post* and I'm tipping this book will be another winner."

— *Philip Robinson*
Winner of five English & Irish Classics, twice Hong Kong champion jockey

"If you ever walk down the streets of Hong Kong alongside Derek Currie, you'd better be prepared to stop frequently. Football fans of various ages, aunties who remember his beard and once-long hair, F&B professionals who encountered him during his time as a marketer for Carlsberg… they all excitedly stop to greet the man they affectionately call 'Yeh-so' (Jesus) because of his iconic look. These encounters are always filled with smiles and genuine affection for a man who symbolised a special era for Hong Kong – a time when sport and showbiz went hand in hand, when East and West met in the exotic, thriving melting pot that was 1970s and '80s Hong Kong. And at the pulsing heart of it all was this twinkling-eyed Scotsman and adopted Hong Konger.

As someone who spent his formative years there, I was privileged to both watch Derek play football and to witness him work his magic at sporting events, press launches, race meets… all of which you will read about here. This is both a captivating story of one man's journey from Glasgow to the Far East and a nostalgic throwback to a magical lost age in a truly unique setting."

— *John Dykes*
Sports television anchor, Singapore

When 'Jesus' Came to Hong Kong

The remarkable story of the first
European football star in Asia

Derek Currie

BLACKSMITH BOOKS

DEDICATION

To the people of Hong Kong who accepted me as a welcome
guest, not an intruder, and made this book possible

When 'Jesus' Came to Hong Kong

ISBN 978-988-76748-0-1

Published by Blacksmith Books
Unit 26, 19/F, Block B, Wah Lok Industrial Centre,
37-41 Shan Mei Street, Fo Tan, Hong Kong
Tel: (+852) 2877 7899
www.blacksmithbooks.com

Editors:
John Charlesworth
Paul Christensen

Contents

Foreword by Craig Brown CBE 7

Preface by Mike Ingham 9

PART ONE: Life of football

1   Learning a lesson 13

2   From Douglas Park to the World of Suzie Wong 17

3   Chickens' feet, kung fu and history in the making 29

4   The good, the bad, and the ugly 37

5   Famous names 47

6   Rules, Proud Mary, and Good Morning, Vietnam 58

7   Looting the Tai-Pan's trophy cabinet 74

8   Sunset over Manila Bay, taming a German giant... and
eventually paying the price. 81

9   Looking good, eating well, and mixing it with the stars 95

10   Time for a change... and a chance to lead a team
against Eusébio 106

11   Ernie's House of Horrors, dancing in the street, and
keeping Hong Kong clean 118

12   The Sport of Kings. 129

13   The Lawman and the Cranhill sounds 141

14   Snakes alive, Fast Wullie and a Double Scotch 152

15   Every shirt tells a story (with apologies to Rod Stewart) . . . 164

16   Beating the Drum... and a legend with a heart of gold 209

17   Interlude: The Yellow Rose of Texas 215

18   Sweet and Sour 230

19   Hall of Fame... or should that be infamy? 236

20   Cordoba Revenge and one night in Bangkok 243

21   A helping hand... or three 252

22   The long goodbye. 264

PART TWO: Life after football

23   Probably the best beer in the world 276

24   The Carlsberg Cup. 288

25   The Jockeys Dash. 302

26   Rugby shorts 307

27   Four World Cups and four European Championships 322

28   Live at the Hong Kong Hotel with Stevie Wonder
and Marvelous Marvin Hagler. 340

29   The Hong Lok Yuen All-Stars. 356

30   Going to the dogs 366

31   The Currie stable 369

32   Lasting impressions 384

      Acknowledgements 402

Foreword

The epitome of Scotland, of Scottish football! That's none other than Derek Currie, the author of this engrossing autobiography. All the trademark Scottish traits are to the fore in the gregarious personality of this popular guy who left Cranhill, not the most salubrious area of his native Glasgow, to forge an illustrious playing career, and extended life, in Hong Kong.

There's an anti-hero syndrome in Derek's native country. You're not allowed to be good at something without the inevitable mistaken notion that "He's too big for his boots, he's making too much money, etc." My experience is that the bigger the star, the more humble he is. Legends like Jackie Stewart, Paul Lawrie, Alan Wells, Stephen Hendry, Andy Murray and football greats like Sir Alex Ferguson, Sir Kenny Dalglish, and Denis Law all have admirable humility. So has Derek Currie.

Having been to Hong Kong on several occasions I've seen the admiration, even adulation, shown to Derek and yet he remains the same level-headed, grounded individual who left Scotland in 1970, aged 21. Back 'home' he was from a sport-minded family as we learn in the book. Oldest brother, Dick, was a Commonwealth flyweight gold medallist and his middle brother John was a professional footballer good enough to be signed for Rangers. Arguably Derek was the star of the family who, as he explains in the text, played for three of the best youth teams in Glasgow, then at junior professional level at the same club as Kenny Dalglish, Cumbernauld Juniors, then Cumnock Juniors. Believe me, he was a much sought-after youngster before he signed for Motherwell FC after excelling in trial matches against Celtic and Rangers.

In the captivating text which follows we learn how Derek responded to an advertisement from Hong Kong to uproot and go abroad. Two super guys accompanied him, Jackie Trainer and the ebullient Walter Gerrard, soon to be nicknamed 'the Water Buffalo'. I had the privilege of meeting this colossus of a guy much later when he had finished playing and was a rep in the licence trade. Both he and Derek couldn't go anywhere without being recognised, with autographs constantly requested. Had it been in the time of 'selfies' they would never have been able to move.

A coaching colleague of mine, Archie Knox, ex-Aberdeen, Manchester United, Rangers, Scotland Assistant Manager and Manager of Dundee, another with the traditional Scottish sense of humour, when asked about Derek told me, "Aye, when I was in Hong Kong he wrote the horse racing column for the *South China Morning Post*. I asked him for any tips and was given two 'certainties'. Neither finished the race!"

Being a lively character there often was controversy when Derek was around. None more than in his first game in Hong Kong when an attempt from Walter Gerrard was looking like a certain goal when it was deflected into the net from the head of Currie. Who was credited with the goal? If I were Derek I think I'd give the goal to his gargantuan teammate rather than alienate the big fellow who was convinced the ball was going in before the additional head-flick.

The excellent read that is this autobiography makes me regret that, although I had the responsibility of the Scotland national team for nine years, I never had the opportunity to rectify the fact that a player of Derek's ability was not the recipient of a Scotland international cap. He did get selected for Hong Kong but I'm sure a deserved accolade from the country of his birth would have been worthy acknowledgement for a man who was a fine player and a thorough gentleman.

Craig Brown CBE
Scotland Manager (1993-2001)

Preface

"I'm going to sidetrack briefly", Derek Currie puts it, tongue firmly in cheek, introducing one of the many memorable anecdotes in this fascinating memoir of a late 20th-century working life. His book is a must-read for anyone who remembers the iconic 'Jesus' of Hong Kong as a star footballer and, subsequently, sports journalist, racehorse owner, Carlsberg representative and all-round city celebrity. However, it is also highly accessible to the younger reader to whom the household names Currie played with or met, and in some cases befriended – Pelé, Eusébio, George Best, Jack Charlton, Kenny Dalglish, and many more, including pop artists such as Rod Stewart and Stevie Wonder – might be less familiar. His fast-paced narrative digressions are somewhat analogous to the swift jinking runs and mazy dribbles that characterised his footballing career in Hong Kong in the 1970s and early 80s, and earned him hatfuls of goals, as defenders floundered in his wake. Indeed, his book is artfully constructed around these sudden changes of pace and direction in the manner of a Best, or a Pelé, or indeed a Currie!

People, events and places are generously highlighted in this retrospective more than Currie's personal achievements. The author engages the reader from the very beginning, offering an inside view of a now-vanished era of Hong Kong history. And this is one of the memoir's major strengths. His recollections evoke a period that I dimly remember with affection from my early years in Hong Kong at the end of the eighties, one without the internet or smartphones.

While he pays tribute to his fellow football players, both Hong Kong Chinese and expatriate Scotsmen, Englishmen, Irishmen and others, Currie also succeeds in painting a kaleidoscopic portrait of a time when East and West most felicitously bonded in the city. Between his arrival in the summer of 1970 on a bumpy plane ride into a sweltering Kai Tak airport at the tender age of 21 up until the early years of the millennium, a dynamic process of economic development and popular culture transformation occurred. It was a process that turned Hong Kong's fortunes around, and changed it from a colonial relic struggling to recover from the Japanese occupation during WWII into one of the most vibrant cities on the planet.

Blissfully unaware of it at the time of his arrival – as a raw but talented recruit to a Hong Kong Rangers team under martinet manager Ian Petrie – he would become part of that remarkable transformation of the city. Dubbed 'Ye So', meaning 'Jesus' in Cantonese, by Hong Kong football fans on account of his long curly hair and beard, Currie was an instant hit. Their love of him in his many games for local sides, as well as for various Hong Kong international XIs, was keenly reciprocated by the 'flying Scotsman'. To judge by the many affectionate references in his book to Hong Kong people and places, Currie quickly formed a strong affinity with the city generally, and not just its football fans. In many ways, his memoir is a paean to the dynamism of Hong Kong at this time, a city he refers to as "my adopted home".

Naturally, the sociable young Currie was delighted to rub shoulders with football greats such as Pelé – whose visit with Santos in Currie's first season in Hong Kong was the magnet that drew him to the city and ensured his signature on the dotted line – but his memoir gives us insights into aspects of expatriate life of the period that entertainingly complement those of more official Hong Kong histories.

His deep affection for Hong Kong people and places shines through: for example, talking of much-loved Cantopop icon, Anita Mui, who for a time was his neighbour, Currie writes that she was "the 'Madonna' of the East and would go on to become one of Asia's best loved singers, until sadly cervical cancer took her young life away at the tender age of just 40. I should have been the one wishing her well! 'Ah Mui' as she was known to music lovers in Hong Kong ultimately became one of their musical treasures." Typically, he acknowledges that although his face was more famous to Hong Kongers at the time and she recognised him, he ought to have been the one wishing her well for her stellar career, had he known who she would become. Likewise, his description of meetings with Hong Kong doyens, such as journalist Richard Hughes at the Foreign Correspondents' Club – the person responsible for the memorable Hong Kong epithet "borrowed place, borrowed time" – is a delightful vignette of a man famously fictionalised by John Le Carré as the FCC-based journalist Old Craw in his great novel *The Honourable Schoolboy.*

When 'Jesus' Came to Hong Kong, with its many skilfully handled flashbacks and flash-forwards, employs a chatty style and an impressive memory for detail. This gift derives undoubtedly from his latter-day career in sports journalism, in which a sharp eye for detail, a flair for finding the right words and an encyclopaedic knowledge of the game are enormous assets to the writer. Currie's memoir paints a compelling picture of a freewheeling, exuberant and imaginative city that the author depicts with wit, verve and a hint of nostalgia.

A football tour to Saigon, then only a couple of years away from capitulating to the North Vietnamese, is vividly depicted: what sounded to Currie and his teammates like fireworks turned out to be live ammunition from the nearby front line! He spares his thoughts for the young South Vietnamese soldiers in the opposition team, destined to return to the fighting after their brief respite. His excursions, to the U.S. to play professional football there for a brief period, and subsequently to Mexico City and then Italy and the U.S. to cover the FIFA World Cup competition for the Hong Kong anglophone press, likewise sparkle with observations.

Some robust 'mistimed' tackles by Hong Kong rival teams are the subject of some of the football-focused first half of the book, as well as appreciation of the flair players of international guest teams. Reference to a Sporting Lisbon jersey exchanged with one such star player segues into a wonderful anecdote about the time Currie arranged a kick-about game on the Happy Valley sports field for football-mad singer Rod Stewart and guitarist Ronnie Wood.

The book's second half is devoted to the author's Hong Kong experiences after hanging up his boots in his mid-thirties. Accounts of meeting icons such as Stevie Wonder (unexpectedly introduced by boxing legend Marvin Hagler) as well as charity events, including an unusual Star Ferry marathon, are woven throughout. His forays into boxing, rugby and especially horse-racing, the sport not only of kings but particularly of Hong Kongers, are described with the same winning blend of panache and accuracy for names and places.

As fellow working-class Scot and Liverpool manager Bill Shankly famously said in response to a journalist's question of whether a football match was a matter of life and death: "It's more important than that!" For Currie, sport, and especially football, has been his life, and he knows he has been a lucky man to have been transplanted to Hong Kong in his youth to fulfil his sporting dreams. Despite his evident affection for compatriots and pride in his nation's sporting achievements (and even its underachievements), Hong Kong comes across as the place that dominated his life. On his return from a three-month stint playing 'soccer' in Texas, he writes, "My heart was really in Hong Kong, not San Francisco, or any other American city. Texas steak knives were replaced by chopsticks; the Yellow Rose by the Bauhinia. I was home again."

Hong Kong holds a special place in the hearts of many expatriates who made their home here. Few, however, have attained Ye So's iconicity and for many his mere nickname awakes happy memories of an exciting chapter in Hong Kong's not-so-distant past. He prefaces his final chapter with the following reflection: "Over the years I've met some amazing people. With some it was just for a chat; others became great friends. All have contributed to a lifetime of memories." For me, these words read like a dedication of his memoir by the 'Jesus' of Hong Kong to all those friends, whether from East or West, that he met on his life journey.

Mike Ingham
Author, *Hong Kong: A Cultural and Literary History*

PART ONE: Life of football

1

Learning a lesson

We left our top floor flat at 123 John Knox Street in Glasgow for the last time. It was late in the evening but a half-moon illuminated the lorry transporting the family belongings.

It was farewell to the cold dark shared outside toilet and the gloomy view of the Glasgow Necropolis opposite, the resting place of over 3,000 souls. The Victorian flat was almost a century old and 200 yards from the oldest house in Glasgow, 'The Provand's Lordship', dating back to 1471.

The Currie family were heading to the newly built spacious housing estate of Cranhill on the city's eastern outskirts. A three bedroom apartment on the top floor of 75 Crowlin Crescent, with wonderful views over the Edinburgh Road towards Carntyne and Shettleston awaited.

I was six years old and fell asleep in the lorry.

It was a new start for the family and there were grassy fields for a youngster to run and play in. I could kick a ball around with new found friends instead of playing hide and seek in the Necropolis. There was a bedroom for my Mum and Dad, one for oldest brother Dick, and the last one I shared with my middle brother John. Most importantly, we had an inside toilet... luxury.

Soon I was enrolled at Lamlash School, where most playtimes I got into fights. My oldest brother was a famous boxer so other kids thought if they could take me down they would be famous for a short while. Later I moved to Milncroft Primary School, also on the housing estate. There were no more scraps, playtime was spent playing football with a tennis ball, two jackets serving as goalposts.

I joined the Life Boys, the junior section of the Boys Brigade, which was similar to the Boy Scouts. I think I joined when I was around eight years old or so. To be truthful I only joined because they had a football team. Despite my age I went straight into the team with kids two years older and I remember we won the Glasgow Life Boys final on one of Lethamhill's ash pitches near Barlinnie Prison. We took no prisoners, and won by 14 goals to 3; I scored five goals and Kenny Aird scored six.

Barlinnie still has inmates; Lethamhill's football pitches are now a motorway.

Kenny Aird would go on to play successfully with St Johnstone and Hearts in later years. He would be acclaimed as the best footballer in Cranhill, although a boy called Jimmy Smith, who went to St Gregory's school could dispute that title. Jimmy, or 'Jinky' as he was called later, became one of the best ever players to grace the colours of Newcastle United.

I was in good company.

A couple of young lads went to the same Milncroft Primary School as me, although a few years after I left to go to Cranhill Senior Secondary. They would become much more famous than Kenny or Jimmy, not with a ball, but with a band called AC/DC. They were called Malcolm and Angus.

I soon represented my school teams and my city at youth levels, also playing for leading amateur sides Glasgow United, Possil YM and Queen's Park Victoria XI as I grew older.

Once I got a trial for the famous youth side Drumchapel Amateurs under-15 side. I thought I played well, but they thought I was too small and lightly built; they didn't know I had only just turned 13 at the time.

I went on to play for Cumbernauld United Juniors, alongside a youngster called Kenny Dalglish, and also played for Cumnock Juniors in Ayrshire.

Ayrshire rivals, Kello Rovers wanted to sign me, but I had already signed an agreement with Cumnock, so they were forced to sign another lad called Quintin Young. Ironically, that year, when the Scotland Junior side was selected, I was beaten by one vote for the outside left position, by Quintin Young.

Quintin went on to join Ayr United under manager Ally McLeod, then to Coventry City, before joining Glasgow Rangers for three seasons and playing over 80 games for the club.

While at Cumnock Juniors I was invited for a trial at Motherwell. Well actually two trials. They were friendly games, both on home turf at Fir Park, the first would be on the Saturday against Glasgow Rangers, the second on the Monday night against Glasgow Celtic.

Playing against both Old Firm teams within three days, something special.

Rangers had a strong team that Saturday afternoon which included Jim Baxter, I was on the left wing, the full-back I was facing was Alex Miller. I had played against him a few years earlier when he was with Clydebank Strollers and knew him and his older brother, Jimmy, quite well; their dad worked alongside mine at John Brown's shipyard.

Alex would spend 15 seasons at Rangers, and that day we had a fine old tussle, but Rangers beat us 3-2. After the final whistle Alex whispered to me "don't do or sign anything, the boss wants to talk to you." The 'boss' was Rangers manager David White.

Knowing a few of the Rangers boys, including Baxter, McKinnon and Miller, I got a lift back to Glasgow after the game on the Rangers team bus and ended up playing cards at the back of the bus.

The Monday night came, it was a farewell game for Charlie Gallacher of Celtic as well as a friendly game under the Fir Park lights with Celtic fielding a strong side. Again, we lost by the same 3-2 scoreline, but I thought I fared well in both games.

So much so, someone must have leaked something to the press, because a few days later there was a back page story in the *Scottish Daily Express* with a headline and picture: "Rangers step in for Currie".

Before I knew it I had Motherwell manager Bobby Howitt chasing me up and asking what was going on? I still had a year of my apprenticeship as a compositor to run and thought I might get a better chance at Motherwell, so I elected to join the Lanarkshire club.

At about the same time, on the other side of the world, a young Chinese lad named Kwok Ka-ming was helping his dad in their family restaurant cleaning dishes and running errands while being enrolled on the junior training course of the Hong Kong Football Association. He joined Hong Kong Rangers and eventually captained the team. He was the first Chinese player I ever met and became a good friend.

I soon learnt that part-time football left a lot to be desired in the upper echelons of the Scottish game, particularly in terms of fitness. I thought I was fit, but working five days a week with just two nights training at Fir Park I was far from it, as I would soon find out. During our training I hardly saw a ball, instead it was up terracing steps or lapping the field with the likes of Peter McCloy and Dixie Deans. The full-timers got their practice with a ball during the day.

I recall playing against Rangers in a reserve match – they used to attract a big crowd in the main stand at Ibrox for such matches. I was running to chase a ball and was about a yard behind Ranger's Alex McDonald, the same man who would become Hearts manager years later, but also a great footballer during his years with St Johnstone, Rangers and Hearts.

Knowing how fast I was, I thought I would make up the yard on Alex easily and win the ball. Wrong – I couldn't catch him. Alex was a full-timer, that's when I realised I had a long way to go to reach the fitness standards required for professional football.

That fitness would come, but I had to go to the other side of the world to achieve it.

2

From Douglas Park to the World of Suzie Wong

It was September 1970 and I was standing on a concrete airstrip 6,000 miles from home. The mid-afternoon sun bore down relentlessly; there was hardly a breath of wind, just the whine from jet engines, and from my companion.

"It's bloody hot and noisy standing here, let's move a bit further away." he said.

We walked 50 metres and stopped.

"It's not just the engines, it's just too bloody hot for me over here, I'll never be able to play football in this bloody heat."

My companion, Walter Gerrard, was a giant bull of a man with a powerful forehead, a square face and a rolling gait. All six feet one and 206 pounds of him. At 27 years of age he was a seasoned journeyman, having enjoyed spells at Barnsley and Berwick Rangers. He clearly felt he would have been better off back at Oakwell or Shielfield Park.

I couldn't blame him. We had landed at Don Muang Airport in Bangkok and the temperature was 94 degrees Fahrenheit (over 34 degrees Celsius).

"It might be the land of smiles", he said, "but I'm no smilin'. I'm getting back on the plane: I need a drink." With that, he headed back to the shimmering sanctuary that was our BOAC jet.

As I followed him, I wondered what life in the East had in store for a boy brought up in a Glasgow tenement.

It turned out the football was only part of an incredible journey.

I had just turned 21 and here I was, on the way to a new life in Hong Kong, along with Walter and a youngster called Jackie Trainer, a lad with stylish dark brown hair above a boyish face. We were to be the first three British footballers to play professionally in Asia.

My contract, signed at the Ivanhoe Hotel in Buchanan Street, Glasgow on August 17, was neatly folded away in my jacket pocket for safekeeping. It promised one hundred pounds a month, with a bonus of five pounds for winning a game and two pounds ten shillings for a draw. With the Hong Kong dollar exchange rate at around fourteen to the pound, that seemed pretty good to me.

A signing-on fee of fifty pounds – worth a lot more than it sounds today – was also appreciated, with a further fifty pounds if the club, Hong Kong Rangers, finished in the top three of the First Division.

You might be wondering why, at the tender age of 21, I had decided to get on a plane that would take me to a place on the other side of the world, about which I knew virtually nothing. My only previous contact being to buy a transistor radio for nineteen shillings and nine pence through a PO Box in North Point, Hong Kong.

Unless of course you count watching movies with my Mum when William Holden was falling in love with Jennifer Jones in the old classic *Love is a Many-Splendored Thing* and drooling over Nancy Kwan in *The World of Suzie Wong* – both filmed mainly in Hong Kong.

At the time I certainly didn't think that just a few years later I'd actually meet Nancy Kwan in person! (I was introduced to her by the man who dated her for quite a while, the jockey Peter Gumbleton.)

But before going off on a tangent like Billy Connolly I should mention that my Dad convinced me early on to learn a trade, warning me of the perils of football: a bad tackle could lead to a bad injury and, ultimately, the end of a dream.

My father worked at John Brown's shipyards and knew how tough life could be. He was playing the each-way card with me, and I appreciated that, so learning a trade it was.

I spent five years as an apprentice compositor in the printing trade – in a football sense perhaps five wasted years, five missed years of training full-time, but I had youth on my side. Despite my slight build and lack of height – just under 5 feet 9 inches – I was quick as lightning and knew how to put the ball in the net.

I always believed I had the ability to make it in the professional game and that my time would come. After all, the Swinging Sixties was the decade of dreams: the music of the Beatles, Rolling Stones, Manfred Mann, and the jokes of Tony Blackburn, on Radio Caroline (before he joined Radio One in 1967), so things couldn't be that bad. Some of Mr Blackburn's jokes were even funny.

I had played football for the Victoria XI, part of the famous Queen's Park Football Club. Steeped in history, it was the only amateur club in Britain playing in a professional league. Posh was not the word: we had to wear a blazer with the club crest to all our games, along with the official tie. We looked more like young bankers than lads going to play football on a Saturday afternoon. It was their centenary year while I was there, so it was a proud time for the Club.

Harold Davis, the ex-Glasgow Rangers stalwart, was the coach. Harold was a tough customer, he had enlisted and fought in the Korean War, got shot in the trenches and had to undergo 18 operations after taking bullets in the stomach and foot. He was nicknamed the 'Iron Man' in his playing days and I learnt a lot about fighting spirit playing under him.

I came from a sporting family. My Dad had been a very good junior footballer. My eldest brother Dick was a bit of a legend whilst I was still in short trousers being a former flyweight Commonwealth Gold Medallist and two-time British ABA Champion boxer. He then became chief boxing reporter for the *Daily Record*, the top-selling newspaper in Scotland at the time.

My middle brother John played at Ibrox for Glasgow Rangers for a time but because he was a part timer never got the jump up to the first team. Just newly married, he had another job, also as a compositor, and two wages went a long way in those days.

I decided to finish my five year apprenticeship before taking my chance for full-time football with a professional club. In my last year in Scotland I was part time with Motherwell.

So, how did I finally get my big break into full-time professional football?

Well, you could say it stemmed from the best World Cup tournament ever: Mexico 1970.

With the heat, humidity and altitude, the pace of the games there might have been slightly slower than usual, but they produced some of the finest individual displays ever seen on a football field. This was especially evident when the masters, Brazil, were playing. They made the game beautiful; movements almost poetic as players glided past opponents with ease and assurance – best illustrated by the greatest footballer of the time, Pelé.

You could hardly say that Carlos Alberto, Clodoaldo, Jairzinho or Tostão were merely part of the sideshow. They were junior royals; but Pelé was the king.

Now in early August of that same year, while the world of football was still swooning over Brazil and their destruction of Italy in the Aztec Stadium in Mexico City, I was heading to Douglas Park, home of Hamilton Academicals for a trial against a scratch side that had been put together by former footballer and writer Doug Baillie.

Doug, who later joined *The Sunday Post* (the Scottish one) as their chief football reporter, had good playing spells with Airdrie, Rangers and Falkirk. A giant of a man, his reports on football always put his readers in a good mood reading his amusing quips and anecdotes of the game. They were few better than Doug.

The offer of this trial had come about because of the disastrous season Hong Kong Rangers had just endured. Professional football was still in its infancy in East Asia, there was no influx of players from Europe and South America as there are today. Hong Kong Rangers' founder and manager Ian Petrie therefore came up with an ambitious project.

After consulting with team officials Dr Chiu But-york, Veronica Chiu (also known as Veronica Chan Yiu-kam, later one of the key figures in the development of women's football in Hong Kong), Willie Jorge and team captain, Kwok Ka-ming, Petrie embarked on a trip to Scotland to bring back quality players to strengthen the team.

Up until then, the main Scottish exports to Hong Kong had been bankers, accountants, policemen and whisky, not necessarily in that order.

An advertisement was placed in a leading Glasgow newspaper stating that Hong Kong Rangers were looking for players to join the club professionally; those wishing to be considered should attend an interview at the Central Hotel in Glasgow at a specified date and time.

A pal of mine told me about the interview and I more or less turned up just to keep him company, although I admit I was a little curious and a game of football was a game of football. A chance to play at Douglas Park on a Sunday morning was great, no matter what the occasion. Plus, there was always the possibility some other scouts might be at the game and I still hoped to get a chance at another club in Scotland on a full-time basis.

Dozens of applicants were interviewed and 20 were selected for a trial. I was one, along with Jackie Trainer and Walter Gerrard.

My trial only lasted ten minutes or so. I had just scored a goal with my head, hardly a common occurrence for me; unlike Walter Gerrard who was built for the aerial side of the game. After gliding the header into the corner of the net I was substituted. Having shown off my trademark darting runs I assumed it was to give other trialists an opportunity to demonstrate their skills.

I knew I had ability and could score goals, and that's what wins games. I was not strongly built, but I had strength in my legs and ran, and looked, like a whippet.

However, that was not what most managers looked for, even today they prefer tall, physically strong lads; except of course if you have the pedigree of a Messi or a Maradona.

I recall playing in a trial for Dumbarton on my 20th birthday – although it was an official Scottish second division game at their old home ground of Boghead Park against Berwick Rangers. The legendary Jock Wallace, whose name those with knowledge of the game will recognize, was Berwick's player manager at the time – he was a goalkeeper. But as the memory dims, I can't recall if he played that day.

We won by three goals to one and I scored two. I did get the ball in the net for my hat-trick, but it was disallowed for offside – not me, but someone standing near the touchline on the left side of the park not interfering with play. Of course that old offside rule has been scrapped now, and rightly so, but it cost me the birthday present of taking the ball home – the accepted prize for scoring three goals in a game, which is still carried forward to the present day.

Anyway, after the game my Dumbarton team mates for the day congratulated me and shook my hand; justifiably, I thought, as I had helped them get their win bonus, plus two more points to help them move up the league table.

The Dumbarton manager, Jackie Stewart, also shook my hand before I left and handed me my £5 playing fee in a brown envelope. He said "well done", but that was all. I felt like a losing ticket on a bookie's floor; obviously no offer was forthcoming despite the headline the next day: "Two-goal Currie seals win against the young 'Gers."

When my eldest brother, Dick, who knew Jackie Stewart quite well, asked him how I had performed his answer was: "Good player, fast and knows how to score, just too small and lightly built."

Does size really count that much if you are fast and can score goals? I was no giant, but hardly a midget. I'll prove these managers wrong I thought. But back to Douglas Park and the Hong Kong Rangers trial.

Petrie indicated that he would like to talk to me after I had showered and changed so I was not to leave the stadium. Half an hour after the game he ushered me to a quiet corner to have a word.

"We think you could be an asset to the club and would like to sign you and take you to Hong Kong" he said.

I asked if he could give me time to think about it. Then he hit me with the knockout punch.

"Santos and Pelé are coming to Hong Kong in December. We think you will be good enough to get into the Hong Kong League XI side to play against them."

"Pelé!" I repeated, mesmerized. My knees went weak, but my brain stayed focused: "Where do I sign?" Everything else went out the window.

An unbelievable opportunity had surfaced: from an interview that I had almost not attended to possibly playing against the greatest footballer of all time, only months after I had watched him on our 18-inch TV at home in Glasgow lift the Jules Rimet Trophy.

The world was getting smaller and I was getting taller.

Walter Gerrard and Jackie Trainer also signed on the dotted line and soon we were heading for the mysterious Far East and the World of Suzie Wong! The flight took 20 hours with stops in Beirut and Bangkok.

As we were just seconds from landing at the notorious Kai Tak, I glanced out the window and almost fell out of my seat as the plane banked sharply to the right. Hong Kong's International Airport was backed by hills and had a landing strip jutting out into the sea from the Kowloon Peninsula. Fortunately during the flight Kwok Ka-ming, the Rangers team captain, had warned us that it could be a scary landing. We soon understood why.

Approaching 'Checkerboard Hill' we could clearly see an orange and white marker painted onto the hillside as a landing guide. On seeing it the captain had to manoeuvre into a low altitude 47-degree turn at almost 200 miles an hour! The aircraft then shot over tall apartment buildings and busy streets, before wheels eventually touched down on the concrete runway, much to the audible relief of all on board.

People who regularly flew into Hong Kong in the old days said on many occasions they saw women leaning over balconies hanging out washing as the aircraft appeared to race between buildings before landing. I never did: my eyes were always tightly closed after the 47-degree turn.

Just before landing Petrie briefed us on what to expect and the enormity of the decision I had made in coming to this fabled city finally dawned on me.

"Guys, when we arrive in Hong Kong there will be a press conference at the airport. There could be a lot of journalists so be prepared. I will handle the introductions, but you must be ready for any type of question."

To be honest, we had little idea of what to expect in Hong Kong, or even what the standard of football was like. No pushing buttons on a keyboard, connecting to the internet, and getting quick answers to questions in those days. It felt like going on holiday to a strange exotic land: a tingle of excitement and a rush of adrenaline.

What we were not aware of at the time was that Hong Kong Rangers had been relegated at the end the previous season, along with the amateurs of the Hong Kong Football Club. Fortunately though, we would not be starting our professional careers in the second division. Petrie had carefully studied the HKFA laws and found that the first division could be extended to fourteen teams from the previous twelve.

Unbeknownst to us, a bitter legal battle had been going on for months between those who were in favour of an extension and those against.

Much of this was political bickering, but initially those against the extension seemed to be winning. Petrie apparently had many enemies in the local Football Association. To settle the many disputes he had engaged Mr Jackson-Lipkin from the lawyers Johnson, Stokes & Master, and eventually the case went to Hong Kong's Supreme Court. At the end of the day the Court ruled in favour of Petrie, and Rangers were given a lifeline.

This was the first time in the history of the Hong Kong Football Association that a case had gone to the Supreme Court. Ian Petrie was a determined man, and quite honestly he was the one who really helped get professional football in Hong Kong started.

A fellow Scot, Petrie had been looking through the advertisements column of a Scottish evening newspaper one bleak winter's day in February 1958 and had come across a job offer with a ship repair company in Hong

Kong. Had he not decided to put pen to paper and fill out an application, followed by interviews in Greenock and London which landed him the job, the story I am writing might never have happened.

Ian Petrie was a controversial character in many ways, but he had a great love of the game, and it was not long after arriving in the city that he formed a youth team, aptly named Hong Kong Rangers due to his Govan background in Glasgow.

Petrie, by all accounts, was a reasonable centre-forward himself. After a trial at the Hong Kong Football Club, under the watchful eye of Jimmy Mair, who went on to become General Manager of the Club, Petrie signed on; but his footballing career never really took off. Instead he turned his hand to refereeing, and by his own admission was a better whistler than striker.

He enjoyed great success with his Rangers youth side, while still finding time for refereeing duties. Eventually he was promoted to Class One Referee status and went on to join the FIFA list of international referees. His Rangers team eventually joined the professional ranks.

In 1961 Tom Finney received an invitation from the English FA to come out of retirement and manage, captain, and play for, an FA touring side to the Far East. In that side was a youngster by the name of Bobby Moore. Finney's penultimate game in the Far East was against Hong Kong and his boys ran out 4-2 winners. The referee that day was none other than, you guessed it, Ian Petrie.

Years later I would see a black and white picture of him and the great 'Preston Plumber' Sir Tom Finney, walking side-by-side out onto the field at the Hong Kong Government Stadium. Petrie was proud of that photograph and it rarely left his office in Causeway Bay.

I have little doubt that when his application for the Taikoo Dockyard job was accepted he could not have imagined that one day he would be walking out onto a football pitch with Finney and Moore.

But back, or rather forward, to September 1970.

After completing immigration formalities we emerged into the greeting area at Kai Tak airport. I can still recall saying to Walter Gerrard at the time, "There must have been someone famous on the plane, perhaps it was Steve McQueen." And we both laughed.

The reason for the comment was that in front of us was a melee of people who, on closer inspection, appeared to be mainly newspaper reporters, many with cameras strung around their necks. For good measure, there were TV crews too.

"They're here for you," Petrie said as the crowd surged forward.

Once a semblance of order had been restored we were asked to pose for photographs, then taken into a large room for a supposedly brief press conference. I am not exaggerating, Pelé couldn't have pulled a bigger crowd.

Petrie introduced us to the reporters in both Cantonese and English, giving a brief background on each player, with some additional help in Cantonese from club captain, Kwok Ka-ming.

He described Walter Gerrard as a strong header of the ball who would score goals and worry a lot of local centre-halves and would more than pay his way at the club. At the time Walter looked more like a heavyweight boxer than a footballer: he had a few stitches on his nose. When questioned by one member of the press Petrie said it was a clash of heads in a friendly match before they left.

In reality, it happened on the big man's farewell night when someone took exception to us enjoying a song in the pub, a thug from a local gang who 'glassed' Walter and turned a peaceful night into a fight. Without going into detail, the person responsible got his due comeuppance.

Boyish 18-year-old Jackie Trainer was described as a great prospect, plucked from under the noses of Queen's Park who had been keen to sign him. Jackie was carrying a Subbuteo set, the tabletop football game, and that certainly added to his boyishness. But the game was not meant to be a toy for him, rather a coaching aid for Petrie who planned to use it for tactical purposes on his boardroom table.

Petrie finally introduced me as playing in the style of Manchester United winger, George Best (I can assure you that description never came from me!)

Then the questions came as fast and furious as last orders on a Friday night in a Glasgow pub.

Not all of them pertaining to football. "Are you here for the women or just the money?" one asked.

"Never met any women and not been paid yet," I replied cheekily.

Rangers officials had already nicknamed me 'Flying Horse', so someone asked me how fast I was?

"Faster than Nijinsky," I replied, referring to the horse who had won the English Triple Crown; not to be confused with the ballet dancer born in Kyiv, I might add.

"Hippy-Haired Currie", was Neil Perera's description of me in the *South China Morning Post* the next day: "the most humorous of the three." Joking soon came to an end when we went through the rigours of Petrie's first training session at Happy Valley a few days later.

After the press conference we were taken from Kowloon to our accommodation on Hong Kong island. Until the opening of the Cross Harbour Tunnel in 1972, the only way to cross Victoria Harbour from Kowloon to Hong Kong was by ferry; either privately owned, or run by the Hong Kong and Yaumati vehicular ferry service.

I vividly recall my first sighting of Hong Kong island as I stood on the deck. As I breathed in the hot, humid air I gazed ahead expectantly; but all I saw was a skyline of never ending neon. I felt a tinge of disappointment.

Although I hardly expected Suzie Wong to be waving to me from a passing sampan, I did expect to see more old colonial buildings; bygone reminders of Hong Kong's swashbuckling past. As we neared the island, however, I did make out a few rickshaws with their two wheels propped up against the wall of the ferry terminal.

After disembarking we were driven to the Alba Hotel in Yee Wo Street, Causeway Bay; a stone's throw from Victoria Park. Along the way we passed tramcars packed with people; this had once been a very popular mode of transport in Glasgow, but they closed that system in 1962. On Hong Kong Island it appeared still to be in great demand.

It was a smartish looking hotel, a good omen, I thought. However, any notions of going upstairs to our separate rooms, relaxing, having a shower, or trying to see if there was any English channel on the television were soon dispelled.

As we rode the elevator with Petrie, he informed us that he had only booked one room.

"Will it not be a bit tight for space and beds?" a worried looking Jackie asked.

"It's okay, there are two single beds, and we've added a camp bed," said Petrie.

There was no tossing a coin to see who slept in the camp bed: seniority ruled.

"Jackie, the camp bed," roared Walter.

In fairness, we took turns to sleep on it during our brief stay.

So there we were, 6,000 miles from home in exotic Hong Kong, Pearl of the Orient. Romantic scenes from the World of Suzie Wong were running though my head. And then Walter started snoring!

3

Chickens' feet, kung fu and history in the making

A burst of light slipped through the cracks in the Venetian blinds on our first morning in Hong Kong; it woke Jackie and me way too early.

"What time is it?" Jackie mumbled.

"Don't know," I said. I still felt groggy, one look at Jackie confirmed he was in the same state; we both looked like death warmed up. Jackie had barely turned eighteen and the flight to Hong Kong was the first time he had ever flown.

"Where's Walter?" said Jackie.

I looked round and Walter's bed was lying empty.

Just at that moment the bathroom door burst open creating a sound not unlike the banging of saloon doors when the legendary cowboy John Wayne made his entrance in *Rio Bravo*.

"I've had a shower, a good night's sleep and I feel great! Time you lazy bastards got up, Petrie's coming soon to take us for breakfast," roared Walter.

"Do you know you snore, big man?" I asked.

"Blocked nose," he replied with a cheeky grin.

Petrie arrived and took us for breakfast at a nearby restaurant. We thought we were going for a good feed of sausage, bacon and eggs, but we were in for a shock. As soon as we arrived we realized an 'English breakfast' was probably not on the menu; the only 'cutlery' on the table being chopsticks.

"It's called *yum cha*," said Petrie as he ordered *har gao* (prawn dumplings) and *char siu bao* (steamed pork buns) together with an array of local favourites. "After games we all go for Chinese food. Eating together as a team breeds solidarity, so you better get used to the local food. I'm not making special concessions for anyone," he added, like a teacher talking to young pupils.

We understood the team unity part, but when the chickens' feet arrived, I thought Jackie was going to throw up!

Later it turned out Jackie actually was sick. Nothing to do with chewy cartilage, just a bad reaction to a smallpox vaccination he had before travelling. It was therefore just Walter and I who turned up to meet our new team mates the next day, our first training session at Happy Valley.

Mid-September in Hong Kong is hot and humid, but thankfully the morning session was restricted to some light exercises and a few laps of the football field. The afternoon session was all ball work.

However, day by day the training got more physically demanding as Petrie upped the work rate. Not exactly like being on the rack in the Tower of London, but the principle was the same. While Jackie rested in bed, we were doing ten laps of the field, just as a warm-up.

Although it was terribly hot, the laps were not too bad for me, I could run all day, but it was not the same for Walter with his bulky frame.

"Does he think we're fuckin' racehorses?" Walter cried on the morning of our fourth training session, while discarding his training shirt. Weighing over 200 pounds in the draining humidity and with sweat dripping endlessly from his forehead onto his hairy torso he was going through the pain barrier, but in fairness, he kept at it.

Walter's comparison to a racehorse could not have been more appropriate; all our training sessions were in the inner area of the iconic Happy Valley racecourse.

After recovering, Jackie soon joined us for training, and as the three of us walked down Wong Nai Chung Road towards Happy Valley one day asked, "Why is it called Happy Valley?"

"One of the lads told me it was originally a swamp, but was turned into a cemetery of some sorts. There's F all happy aboot it," said Walter.

Nine days after arriving in Hong Kong we were to play our first game at a ground on the other side of the harbour in a place called Kowloon.

The ground was on Boundary Street – so named because it followed the original boundary with China – and belonged to the Police Sports Club. Wooden tiered seating meant just over 10,000 spectators could legally be accommodated.

The vast majority of local fixtures were played at Boundary Street, only high profile games being played on Hong Kong Island at the Government Stadium which housed 28,000. A handful of games were also played at the Hong Kong Football Club and South China stadiums.

The opponents for our first match were ironically called Happy Valley. They played in an all-white strip and were considered a very good side by Hong Kong standards.

On the Saturday of the match, we took the ferry from Hong Kong Island over to Kowloon, arriving at the stadium about an hour before kick-off. There were already thousands of people queuing up to get into the ground.

As kick-off neared the stadium was full to capacity and fans were turned away. Many secured places on the roof tops of adjoining buildings or headed for the rugged hillside on the opposite side of the ground. This was steeply banked and not easy to gain access to, but fans seemed to throw caution to the wind in their eagerness to watch the game.

The stewards of the Hong Kong Football Association had also allowed a line of spectators two deep to sit on the grass, a yard or so from play. Not a blade of grass around the pitch was unoccupied. It might not have been the Maracaná Stadium with 200,000 people, but it felt like a junior version of it that day.

In hindsight, the game should have been played at the Government Stadium, but the Police Ground bursting at the seams, with hundreds on rooftops and thousands on the hillside, added to the spectacle.

In the spirit of the occasion, it being our first appearance, Walter, Jackie and I each kicked autographed footballs into the stands prior to kick-off. That friendly gesture nearly sparked a riot as fans grappled with each other for the balls.

So to the game. Everyone wanted to see if Petrie's new signings were up to the task and if professional footballers from overseas were good for the game in Hong Kong and, to a larger extent, Asia. It might have been our first game, but it was a mighty important one, and, judging by the huge numbers of fans attending, they thought so too.

When referee Fred Pratlett blew his whistle it was not only to start the match, but also to herald a new era in Hong Kong football and a minor piece of footballing history. In a tiny corner of Asia, the electrifying atmosphere that had engulfed the stadium ignited a huge roar as the game got under way.

Like boxers in the opening round, sparring and trying to gain an early advantage, the two teams probed away looking for a breakthrough. It came in the 10th minute. And it went our way. Kwok Ka-ming got the better of his marker on the right wing and sent a delightful looping cross into the 18-yard box. Walter rose majestically to meet the ball, just ahead of his marker, Ip Kam-hung, and sent a diagonal header from about 12 yards out towards goal.

I was roaming in the box, and as I followed the flight of the ball, I raced to meet it, and, with a flick of the head, nodded it into the back of the net. I can still recall that lovely 'swishing' sound as the ball made contact with the net.

The first thing I heard, before my team mates had time to throw their arms around me to celebrate, was a Glasgow accent: "You little bastard, that was going in."

"Just making sure, big man," I replied through the noise of the crowd.

A yard or so out from goal, with a posse of Happy Valley defenders lurking, my predatory instincts had taken over. Walter's header might have gone in, but it could just have easily have hit the post or been cleared by a defender. You can't be polite when it comes to the business end of the game, you just finish the job, as you were taught to do.

There have been lots of wind-ups over the years regarding that incident. One of Walter's pals, businessman Roger Perrin, delighted in getting

Walter going by asking, "Walter, who scored the first goal in Hong Kong with his head? You or Derek?" A red flag to a bull springs to mind.

Sadly, Jackie Trainer had to be substituted in the latter stages of the first half as he still hadn't fully gotten over the effects of his vaccination jab.

Happy Valley, to their credit, came roaring back into the game and equalized shortly afterwards and were unlucky not to be ahead at the break.

Petrie gave a blast to a few players in the changing room at half-time and we were a different animal in the second half; we made the Happy Valley side look as if they had been tranquillized by the blazing sun.

Our superiority eventually forced a few Valley defenders into making some over-enthusiastic tackles in an effort to slow us down. I took a few knocks, but my speed was my saviour in avoiding the occasional bad, late challenge; but not so the big man. Walter would be the first to admit, he was not blessed with speed and he took some terrible punishment from the Valley rearguard. It was only when referee Fred Pratlett cautioned a few of them that things quietened down.

We got our second goal in the eighth minute of the second half: a cushioned pass from me to Walter and he steered the ball past the Valley goalkeeper. I was almost tempted to say, "That ball was going in", but thought better of it. Yau Kwok-leung, who had come on to replace the under-the-weather Jackie, got the third goal some six minutes later, from a cross by Kwok Ka-ming.

In the last minute of the game the constant fouling on Walter resulted in us being awarded a penalty. As designated penalty taker, my role was to finish the job, which I did. The final whistle sounded shortly after and we had won 4-1.

A good start, for the team and for us.

For me, Walter was the architect of the victory. He played a leadership role in taking all the attention and knocks from rugged, uncompromising defenders, allowing Kwok Ka-ming and me the freedom to make good use of the space afforded us. Walter was built like a Sherman tank compared to the local lads, but was nevertheless aching from head to toe after the game.

However, after several cold lagers in the Police mess next to the ground he was soon feeling no pain. He even forgot that I had scored the first goal. I thought it better not to remind him.

You can't rest on your laurels and on Sunday week we were in action again.

We had leapt the first hurdle in our opening test, but this was not a five furlong sprint, rather a test of stamina, like the Grand National, and we couldn't afford to fall at any of the obstacles ahead.

We knew we would be under intense scrutiny in every game and would come up against a lot of tough tackling teams and, to a degree, jealousy from some local players who may have believed that we were infringing on their turf – this was totally unfounded, all we wanted to do was play football, regardless of any ethnic consideration. But, mainly, we wanted to prove we were more than 90-minute 'one hit wonders'.

The local lads in our team were great and made us feel right at home from day one. Some of them would teach us snippets of the Cantonese language. Such as *Jo San* ('good morning') and the occasional not so polite colloquial swear words, but I won't repeat them here.

We had moved out of the Alba Hotel in Yee Wo Street and were now residing in the Rangers clubhouse at 24 Leighton Road, along with all the other players in the squad. The Clubhouse took up almost the whole first floor of the building. The local boys were in bunk beds in various rooms, but, while we had our own room, there were still three of us in it! A small wardrobe to share and suitcases under the bed comprised the storage space. Not the Hilton, but hey we had just arrived and hoped the room would only be temporary, just like the Alba Hotel had been.

Sunday came along and our next game against Fire Services. I can tell you it was not water they threw at us once the opening whistle blew. It was a Golden Jubilee Cup tie at the Government Stadium and around 15,000 were in attendance, a good crowd for a first round tie in what later became known as the Hong Kong FA Cup.

Like the famous Leeds v Chelsea fiery encounter, which had been played five months earlier at Old Trafford and widely considered to be one of the most brutal of all cup games, our match was also explosive.

The boss of the Fire Services team was Colin Green, arch enemy of Ian Petrie, and the main protagonist against Petrie extending the league to avoid relegation at the end of the previous season. If our blue shirts invited comparison with Chelsea, then Fire Services were a parody of Leeds United: not a side of magnificence with muscle to match, they were merely downright crude.

When Jackie Trainer was hacked down from behind by a Fire Services defender after just 10 minutes we knew what was in store.

I scored the first goal in the 20th minute, but rather than me telling you about it, I'll defer to journalist Neil Perera and his description in the *South China Morning Post* the next day.:

"Currie pounced on a through-pass from the centre and clutched his stomach as Chan Shui-hung's right boot crashed into it. But the young Scotsman gathered himself up after a brief pause and slashed the ball in to score."

Cheung Chi-wai, regarded as one of the stars of Hong Kong football, got the equalizer for Fire Services just after the half hour.

In the 64th minute I hit a scorcher from 20 yards into the low right hand corner of the net to make it 2-1.

Five minutes later Chi-wai also got his second to level the game at 2-2.

Shortly afterwards, one of the Fire Services players left a five-inch gash on the back of one of our players and was sent off. We were now on the receiving end of some terrible challenges and local referee, Lam Kim-cheung was not up to the task of controlling the game. Punches in the ribs and sly kicks away from prying eyes were the order of the day.

Walter Gerrard was quoted in *The Star* newspaper the next day as saying: "the last straw was when somebody kicked me when the ball was nowhere near, I just couldn't believe they got away with it."

The game finished 2-2 after 90 minutes. In fairness to the referee, he found the game almost impossible to get a grip on and I think he was on the verge of abandoning it. But being a cup tie we had to go into a designated 20 minutes of extra time.

However before that took place sanity returned when the HKFA Chairman himself, Mr Liu Lit-mo, walked up to the players before the game resumed. With a finger-wagging towards the Fire Services players he warned them to restrain themselves.

There were no more goals in extra time and a replay was on the cards for a few weeks later, to be played at a venue yet to be decided. Perhaps a boxing ring with the Firemen in the red corner?

An irate Ian Petrie was quoted in the *SCMP* the next day: "This is the dirtiest, most provocative football I have ever seen in Hong Kong." Colin Green, the Fire Services boss, was remarkably quiet.

Funnily enough, some time later I would become friendly with Colin, but for now he was *persona non grata*.

A bruising encounter. They had tried to provoke us, particularly Walter, Jackie and me, but we were prepared and not easily sucked in. Full marks to our young Chinese team-mates for showing remarkable restraint and not retaliating to the one-sided brutality being dished out that day.

Without dwelling on it, there was more to come when we faced Eastern a little later.

But for now half the team had appointments with our local Chinese herbalist for treatment, and we had only played two games!

4

The good, the bad, and the ugly

Remarkably, by the time our next match came around injury problems had receded. Our opponents were to be South China, or the 'Caroliners' as they are known, due to their cosy clubhouse and ground both being located on Caroline Hill Road. Anyone who has attended the famous Rugby Sevens will know that hilly road well: it's the main route up to the Hong Kong Stadium.

Occasionally league matches were played at the South China ground, but because of capacity restrictions due to the age of the old stadium, the HKFA had transferred our game to the 28,000-capacity Hong Kong Stadium as there was city-wide interest. Just as well: it was a sell-out.

We had added a new player to our ranks and there was a whiff of the 'cloak and dagger' around his signing.

Six foot plus, Ron Tinsley was a centre-half who had once played for the British Combined Services, known today as the UK Armed Forces, and made up of the best footballers in the three services: Royal Navy, British Army and Royal Air Force.

As a recent new recruit to Hong Kong and based at RAF Kai Tak, Ron's arrival, and word of his ability, were passed on secretly to Petrie by a friendly admirer of Hong Kong Rangers, so he was signed quietly, under the radar so to speak.

Jardine Sports Association, the current league champions (and known generally as Jardines), had also discovered his presence and were believed to have been anxious to sign him; but Petrie beat them to it, securing his signature, perhaps not under cover of darkness, but certainly from under their noses.

Tinsley's first game was to be the South China encounter.

Nam Wah, as they are known in Cantonese, were historically the most successful football club in Hong Kong, founded as far back as 1904. They are known for their sportsmanship, and highly respected for their honesty, integrity and sense of fair play, traditionally seen as British virtues.

All our contests with South China, and there were many over the years, were tough but fair, with well-merited handshakes at the final whistle.

After all these years I take my hat off to the South China organisation, a class outfit.

Since foundation South China had had a policy of only fielding Chinese players, nothing racist, just a grand old respectable tradition.

The only foreign players the club would sign had to have Chinese ancestry: for example, Malaysian international goalkeeper, Chow Chee-keong.

However, in the face of increasing competition. that policy would eventually change ten years later. European players were seen as increasingly beneficial, and, ironically, I was involved in one of their early signings: Alex Miller, the former Aberdeen and Hibernian manager, who was also assistant manager to Gérard Houllier at Liverpool at one stage. Alex was a full-back at Glasgow Rangers for fifteen years and I recommended him to South China.

But back to the match.

When we looked out from the windows of our changing rooms on match day all we could make out was a sea of faces. It was as if we were in a Roman amphitheatre, such was the structure of the old stadium.

We learned afterwards that flags flown in various sections on top of the wall surrounding the stadium indicated the ground was full, though the Hong Kong Football Association said in the newspapers the next day that hundreds of fans had climbed over the walls illegally, desperate to watch the match.

As the two sides walked onto the pitch we received a tremendous reception in anticipation of an exciting match. It could have been a Wembley cup final. It probably was for us.

We kicked off and the crowd quietened down, but just a minute into the game there was a mighty roar: we had been awarded a penalty!

Our opening attack had caught the South China defence in disarray and in panic one of their defenders clumsily handled the ball inside the 18-yard box. The South China players and fans thought it was accidental, the Rangers fans were sure it wasn't.

When the dust settled the penalty stood, and rightly so, the defender, Chan Chi-kai, had unquestionably handled the ball.

I took the ball and placed it on the spot. There might have been 28,000 people inside the stadium, but as I stepped up to take the kick I swear I never heard a sound. I had trained myself from a young age to take spot kicks and, as far as I was concerned, it was a free shot at goal.

I will not go into the styles of taking penalty kicks, except to say that, provided the goalkeeper stays on his line before the ball is kicked, nine times out of ten a good player should score, barring an act of God perhaps.

I once took five penalties against Peter Schmeichel, the great Dane who played for Manchester United. But that's for later.

I made no mistake from the spot and we were 1-0 up and only a minute of playing time on the clock.

The fastest goal in a first division match by a European in Hong Kong football history? Certainly at that time, but perhaps not today. Regardless, we sensed we were on our way to victory.

The second goal came twenty-one minutes later. Walter laid off a nice pass to former Hong Kong youth international Cheung Kai-ming. He carried the ball into the heart of the South China defence then released it to me on the left wing.

I beat my defender and sent over a raking cross to Jackie Trainer, placed perfectly inside the six yard box, and the youngster headed brilliantly past the Caroliners' goalkeeper, Lau Kin-chung, to put us 2-0 up. Rangers fans roared their approval, but more was to come.

On the half hour mark, Jackie split the defence with a masterful pass to me. This time I had no one to beat, Jackie's through ball had left me in the clear. All I had to do was float a nice cross over to the waiting Walter Gerrard and with a powerful downward header he beat the keeper. We were three goals to the good. Another huge roar from our supporters; the South China fans were stunned.

Complacency in defence a minute before half-time allowed Chan Chui-kee to pull one back for South China and give their fans some respite during the break.

The second half was fairly uneventful and the pace of the game slowed, mainly due to the efforts in the highly-charged first half.

Mind you, had Yeung Chun-chin not headed a ball off our goal line from a header by South China's Chan Sik-cheung, it might have given the Caroliners the impetus to come back at us.

Thankfully that was not the case. I almost got a fourth goal when I went on a solo run with four South China defenders at my heels, but my shot was saved by keeper, Lau Kin-chung. That was the last chance of the game and it ended 3-1 to us.

Afterwards the team celebrated at a nearby Chinese restaurant in Yee Wo Street. By then the three of us had just about mastered chopsticks, but getting the skin off the chicken proved more difficult than beating South China.

Ron Tinsley had come through the game fairly well for his first appearance; still a good bit off the mark fitness wise, but he looked a good asset for the future.

The report in the *South China Morning Post* the next day praised our second and third goals saying they were, "as good as any that would be seen at the stadium this year." No mention of any pressure on me taking a penalty after one minute in front of 28,000 fans!

But yes, it was a satisfying win. Jackie, Walter and I had played our part in all three goals and if any doubters thought that our stay was going to be temporary, whether through any misconception of our ability, or by thinking we might succumb to bullying and kicking, they were wrong. We were here to stay, no matter what was thrown at us; there was no mistaking our determination and endurance, even in the heat.

When the three of us arrived for the 1970/71 season we were the first full-time players from Europe to play professionally in Hong Kong and Asia. But that was not the first season professional football had been played in Hong Kong.

For many years select individuals had played as amateurs, being paid under the table to play for certain clubs.

To stop this 'shamateurism' and wipe the slate clean professional football was introduced in Hong Kong for the 68/69 season. From then onwards a club could engage an all-star line-up for a relatively small outlay and be successful.

In the 69/70 season Petrie signed a Thailand youth international centre-forward called Eakchai Sonthikan. Initially he scored goals for Rangers, but towards the middle of the season his form dried up and he got homesick, he had nobody to talk to in his native language. As Hong Kong turned slightly colder in February and temperatures dropped, he asked Petrie to return him to the warmth of Thailand, and Petrie let him go back.

I met Eakchai several years ago in Bangkok, at a game when Tim Bredbury, a good chum of mine and also a well-known former Hong Kong footballer, was coaching a team from Hong Kong. Tim's side were playing a friendly game against Thai first division club Port Authority in Bangkok.

Eakchai told me, looking back on his stint in Hong Kong, that home sickness was the main reason for leaving, and yes, the Thai weather was much more suitable. He also mentioned he found it very physical playing against certain sides, without mentioning any by name. I could easily have named at least half-a-dozen candidates!

That same season Petrie signed Jimmy Howard from Hong Kong Football Club to play centre-half. Jimmy was a regional manager with Rentokil (a pest control company), not a professional footballer, and retained his amateur status – he confided to me that during the professional season he had with Rangers he never received a 'brass razoo'.

To this day he is known by many of a sporting persuasion in Asia as the legendary 'Ratcatcher'. A top bloke whom I first met in Manila in 1971 on a football tour and in his heyday a tidy player, and also pretty good at a collection of sports, including rugby.

A keen Arsenal fan, which I suppose accounts for him perpetually wearing a pair of red socks, I occasionally meet him for a beer or three in the seaside town of Pattaya, as Jimmy resides in Sattahip, only a short drive away.

During that season, Petrie signed another two Thailand players, Udom Chungpoonswasdi and Chatchai Paholpat.

Udom, whom Petrie apparently signed unseen, was a goalkeeper, but mediocre, as Petrie soon found out; however Chatchai was Thailand's youth team captain.

After playing one game against Sing Tao, and receiving some rough treatment, the young Thai player did a 'moonlight flit' back home and was never seen again. Clearly he thought his legs would be better protected back home in Siam. Udom went with him.

There was another overseas player who graced the first division around that time, but like Jimmy Howard, he initially played as an amateur. His name was Tony Gurka who played for Tung Sing.

Tony arrived in 1965 with the British Army and was a corporal in the Military Police. A keen sportsman, he left the Army and formed his own company investigating trademark and copyright infringements. He was a useful defender, playing mostly as a part-timer because of the nature of his job and he would play part of the 1972 season alongside me at Seiko. Tony also featured in a League XI side alongside me against Benfica that year.

He sadly passed away at the relatively young age of 62 in 2003. St John's Cathedral in Garden Road was packed the day we put him to rest, and there were quite a few old local football faces from his Tung Sing and Seiko days there to remember him, which was fitting.

For a time during my era the Police had a side in the first division, but the boys in blue who upheld law and order at work had defenders who did not always uphold it on the field and quite often you could end up black and blue playing against them.

Not all their team were 'old bill' but their star player certainly was. Policeman Ken Wallis who had arrived in Hong Kong in 1962. Ken represented Hong Kong in various select sides as an amateur, such as at the 1964 Merdeka Tournament in Malaysia, and was a damn good striker.

However it would be in Lawn Bowls where Ken would make his international mark. He would be the one of the last Hong Kong representatives to win a Commonwealth Games medal, in Canada in 1994. For good measure he was also the last man to carry the Hong Kong flag at the closing ceremony that year as Hong Kong's participation at the Games ended due to its 1997 return to China.

But back to the 70/71 season. Three days after our success over South China we were brought back to earth with a bump in front of 27,000 fans in a thrilling match against Fire Services in the Golden Jubilee replay at the Government Stadium.

Neither side gave an inch in a game which produced seven goals. Unfortunately they scored one more than we did.

Walter missed the game due to an ankle injury and his aerial strength was sorely missed. I had been given the task of spearheading the attack in his absence, However my pace was nullified somewhat as I had two central defenders hanging around me like a bad smell.

Unlike the previous encounter, which forced the replay, Fire Services were on their best behaviour, and this was highlighted in the *South China Morning Post* report the next day:

"It was a titanic struggle, hell for leather, played at a tremendous pace, but with both sides showing commendable regard for the laws of the game and common sportsmanship," wrote Jock Sloan.

At one stage we were 3-1 down then 4-2 down before Kwok Ka-ming netted in the 75th minute, to make it 4-3, despite going all out after that we could not find the equalizer and were out of the Jubilee Cup.

Robin Parke writing for *The Star* newspaper the next day commented that we had paid the price for a suspect goalkeeper and bad defending, while also missing Walter Gerrard.

Cheung Chi-wai had a great game that night, the former Vancouver Royals player scoring a hat-trick, but although I admired him as a player, I could not always respect his attitude.

In the *China Mail* tabloid the next day he was quoted as saying, "I don't like the way people have praised the foreign players, it makes Hong Kong footballers look small fry. I hope people will not look down on us again." He did clarify that somewhat by saying "I have no ill-feelings against overseas footballers playing in Hong Kong."

Nobody I know has ever looked down on local footballers, I think he was just stirring the pot! Mind you, I suppose we would all like to retract some of the foolish things said through life, myself included. In fairness to Chi-wai, I think the afternoon tabloid dramatized the story.

Chi-wai was a great player and to this day we are still friends off the park, but in truth, at that time, I don't think he liked sharing his leading role on the football stage with the new acts in town. I can understand that: it's human nature.

The young boys in our team made mistakes in the game but they would learn from that defeat as the season progressed and we bounced back with a 5-0 win in our next game over the Hong Kong Football Club side at their Sports Road ground.

Sing Tao held us to a 1-1 draw a week after the Club win in front of 24,000 fans. To be honest it was a fair result, but it seemed that in every game against us the opposition played as if it was a cup final for them.

There was nothing fair about our game against Eastern the following week at Boundary Street. It would turn out to be the roughest encounter we had faced since our arrival some seven weeks earlier – I took more hacks than a chicken on a butcher's slab.

Lee Wai-kit writing for the *China Mail* the next day said: "the Fung brothers, Ki-kong and Ki-tong repeatedly clashed with Rangers

Scottish forward Derek Currie, with some serious deliberate and vicious tackling."

Fortunately, I was able to avoid most of their crude tackles by using my pace, otherwise it would have been a hospital job for me, I kid you not.

We had a tough and well built full-back called Chek Chi-wai and he was far from pleased by the assaults on his team-mates. Unfortunately, he decided to take the law into his own hands by flattening one of their players just a minute from half-time. He was shown a red card and had an early bath while we talked tactics for the second half.

As we started the second period the scoreline was 1-1. Jackie Trainer had scored with a direct free kick and Eastern had equalized five minutes before the break.

Despite being down to 10 men we outplayed Eastern in the second period to run out 5-2 winners.

The *SCMP* tells the story: "Rangers and Eastern players waged a brutal soccer battle at Boundary Street yesterday – a battle which kept team trainers as busy as Medical Corps men after a guerilla ambush."

The paper went on to say: "the match was worst in the melting minutes of play. Fung Chi-ming ankle-tapped Currie and brought him down. Gerrard tried to intervene and fists began to fly. The situation got vicious. Players of both teams squared up. Then Lo Kwok-tai of Eastern kicked Ron Tinsley in the back and the referee signalled for the riot police to move in."

Getting the riot police to come on the field was one of the few things referee Luk Tat-sing got right that day. His lack of control had been the catalyst for much of the trouble during the game. Ian Petrie did not mince his words afterwards, "soccer will not develop in Hong Kong if these sort of events are allowed to continue."

Despite the bruising encounter we still had the class to get the points, though most of us suffered a variety of cuts and bruises. However, we accepted the pain as the price paid for winning the war, and that's what it was that day!

Let me say here and now there were a lot of skilful players in Hong Kong, but up until then, many defenders thought there was only one way to stop the *gweilos*.

Despite the brutal game, three days later I would play in a game which would define my career in Hong Kong.

One in which I would be christened with a name, the use of which may be frowned on in some quarters, but by which I am still known to this very day. It was one of my finest games in Hong Kong – perhaps the Eastern game had sharpened my reflexes – and fittingly it would be the first game in which I would represent Hong Kong at any kind of international level.

5

Famous names

I had been selected by the Hong Kong Football Association to represent the League XI in a 4-3-3 system to play against visiting top Stockholm-based football club, Djurgårdens.

The date was November 8, 1970.

They say 8 is a lucky number because in Cantonese it is pronounced 'baat', which also sounds like the word for prosperity or wealth. Being born on February 8, I was hoping the date would be doubly lucky for me and my League XI team-mates.

We would need all the luck we could get as the crack Swedish side included in their line up three World Cup stars, two other full internationals, and two youth internationals.

Mind you, our side were no slouches. We had Cheung Chi-doy and eight other more than capable Hong Kong-born players alongside Malaysia's international goalkeeper Chow Chee-keong, and me, the lone Scotsman. Rangers manager, Petrie had demanded an insurance package be arranged by the HKFA in case I got injured. I felt like a prized racehorse; perhaps I was to him.

The official attendance on that day was 24,279 and they paid HK$147,500 [Hong Kong dollars, just $ from here on] to watch. None would go home disappointed, unless they had a penchant for anything Swedish.

Acclaimed singer Matt Monro had flown in for an appearance at the Hilton Hotel, and I was told he was one of the fans in the stadium – Matt had spent some of his early years residing in Hong Kong.

As the only non-Chinese player in the League side I was pleased to hear the crowd give me a warm welcome as I took my position on the left wing. I waved to show my appreciation. I had come a long way in a short period and my love affair with the Hong Kong fans was about to blossom.

Jock Sloan, under his pen name of I.M. MacTavish, covered the match for the *SCMP* and his description captures the essence of the game: "The Swedes were early attackers, but Currie, in his busiest mood, was soon worrying their defenders."

We fell behind, against the run of play, when Chow Chee-keong got caught far from his goal and Lindman easily lobbed the ball over him to put the Swedes one up.

Four minutes later, after a lovely pass from Wong Man-wai to Chi-doy, the ex-Blackpool player beat World Cup goalkeeper Larsson with a stunning low shot and we were back to all square.

"Once on level terms Hong Kong gave much more than they got and it was a sad moment when Currie out-jumped the defence to beat the goalkeeper with a superb header, only to see the ball strike the post and rebound into play," wrote Sloan.

Did I say I was crap in the air? OK perhaps not quite Denis Law.

The visitors switched goalkeepers at half-time with Mattsson replacing Larsson. They then took the lead again in the 58th minute when a misunderstanding between our centre-half, Fok Pak-ling and Chow in goal, left Leif Eriksson with an open goal; the Swede did not miss.

We threw everything into attack and were unlucky not to equalize quickly, but eventually we did so in the 75th minute. In a goalmouth scramble, with the ball bobbling about, I eventually crashed it goalwards in typical 'Gerd Müller' fashion, from three yards out, forcing their defender, Cronqvist, to use a hand to try and prevent it hitting the back of the net. But there was just too much power in the shot and it crossed the line to a huge roar from the home fans, and the goal was given.

Over to Jock Sloan: "It was now all Hong Kong and with the crowd giving them tremendous encouragement the local boys responded splendidly." He added, "Currie had four good tries, Cheung Yiu-kwok and Cheung Kwok-gun had one each, Cheung Chi-doy set up Lee Kwok-keung twice with the goal at his mercy, but the sinner-in-chief somehow contrived to miss."

But the winner did come, and it came in the final seconds of the game. I can recall it as if it were yesterday.

I broke clear inside the box from the left, as I raced at a slight angle towards their goal my idea was to bluff the keeper and make as if I was going to clip the ball with my left foot past him, while in reality, I was only going to drag it past him and open my body up to score with my right foot.

Change of plan: out of the corner of my eye I saw one of our players standing square to me, so I passed the ball with my left foot and he had the simple task of side-footing it into the net, giving us a merited victory. It was almost the last kick of the game so the timing could not have been sweeter. Predictably, the stadium erupted again. When I rushed to embrace the goalscorer, I saw it was Lee Kwok-keung; the sinner-in-chief now had his sins absolved.

I was always taught that the hallmark of a good player was not to be selfish. An attacker always has a selfish hunger to score, but if a team-mate is in a better position, as Lee was that day, then pass, it's as simple as that.

A huge banner headline in the *SCMP* the next day read: "CURRIE AND SPICE," with a sub-head: "Storybook win for HK over Swedes." The report said the League XI had played with a spirit of determination not seen since they had beaten Peru 3-2, two years earlier.

"This was a thoroughly professional Hong Kong side, inspired by the strength and intelligence of Cheung Chi-doy and the enterprise and never-say-die spirit of Derek Currie. Together, these two tore the Djurgårdens defence apart and it was fitting that both of them got a goal. Chi-doy was the spice that complemented the Currie," Jock Sloan concluded. It was an amazing day, but it wasn't finished for me.

I came out of the Stadium after showering and there were a few hundred fans or so still lingering, a good half-hour after the game had finished. I was just about to descend the steps from the stadium entrance when I was lifted off my feet; seconds later I was being carried head high by a throng of jubilant fans. My feet never touched the ground all the way down Caroline Hill Road until I got to the steps of the Lee Gardens Hotel, a mile or so from the stadium.

There was an official Chinese-style dinner that night, with a traditional 8-course menu – there's that 8 again – which included abalone, shark fin soup and other dishes that these days would be frowned on. I had to show some of our guests from Sweden the correct way to hold chopsticks; by then I was pretty good with them. The banquet in Djurgårdens' honour was held in a Central District restaurant and was attended by the Swedish Consul General and Henry Fok, then President of the HKFA.

There were toasts to accompany each new dish as it was laid on the table. And there was a band to provide entertainment. The toasts were made with mugs of beer, which were slipping down a treat. This encouraged some of my League XI team mates to suggest that I give them a song. Never slow, I took to the stage and gave them the old Sinatra classic, *My Way*. It's not every day that you get to sing in front of probably the richest man in Hong Kong, as Henry Fok was at that time.

Talking of singing, earlier I mentioned Matt Monro, whose real name, you might be surprised to know, was Terry Parsons. What's more, his career was actually launched in Hong Kong, when he was on National Service in the British Army and stationed in Hong Kong in the early 50s.

'Uncle' Ray Cordeiro, the famed Hong Kong man of music, had a weekly radio show for amateur talent – there was a prize of 200 cigarettes to the winner as the show was sponsored by a tobacco company. Terry won every week for two months and in the end Uncle Ray had to give him a 15 minute show of his own in order to give other contestants a chance!

Terry Parsons may have changed his name to Matt Monro, but it was in Hong Kong that 'The Man with the Golden Voice', as he was often known, started his singing career.

That night Mr Monro might have been singing only half a mile away at the Eagle's Nest nightclub in the Hilton, belting out *Born Free* to paying customers. But little did he know that he had competition at the Djurgårdens banquet where I was belting it out for free!

The next day, the Chinese-language footballing newspapers had banner headlines in Chinese characters, *Ye So da gow heung gong*, translated as "Jesus saves Hong Kong". I had been christened 'Ye So' or 'Jesus'. Amazingly the name stuck.

When I later played in games which were aired live on TV, local commentators used this nickname.

I'm sorry to say that on more than a few occasions I heard that the Catholic Church had complained about the reference; but in the soccer-mad town at that time *Ye So* remained, much to the consternation of some in the holy order.

There's a postscript to being nicknamed 'Jesus'.

Just over three weeks after the Djurgårdens game Pope Paul VI was to be at the Hong Kong Stadium to bless a gathering of local Catholics during a three hour stopover. The 73-year-old pontiff had just visited the Philippines and Australia and there were to be 50,000 people crammed into the Government stadium for the open-air mass, with many watching outside the stadium on a TV link-up. The pontiff flew to the stadium in Happy Valley from Kai Tak airport by helicopter – I believe it is the only time in history that a pope has visited Hong Kong.

One local newspaper cartoonist decided to have some fun. A cartoon showed the Pope addressing his cardinals, with a likeness of me hiding between cassocks. The caption had the Pope asking "Now gentlemen, what's all this about Jesus playing football at the Hong Kong Stadium?"

During my days growing up I was fortunate to actually see many of the great players in the flesh. I especially remember a Wednesday evening in May of 1960.

The sadly departed mercurial wordsmith Hugh McIlvanney described the 1960 European Cup final in Glasgow, between Real Madrid and Eintracht Frankfurt, as a watershed moment for him. Writing about that memorable 7-3 win for the Spaniards he put it quite simply: "here was a game as we had always known it could and should be played."

McIlvanney was not alone in admiring the flawless display by the white-shirted Spanish team. 127,621 fans stayed on well after the final whistle to applaud the greatness they had witnessed, while also acknowledging the part the spirited German losers, in red shirts with white sleeves, had played on that magical Wednesday evening in May. I was one of them.

I was alongside my Mum and Dad watching another hero, Alfredo Di Stéfano, in what was considered to be the greatest game in the history of the old European Cup.

When the gates opened some two hours before kick-off, we had already been queueing for well over an hour so we could get a good spot in the open area under the towering North Stand at Hampden. Tea from a flask and sandwiches prepared by my mother kept us from hunger and once the turnstiles opened at 5.30pm I sprinted down to the front, adjacent to the halfway line. I was one of the first hundred or so inside the stadium and managed to secure a prime spot for my Mum and Dad.

When they duly arrived at the white-painted front wall separating us from the field, my Dad brought out a little wooden stool. He had made it at his workplace and when the folded legs were straightened and I stood on it I was eight inches taller and able to see the field of play clearly. At eleven years of age I still had some growing to do.

My whole family was at that game: middle brother John was behind one goal and older brother Dick, who had managed to get us all tickets for the game, had a prime seat in the main stand, sitting alongside the then Tottenham Hotspur manager, Bill Nicholson.

The football that night was scintillating and a Glasgow newspaper described it as Citizen Kane on grass, Swan Lake in studs, and the Mona Lisa in Mount Florida (the area where Hampden Park is located).

In many ways it was the birth of the new game of football that McIlvanney had envisaged and it was the first European Cup match to be broadcast live, both on national TV in Britain and to 12 other countries on Eurovision. Over 70 million viewers watched the game that night.

Many, many young up-and-coming players took inspiration from that game. It was the match that lit the 'blue touchpaper' and motivated many a future star; including a young 15-year-old Scot called Jimmy Johnstone, who later became one of the Lisbon Lions with Celtic, winning the European Cup in 1967.

In later years Johnstone said "that match remained the biggest influence on my career." His captain of the Lisbon Lions, Billy McNeil, was also at the game, as was a young teenager named Alex Ferguson, and in their autobiographies both agreed with Johnstone that the game was inspirational.

The great Bobby Charlton said at the time, "It was football on a different level than I'd been taught," and Jimmy Greaves joked, "the match has been edited, these players are doing things that are not possible."

That game invigorated the football world, and the names of Real's dazzling forward line: Canário, Luis del Sol, Di Stéfano, Ferenc Puskás and Francisco Gento, slip easily off the tongue, along with that of their centre-half who was at the heart of the Spanish defence, the aptly-named José Santamaría.

I was fortunate enough to meet Santamaría in later years when he came to Hong Kong while managing the Barcelona-based club, Espanyol, and I told him the joys he had given to a young 11-year-old watching Real Madrid win their fifth consecutive European Cup on that magical night. "*Gracias*", he modestly replied.

I must admit as a forward I also liked Puskás and Gento, but really my hero, before Pelé and Eusébio, was Di Stéfano, known as 'The Blond Arrow'. I would have loved to shake his hand and tell him the pleasure he gave me while growing up. Actually, I did meet him, but never realised it at the time, until it was too late.

It was in the Olympic stadium in Rome during half-time in a group stage match between Italy and the USA at the 1990 World Cup finals. I went to the bar to get a coffee and something to eat just before the half-time break and there was only one other person standing there, just to the left of me.

He gave me a friendly smile and I nodded to him as I perused the menu. I gave him another look, and he smiled again, as if he knew I was trying to recognize him.

The waiter came and eventually took my order, and by this time I had worked out who the stranger was: Di Stéfano, a tad older, but I was sure it was him! I looked left again, but he had vanished into the night.

I checked around but could not see him anywhere, and at that moment a journalist I knew arrived on the scene and could see my darting eyes.

"Looking for someone?" he asked.

"Di Stéfano," I said, "I am sure I just saw him."

"Yes, he's here, one of the Spanish journalists interviewed him earlier," he said.

Damn, so close to my hero, but at least I got a smile from him. I was 41 years of age at the time, but you are never too old to salute your childhood heroes, or legends of the past. A shake of his hand would have been an honour.

So, two weeks before Xmas of 1970 I was no longer that young boy watching greatness at Hampden. I was going on to the field, playing against it. It was what had persuaded me to embark on the long journey to Hong Kong in the first place: to play against the king himself: Pelé.

My earliest image of Pelé was in 1958, when as a nine-year-old I watched him on an old black-and-white Bush television set, which my parents had bought originally to watch their eldest son, Dick, compete in the 1954 Vancouver Commonwealth Games, four years earlier.

It was the final of the 1958 World Cup in Sweden. Pelé chested the ball onto his knee, then flicked it over the centre-half's head and ran around the Swede to volley the ball into the back of the net. "Who is this 17-year-old?" the footballing world cried out: he had just scored two goals in a World Cup final and become the youngest player ever to play in one!

Brazil also won the World Cup in Chile four years later, but a torn thigh muscle when he was playing against Czechoslovakia in the group stages robbed us of seeing the then 21-year-old again in the tournament.

Four years later in 1966 he was brutally injured by diabolical tackling and virtually kicked off the field in vital games against Bulgaria and Portugal. By his own admission he was so disgusted by that, and also by the terrible English refereeing in the tournament, that he would never play in another World Cup game.

I still cringe today when I see the brutal double foul by Portugal's Morais on Pelé; many will recall that iconic picture of him being helped off the field by Dr Gosling and Mário Américo, the premature end to his 1966 World Cup.

At Goodison Park that day the indulgent English referee, George McCabe, did not even give Morais a yellow card, when the Sporting Lisbon club player should have been shown red.

Thankfully, Pelé did rescind his decision and played World Cup football again; if he hadn't, we might never have had the glory of Mexico 1970, for me the greatest World Cup finals in the history of the tournament.

It was surreal to think that only six months before I lined up against him, he had set the football world alight once again, along with his magnificent Brazilian team mates, to capture the World Cup for the third time.

Who can ever forget the header that forced Gordon Banks to make that incredible save in Guadalajara, or the lofted shot from 60 yards out, when he noticed the Czech goalkeeper was off his line, the keeper frantically running back as if the last train had just left the station, and then, to his relief, seeing Pelé's shot eventually fluttering a mere foot wide of the post.

Or that great header to score the first goal in the final against Italy, when he met Rivellino's cross to nod the ball past the outstretched fingers of goalkeeper Albertosi inside a packed Aztec Stadium.

The great man was now in Hong Kong and, for good measure, so was his World Cup team-mate, Clodoaldo.

I can tell you, there was some nervous tension in the changing room at the Hong Kong Government Stadium prior to kick-off, but I had put my first plan of action in motion.

I had arranged a photographer to be on standby after the teams had come on to the field. No thought of how the game could develop, that would take care of itself. My only thought was a picture with the great Pelé, a dream come true.

I was never nervous going onto a football field, in any grade. I knew as long as I was as fit as I could be, my ability would take care of the rest; but a picture with Pelé, that was something else.

I needed that picture. Playing against Pelé was why I had really come to Asia in the first place, and why I left my friends and family behind.

I need not have worried. As the great man and I came in close contact in front of the main stand, I asked him if we could have a picture together. He obliged with a smile. As Pelé put his right arm around me for the picture, I remember it was like standing next to a middleweight boxing champion, he was all muscle, and he was Pelé!

The sun was shining and the old stadium was bursting at the seams with 28,000 fans packed inside ready for the action.

We lost by five goals to two, but we were always in it.

I thought I played as well as I could, best summed up I suppose by reports in the *South China Morning Post* and *The Standard* the next day. Jock Sloan again penned the match report for the *Post* and said:

"The persistence of Currie was always a source of worry to the visitors and his move which gave Hong Kong the equalizing goal at two-all would have been hailed as the supreme effort if it had come from Pelé himself."

He described the move in greater detail: "Six minutes later the Stadium was in uproar. Cheung Yiu-kwok sent a short free-kick to Cheung Chi-doy out on the left and as the Jardines star moved forward, Currie raced goalwards.

When Chi-doy's shot came his way the Flying Scotsman sold goalkeeper Cejas a brilliant dummy and the ball flashed low into the net for an equalizing goal that must have won the approval of Pelé himself."

The Standard reported: "Full pride for Hong Kong's performance must go to the Cheung brothers, Derek Currie and 18-year-old Tang Hung-cheong.

They all turned in top class performances, but one could not help feeling that had Currie not been denied the ball when he deserved a pass, the score could have been much different. Currie played like a demented man taking every and any position but he was not given the co-operation of the other forwards."

Looking back, I suppose everybody wanted to play well on such a memorable occasion and perhaps I was denied some goal scoring chances by over zealous team-mates seeking personal glory. I would have to say though it was one of the happiest days of my life, despite losing, as daft as that sounds. The scoreline did slightly flatter them, and of course Pelé got the fifth goal, three minutes from time with a penalty.

I would have loved to have been on the score sheet despite getting the credit for the second goal, and yes, I daresay if some team-mates had been more generous with better distribution of the ball, it might have happened, but it was still a happy Glaswegian who walked off the field carrying Pelé's jersey.

6

Rules, Proud Mary, and Good Morning, Vietnam

Almost a week after Pelé flew off into the sunset there was a bit of a break for the Christmas holidays.

Although there were no upcoming fixtures that did little to stop Petrie from working us hard in training. He didn't like to see us with spare time on our hands, or for that matter, having a bit of fun. The tyrant ruled with an iron fist.

One day he took the whole team to prison.

All the players and officials were loaded onto a bus and driven to Stanley Prison. Fortunately it was not to be locked up, although the gates were closed after we drove through, but rather to do our bit for society.

Willie Jorge, the Chairman of Hong Kong Rangers, who was previously very senior with the Prison Services (he might even have been the boss of Stanley Prison at one time), had arranged an afternoon game for us against the prisoners and prison staff.

It was to be a reward for all the inmates who had been on good behaviour. I almost forgot the story until Kwok Ka-ming reminded me, but how could I forget?

The referee was an Italian who was doing time for forgery – or was it smuggling? – but it's what happened before the game started which was the highlight.

The prisoners were sitting almost three deep around the perimeter of the field, marshalled by prison officers. We ran out onto the pitch as normal, but there was nothing normal about our shirts, they looked so big and bulky you would have thought we were at the North Pole.

On a signal we ran towards the seated prisoners, pulled up our jerseys and out fell packets of cigarettes. There was stunned silence for a split second. And then the inmates scrambled to scoop up the treasure. (Fortunately the prison staff were in on the escapade so it was quite good natured).

After that, the prisoners cheered our every move on the pitch and we won over a few thousand more fans that day.

It was a charm offensive and brought some relief to those inside… but we were happy to get out of the gates at full-time!

Kwok Ka-ming, our right winger, often used to act as middle-man between our local players and Petrie, helping to settle countless disputes: such as Petrie failing to pay salaries on time, or making deductions from wages for often frivolous matters.

Ka-ming summed up Petrie when he said in a podcast a few years ago, "Petrie's rules were basic: you had to train every day, apart from match day; no girl-friends, and no smoking. But you were allowed to drink, because he did."

There was also an unwritten law that you could not even speak to a member of the opposite sex on match day. I recall midfielder Ma Ying-cheung talking to his girl-friend two hours before a match; he was noticeably missing from the line-up that day. Nothing wrong with being a disciplinarian, but it could only go so far and, like most tyrants before him, it was to prove his eventual downfall.

We had a fair bit of free time between training sessions and there were an abundance of movie theatres in Causeway Bay: the Lee Theatre, Hoover, New York, all with five showings a day, the last being around 9.30pm.

However, if you went to that last showing it wouldn't finish until around 11.30pm and, under Petrie's rules, you had to be home by 11.30pm, or be locked out and hit with a mammoth fine. Even if we had an afternoon match and went out afterwards we still had to be in by then, no extra time!

Next door to our clubhouse was a restaurant, fashionably called the 'Café de Loren'. It was a bit of an institution, well known as a late-night drinking spot and often open until four in the morning.

Now there just happened to be an alley that separated the restaurant from the clubhouse. Our room was on the first floor, and the proprietor of the restaurant would conveniently park his car in that alley, just below our bedroom window.

I say conveniently, because it allowed us the opportunity, when arriving home after 11.30 pm, to propel ourselves onto the top of the car, reach up for the ledge, and climb through the window into our room, all unbeknownst to the boss.

Jackie slept nearest the window and it was agreed that he would keep the window unlocked at night so that if we missed curfew, a couple of athletic moves and we were inside.

The first time we tried the ruse things didn't quite go to plan. Jackie's bed was right up against the window and so made the perfect landing area; the only problem was that Jackie was fast asleep in it that night! A piercing shriek suddenly rent the air. Completely forgetting the ruse Jackie screamed, "for Christ's sake, we've got a burglar, I can't move, get the light on."

I jumped out of bed, sprinted to the light, and turned it on; there was Walter spread-eagled on top of Jackie like a 'fish supper'. But that wasn't the end of it.

After Walter had completed his 'Edmund Hillary' exploit, navigating up to the ledge and then down through the window to the comfort of a soft landing on top of Jackie, he mumbled something, closed his eyes, and immediately fell asleep.

I advised Jackie that it would probably be better to let the fallen soldier lie where he fell. I then proceeded to help him struggle out from underneath the slumbering giant and suggested he sleep on Walter's bed for the night.

After that, if either Walter or I were not home by 11.30pm, Jackie would read a book until all three of us were safely tucked up. In truth, it didn't happen too often, but it came to an abrupt stop one night when Walter, at 27 years of age, decided his climbing days were over and banged on the front door of the clubhouse and told Petrie to "open the fuckin' door!"

Petrie initially fined Walter a week's wages, later rescinded when Walter pointed out that he was a grown man, not a 15-year-old kid. Eventually accommodation away from Leighton Road was found for Walter and me, alongside two of our Chinese team mates. One of whom, we strongly suspected, was a 'mole' planted to report back to Petrie on our nightly movements. We occasionally referred to our mole as 'Philby', but he had no idea what we were talking about when we addressed him by that name, despite his excellent English.

Midway through the season Petrie acquired another British recruit – 25-year-old Irishman Eddie Simpson who had light-coloured hair and long sideburns – and he also joined us in our new abode. Jackie, being only eighteen, was deemed to be too young to leave headquarters in Leighton Road.

We were billeted opposite the Hoover cinema, overlooking Yee Wo Street, five of us in a large room, plus the odd rat or two running around in the small kitchen looking for scraps during the night. Next door was Jardine's Bazaar, a street so narrow sunlight fought for a place to shine through – our place was no better. Freedom always comes at a cost!

I mentioned earlier that we had a lot of free time prior to Xmas; well, if I rewind, it was about a week before Xmas when I saw one the best live music concerts I have ever witnessed.

I had made pals with the entertainment features writer of *The Star* newspaper, a chap called Terry Geary. A friendly clean shaven Englishman, with long straight hair often flickering over his eyes, who walked even faster than me.

Terry liked his football and I would occasionally get him tickets for games; he would reciprocate by taking me to press conferences, featuring the likes of Tom Jones and other superstars who visited the city. Many were big names in the UK and the USA, but some were still relatively unknown in Cantopop Hong Kong.

While I was still staying at the Rangers clubhouse, on December 19, 1970 I went to see one such act at the Princess Theatre in Kimberley Road, at the junction of Nathan Road, near the Miramar Hotel in Kowloon.

A few days earlier I had been with Terry and an American entrepreneur, Frankie Blane, who was then based in Hong Kong; he told us that he had a show that we must attend, "it will blow your mind" were the words he used.

"OK, so what's the show?" I asked the towering American, who was built like an NFL quarterback.

"The Ike and Tina Revue," he said, "and you get front row tickets alongside me!"

Well I knew the names, and the song *River Deep, Mountain High* had hit the top three in the UK charts but bombed in the US of A; but I knew little else about the pair.

I need not enlighten you as to what Tina Turner has done since then – she's the undisputed Queen of Rock 'n' Roll – but I was fortunate that night in Kowloon to see first hand the talent that would eventually conquer the music world.

It was one of the earliest live performances where they did their rendition of the Creedence Clearwater Revival song, *Proud Mary*. That rendition would go to number 4 in the Hot 100 in the month of March 1971; just a few months after I had watched them perform it live – undoubtedly one of the warmest and most engaging performances I have ever witnessed.

The song started off in a slow sultry tone with Tina saying they were going to start "nice and easy, but we never do anything nice and easy and we will finish nice and rough". Ike started playing his guitar in slow mesmerizing fashion, but suddenly the song was transformed into a frenetic rock 'n' roll classic with Tina and her backing singers, the Ikettes, delivering gospel-like vocals. By that stage the entire audience was on their feet clapping along and Tina, in her tight clinging dress, was strutting her stuff, the way only Tina – or Anna Mae Bullock as she was born – could.

I climbed on top of a car parked in the alley in Leighton Road that night to get home to bed.

———————

It was just as well that the war movies *Apocalypse Now* and *Platoon* had not been released at that time, or my team-mates and I might have had second thoughts about boarding an Air Vietnam flight to Saigon on the afternoon of January 4, 1971.

Naturally we knew there was a conflict taking place in Southeast Asia involving Vietnam, Laos and Cambodia, and that the US had entered into the fray some years earlier. But hey! we were told that we were just going to participate in a semi-friendly football tournament and our safety was 'doubly' guaranteed.

Youth is an amazing thing, you are invincible and gullible at the same time, nothing in the world is going to happen to you, somebody else perhaps, but never you. Ian Petrie had arranged a dinner for the night before the flight at the wonderful old Sunning House Hotel in Hysan Avenue, Causeway Bay, to give us all the details of the trip ahead. By then it was a bit late for second thoughts.

Sunning Court and Sunning Plaza now stand where the quaint old Sunning House Hotel, with its white-painted facade, once stood. But like those who knew it, stayed in it, or dined there, I'm left with great memories.

We were told to wear our new tailored blue jackets and grey slacks, specially made for the tour. There was a group picture on the steps of the old hotel and we all looked prim and proper; but in truth, shorts and Hawaiian shirts would have been more appropriate for the heat and humidity of Saigon.

It was a happy bunch who climbed the steps the next day to board South Vietnam's first commercial air carrier. Perhaps there would have been more trepidation if we had known of the accidents that had occurred with some of their aircraft a few months earlier. But enough of that.

It was also a cheery bunch that arrived safely at Tan Son Nhat airport in Saigon some two-and-a-half hours later and breezed through a quick immigration process like VIPs – mind you, there can't have been too many football teams flying into that war zone.

We were met by a dozen Vietnamese girls in traditional *ao dai* dresses, each holding a garland of flowers, which with a smile they placed around our necks. Now, did I not say that Hawaiian shirts would have been a much better dress code?

We boarded small buses, really pick-up trucks with canopy roofs, open sides and seats along each side. Very similar to the Thai baht bus or *songthaew* as it's called in Thai, which normally frequent the seaside towns of Pattaya and Phuket.

The welcoming Vietnamese girls, with their charming smiles, also hopped on board. But as soon as Petrie arrived he said to the local Vietnamese official meeting us, "Get the girls off the buses." Sadly they disappeared along with their smiles. Not that anything unbecoming was going to happen, Petrie just did not like women; we had heard rumours about him, but nothing substantiated, if you catch my drift.

It was hot in the vehicles so blue jackets were soon discarded and ties loosened even though it was almost dark by that time and the trip to our hotel, the Bat Dat, only took half an hour or so. On arrival we were greeted at the door by a gunner in fatigues, strategically tucked behind an emplacement of bulky three-foot long sandbags, a machine gun perched above them with a fully-loaded feeding device and a magazine of cartridges to reinforce the point. That's when I felt my underpants getting wet!

It was a 16-player squad for the tour and I shared a room with Walter Gerrard, while Jackie bunked with Archie McCuaig, a new signing Petrie had brought out from Scotland to strengthen the team. Archie had played with St Mirren, a Scottish first division club side from Paisley.

Archie had flashing eyes, refined features and a prominent moustache, almost a young looking Omar Sharif, but he quickly turned a bit pale when he saw the acting 'doorman' at the entrance to the hotel. Although no stranger to seeing the odd skirmish in Paisley, it was only punches that were thrown there. In Saigon it could be a grenade!

The other twelve Hong Kong-born players shared rooms as well. We were all told to keep the lights off during the night! Made me think about my mother's stories of the blitz.

Kwok Ka-ming, Petrie's right-hand man and interpreter, looked a bit gloomy at the breakfast table the next morning, as did quite a few others – I don't think they got much sleep!

"Did you guys hear cannon fire in the night, and what sounded like bombing in the distance?" Ka-ming asked. As if we didn't! Later in the day we were informed by a military official that it was quite normal. Just get used to it he told us, it was their own army firing the cannons as a show of strength to the enemy. Well, knowing that was a great relief!

But, funnily enough, we soon got used to the odd blast of cannon fire during the night, not that we had an option!

Little was known about the format of the tournament that we were to play in. However there was to be an official dinner that evening, to be held at a floating restaurant not too far from the hotel, hopefully, we would find out the details then.

Before though we were to enjoy a sightseeing trip around the wonderful old city with its century-old French architecture. It had been ceded to France in the mid-19th century, before being handed back after South Vietnam's independence in 1955.

Saigon, once known as the 'Pearl of Indochina', had in essence been the capital of French Indochina; which accounted for the beautiful French-built colonial villas and monuments. Not least, the imposing Saigon City Hall in Nguyen Hue Street, built at the turn of the 20th century, and also the Notre-Dame Cathedral Basilica of Saigon, the largest church ever built in the French colonies.

We drove around Lam Son Square, past the soon to be famous Continental Hotel. This venerable old establishment was, unbeknownst to us at the time, the current 'in place' in the city, where the elite, rich and powerful met; besides being a popular spot for CIA operatives and military personnel.

It was also popular with foreign correspondents as it was situated in the centre of the city, and was the place where author Graham Greene stayed when writing his anti-war novel, *The Quiet American*. I had read the book, so it was interesting to see where his main character, Fowler, had supposedly enjoyed his ritual nightly beer.

We saw defence batteries around all the old buildings, but I'll refrain from describing them as, although worrying, they were so commonplace eventually we hardly noticed them – if you'd seen one, you'd seen them all.

When we arrived at the floating restaurant on the Saigon River for the official dinner we again saw a strong military presence. I don't recall the names of the prominent officials who greeted us at the dinner, but they eventually informed us that we would be playing for the 'Spring Tree' Cup. The other teams in the tournament were to be: Saigon SV Civilians; SV Military; and the Khmer Republic.

We later found out that the takings from the matches, to be played in the city's 16,000 capacity stadium, would be given to the combatants 'Spring Tree Fund'; so in essence it was a benefit tournament for army personnel injured or maimed during the war.

I think it was also a chance to give the football fans of Saigon a break from the daily reminders of the ongoing agonies of the war which had raged in the city and countryside for years.

After an enjoyable dinner, with copious amounts of delicious prawns three times the size of any found in a Chinese restaurant in Glasgow, we left the My Canh restaurant and returned to the hotel.

It was only much later that we heard about the unfortunate history of the restaurant: two bombs exploded in a bloody attack some years before, tragically killing 32 and injuring 42 others.

Had we known that earlier, the prawns probably would not have tasted so good, nor the friendly atmosphere been so conducive, instead it would have been squeaky bottom time again.

The heavy military presence gave us some kind of assurance, but at the same time it was also scary: if it was necessary, then were we really safe?

Traffic in many parts of Saigon is a nightmare, especially if you are in a rush to get to any destination in the daylight hours. It certainly was in 1971 and people tell me it still is today.

The road outside the Bat Dat Hotel was roughly 8 metres wide, but it could take anything from 20 seconds to a few minutes to cross. There was a constant stream of bicycles, mopeds and motorcycles, inches apart in an endless procession of moving chaos. Only when you spotted a brief break in the traffic would you dare to cross and sometimes, when halfway across, a hand in the air was your only recourse to temporarily stop the next wave of traffic and get safely to the other side.

There were obviously restrictions imposed on us, including not straying too far from the hotel, which was understandable, but sometimes we needed to stretch the legs.

One day after lunch, Walter, Jackie, Archie and I left the hotel, waving a friendly greeting to our guardian manning his machine gun at the front door – we had nicknamed him 'Tommy' – and headed out for a stroll. Exiting the hotel we turned left and walked 100 metres down the road. There was another street leading off to our left and we thought this would be safer than another perilous trip across the main road which we had now named 'No Man's Land'. About 20 metres down the street we noticed there were two bars with girls outside wearing cheongsam-like dresses and waving seductively at the four of us.

We put the brakes on. I said to Walter, "No way, Big Man!" in case he suggested we go in for a laugh; a beer was definitely off the agenda. But I needn't have worried, Walter had heard all the 'Vietnam Rose' stories, so the girls were no temptation for four healthy young athletes, who were out, after all, just for a stroll; we quickly turned around and headed back to the sanctuary of the hotel.

Match day came around on Thursday, our first game was against the SV Military side; later in the day the Saigon SV Civilian side faced the Khmer Republic.

Matches were to be played in the Cong Hoa Stadium, only a kilometre and a half from our hotel. With a military escort, and flashing lights, traffic parted like the Red Sea.

The opening games were to decide the semi-final pairings: the winner of one game playing the loser of the other and vice versa. Obviously the two Vietnamese sides included a number of the best local players; either military conscripts, or those who had civilian war duties.

The third side we might face was the Khmer Republic, representing the pro-United States military led republican government of Cambodia – an entity only formally declared three months before the tournament. This would be their first ever overseas football match. In reality, it was Cambodia, under another flag.

We won our opening game 1-0 in a three-quarters full stadium. The other match was won by the Cambodians with the same scoreline – the first ever victory for the newly-formed republic.

We had battled against some dodgy decisions in our game and, since there were no neutral officials, we did well to actually win the game in extremely hot and telling conditions. However, the next day, the Friday, our game would be engulfed in controversy.

We were the second game that day, so we left our hotel slightly later to avoid sitting in the stadium heat.

Sirens and flashing lights from the accompanying military jeeps again escorted us to the stadium and we arrived in just twenty minutes.

On arrival we found things were going well for the SV Military side against the Khmer Republic as they were holding a healthy two goal lead. They eventually won by three goals to one. One local side into the final; hopefully we would stop the other from getting there too.

Our game ended in a 0-0 draw, meaning it would be sudden death extra-time – the first team to score winning – and that's when the fun started, but it wasn't us who came off the field laughing! I can still recall the controversy surrounding the incident which eventually left a sour taste in the mouth.

Their keeper rushed out of goal and collected the ball just ahead of a speedy advance by me into the penalty-box. I noticed that he was hoping to kick a long ball downfield from just inside his 18-yard-line.

Standing two yards or so outside the box, I turned my back on the goalkeeper. He miskicked the ball, which hit me on my back and rebounded past him. I immediately turned and went round him, his pace was no match for mine, and steered the ball into the open goal for what should have been passage into the final. But it was not to be. The local linesman waved his flag for an infringement against me; the referee came over, discussed it with him, and disallowed the goal.

Petrie was incensed and wanted us all to walk off the field in protest. Most of our players followed his orders, particularly our defenders. As they were leaving the pitch, a player from the Vietnamese Civilian side played a long ball up field from the spot where I had been penalized. With no defenders to thwart him one of their forwards tapped the ball into the empty goal, and they were awarded the match.

Petrie looked like he had a purple vein ready to explode on his forehead and ordered us all to get straight onto the bus and go back to the hotel.

Fortunately cool heads eventually prevailed and there were apologies from Vietnamese officials. Although when the third-place game against the Khmer Republic came round on Sunday Petrie was still seething and only put out fringe players to represent us, they lost 4-0.

As players, we were angry at the time, for what we thought was an injustice: beaten by 'home' officialdom. I was outside the box when the keeper made his clearance and it was not my fault he mistimed his kick; but, it was no good crying over spilt milk as the saying goes.

For the record, the Saigon Military side, who we had beaten in our opening game, defeated the Civilian side 1-0 to win the 'Spring Tree' trophy.

Karma perhaps?

We might have lost to a dodgy decision, but it was a trifling injustice compared to the questionable decisions and real injustices the people of

Indochina suffered during a protracted conflict that lasted, substantially more than ninety minutes!

The Saigon experience seems a long time ago, and to put it into perspective, *Grandad* by Clive Dunn was number one in the UK charts and George Harrison's *My Sweet Lord* was topping the airwaves in the US of A.

My only connection today: I'm now a grandad.

I have not been back to Vietnam since that trip in 1971, though I have lived in Asia for over 50 years. I continue to hear good reports about life in the united country, as it is now, and I've promised myself that I'll go back there in the not too distant future.

When I lived in Hong Kong, a visit to the bar of the Foreign Correspondents' Club often reminded me of my trip to Vietnam, but my memories are like a small note on a postcard in comparison to the fascinating stories of Saigon told by experienced 'hacks' who had covered the entirety of the war.

Men like the seasoned war correspondent, Alabama-born Charlie Smith, who worked for UPI in Saigon during the war. Charlie's magnetism at the bar would draw people into earshot whenever he was recounting moving stories of the conflict in his soft southern drawl.

Alongside him at the bar would be Bert Okuley, a native of Detroit and very much a regular at the FCC; he had been Charlie's bureau chief in Saigon.

Bert was actually the man responsible for Dutch-born photographer Hugh Van Es taking that iconic picture of an Air America Huey helicopter, perched on the roof of a building, with people climbing up a makeshift ladder, frantically trying to escape the fall of Saigon on April 29, 1975.

The building in question actually housed CIA officials and their families, but Van Es's historic photograph was often captioned, incorrectly, as the building housing the American Embassy in Saigon. Hugh was the UPI photographer and he was in the office that day developing film when Bert shouted out to him, "Van Es, get out here! There's a chopper on that roof!"

I heard that story several times from the horse's mouth while having a drink at the bar with Bert, who also used to throw me the occasional tip for the races at Happy Valley, always from an unknown source. Clandestine as ever.

Hugh Van Es had been in Vietnam for a great number of years and must have taken many moving combat photographs, but his rushed shot that day, at the command of his bureau chief, became the defining picture of the 'fall of Saigon'.

Australian Ray Cranbourne, or 'Cuddles' as he was affectionately known, was another photographer who covered the hot spots of the war through his camera lens.

He shrewdly used a Vespa scooter for getting around the country, and found carrying cartons of cigarettes would often get him fuel in areas where gasoline rations were scarce.

I never met any of these characters while I was in Saigon, but got to know them all pretty well in later years, whether at the bar of the FCC in Hong Kong or on one of the frequent golf tours to Manila. Sadly, none of these charismatic gentlemen are still with us, but their stories are indelibly etched in conversational history.

There is, however, at the time of writing, a living veteran from that period whom I still see from time to time in Thailand.

Israel Freedman – known to everyone as Izzy – was an Air America pilot, and one of those who evacuated people by helicopter from the US Embassy when it fell that day in April 1975.

Izzy had been in Vietnam since early 1963 and it's fascinating to listen to the stories of his many missions during the war. He originally piloted a Fairchild C-123, which was used to carry troops and deliver supplies and evacuate the wounded.

On one occasion, Izzy flew his plane alongside two other transport planes carrying troops, as backup to the plane carrying the then United States Secretary of Defense, Robert McNamara, who was on a fact-finding mission to Vietnam.

"McNamara was in this bulky white C-123 plane, and we dubbed it 'The White Whale' because of its shape and colour," Izzy told me with a wry smile. "Our three planes flew alongside in case of an emergency and we had troops ready to deploy from within our aircraft."

After two tours, Izzy joined Air America and flew helicopters until the end of the war. One day, decades later, we shared breakfast in Bang Saray, a fishing village near his home, and I asked him how many helicopter missions he had taken part in.

"Hundreds and hundreds; some lasting just seven minutes and others for an hour, depending on the mission."

When he settled down in Thailand Izzy opened a bar in 1984 in the infamous Patpong district of Bangkok. Called the Crown Royal, it was a popular after-work spot with local expats, particularly on a Friday night, when it was often three deep at the bar with customers. They had a bell just above the bar, which, when rung, signalled drinks for all the female staff; it normally peeled once or twice a night, but most Fridays it rang every twenty minutes or so.

After finally selling his bar Izzy moved to the fringes of Pattaya, and has lived there ever since. One of the most warm-hearted characters you could ever meet, he still has some old war-time buddies who live near him and we have a group who play annually for the 'Izzy Freedman' Trophy, normally at Burapha Golf Course or Phoenix in Chon Buri.

Izzy's golf days are behind him now, but the trophy is in honour of his friendship to the many who know him.

When we packed our bags to leave the Bat Dat Hotel – in what is now Ward 11, District 5 of Ho Chi Minh City – that Monday in 1971, we never had anybody to say goodbye to except a youngish Vietnamese man, and there was a twinge of sadness about that.

He was our 21-year-old liaison officer, whose duty had been to look after the team; he had apparently been brought back from the war front just to look after us. His English was pretty good, albeit with a slight American twang.

He called himself 'Dung', but preferred to be known as 'Johnny', probably his assumed name when mixing with his G.I. buddies in combat conditions. He was always neatly dressed in his fatigues and peaked cap.

His time with us, sightseeing, accompanying us to matches and dinners, must have seemed like a 'get out of jail' card for a while. We could not imagine the horrors he might have witnessed, so we never asked, and he never said.

We made him as welcome as possible when he was with us, chipping in to buy him the odd gift, like a carton of cigarettes. When we said our final goodbyes to 'Johnny' I think the gift he treasured most was a picture we gave him.

One of our boys had a female pen-pal in America and she had sent him a picture of herself. Johnny had seen the picture and it was obvious that he liked it, so it seemed a suitable departing gift for the young trooper; especially as he seemed to like everything American. We gave it to him just as we were departing and you could see the joyous look on his face as he carefully tucked it into a sleeve of his thin leather wallet.

He probably told his buddies when he went back to the front that he now had a pen-pal. Why not, it was probably the last thing he looked at before closing his eyes each evening, not knowing what the next day would bring, or whether he would survive it.

I don't know if 'Johnny' made it through the war; it would be nice to know that he did. Slim chance, perhaps, but somewhere an anonymous American girl would never know that her picture made a young Vietnamese soldier's life that bit more bearable during a very cruel war.

7

Looting the Tai-Pan's trophy cabinet

After returning from our sortie to Vietnam we cruised past KMB winning 6-2 with a brace of goals each from Walter, new recruit Archie McCuaig, and me.

However, the big crunch game was to come on February 12: could we topple then current league title holders, Jardines, considered to be the 'Real Madrid' of local football.

They had a star-studded side that included Cheung Chi-doy – who had played in the top flight of English football with Blackpool – and were backed financially by Jardine Matheson, one of the original wealthy trading houses, or 'hongs', that dated back to Imperial China.

History tells us that Jardines were one of the most influential companies in the development of Hong Kong, but they only intermittently got involved in local football. They had a club side in the 1950s for a brief period, but it was not until the 1968/69 season that they dabbled in local football again; their team winning the Senior Shield that season.

The following year they were totally dominant and won four trophies, including the league title. All four were proudly exhibited behind a protective display in a window at the company's headquarters, Jardine House, then located at the corner of Des Voeux Road and Pedder Street in Central District. (The Connaught Centre, which is now known as Jardine House, would come two years later, in 1972).

The trophies were a symbol of their superiority in local football, but also a great advertising vehicle for the proud old company and their young tai-pan, the 32-year-old Henry Keswick; who would in later years be deservedly knighted – he was plain old Henry at that time.

I recall walking in Central one afternoon, shortly after arriving in Hong Kong, and stopping at Jardine House to look at the gleaming trophies.

Now, barely a year later, we were plotting to take them away from their elegant throne.

First though we had to beat Jardines on the field; not quite a 'Churchillian' phrase, but, as it turned out, some of the opposition did think it was war that Friday evening in front of a record crowd for a First Division league match of 28,382.

Some of their tackling that night was deplorable – their cause had not been helped by the fact that their star player, Cheung Chi-doy had pulled out of the game injured. In his absence their motto appeared to be: "if we can't beat them, stop them."

They were reportedly on a win bonus of $200 per player, a lofty amount in 1971, so they did have quite an incentive. In those days it was two points for a win and victory for Jardines would have consolidated their lead at the top of the table. But we had other ideas.

The report in the *SCMP* the next day summed up the game well: "Rangers knocked a lot of the pomp and pride out of Jardines, the reigning champions, when they beat them even more decisively than the 4-2 scoreline suggests, before a thoroughly entertained and record capacity crowd at the Hong Kong Stadium last night.

It was a blood-tingling and spine-chilling encounter. Jardines lost more than a game and two vital points, they lost a host of friends by their often crude and frequently crippling tackles, particularly in defence.

Not unexpectedly, Derek Currie was the main target for much of the abuse and goalkeeper Chow Chee-keong, who had yet another shocking game, seemed more interested in his physical attacks on the flying Scotsman than in his main job of keeping the ball out of the net."

Chow Chee-keong was a Malaysian international goalkeeper and he got further criticism from writer Lee Wai-kit in the *China Mail* newspaper the next afternoon. Lee claimed it was Chow's worst performance as a goalkeeper and one of the darkest days in his career.

"He was booed and jeered repeatedly in the second half for his cruel and rough play, but he managed to get off without any punishment in the face of lenient refereeing by Ivor David."

I hasten to add, Chow was more or less restricted to his 18-yard line, the war zone was even tougher further up the pitch! But we came through it and I scored a hat-trick – you'll hardly be surprised when I say that two of them came from the penalty spot! Tang Hung-cheong got the other.

Let me also say though that I bear no grudge against Chow, he went on to become a good friend and we became team-mates in many games in later years for the Hong Kong League XI, with considerable success.

Chow was rash in those early encounters, but I was almost always fortunate enough to get the better of him, even in later years when he played for South China. In certain quarters he was known as 'the Flying Sword,' because of his bravery guarding his line; and like Zorro, he left his mark. Walter, Jackie and I were the new kids in town and everybody wanted a piece of us, literally! In another game, not long after that first encounter, Chow left a stud mark in my thigh, which, although fading, still shows as a small scar today; and I am now 73 years of age.

As a forward with an eye for goal you have to expect challenges, and all I expect in return is for the referee to do his job; unfortunately, that is not always the case.

Sadly Chow passed away a few years ago. When asked by a journalist for my thoughts on him, I replied, "We were the worst of enemies and the best of friends."

The Jardines game was a turning point for Rangers and we were now real title contenders. We also had more and more local fans supporting us, because as a club, we always gave 100% and played within the spirit, laws and boundaries of the game. There now looked a real chance that some of those trophies on show in Central might soon be moving to a clubhouse in Causeway Bay.

The win over the current champions gave us added momentum and we continued upwards in our quest for the league title, which, if we managed it, would be the first ever for Petrie's Hong Kong Rangers. But before that, we had another chance to pick up silverware, and our opponents were South China.

We had reached the final of the Senior Shield, the oldest football knockout tournament in Asia, first played for in 1896 on the football fields that lay inside the Happy Valley racetrack.

The old, moth-eaten records show that in the final that year Kowloon FC defeated HMS Centurion 3-0 in front of 2,000 spectators who were accommodated in open, temporary stands.

You might ask: who were Kowloon FC?

Well, they were principally engineers who found themselves working on the wrong side of the harbour, while the *HMS Centurion* side were picked from the 620 sailors on board the flagship of the colonial China Station, which was based in Hong Kong.

I should mention that the sailors got their revenge the following year, beating the engineers 2-1; again the game was played at the Valley, with a similar large crowd in attendance.

As I am still an absent member of the Hong Kong Football Club, I should proudly also mention that the grand old Hong Kong Football Club team won the Senior Shield, after extra time, in 1899, the competition's fourth year. Old press reports show a chap by the name of J.F. Noble, who worked for HSBC, put a "lightning shot into the net". I believe it was the first ever silverware of any kind won by the Club.

All a far cry from us in 1971 lining up to play South China in front of over 26,000 fans at the Government Stadium. It was still the same old Shield, and just as important to the players of both sides as it would have been to those long ago players at the end of the 19th century.

Like a Hitchcock thriller, our game built up to a dramatic ending: we came back from the brink of defeat to score two goals in two minutes towards the end of full-time and shatter South China's hope of adding another trophy to their name.

The late goals gave us a 3-2 victory, but we had to work really hard to achieve success that day. Reports in the press said, "The Senior Shield will stand on Rangers' sideboard as a tribute to the professionalism of their overseas players, who had to do two men's work, as some of the young

Chinese boys in their side crumpled under the pressure of trailing by 2 goals to 1 with defeat staring them in the face."

A bit cruel, but the heads of some of our players did go down due to lack of experience, and I like to think our fighting spirit taught some of them a valuable lesson. The old adage 'the game is not over until the final whistle' comes to mind. Our fans cheered loudly when the final whistle went, while South China fans groaned, as did their players; the game had been turned on its head in a frantic final 10 minutes. Our first trophy for Petrie and we certainly celebrated that night; probably as much as Kowloon FC did 75 years earlier.

Another much sought-after trophy was the Viceroy Cup. It was introduced in 1969 and was the first time that the Hong Kong Football Association had opened its doors to commercial sponsorship; BAT (British American Tobacco) were first in and Viceroy was one of their biggest cigarette brands in Asia.

Not quite a breath of fresh air by today's commercial standards, but back then their promotion of the event was welcomed and added a bit of colour to the game; as well as putting up enough prize money to dangle an enticing carrot in front of clubs and players. In later years BAT would bring out well-known footballing figures to add a little glamour to the prize presentation on the day of the final.

Jardines won the inaugural event; the trophy being one of the four displayed in the window at Jardine House. It very much resembled the English FA Cup and was similar in size. In those days the tobacco companies spent huge amounts on advertising; and apparently for buying silverware as well.

The competition format for the 1970/71 season – the first year Rangers participated – saw two groups of four teams, labelled A and B. The winners of group A would meet the runners-up of group B, and the B winners would meet the A runners-up in the semi-finals. In later years it would be a straight knockout competition for Division One clubs; but in the first year of Rangers participation only eight teams entered.

Since there was prize money involved, clubs like South China and Happy Valley, who were not fully professional, did not enter sides in the first two seasons of the competition. However by the time the 71/72 event came round, all 14 teams had joined in.

We got to the semi-final and beat Jardines 1-0 and would face our old enemy Eastern in the final; they had defeated Sing Tao 3-2 in the other semi-final tie.

Full marks to Eastern, they pulled off the upset of the season by beating us 2-1 and, to make it worse, they came from 1-0 down to win. Drawing 1-1 at full-time, the game went to extra time and unfortunately we conceded a penalty.

Our Irish recruit, Eddie Simpson, who had been out for some time with an injury, and was only just back in the team, brought down Eastern's Tse Kam-wah. The penalty was awarded in the third minute of extra time. Their veteran skipper, Lo Shun-kong, made no mistake from the spot, and that's how it ended. Naturally, Eastern were delighted – and we were utterly despondent!

Two trophies would have been great, but hey, we still had a good chance of winning the big one, the league title, to add to the Senior Shield.

I was top-scorer in that Viceroy Cup, despite losing to Eastern, with six goals from five matches. My team-mate Kwok Ka-ming was runner-up with three goals. It hardly made up for losing in the final though, a bit like being the best man at a wedding, with no honeymoon to look forward to.

The season moved on towards the business end of proceedings and our pursuit of winning a first ever league title for Rangers. We were still on an upward trajectory after a hard-fought 4-3 win over Happy Valley, followed by an amazing 7-2 win over South China, a game in which Walter and I both scored hat-tricks, the other goal coming from Tang Hung-cheong.

Tang had the nickname 'Mamo' – which literally means horse hair – as he loved gambling on the horses at Happy Valley. He was always asking me for 'tipsy', as he would say in his broken English; he was well aware that I had a few close links with several jockeys riding in Hong Kong. He was a talented player who modelled himself on George Best and would often say at training 'me Jorgee Bestee.'

He was brilliant in a game for the League XI, when we lost to Santos 5-2, and was a key player in our hunt for the league title. He had loads of talent, and was never scared to dribble past opponents – the sign of a good mid-field player.

Although we faltered slightly at the end of the season, we won our last game game of the season by six goals to two, and clinched the League title. It was the first and only time Rangers would win it in their history.

Admittedly it was not quite as comfortable as we had hoped: Jardines finished a mere two points behind us in runner's up spot. But it was a truly wonderful season for the club and also for Walter, Jackie and me, considering all the pressure heaped on us as the new boys in town.

It was a season, I will never forget and neither would any of my team-mates.

Hong Kong Rangers had only won four league games in the season prior to our arrival. In winning the title, we only lost four games!

Walter and I scored 30 goals each that season, but unfortunately for us, Chan Chui-kee of South China, scored 31 to pip us for sharing the top goal scoring award. Tough, but I would win that title the next season, despite an under-par performance in the league by Rangers.

Sadly, Walter had a huge fallout with Petrie over conditions. Particularly Petrie's high-handed attitude, combined with the 'schoolboy rules' he forced on him. After all, Walter was 27 years of age! The 'big man' left the club and headed for new pastures in Australia; but it wasn't long before he would return to his adopted home.

For Jackie and I, it was time for a well earned holiday and back to Glasgow to see our family and friends, telling stories of the 'Fragrant Harbour' that few, if any, would believe.

8

Sunset over Manila Bay, taming a German giant... and eventually paying the price

Returning from a break in Scotland, it was a long flight back to Hong Kong for a new second season in the city.

Despite differences with Petrie, Jackie and I had agreed to play another season with Rangers, but I managed to negotiate moving out of the annex club house in Yee Wo Street and into a shared flat in Tin Hau Temple road, a short walk up the hill from the Park Cinema, across from Victoria Park.

Accommodation was fairly expensive in Hong Kong in relation to salaries, so it was best to share the costs.

An ad in the *SCMP* listed a vacancy in a three-bedroom, Tin Hau Temple Road flat. The location was great for me: a twenty minute walk – or an eight minute taxi ride if I was late – from training at Happy Valley.

On viewing the flat I found it was shared by a man and a woman, both working in Central district.

Deborah was from England – apart from her day job she also played cello in the Hong Kong Philharmonic Orchestra. But it was the chap who interviewed me to see if I was a suitable tenant; at the same time I checked them out as I didn't want to stay with a couple of rockers who played music and partied all night – being a young athlete I needed rest and peace! The cello was acceptable.

The chap was Dean Barrett, an American from New London in Connecticut, who wrote for the renowned Asian art and culture magazine, *Orientations*. An interesting character, as I found out in later years. He joined the Army Security Service, trained as a Chinese translator and served in Thailand during the Vietnam War, and then earned a Master's Degree in Asian Studies at the University of Hawaii.

For those who do not know his writing, Dean has published a number of novels, many set in Asia, including *Memoirs of a Bangkok Warrior*, *Skytrain to Murder* and his Hong Kong classic *Hangman's Point*, set in colonial Hong Kong in 1857. Dean told me it took him two years to research the latter, including several trips to London to visit libraries that housed old historical documents. Dean has spent a large part of his life in Asia, mostly in Hong Kong and Thailand, and, like me, is now retired in the land of smiles.

It was almost 30 years since I had seen Dean, then, out of the blue, I bumped into him one day outside the Hyatt Hotel, near the Foreign Correspondents' Club in Chit Lom, Bangkok. Since then we have caught up on several occasions, the last in the Robin Hood pub when I was researching this book. Dean is a man with a great affection for Asia; very much like myself.

So after moving in with my new flatmates and getting used to my new surroundings, it was time for football again. With Walter Gerrard moving away, Petrie had gone back to Scotland to find new recruits for the 71/72 season. Defender Eddie Simpson had not been given a new contract and Archie McCuaig had decided to go back to Scotland.

Sadly, Archie had complications with a bout of pneumonia a short time later and died in his homeland. Those of us who knew and played alongside the friendly, but tough mid-fielder, were sad when we got the news, it was heartbreaking that Archie, a former player for St. Mirren, died so young, he was the epitome of a great bloke. Life can indeed be cruel.

Petrie returned with his new recruits, almost a year to the day after Walter, Jackie and I had disembarked at Kai Tak Airport. They were midfielder Jimmy Hughes, forward Gus Eadie, and defender Hugh McCrory.

I knew Gus Eadie from my Glasgow days and played against him for Motherwell when he was playing for St. Mirren alongside Gordon

McQueen (another who would eventually play in Hong Kong). I knew little about Jimmy Hughes, other than that he was a battling mid-field player.

McCrory was a 17-year-old youngster who had spent the previous two seasons at the Manchester City youth academy. When I was back in Scotland I had watched a trial game that Petrie had arranged, and mentioned to him that the young left back would be a good asset to the club. Petrie duly signed young McCrory. Being the youngest, he was soon nicknamed 'Junior', and that's how I will refer to him from now on.

Junior would play a season with me at Rangers before I left for Seiko; after that we developed a healthy rivalry, opposing each other in many matches, him being a defender and me a forward. I should mention that although Junior was a talented player with a great left foot, he could also produce crunching tackles, and I was on the end of some of them! Funnily enough, we would end up playing alongside one another at Seiko and eventually become good buddies.

Petrie also brought out other players during the season, including Stewart Gilmour, and an old pal of mine from Glasgow, Andy Savage, a very handy footballer.

Before the season started, Petrie arranged a pre-season tour to Manila in the Philippines. It was my first trip to the Philippines and the densely populated city on the island of Luzon, but, following in the footsteps of General Douglas MacArthur, who vowed, "I shall return" when he was evacuated during World War II, I did return, many, many, more times than the great general himself.

Petrie had signed a mild mannered and quietly spoken centre-forward, Victor Koliczew, an American-born player of Brazilian parents, who was strongly built and, according to Petrie, came with a big reputation. However, he failed to live up to it, and Victor would eventually drift away into anonymity as far as his playing days with Rangers were concerned. But for now, he was on the tour alongside us.

We flew into Manila International Airport and were met by representatives of the Philippines Football Association who quickly whisked us through immigration – I would learn later, not everything was quick in the Philippines, especially the traffic. On the journey to the hotel we were amazed at the number of vehicles on the road; our bus driver made good use of his horn as cars and jeepneys zig-zagged around us.

The jeepneys were basically jeeps left behind when the American forces left the Philippines at the end of World War II. They were converted and recycled as mini-buses, their steel bodies gaily painted with pictures of film stars, musicians, religious figures and anything that could add colour. They were a popular way to get around the city for the locals and seemed to stop anywhere and everywhere.

Our bus finally turned onto Roxas Boulevard, the vast promenade and major highway that runs along the shores of Manila Bay lined with towering coconut trees swaying in the breeze – a sharp contrast to many of the other roads in the city!

We were bunked in the Aloha Hotel right on Roxas Boulevard, overlooking the scenic bay. I shared a room with Gus Eadie and Ron Tinsley.

Gus I soon realized was a bit of a rebel, and one night tried to make it four in our room. Petrie got wind of it and, despite Gus claiming he was stiff after the flight and only wanted a massage, Petrie kicked the masseuse out. Several months later Gus himself would be kicked out of the club, but ended up playing for another Hong Kong side. A pity, because Gus was a good footballer, but 'Cool Million', as he was later nicknamed, did not fit in with Petrie's house rules.

The two matches we played in Manila were against the newly formed Philippines national team, coached and managed by a Spaniard, Juan Cutillas, a former Atlético de Madrid player.

Andrés Soriano, the family head of the San Miguel Corporation, had brought Cutillas over in the hope of strengthening the appeal of football in the country. At that time the Philippines was very much influenced by American sports, especially basketball, and Soriano wanted a more even balance with European sports – the irony at the time being that the average height of a male Filipino was just 5 feet 4 inches, yet the national sport was basketball!

Mind you, the Philippines came up with some great boxers over the years: Flash Elorde, Luisito Espinosa and more recently Manny Pacquiao. However football lagged behind in popularity and Soriano wanted to address that and see some improvement in the local players.

It was Soriano and San Miguel that had sponsored our trip, with a little help from Cathay Pacific Airways.

In a move reminiscent of Petrie in Hong Kong, Cutillas, who had obtained a national coaching licence in Spain, decided to bring some young Spanish footballers to Manila. He brought over four players to play in exhibition and unofficial games, hoping their skills would somehow rub off on the local Filipinos and attract more interest, and spectators, to the local game. It actually worked for a short period.

Manuel Cuenca and Tomas Lozano were two of these players and, ironically, two years later they would be playing alongside me at Seiko. A lack of financial resources caused a decline in Filipino football and with basketball's influence again in the ascendancy the pair eventually moved to Hong Kong.

Manuel was a tricky winger who liked to dribble to the touchline and then cross balls into the penalty box; while Thomas played as an inside-forward.

As with our first days in Hong Kong, some of the local Filipino food took us a bit by surprise. One of the lads, being a bit conservative, decided to play it safe, so when he saw a man selling 'boiled eggs' he bought a couple.

On cracking one open he was shocked to find a well-formed duck embryo inside; it even had its tiny wings! He thought he had been done by the seller and was about to chase after him when our guide, who thought this was hilarious stopped him, explaining that it was a snack called *balut* and that was the way it was supposed to be. He went on to say it was quite a local delicacy. We refrained from sampling it.

At dinner one night we were served another Filipino classic: chicken *adobo* – there's also a pork version – a kind of Filipino stew where the meat is marinated and cooked in vinegar with garlic and spices and served along with rice. After a few tentative bites, we found this to be delicious and much more to our liking.

Our two friendly matches took place at the Rizal Memorial Stadium, named after the Philippines national hero, José Rizal, and located in the Malate district of Manila. The games attracted only a few thousand spectators – unlike five years earlier when the Beatles came to town and played in front of one audience of 50,000 in the same stadium; it was the Beatles' second biggest attendance ever at a concert.

Okay, we were not the 'Fab Four', but we had expected a bigger crowd and a few of us certainly had hair long enough to match McCartney and company. The Beatles combined audience was 80,000 at their two Rizal concerts in 1966; we had just over 4,000 for our two matches, one we won and the other we drew.

Jimmy Howard, alias the Rentokil 'Ratcatcher' who played as an amateur for Rangers in 1969, was now living in Manila and offered to take a few of us out on the town after our last match, when the sun had gone down over Manila Bay.

Jimmy promised Petrie he would look after us and uncharacteristically Petrie gave his blessing. Jimmy whipped us down to the Mabini district for a whirlwind tour of the nightlife. Copious amounts of San Miguel beer were downed, and we all ended up in a bar called the 'American Eagle', one of Jimmy's favourite haunts. A bar steeped in history, but sadly past its glory days now.

Then the bar was still fairly fashionable: it had a huge sculptured eagle on display and a combo playing music on a small stage with long curtains dangling from the ceiling. There were also ladies around who were happy to have a drink and a dance. Getting back to the Aloha Hotel was a bit hazy that night: I'm sure someone must have 'shown me the way', and it wasn't Peter Frampton.

After enjoying more than a few tipples in Manila, Hogmanay on the eve of 1972 was as dry as the Sahara for me.

The mighty Bundesliga club, Hamburg, were in town and I had been selected to play for the Hong Kong League XI against them two days later. I did however attend the traditional New Year's Day race meeting at Happy Valley racecourse – coming out a few hundred dollars to the good. I slept well that night.

Hamburg were a top side, the squad included two players who had played for West Germany against England in the 1966 World Cup final at Wembley: Willi Schulz and West German captain Uwe Seeler.

Just under 28,000 flocked to the ground when we faced Hamburg, hoping that the League XI could topple a crack Bundesliga side that also included another four West German internationals in their line-up. The game was also live on TV throughout the city and later reports showed it drew a huge television audience.

Their goalkeeper, Özcan Arkoç, was a former Turkish international who had played with leading sides Fenerbahçe and Beşiktaş, so Hamburg had no shortage of experience from back to front.

Mind you, our League XI side were no slouches. We had the Cheung brothers, Chi-wai and Chi-doy, leading the line, me on the left wing and Kwok Ka-ming on the right.

Malaysian international Chow Chee-keong was our goalkeeper and at the heart of defence were Fok Pak-ling and Lau Chi-wai, supported by full-backs, Tse Kwok-keung and Chan Shui-hong. The tigerish Tsang Keng-hung was in midfield alongside Chan Hung-ping. Anyone who knew their local football could see that this was not a bad side; and so it would prove against the Germans.

When referee Lee Kan-chee blew his whistle at half-time the game was scoreless; there had been a few niggling challenges in the first half and Schulz had been booked for a bad challenge on Cheung Chi-doy.

Hamburg had assigned full-back Caspar Memering to tight marking duties on me. Although his close attention made it slightly difficult, it didn't blunt my enthusiasm or effort: I still spent the first 45 minutes prodding and stabbing at the German defence looking for openings.

Memering at that time was a relatively young player; later he would move up to play in midfield, and be a member of the Hamburg side that won the Cup Winners Cup in 1977 and also in the West German side that won the Euro Cup in 1980. However, my pace would prove greater than his on this particular day.

The breakthrough came in the second minute of the second half, following a clever move between Chan Hung-ping and Cheung Chi-doy. The ball reached me inside the box, but my quick shot was blocked by keeper Arkoç. There must have been at least three defenders around me and the momentum from one of them had pushed me partially to the ground. But the ball the keeper had parried was still to be won.

Somehow I sprung back up like a toy soldier on a spring, and before any Hamburg defender could get to the ball, blasted it goalwards. It hit the roof of the net and the stadium erupted, as, apparently, did many households across the territory.

There is a photograph of me, just before the ball found the net, lying on the ground with German defenders all around me. To this day I still don't know where I got the speed, or effort, to pick myself up, beat them all to the ball. 'Jumping Jack Flash' springs to mind.

Journalist I.M. MacTavish (alias Jock Sloan) described the moment the next day in the *SCMP* "Currie, 'Jesus', tormented the German defence with his pace and persistence, and his goal, created out of half a chance following a delightful inter-change between Cheung Chi-doy and Chan Hung-ping, must have given him much satisfaction, as it did to the 27,565 fans who packed the stadium." Despite strong Hamburg pressure, and with a couple of great saves by Chow Chee-keong in the League XI goal, we held on to beat the crack German side 1-0.

The Hamburg coach, Klaus-Dieter Ochs, was quoted in *The Standard* the next day as saying he was disappointed by his side's performance: our packed defence and good saves by our goalkeeper had kept his side from scoring. Well, that's the job of the defence and the goalkeeper, is it not?

However he did have a few kind words, saying: "The League side was equal to many sides that play in the Bundesliga, and would hold their own." That was much appreciated, although perhaps a slight exaggeration. It was a great victory for Hong Kong, but more than anything, it gave the many fans a great feeling of pride, as I would find out two weeks later.

Ian Petrie had taken us to Shek O, a little seaside village with a lovely beach on the southern side of Hong Kong island. We had done some leg work on the sands and afterwards retired to one of the many little huts in the village that served *yum cha*, a nice selection of Chinese tea and *dim sum*.

As we were having our noodles and pork dumplings, Petrie was engrossed in a conversation in Cantonese with an elderly villager who had a tanned and deeply lined face and who, for some reason, was pointing at me.

Petrie then repeated to me in English what the villager had said. "He told me that most of the village watched the game against Hamburg on TV; when you scored everybody stood up and cheered loudly... and when the game finished they all got drunk."

To this day, that was one of my proudest moments and thinking about it still brings a lump to my throat. It was not in a Scotland jersey, playing, or scoring at Hampden, but in my newly adopted home, and for the people of Hong Kong.

I had done it for them, and was as proud as they were that day. I went over and shook the old man's hand and thanked him kindly.

Hamburg would return to Hong Kong in late 1978, with arguably one of the best club sides in Europe, or the world for that matter. I would score against them once again, but things would not work out quite as well as our previous encounter. Thankfully, the game was not covered live on TV in Hong Kong, or in Shek O!

The galaxy of stars in the Hamburg team included Keegan, Kaltz, Hrubesch, and Magath. That four between them would collectively amass 250 international appearances for Germany and England.

To say they were on a revenge mission was an understatement, they were hell bent on redressing their defeat in 1972. Their opponents this time would not be the League XI but Seiko, the club I joined at the end of the 71/72 season.

The 'Watchmen', as we were known, had a good side, but the weaknesses around our defence would be as exposed as the Maginot line was for France in the last world war. Perhaps I was to blame. After 10 minutes I scored a goal, that seemed to make them angry.

Team-mate Billy Semple had slipped the ball to me at the edge of the 18-yard box, inside full-back Manny Kaltz and, after taking a few steps, I drilled it past goalkeeper Rudi Kargus. Seiko were 1-0 up against the side which would win the Bundesliga title that season. Sadly, *déjà vu* it was not to be, our glory would be fleeting.

Someone later told me that they were flying from Hong Kong to London on board a Cathay Pacific jet that same night. After take off, the Captain came on the passenger address system and announced that I had just scored a goal and Seiko were leading Hamburg 1-0; a rousing cheer followed. It just showed that there was a lot of local interest in the game but, thank goodness, when the plane was out of Hong Kong airspace there were no further dispatches.

It's fair to say the game was a big occasion in Hong Kong that evening; particularly with European footballer-of-the-year Kevin Keegan playing. However, my goal was like a red rag to a bull. They came at us like a bat out of hell and put four past us before half-time!

Ours was not a happy changing room at the interval and the club boss, Wong Chong-san, let us know his thoughts. "I do not want to see you defending so much, you are all on $10,000 a man, win or lose, so go out in the second half and attack them." There were good intentions behind the words of C.S., as he was known, but it was the worst thing he could have said. If we had tried to keep possession, restricting their space and control, then we might not have conceded another five in the second half!

Their giant of a centre-forward, Horst Hrubesch, often finding himself unmarked, scored three in the second period and instead of Manny Kaltz, my direct opposite number, marking me, it was soon me chasing him down the flank to stop his overlapping runs.

It was a disaster of epic proportions! The final score: 9-1 to Hamburg.

My worst defeat in any grade of football; they had beaten us by the width of the River Elbe. To cap off our disastrous night their ninth was an own goal by defender, Hugh McCrory. He was so upset by the lack of marking from his fellow defenders that in the last few minutes of the game he blasted the ball into his own net in sheer frustration.

As the players were walking back to the centre-circle Kevin Keegan said to our Scottish centre-forward – the six-foot plus Ian McWilliams: "This reminds me of a Scotland v England game," referring to the humiliating 9-3 defeat Scotland suffered at the hands of England in 1961.

Not appreciating the remark, McWilliams, who incidentally was legendary coach Jock Stein's last signing for Glasgow Celtic, growled at the former Liverpool star. "I'll kill you, you little shit." Not likely that he would have, but Keegan was concerned enough to turn to me and say, "tell him I was only joking."

Keegan actually looked quite worried. McWilliams at 6' 5" was considered Britain's tallest player when he signed for Celtic and was an imposing figure. Secretly though he was a gentle giant, but I never told Keegan that. I just said, "no problem, just buy him a pint after the game."

Funnily enough, when I was covering the 1998 World Cup finals in France I bumped into Keegan, also covering the event, in Bordeaux at the Stade Chaban-Delmas, prior to a group match between Scotland and Norway. We had a chuckle recalling the 9-3 conversation in Hong Kong almost twenty years prior, which amazingly he actually remembered.

After the game against Hamburg I was ambushed by a German television commentator and his cameraman who asked if I could be interviewed. The interview went like this:

"Mr Currie, you scored the goal in the one nil defeat the last time Hamburg played in Hong Kong and you also scored tonight, anything to say?" I spoke a little German and replied, "Heute abend, Hamburg über alles" which literally means in English "Tonight, Hamburg above all" – a play on the words of the German national anthem put to music by Haydn.

Expecting me to speak in English, he was taken aback and immediately cut the interview and said to me, "perfect."

It might have been perfect for him, and German television, but it was more than a tad humiliating for me and my team-mates!

If someone had said to me I would be playing against Eduardo Gonçalves de Andrade over Chinese New Year in 1972, the answer would probably have been, "who?" A further clue that he played for Brazil would be of little help.

That he played for Brazil in the 1970 World Cup final against Italy would narrow down the likely candidates. But had they given me his nickname, 'Tostão' (little coin), well, who didn't know him!

Many of the great Brazilian players were given nicknames early in their careers, some even before they entered their early teens. These names would often stick, and for many, like Tostão, their given names and family names would never be on the radar, or the back of a jersey. Pelé and Kaká are prime examples. Tostão was a young 19-year-old when he made his debut at the 1966 World Cup finals against the Hungarians at Goodison Park, replacing Pelé who had been injured in the previous match against Bulgaria. Although he scored, it was not a happy debut for the youngster: Brazil lost 3-1. However his fortunes would change four years later, winning the World Cup in Mexico.

I always felt Tostão was something of an unsung hero in that great Brazilian side; mind you, it's easy to be overshadowed when you're playing alongside Pelé, Gérson, Jairzinho and Carlos Alberto.

I had already played against Pelé and Clodoaldo, two of that World Cup winning side, in the game against Santos. Now I would face two more of the players who defeated Italy 4-1 that day in Mexico City. Hong Kong Rangers were to play Belo Horizonte club side, Cruzeiro at the Government Stadium. Tostão's close skills were superb, he had great technique, and vitally, he had the vision for making the killer pass! He shielded the ball as well as anyone; few, if any, could dispossess him, and he could score goals. But his real talent was in setting up chances for his teammates; as when he nutmegged England captain, Bobby Moore in Guadalajara, when Brazil beat England 1-0 in the World Cup group stages, setting up the goal eventually scored by Jairzinho.

I suppose today Tostão could be called a false number 9, an unconventional centre-forward who often dropped deep to find the ball.

He would set up two of the goals in the 3-1 victory over Uruguay in the semi-final in Mexico; previously having nabbed two goals himself in Brazil's 4-2 quarter-final victory against Peru. For good measure, he was top scorer with ten goals in Brazil's qualifying games for that World Cup.

I mentioned earlier that there were two members of that victorious Brazil 1970 side in the Cruzeiro team I was about to face. The other, Wilson Piazza, played in the centre of defence for Brazil in Mário Zagallo's faultless, 4-4-2 system.

Fontana, another defensive player in the Cruzeiro team, was also a member of that 1970 squad. He played in Brazil's group game against Romania, but didn't make the team for the final. Cruzeiro also had Argentinian central defender, Perfumo, who played for his country in both the 1966 and 1974 World Cup finals, including, captaining the side in the 1974 finals in West Germany.

It was hard to fancy our chances of beating them, or indeed troubling their high quality defence for that matter.

They were on a long tour that had already taken them to Australia to play in a tournament – for history buffs, they were the first Brazilian club touring side ever to play in Australia.

Cruzeiro were scheduled to play four games in Hong Kong to celebrate the Lunar New Year holiday welcoming in the 'Year of the Boar'.

They started by beating a Hong Kong League XI side 3-0. No Rangers players were eligible for that team because none of us had turned up for a designated training session, our manager had banned us from attending!

That was because of politics between the HKFA and Petrie. It's not worth going into here, but it cost me and some team mates such as Tang Hung-cheong and Kwok Ka-ming the opportunity of playing in the League XI side. However, it was nice to see some journalists later writing that we had been badly missed.

The Hong Kong National side, riding their luck at times, managed a well-earned 1-1 draw in Cruzeiro's second game. In the third game, they beat a Hong Kong Chinese-combined side by two goals to nil. Their final match was against us on February 23.

On the night, it turned out that their strength, as expected, provided too great for our young Hong Kong Rangers side. However, it was an opportunity for the local youngsters in our side to rub shoulders with some of the great players in world football, it would hopefully be the start of a learning curve to improve their own skills.

We lost 3-0 and, although I never managed to swap shirts with Tostão that night, I did get a photograph with him and Perfumo after the match – one for the scrapbook. It was a privilege to be on the same field as the left-footed genius and, unlike Bobby Moore in Guadalajara, Tostão never nutmegged me in Hong Kong.

I did mention that to Bobby once in jest... only once mind you!

9

Looking good, eating well, and mixing it with the stars

A way from the football side of things, my early years in Hong Kong left me with a lot of free time to roam the congested streets of Causeway Bay. There were many things to spend your money on during the daytime – leaving aside the nightlife for a moment.

Tailors' shops seemed to be everywhere – it was estimated that there were some 15,000 doing business in the territory during the late 60s and early 70s – but, unlike some of their clothes, their names were not very creative: Good Tailor, Very Good Tailor, Pretty Tailor, Fancy Tailor, Best Tailor.

In 1972 it cost just $15 or so for a made-to-measure shirt, about £1, hardly an arm and a leg. Choose your style, fabric, colour, collar – button down or straight – and the shirt would be ready within a few days. Of course a smart business suit cost more, but because of the climate safari suits were both fashionable and reasonably priced.

With a combination of low prices and quality tailoring Hong Kong was a happy hunting ground for tourists looking to buy clothes to take back home.

Some tailors were very highly regarded. Sam's Tailor in Burlington Arcade for instance catered to American presidents, famous singers and movie stars: Ronald Reagan, Cliff Richard and Richard Gere all shopped there; but Sam's shirts cost a tad more than the $15 ones you could get in a Causeway Bay alley.

Sam's shop was a bit of an institution. Just off Nathan Road in Kowloon it opened for business in 1957 and was named after its founder, Sam Melwani. Over the years I got to know his son Manu, who eventually took up the day-to-day running of the shop. Manu fitted out Michael

Jackson, Prince Charles and David Bowie; he would also cut the odd cloth for me too.

My neck of the woods however was chiefly Causeway Bay. When it came time to eat, this area had it all. As well as an abundance of Chinese restaurants there were some very good European ones too and you could get a three-course set meal, with a drink of your choice, for under $10.

The inappropriately named American Restaurant at the corner of Leighton Road and Percival Street (not to be confused with the one in Lockhart Road) was a favourite of mine. They cooked a wonderful Malaysian-style curry, which brought perspiration to the brow of many a customer – it was so good I remember my teammate Walter 'the Buffalo' Gerrard often scoffing two orders at one sitting.

I should mention Walter was nicknamed '*Dai Sui Ngau*', 'big water buffalo'. by the local fans. I used to say to him it was for his lack of speed and not his size, which often got me a clip on the ear.

The Café Goldfinch in Lan Fong Road directly behind the Lee Gardens Hotel was another favourite; as was the Queen's Café, which had been around since 1952 and was justifiably famous for its wonderful borscht.

Hong Kong was a gourmet's paradise and there was always a restaurant to suit the size of your wallet. Chinese restaurants were not expensive; the Ying King, at the junction of Johnston Road and Fleming Road in Wan Chai, was just one of the many popular Cantonese eateries with very affordable prices.

Despite Hong Kong's frenetic pace, dining itself was often a leisurely affair, especially when it came to local food. At breakfast or lunch a Chinese meal could last two hours; customers would sit and read the papers and discuss the news and latest gossip with their friends, while intermittently ordering dishes from the menu. Some brought along their pet birds, hanging their cages on hooks outside the restaurant.

If you wanted to open the purse strings, then establishments like the Fook Lam Moon served some of the best Cantonese cuisine in town. In need of a good steak? Jimmy's Kitchen or the Diamond Horseshoe in O'Brien Road were just a couple of options.

When the sun set and the moon rose there were not too many traditional European-style pubs – I'm taking the somewhat seedy Wan Chai bars out of the equation.

When I first arrived I did find a pub in D'Aguilar Street. It was simply named 'The Pub' and was run by a former Aberdonian sea captain called Eric Dunbar – a man with a very large frame.

Now the *South China Morning Post* newspaper office was just a few steps away from this establishment, so it was frequented by many of their hacks, including Jack Spackman and Lex Fullarton, who from time to time caused the publican considerable grief with their antics.

In one incident, 'Lexy', as he was known, poured a pint over Eric Dunbar. No one was sure why he did it, not even Lexy. He was subsequently banned, until apologies were rendered.

There were plenty of establishments selling alcohol, but they were not like the bars back in Glasgow. Pubs as we know them, like the Bull & Bear in Hutchison House and The Jockey in Union House, did not appear until late 1974 or early 1975.

Of course there was always seedy Wan Chai, where you could have a beer and buy a drink for a lady – who could be any age from twenty to sixty – although the drink you bought for her was more than likely to be cold tea in a glass, rather than the expensive alcohol you thought you were paying for.

Plenty of people thought of opening bars in the city; some who'd never even lived there. I remember receiving a phone call one day in late 1972. It was long distance and the caller on the other end was none other than one of Scotland, and Europe's, finest players of his day, Jim Baxter, affectionately known as 'Slim Jim'.

"Derek, I am thinking of coming over and possibly opening a bar in Hong Kong. What do you think?" he asked.

Now I had known Jim for quite a few years, had played against him, and he was friendly with my two brothers, he'd got my telephone number from one of them.

"Jim," I said, "I am not sure Hong Kong is the place for a pub using your name. To be honest, I am probably better known here than you, so I'm not sure your name would bring in customers."

Although Jim was a superstar to many in Scotland, in cosmopolitan Hong Kong his name was only known to expatriates who followed football. Was that enough to succeed?

Opening a pub in the way Slim Jim fancied did not seem financially viable: never mind the cost of setting it up, renting premises in a prime location and paying his own accommodation would make margins tight to say the least. Baxter took my advice, and that was that. Was it the right call? Who knows? It might have worked in later years when the bar business started to boom, but in the very early 70s, I think, perhaps not. Wan Chai then was still the star attraction.

The former Glasgow Rangers star did eventually open a pub in Glasgow, which I think was the right place for it – he was a city icon, though perhaps not to the green half.

Over the years I often toyed with the idea of opening a pub myself. Either in Hong Kong or Macau. But in the end realised it would be a tough life – too time consuming it could often be a dangerous occupation, particularly when your pals came in. You have a drink with them, and before you know it, you forget you're the owner. It's not about drinking the profits, it's more about the state of your liver and looking after your fitness.

So it was me who gave the red card to Baxter's Bar in Hong Kong, and I gave one to myself, just for good measure.

––––––––

There were two mainstream English-language newspapers in Hong Kong in my early days: the *South China Morning Post* and *The Standard*.

But there were also a couple of afternoon tabloids: *The Star* and the *China Mail*.

The Star in Pennington Street in Causeway Bay was founded in 1965 by Graham Jenkins, a gruff Australian who was previously Reuters' manager for South-East Asia. He was a no-nonsense newspaper man who had been around Asia for a long time – during the French Indochina war he was a correspondent in Saigon. He was an interesting character if you ever decide to research his history.

The English-language version of *The Star* (which also had a Chinese edition) had a host of well-known scribes working on it over the years, including Kevin Sinclair, Geoffrey Somers, Peter Owen, Henry Parwani and a young Mike Rowse, who would go on in later years to become the Director-General of InvestHK, a department of the Hong Kong Government.

Late one morning, Terry Geary, my showbiz writer mate on *The Star* called me to ask if I was free to attend a press conference at the Hilton Hotel in Central District.

I had played a match the day before, so was available. "Who's the press conference for?" I asked.

"The Carpenters."

"Fine, meet you at *The Star* office," I told him.

When we got to the Hilton conference room there were only a dozen or so present. I had expected more, a lot more. In 1970 the talented American vocal and instrumental duo had big hits with *Close to You* and *We've Only Just Begun*.

They were very much the new, and popular, kids on the block by 1972 and I confess I enjoyed listening to the warm voice of Karen Carpenter; with the right amount of tone quality, she was almost angelic when she sang. I also loved listening to the Carpenters' version of *Ticket to Ride*, sung as a melancholy ballad which is as pleasant today as when they recorded it in 1969. So, in truth, I was looking forward to seeing and meeting the talented duo from Connecticut; after all, Jesus was a carpenter. They had just completed a sell-out tour of Australia and were in town for a concert on May 30, before flying on to Japan. When they entered the room both were dressed smart-casual, and had warm smiles.

The thing I recall more than anything about that press conference was their answer to a simple question: "Who, or what, was the greatest influence on your musical career?"

In unison they answered: "The Beatles". Not the answer I had expected.

Mind you, three years later they had another major hit with a remake of the Marvelettes' chart-topping 1961 single, *Please Mr. Postman*. With no disrespect to the Marvelettes, a great Motown group, I think Richard and Karen might just have had the Beatles in the back of their minds when deciding to record that song.

The 'fab four' from Liverpool had recorded it in 1963; and the Carpenters would have success performing another cover version of a Beatles hit.

Sadly, the wonderful voice of Karen Carpenter was silenced in 1983 when she died of heart failure, brought on by complications from anorexia. A life cut short. But, thankfully, the one thing about music is that it never dies and neither will the legacy of Karen Carpenter.

An afternoon trip to the Hilton Hotel, listening to the famous brother-and-sister duo being interviewed was enlightening. To also have a chat with them after the conference concluded was an unexpected bonus. It might sound corny but it seems like *Only Yesterday*!

Away from the city, a trip to Repulse Bay was one of the main recreational attractions. Though there was a bus route from Central to Repulse Bay – which still remains today: the number 6, one of Hong Hong's oldest bus routes – it was quicker and easier to share a red taxi with friends or team-mates.

A 10-kilometre trip from Happy Valley or Causeway Bay, up over Wong Nai Chung Gap Road, then down the winding Repulse Bay Road would take you to the sandy haven.

Deep Water Bay was an alternative, but Repulse Bay was the more popular, the beach stretching out in front of the imposing old colonial building that was the Repulse Bay Hotel.

Not that we often passed through its magnificent portals, skimpy shorts, T-shirt and flip flops were not quite the appropriate dress for this palatial hotel which first opened its doors on New Year's Day, 1920.

Over the years Ernest Hemingway and Marlon Brando stayed there; and it was where William Holden and Jennifer Jones stayed during the making of the film *Love is a Many-Splendored Thing*. It played host to many other famous names, some I believe quite notorious... ah, if only walls could talk.

Below the hotel, the first building you saw as you turned onto Beach Road was the Lido Complex. A two story edifice that was primarily used as a restaurant with bathing booths and changing rooms.

At the other end of the beach was a Tin Hau Temple; dedicated to protecting fishermen, its tall colourful shrines were a favourite spot for photographs. It also had a little red bridge, the 'Longevity Bridge'. Every time you crossed over it your life would be prolonged for three more days, or so was the claim.

Repulse Bay had a lovely beach, perfect for laying down your towel and stretching out to soak up the sun. Of course you needed plenty of the suntan lotion or the strong rays could quickly make you as red as a lobster, rather than giving you the cool tan you were hoping for. When it did get too hot, there was the big beautiful sea to cool off in.

It was rumoured that Repulse Bay was once the home of pirates and that the Royal Navy had purged them from the area to safeguard merchant trading ships. It was also rumoured that many pirates couldn't swim as they were originally landlubbers who had been shanghaied.

And that leads me to a scary story about one of my fellow footballers. Someone who would go on to become the second foreign professional to represent Hong Kong at international level. Had the day in question panned out differently, he might never have made it or seen daylight again.

David Anderson was his name; but fellow Glaswegian and Caroline Hill team-mate Andy Savage nicknamed him 'Lobey' after a fictional cartoon character from a Glasgow newspaper.

Lobey Dosser rode a two-legged talking horse called El Fideldo and the cartoon drew heavily on the Glasgow vernacular: Lobey was depicted as a really laid-back character, just like Davie Anderson, and the nickname stuck, although the cartoon character Andy Capp might have been just as appropriate as he always seemed to have a cigarette in his mouth.

The story I am about to relate was told to me by Andy Savage the day after the incident.

Andy was sitting on Repulse Bay beach with Brian Harvey and some Caroline Hill team-mates enjoying the sun. Lobey had gone into the water to cool off. By sheer chance Andy looked out to sea a few minutes later and spotted him quite a long way out. Turning to his team-mates, he said: "look at Lobey with his arm in the air trying to keep his fag dry."

Unbeknownst to them, the current had gently eased Davie out of his depth. His arm was not in the air to keep his cigarette dry, he was actually waving frantically for help, but none of the boys were aware of this at the time. They just laughed at the lengths he seemed to be going to to protect his cigarette.

Lobey however could not swim!

It was only when his head went under water for several seconds that Andy and the boys realised he was in trouble. They quickly called the lifeguard and then scrambled though the water to reach Lobey, whose head kept disappearing under the waves.

They dragged him from the sea and thankfully he was revived by the life-guard. He was a lucky boy that day Andy told me. The first thing he asked for after coming round? A cigarette!

Happily, Lobey did eventually learn to swim.

After soaking up the sun it was time to head over to a nice little restaurant and bar called the Drift Inn. The bar had wood panelled walls and cool air-conditioning, the perfect place to have a shandy before heading back to the city.

In later years, when suitably attired, I would occasionally venture into the Repulse Bay Hotel to have a drink on the terrace. Gazing out over the bay, it was easy to imagine seaplanes bobbing on the waters; as they had done some fifty years earlier when flights from Hong Kong to Macau flew from that very shore. It was rumoured that some of the pilots had a stiff drink at the hotel bar before setting off, just to settle the nerves.

Celebrities of all kinds stayed at the grand old hotel over the years – before it was demolished in 1982 and then rebuilt – and I can say that I had something in common with royalty: Prince Juan Carlos and Princess Sophia stayed there on their honeymoon, and so did I, for one night in 1974 after my first marriage. I wonder if their bed creaked too?

Finally there was the movies. I previously mentioned Hong Kong had an abundance of good picture houses with comfortable seats and reasonable pricing, but it wasn't just watching movies, it was starring in them. Well, starring might be a slight exaggeration!

There was a thriving film production industry based out in the New Territories, but there weren't too many European actors… which is where I came in.

No Academy Awards

I bumped into one of my old Mum's favourite actors one afternoon at Sha Tin racetrack. I suppose he was one of every mum's favourite actors for a while.

He was standing in the paddock at the International race meeting. His horse, Don Bosco, was running in the feature race. As I approached he smiled, shook my hand and was gone. I felt like Sir Alec Guinness watching him leave, as he did at the conclusion of Doctor Zhivago. He was, after all, Omar Sharif.

Sadly my own acting ability never reached the dizzy heights of that great Egyptian actor… but I had a lot of fun along the way. In those days footballers and journalists substituted for professional Caucasian actors. Some turned out to be naturals, others were… well the less said the better.

Unlike Omar Sharif, there were no romantic epics for me. I mostly ended up getting beaten up by the likes of Sammo Hung, as I did in

Enter the Fat Dragon, a satirical version of the Bruce Lee movie, *Enter the Dragon*.

Although I did a fair bit of TV work as a sports commentator, some commercials and a few sketches with the Hui Brothers, Sam and Michael on TV, movies were a new front.

The first I ever appeared in was called *Bruce Lee in New Guinea*.

However, it was not made in New Guinea, nor was Bruce Lee in the movie. It was shot in 1977 in Sai Kung with someone who had more than a passing resemblance to the real Bruce Lee.

It had the singularly named Dana as the sexy Queen of the Snake Tribe. Bolo Yeung who starred in *Enter the Dragon* co-starred. The feature was one of many made after the death of Bruce Lee in 1973 that used his name or character.

In one scene I was supposed to be written off in a snake pit. However due to my ophidiophobia with the wriggling creatures it was given to another fellow actor who was not so squeamish.

They had assured me beforehand that the snakes were harmless, but no way was I going into that pit; with the snake queen alone, sure, but not with twenty of her snakes!

Instead, while I was attacking Dana in the last scene, the Bruce Lee lookalike finished me off with a couple of kung fu kicks to the throat.

I had a brief role as a cowboy, which I really enjoyed, in a Chow Yun-fat movie called *The Head Hunter*. Wearing a Stetson I had got in San Antonio and a checked shirt I looked every bit the part.

In my main scene I shot a character played by Wan Chi-keung, a popular football player for South China who was also a part-time actor due to his good looks.

"Make my day" I felt like saying in my best Clint Eastwood voice as I aimed my gun at him… firing blanks of course. It was only a fleeting appearance however, so I won't get carried away with my performance.

The last movie I made was quite successful: *All the Wrong Spies* produced by Cinema City in 1983. It was a spoof of a detective film set around the eve of World War II, very much in the vein of *Casablanca*.

A galaxy of local stars including Teddy Robin, George Lam, Brigitte Lin, Tsui Hark and Eric Tsang featured. Loads of Hong Kong celebrities also had cameo roles: Sandra Lang, Joe Junior, Anders Nelsson and even legendary D.J. Ray Cordeiro.

Walter Gerrard and I played two bungling German spies in black trench coats with hats to match.

My favourite memory was a bit that sadly never made it into the final version. Walter and I were squeezed into a phone box together, about to make a call that could change the course of history; unfortunately Walter passed wind and we burst out so fast the director never had time to say action let alone cut! Well, it was meant to be a comedy!

10

Time for a change... and a chance to lead a team against Eusébio

I was on holiday in Spain with my parents, eldest brother Dick, his wife Irene, and their two young boys, Fraser and Stewart, when I heard speculative reports that I was possibly on the transfer market.

It was early July 1972 and Petrie had requested a meeting after my holiday break in Benidorm. There were rumours that newly-promoted football club Seiko had me high on their recruitment list.

But for now I was enjoying strolls along palm-fringed boulevards by the sea and sampling the odd jug of fruit-laden iced Sangria in one of the many terraced bars overlooking Playa de Levante beach. My Dad and brother were having their usual *cuba libres*.

It was a time for relaxing after my second season in Hong Kong; a chance to spend quality time with family. Little did I think that I would end up playing football in Benidorm during that summer break, in what would be my one and only match on Spanish soil.

My Dad had been unable to book us all into the same hotel, so I stayed elsewhere, with interesting results. In 1972 Benidorm only had a fraction of the hotels it has now. Thankfully in the early 70s it was still ten years away from earning a reputation as a haven for British 'lager louts' and being dubbed 'Blackpool with sun'. Back then it was still a semi-sleepy resort on the south-eastern Costa Blanca coastline of Spain.

If memory serves, it was the Hotel Madrid where I stayed; and, as I later learned, it was not too far from a football ground. The hotel was three-four stars with predominately British tourists as guests – I particularly recall two elderly ladies, each of whom could easily be described as a double for the fictional 'Miss Marple.' I remember because as they passed me from time to time they used to say in unison, "Hello Jason," followed by a little giggle.

"Jason?" I thought.

Eventually, intrigued, I stopped them as they were leaving the hotel one day and asked: "Ladies, why do you call me Jason?"

"You look just like Jason King," one of them replied.

Seeing the blank expression on my face, the other one explained Jason King, played by actor Peter Wyngarde, was a character in a very popular series at that time in the UK.

"Okay," I said, "my name is Derek, but if you prefer Jason, so be it."

"Bye Jason," they said in unison, and had another little giggle.

Was there a slight resemblance? Having been out of range of British television for two years I really had no idea who Jason King was, but then I never told the pair I thought that they looked like doppelgangers for Jane Marple!

One problem I had at the hotel was getting served in the restaurant. Oh there were plenty of waiters, but they were like flies around a jam pot rushing to serve the young British girls who only had to flutter their eyelashes. My cries of "waiter, waiter" fell on deaf ears and I always seemed to be one of the last to get served. However, that would all change after a trip to the football field.

There were three other young guys from Glasgow staying in the hotel and in conversation we all agreed that we were poor seconds when it came to service.

One morning, one of the lads told me that there was to be a game of football the next day between our hotel and a rival one who had a habit of always beating them. Knowing what I did for a living he suggested that we all asked to represent our hotel; it might help to improve our relations with the staff. I decided to play as it would help keep me in shape.

In the late afternoon sunshine our team made the ten minute walk from hotel to football pitch. It took us up quite a steep hill to the ground, and I noticed that there was also a steep incline on the playing surface.

I had told the Glasgow boys not to mention to our hotel staff team members that I played professionally.

We won the game 9-2 and I scored seven goals.

At dinner that night I had two or three waiters around me from the moment I was seated. I felt like royalty. Across the dining room I could hear the plaintive cries of teenage girls: "waiter, waiter" which brought a wry smile to my face.

All the waiters wanted to do was talk football with me. Suddenly I was the star attraction at meal times and the waiters simply brushed aside the young ladies with the words: "*momento momento*". The worm had turned.

All too soon though it was time for a flight from Alicante to Glasgow and a meeting with Petrie to discuss my future, and to ask why I had not been paid my salary for June. The holiday was over.

Our meeting was in the Ivanhoe Hotel in Buchanan Street, Glasgow; the same venue where I had signed on the dotted line for Rangers two years earlier. But the mood was very different.

Petrie told me that he had been approached by Seiko who had offered a substantial transfer fee for my services – although he never said what that fee was. He asked me to give the matter some thought, but insisted that he was still undecided as to whether he would release me.

I found out later that he was bluffing, he had already signed an agreement with Seiko and accepted a fee for my transfer to the newly-promoted club. All that was pending was my agreement.

Petrie knew my desire to leave, mainly due to the self-inflicted problems he had caused the club. Walter had left in disgust, as had Jackie Trainer. It was time for me to move on too.

However, at that moment he seemed to have the idea that he still had power over me, although in actual fact it was the other way round. If I turned the lucrative offer down, he would be in financial trouble as he would have to return the fee to Seiko within 10 days. When it came to it, my consideration didn't take long. I said "Yes".

So, officially, I became a Seiko player, although he refrained from disclosing this to me. If he thought he was being clever I had an ace up my sleeve which would trump any card he cared to play.

I won't say what it was; though I will say it had nothing to do with anything of a seedy nature, rather it was something he had asked of the team during my second season with the club, and it was morally wrong.

So much so that I had discussed the matter with two senior Hong Kong policemen I knew, Paddy McMahon and Martin Cowley, and they had it on record if I wanted to pursue the matter. Martin Cowley, retired and now residing in Perth, Australia told me he still has my original written statement.

The same Martin Cowley who, when at Hong Kong Police Training School, had a young recruit under him who addressed him as 'Sir'. That young recruit is now Chief Executive of Hong Kong, John Lee. I believe Martin now addresses him as Sir!

Anyway, back to Petrie: two can play your game, I thought.

Mind you, he did eventually cough up my June salary. Perhaps he was worried that he might have been in breach of contract which would have made me a free agent; meaning his big payday for me could have turned to dust in the wind.

Petrie delayed booking my trip back to Hong Kong for a further week, seemingly to keep me away from Seiko officials, saying my transfer needed to be discussed in Hong Kong. It was total bollocks. He was hoping to sign a replacement for me and announce this to the press when he got back to Hong Kong ahead of me, but his new marquee signing had not yet materialised, hence the delaying tactics.

When I did get back to Hong Kong I could not get hold of Petrie, but was contacted instead by Seiko officials who asked me to go to their office on the top floor of the Stelux Manufacturing building, next to Kai Tak airport.

I was met there by Wong Chong-po and Wong Chong-san who ran a business manufacturing watches for Seiko, the iconic Japanese brand.

Their friendliness was the first thing to strike me and that friendship has lasted to this day.

The two brothers were born in Bangkok, as was their father, Wong Chue-meng, son of a Chinese immigrant who had settled in Thailand. Wong Chue-meng moved to Hong Kong and founded Stelux Holdings in 1963. The two brothers – C.P. being the elder by nine years – eventually took over the running of the company from their father.

Both loved football, and the Seiko team was formed using an advertising budget from the Japanese conglomerate. Over time, that would prove to be a master stroke as the advertising they got through the Seiko team name's exposure in print and television would prove immeasurable.

Sadly, C.P. died in mid-2020 in his 80th year. At that time he was Chairman of Bangkok Land and also owned the Impact Arena, a mammoth convention and entertainment complex in the Muang Thong Thani district of Bangkok. Anant Kanjanapas was his Thai name and I respectfully attended the Thai funeral rites ceremony held in his honour

His brother, C.S. is also now based in Thailand – Keeree Kanjanapas is his Thai name – and he is more or less retired. His son, Kavin now runs the day-to-day business of his company, the BTS (Skytrain) Group in Bangkok.

Without doubt, the BTS has changed the face of travel in Bangkok and although it was a rough ride for him at times, C.S. gave Bangkok the wonderful mass transit railway system that it has today.

They own hotels under the Eastin brand name in Bangkok, and the Thana City golf course. They also have many other ventures, as well as hotels in Europe, and, for good measure, their own private jet.

My visit to their office at Kai Tak was the first time I met the brothers, and they asked, "Are you ready to sign the contract?"

"Indeed I am," I replied.

As far as the brothers were concerned on that day in July 1972, all was in order, contrary to what Petrie had told me, and I signed there and then and considered myself a Seiko player henceforth.

I would go on to win 20+ trophies with them over eight wonderful seasons – apart from a short three-month stint in the USA with San Antonio Thunder in the NASL.

After signing we had a brief chat about the club and their plans for the new season.

The club had just successfully negotiated promotion from the Second to the First division, but signing good players would be key to a successful future. I mentioned that there was a young lad who had played for Sing Tao, and was now with South China, who looked useful. "His name is Wu Kwok-hung."

"We are already talking to him," they replied with a smile.

They were more than smart businessmen, I thought, they also knew their football. Wu would go on to become one of the greats in the history of Hong Kong football and we played well together – he wore the number 10 shirt, while I wore number 11.

As I said earlier, Petrie had already signed the contract with Seiko and received $30,000 as a transfer fee, as well as extras for my air fare from the UK to Hong Kong, plus some other add-ons, bringing the total to around $34,000. It might even have been a record transfer fee for the time in that part of Asia.

However, just when I thought I was finally a Seiko player, Petrie popped up again to suddenly claim that he had not cancelled my registration form for the club, and until he did, I was still in the Rangers camp. He was reported in the press as saying that he would only consider selling me for $40-50,000, even after he'd made the agreement with Seiko!

I think Petrie might have been trying to squeeze more money out of Seiko, so I passed on my 'ace card' information to their officials, who I think then hinted to Petrie that I might make an embarrassing legal challenge against him.

Anyway, on the eve of Hong Kong Rangers' pre-season trip to the mainland, Petrie reluctantly finally agreed to let me go. Although I loved playing alongside my Rangers team mates, it was like getting out of prison!

For two years I had given him everything on the playing field, and scored almost seventy goals for the club. He received good money for my transfer so I thought he might have shown a little gratitude. He did not.

Success was instant, and timely, for Seiko: we won the season opener, the seven-a-side Stanley Shield, which was contested by all first division clubs and played at the old Hong Kong Football Club ground in Sports Road, Happy Valley.

A comfortable 4-2 victory over South China in the final had us in good spirits for the season ahead.

Ho Yung-hing in goal, Au Wing-hung, Lai Po-chung, Chan Hung-ping, Ho Sun-wah, Wu Kwok-hung and me were the magnificent seven who gave the 'Watchmen' the first silverware in their inaugural year in the First Division – the 72/73 season.

The other good news was that Walter Gerrard, who had played half the previous season with Caroline Hill, was returning to Seiko; I would once again line up alongside my old team-mate and buddy.

Our season opener was against a strong Police side at Boundary Street in front of a full house; fans keen to see how the newly-promoted side would perform. We hammered them 5-0, with Wu Kwok-hung scoring one and me getting the other four. A great start. The next day newspaper reports were all of the same opinion: Seiko had spent their money well!

We continued to win games, helped by the two Spaniards we signed, Manuel Cuenca and Tomas Lozano, who had left the Philippines and moved to Hong Kong. We now had a strong side and C.S. took control of the club. Still having good connections with his country of birth, he decided that our first overseas tour would be to Thailand to play in the Queen's Cup tournament.

Now I explained earlier that the nickname given to me by local fans was *Ye So* – 'Jesus' in English – and my hair was undoubtedly pretty long in those days. I was therefore ordered to get a haircut. Not by team officials, but by Thai Immigration who had informed C.S. that Mr Currie (or 'Jesus') would not be allowed into Thailand unless he did something about his hair.

A new look was called for. My long mane had been synonymous with me since my arrival in Hong Kong and I was disappointed to lose it, but it was time for the shears to come out. Linda Foster, a hairdresser from England, gave me a new look and, though my hair was still a debatable length, Thai Immigration gave me the all clear.

The Queen's Cup was to be played at the National Stadium in Pathum Wan, which is still in use today and stands not far from the modern MBK shopping centre – a place many who have visited Bangkok will I'm sure be familiar with.

Nowadays, most important games in the capital are played at the newer Rajamangala stadium – situated half way between central Bangkok and Suvarnabhumi airport – which opened in 1989 and holds roughly 50,000 spectators.

The Queen's Cup tournament was named in honour and recognition of Queen Sirikit, the Queen consort of King Bhumibol Adulyadej (Rama IX) and the mother of the current king of Thailand.

We would lose in the semi-final 3-2, after extra time, to the side who would go on to win the competition, Raj Pracha, but it was in controversial circumstances.

I had twice put Seiko into the lead, only for the Thais to come back and equalize each time. It looked like going to penalty kicks after extra time, until two minutes from the end when the Thai side were awarded a corner.

At the time our centre-half, Fok Pak-ling was lying injured on the ground and needing attention. Our medical staff were looking to come onto the field, but the Thai side took the corner quickly. From the resulting goalmouth scramble, and, despite our pleas to the referee, they managed to get the ball over the line.

We were not happy, but the goal counted, and we had lost.

We protested, but the referee ignored us, and despite our manager, C.S. Wong, making a strong protest to the Organizing Committee, the result stood, and that was that.

However, it was not all bad for me. The Organizing Committee had to select an All-Star side from the participating teams to play a final match against the Queen's Cup winners and I was the only player selected from Seiko, which was a great honour as I would become the first *farang* (Caucasian foreigner) to be selected as a Queen's Cup All-Star. I still have the lovely souvenir I received proudly displayed in my home in Bangkok.

Once back in Hong Kong, a long football season ensued, but Seiko would soon become a household name. In our first year in the top division we would go on to win almost every honour, including the League title, Senior Shield and Viceroy Cup, only missing out on a clean sweep by losing in the final of the Golden Jubilee Cup. The new kids on the block were here to stay.

For me, one of the highlights that season was being selected to captain the Hong Kong League XI against the mighty Benfica, led by the legendary man from Mozambique: Eusébio.

(How things had changed from being a part-timer at Motherwell.)

The game was to be played on February 5 as part of the Chinese New Year celebrations, just three days before my 24th birthday. Benfica had thrashed the Hong Kong National side several days earlier, so I wasn't expecting any birthday presents from them. But, as it turned out, it wasn't that bad a day.

I had been tucked inside the commentary box as a guest commentator for RTHK at that opening game that ushered in the Year of the Ox. Dragon dances were part of the pre-match celebrations at the Government Stadium; but it was the Portuguese side which supplied the firecrackers, putting 11 goals past the Hong Kong side, with no reply.

I can't recall who was the RTHK anchor that day, but I do recall the question asked of me when the final whistle was blown:

"Derek, you will lead out a League XI to play Benfica in a few days time, what are your thoughts?"

"I'm heading for Kai Tak to catch the first flight out of Hong Kong," I joked.

Despite the National side being whipped, there was a huge crowd of 27,804 on the day we faced Benfica. Was that because of the attraction of Eusébio, or did they think we had a chance?

Benfica's lineup also included Rui Rodrigues, Adolfo, Simões and Nené. Nené was their right-winger and a player who was capped for Portugal on 66 occasions. However, the star of the show was undoubtedly Eusébio, a long-time hero of mine. He had pace, technique and a ferocious right foot that had made him top scorer at the 1966 World Cup finals.

He had also been top scorer three times in the European Cup during the mid to late 60's – the earlier version of the revamped Champions League as we know it today. He would also go on to win the 'Golden Boot' award as top scorer in Europe in 1973, with 40 goals.

It was a great side and their strength could be measured by the fact that they had won the Portuguese championship for the past two seasons, and would go on to win it again in 1973, becoming the first Portuguese side to go through a season undefeated, winning 28 games and drawing two. To say that we were the underdogs was somewhat of an understatement!

I was made captain for the day, and led out a team that contained mostly Scottish and English players, with one Spaniard and four Malaysians.

Our squad consisted of Scotsmen Davie Anderson, Jackie Trainer, John McGunnigle, Andy Savage and Davie Breen. Our English boys were Tony Gurka, Brian Harvey – brother of Colin of Everton fame – and Liverpudlian Tony McLaughlin.

My Seiko team-mate Manuel Cuenca was the lone Spaniard and Chow Chee-keong, Wong Kam-fook, Khoo Luam-keng and Chan Yoon-cheong were the Malaysian lads.

The players knew the importance of the game and we badly wanted to give the Hong Kong fans some pride back after the national side's thrashing.

Six minutes gone, and we were 1-0 down!

Ever reliable centre-half Davie Anderson mis-hit his back-pass to our keeper, laying the ball directly into the path of Benfica's Jordão.

Two minutes later, Eusébio cut diagonally across our penalty area and swept a brilliant shot into the corner of the net.

Two down in under ten minutes.

But we then defended like Davy Crockett at the Alamo, and slowly settled into the game. Tony McLaughlin and I were causing some problems to the Benfica defence and I lobbed a shot which sailed just over the crossbar. However, just when we thought we had weathered the storm to go in at half-time only two goals behind, disaster struck again.

Jackie Trainer was left stranded by Nené whose cross from the right wing was missed by Eusébio, but Jordão, following up, put it into the net. We were down by three at the break.

During half-time I told the boys in the changing room that I thought we had played reasonably well, apart from a couple of careless slips.

I emphasized that in the second half we needed to slow the game down and keep possession. If we had the ball, there was nothing they could do to hurt us. Easier said than done.

I told them that we needed to believe in ourselves: we were good players. It worked a treat.

Davie Anderson made up for his costly error at the start of the game with a stunning second half performance, as did all the lads in that second period.

Late in the half we finally got the goal we deserved, brilliantly set up by Tony McLaughlin. He brushed aside two Benfica defenders and slipped the ball to me just inside the penalty box. I controlled it, took a couple of steps, and swept an angled shot wide of Benfica goalkeeper José Henrique. He stretched his arms, but he was never going to reach it; as it hit the inside of the rigging the crowd roared their appreciation. Despite some other close efforts there was no more scoring in the game.

We walked off the field that day with our heads held high, cheers from the crowd ringing in our ears.

I shook hands with Nené afterwards and he said, "Good game." He was someone I had got to know quite well on the field because every time there was a kick-off, he and I would face one other, him being their right-winger and me being our left-winger and sometimes we shared a little friendly banter. When you talk of great Portuguese wingers, Ronaldo and Figo might spring to mind, but believe me, Nené was up there with the very best.

It's not often you get cheered off the field for losing a game 3-1, but we all felt like winners that day against Portugal's finest, and so did the fans.

11

Ernie's House of Horrors, dancing in the street, and keeping Hong Kong clean

The 72/73 season saw rivals Eastern FC sign some good players, including Ernie Hannigan, a teenage sensation in Scotland when he was just seventeen.

Playing alongside former Scotland star, Neil Martin, he had helped Queen of the South get promoted to the First Division in 1962. Ernie left the Palmerston club and signed for Preston North End for £15,000 at the age of twenty, playing three seasons for them.

Coventry City would then sign Ernie in 1967 for £55,000 and he moved from Deepdale to play under the managership of Noel Cantwell – a man who made 123 appearances for Manchester United and also managed the Republic of Ireland on 36 occasions. He also signed Neil Martin, Hannigan's old playing partner at Queen of the South, from Sunderland for £90,000.

Ernie was a 'George Best' type of player, with hair to match. He liked to take defenders on, but all Cantwell wanted was for Ernie's first touch to be a cross into the box for the tall forward partnership of Tony Hately and Neil Martin.

Needless to say they argued, fell out, and Ernie moved on, having spells with clubs in Scotland, South Africa and the USA, before finally landing in Hong Kong. He was 29 when he arrived and soon became known as the 'leader of the Eastern pack'. Let me explain why.

Eastern's foreign players were housed at their clubhouse in Gloucester Road, very close to the Excelsior Hotel. There were two bedrooms in the flat and neither had air-conditioning; in hot and humid Hong Kong that in itself was enough to make anyone slightly crazy. Ernie shared one of the bedrooms with Stan Forster, a talented, one-touch forward who as a youngster played for Crystal Palace.

The other bedroom accommodated four: Davie Breen, easily distinguishable by his walrus moustache; the slightly balding Aitken 'Aiky' Cairns; Billy Buchanan, known as 'Buckie'; and my former team-mate at Hong Kong Rangers, Jackie Trainer, alias 'Big Jake'.

In the flat above were two more Scottish lads, Billy Mullen and Andy Cumming, who played for rival club Fire Services – I had played alongside both as a youngster at Queen's Park. I especially remember playing against Andy in schools football, simply because of his height: he was 6 feet tall when just 13 years of age and represented the Scottish schoolboys team. Andy only grew another inch or so, otherwise he might have chosen to play basketball.

Although the Eastern boys were a good footballing side, and unlucky not to win the Senior Shield that season, losing 2-1 to South China in the final, it was their exploits off the field that earned them their reputation. To understand the characters involved requires brief descriptions:

Davie 'Neebs' Breen was a friendly guy who had a spell at Wigan and was a great distributor of the ball on the football field; but off it he had a penchant for afternoon naps, which probably explained why he could tell stories long into the night, while constantly playing with his drooping moustache

Aiky and Buckie were the 'Bonnybridge mafia', both from that small village in the council area of Falkirk. Aiky played as a central defender for Eastern, and played well. He was brought to the club on the recommendation of Buckie, who told the powers that be he was better than Jack Charlton!

Jackie Trainer tells of meeting Aiky on arrival at Kai Tak airport. After the build up from Buckie, he expected to see a giant god-like centre-half; but Jackie's description was somewhat different: a tall, thinnish, balding guy, wearing purple-hooped socks. Not quite the imposing figure Buckie had everyone believe.

Things didn't get any better when the assembled media asked Aiky where he came from and what was his background?

As honest as the day is long, Aiky replied, "I'm a postman from Bonnybridge." Not quite the answer the press were expecting! In truth, Aiky played with Bonnybridge, a decent junior club in Scotland; but being only part-time, his main job was local postman. "At least he'll be fit," Jackie quipped. Clearly a little PR exercise was required by Eastern.

In fairness, Aiky did a job for the club in helping them get to the final of the Senior Shield, no mean feat in itself.

Then there was Billy 'Buckie' Buchanan. He could sell snow to the Eskimos. Buckie loved the game, and although a mere 5 feet 4 inches tall, which restricted him in some areas of the game, he balanced it by always giving 150 per cent in effort. A real jack-in-the-box who got his fair share of goals for the club. He was also one of the funniest people I ever met, always able to make you smile at his stories and you never knew if they were fact of fiction.

I first met him, of all places, on the beach in Tossa de Mar in 1966 in an impromptu kickabout.

Little did I know we would catch up again six years later in Asia.

Jackie Trainer was the fourth member in that room and became chief storyteller, keeping me up to date as to what went on in Ernie's house of horrors.

Finally, there was Stan Forster, Ernie's room-mate Stan had a somewhat squeaky voice and was always ready with a little gripe about something or other; but as a player, he was like a miniature Tostão, trapping and shielding the ball well, he could also score goals.

I recall playing alongside him once in a Governor's Cup game between an all European XI, representing the HKFA, and an all Chinese team, representing the Chinese Athletic Association XI, which included seven South China players, as well as Fire Services Cheung Chi-wai up front.

I was made captain for the day and scored both our goals in the eventual 2-1 win; which was actually much more comfortable than the scoreline suggests. Stan set up one of the goals for me on a plate and I was impressed by his style of play, I would have liked to have played alongside him more often.

But back to life in the Eastern flat. 'Squeaky' Stan was Ernie's designated 'Sergeant at Arms,' while Ernie was the ringmaster who ran the circus, animals and all.

One night the four boys who shared a room had gone to sleep, lying in peaceful slumber; that was until Ernie put a snake under the door! Typhoon signal No.10 could not have created more havoc. Screams of, "for fuck's sake, there's a fucking snake in the room!" reverberated around the walls, and even the sleeping walrus awoke with a start.

"For flip's sake, what's going on?" Neebs called out, his face turning a whiter shade of pale as he suddenly registered the reptile slithering and hissing across the floor.

"Jesus Christ, it's a snake!" he shrieked.

The poor reptile, undoubtedly using its hissing as a defence mechanism, was probably more scared than the players; though in their moment of panic they failed to realize this, nor did they know if it was venomous or not.

More hissing saw the four valiant Scottish professionals standing on their beds holding pillows in front of them to defend their privates, as valiantly as they would have done against a free kick in the last minute of a major cup final.

"Open the door for Chris'sake," shouted Jake in desperation, not realising that Ernie had cunningly locked it to add more drama to the petrifying scene inside.

"Think we should open it Ernie?" a squeaky voice was heard to say.

"I think it's jammed Stan," Ernie replied, enjoying every minute of the trapped denizens' torment.

Eventually, Ernie opened the door and grabbed the snake like a professional snake handler.

"Do ye nay like ma wee pet? It's nay poisonous, it just wanted to say hello," he mocked.

Jackie relayed that story to me in great detail. Apparently after Ernie had taken the snake out of the room, the boys stuffed towels in the small gap under the door, locked it from the inside, and pushed a sideboard up against it for good measure, securing their sanctuary from any more intrusions. Only then did some semblance of order return.

According to Jackie the snake was never seen again. Ernie probably took it back to the pet shop where he bought it. Then again, he could have just released it outside on the landing; one never knew with Ernie.

Ernie was a tough bugger, so it was always best to be on his good side. He and I got on well as he liked the fight game and with my brother being an ex-boxing champ we would chew the fat over a beer now and again, trying to decide whether Ken Buchanan or Walter McGowan was the better boxer.

Another of Jackie's tales about Ernie concerned a visit to a bar in Wan Chai after a match they had played earlier in the day. Ernie got involved in a heavy-drinking competition with an enormous African-American G.I. who was on a five-day R&R from Vietnam – alternatively referred to by many enlisted men as 'I & I', intoxication and intercourse.

After 15 or so whiskies they were swaying like Ali and Frazier in the last round of the 'Thrilla in Manila.' The G.I. eventually folded. He didn't need a referee to count him out, he simply slumped over and fell into a deep sleep, capable only of dreaming about the intercourse part of his trip.

Never one to give in when faced with a challenge Ernie had outdrunk the soldier, but it had taken its toll on the Scotsman. Jackie told me it took all five flat-mates to get the champ into the back of a red taxi and take him home. He was totally oblivious to his success.

Where are these Eastern characters now you might ask, a half-century later?

Sadly three of them are no longer with us:

Ernie died in Perth, Australia in 2015, he had been inducted into the Western Australia Football Hall of Fame in 2004.

Stan Forster passed away in Melbourne, a few years after Ernie.

Aiky returned to his native village of Bonnybridge, but died from dementia several years ago.

Of those who remain:

Neebs, last I heard, was residing in Perth, Australia with his wife and family.

Jackie, who originally arrived with me and Walter in Hong Kong, would also go on to play for Seiko and Bulova and after retiring would spend 18 years coaching at Bolton Wanderers. He now works full-time at a Manchester university, and is based at the Etihad Stadium where he is responsible for the practical coaching development of students on sports degree courses.

Billy 'Buckie' Buchanan became the Provost of Falkirk! Funny the way things work out.

For instance, if someone had said to me in Glasgow, prior to the ringing of the New Year's bells in 1969, that three years later I would be making a TV commercial for Bell's whisky in Hong Kong, I would have thought them comfortably inebriated!

Then again, Hong Kong was always full of surprises, and this time it came from a Danish trading company: the East Asiatic Company, better known as EAC.

Two of the senior Danes, who ran the company from an office in Central District, John Madsen and Erik Christensen, just happened to be fond of football.

The pair were no slouches themselves on the field, particularly Madsen, a talented individual who played regularly for the Hong Kong Football Club first team.

Walter Gerrard and I became friendly with the pair and would pop into their office for a chat every now and again. One day, John Madsen asked Walter and me to come to his office for a meeting, he wanted to discuss a proposal.

Well, that proposal just happened to concern making a commercial for a Scottish product: Bell's whisky. EAC had just taken over the distribution rights for Hong Kong and Macau. Madsen wanted us to promote the product through a TV commercial. We were readily recognized in Hong Kong as being both footballers and Scotsmen, so in a way, it made sense to feature us, the advertising shoe fitted nicely.

He also offered us the opportunity to become part-time salesmen for the product. I declined, but as Walter was getting nearer to retirement, with his knees telling him it was time to look elsewhere, he happily accepted.

Now, I will say, selling whisky in Hong Kong at that time was not easy. At all the big Chinese dinners and wedding parties, cognac was the spirit of choice for the many toasts and *yum sings*. It was rumoured among the Chinese community that brandy, distilled from grapes or a fermented fruit mash, was good for your sex drive. Whisky on the other hand was termed *luk deem boon* or 'half-past six' – I'll leave you to work out what that means – and, sadly, many local consumers actually believed it. I suppose an ad featuring two athletes might help dispel that thinking, perhaps that was part of the strategy, although an orgy to prove it was sadly not forthcoming.

As it would turn out, our relationship with the two Danes would help both our post-football careers: Walter would go on to be a successful product manager for EAC, and I would end up as Public Relations Manager for Carlsberg Brewery in Hong Kong.

The commercial was to be shot in Big Wave Bay on the eastern coast of Hong Kong island. We had to wear short-sleeve white shirts for the shoot, with tartan ties, and full matching kilt and sporran. That was to prove a slight problem for me! With his size and build the kilt looked a treat on Walter, but mine came down over my knees.

I should mention that the kilts were on loan from a Scots regiment stationed in Hong Kong at the time – there was always one or another on a tour of duty in those days – but clearly there was a mistake in sizes when procurement took place.

In the opening scene we were supposed to be gaily dancing down a hill towards the beach, arms aloft, expressions bright – a scene familiar to all those who remember British TV's White Heather Club.

No problem for Walter, just another day for him; anything but for me. Those kilts, beloved though they are by all Scotsmen, are heavy and unwieldy at the best of times, like wearing a duvet, and though I tried to swirl and twirl, it took all my athletic strength and agility to eventually satisfy the commercial's director. Certainly not the attire for the heat and humidity of the Far East.

The next scene had us sitting at a table on the beach and ordering a whisky from a local Chinese waiter. The commercial was to be shown on both the Jade and Pearl TVB networks in a campaign backed by hundreds of spots and supported by promotional material.

That meant we had to ad-lib in both English and Cantonese; the voice-over would also be recorded by us, but synchronized in a recording studio later.

"*Foh kei, gum ling wai si gay, m'goi,*" (Waiter, Golden Bell's whisky, thank you) was the line in Cantonese.

I should also mention that we had to call it Golden Bell's in Cantonese as Bell's on its own, had a translation with a deathly ring to it.

The waiter would return with two glasses of whisky and we would smoothly down them, and, with delight on our faces, praise the taste. Well that was the plan, but the Director was not happy with the performance from Walter.

In case you are thinking that we were drinking cold tea, a substitute often used in such commercials, then you would be wrong. This was Hong Kong, we were drinking the real McCoy, Arthur Bell's finest.

"Mr Gerrard," said the Director, "when you are drinking the whisky, can you please look as if you are enjoying it."

"Okay. We'll try again, fill the glasses once more," he ordered.

Now Walter liked drinking whisky, but he had an unusual way of reacting to the taste: a shake of the head and closing his eyes. That was certainly not what the Director was looking for.

Walter leaned over to me and said cheekily. "Look as if you're enjoying it? The boys back home would nay fuckin' believe I'm getting paid for drinking it."

I said, "Walter, he wants you smiling at the camera, not how you swoosh it down in a pub in Milton" (a district in Glasgow).

"Okay, I get the point, but the silly bastard hasn't realised I was only faking it so I could get another glass," he laughed.

I'm not sure if the reel of that ad still exists, I'd certainly love to see it again. Sales did go up and hopefully so did *luk deem boon*!

In the very early 1970s, a telephone call from Hong Kong to the UK entailed a pilgrimage to Mercury House, the home of Cable & Wireless, and just a stone's throw from the colonial-style Hong Kong Club building. Although Alexander Graham Bell, a fellow Scot, had pioneered long-distance telephone calling a century or so before, in Hong Kong it still meant a trek to Central to make a booking for a three-minute call to my Mum and Dad's home in Glasgow, a procedure not only laborious but also costly.

Alternatives were fairly limited: the next best thing was an airmail letter, a thin, lightweight blue sheet of foldable, gummed paper with the letter and envelope as one piece, at least it was economical and considerably cheaper.

In early 1973, while writing out my parents' address on an airmail letter inside the old Edwardian structure that was the General Post Office in Pedder Street, I felt as if someone was staring down on me. My eyes darted upwards and I was shocked to see this scruffy-looking face, with masses of long hair, looking down from a poster and telling me, in no uncertain terms: 'Keep Hong Kong Clean'. Unnervingly, the face was mine!

Now, I knew I was part of the Government-backed campaign to keep the streets of Hong Kong free from rubbish, and had been photographed some months earlier, but I was not prepared to see myself prominently displayed in the halls of the 'Old Lady of Pedder Street', as the Post Office, constructed in imperial splendour of granite and red brick, was affectionately known.

Indeed, in the days following, that same untidy-looking face would appear at bus stops, public libraries and office notice boards across the city. Perhaps it was time I got a haircut and cleaned myself up, or was that the point?

Let me backtrack to how it began. Ted Thomas, a well-known local broadcaster and PR guru had summoned me to his office one day. Ted was in charge of the PR for the ongoing campaign to tidy up the city, organized and coordinated by the Urban Council. He told me that they were looking for well-known sporting personalities and movie stars to endorse the 1973 clean up campaign. Cheung Chi-doy and I – assuming that I agreed – would be the sportsmen; David Chiang (Chiang Wei-nien), a martial arts superstar would represent the movie world.

The original campaign had been launched in 1972 with the aim of generating public concern for environmental cleanliness through civic pride. With the rise in Hong Kong's population had come a rise in rubbish on the streets, and that was a serious concern for the Government.

The campaign had begun with a cartoon created by Arthur Hacker, an artist and historian, who was then working for the Hong Kong Government as creative director in their Information Services Department.

Arthur was an intelligent, unassuming character who spoke in a slow, humorous drawl; he was also damn good company, particularly at the bar of the Foreign Correspondents' Club – in those days on the fourteenth floor of Sutherland House – which just happened to be next door to Mercury House. Handy for a drink, after calling Mum and Dad long distance.

Some might recall the opening lines of John Le Carré's classic novel, 'The Honourable Schoolboy,' describing a Vietnam War reporter looking out from the 14th floor toilet of the FCC.

That same toilet became famous as it offered a wonderful view of the harbour from within the club premises, there was no better view in Hong Kong while one was having a piss!

I once asked Arthur if he got his inspiration for cartoons whilst enjoying the harbour view from the men's room.

"Currie," (he addressed everyone by their surname), "I do not work when I am in the FCC, it is not a place for thinking, or sobriety."

Staying with surnames, but going back to Hacker's original 1972 'Keep Hong Kong Clean' campaign, he created a vile, green, long-snouted monster with red spots and a forked tail and named it 'Lap Sap Chung', (in English, 'Rubbish Chung'), which would become an iconic folk villain. The deliberately repulsive cartoon character was meant to shock people. It worked. By the late 70s there were no cleaner cities in the world, except, perhaps, Singapore.

To this day in Hong Kong, if anybody throws litter, they are greeted with a chorus of "Lap Sap Chung," a legacy of Arthur Hacker.

When I look at that old poster of me during the 'Keep Hong Kong Clean' campaign, I hardly looked the ideal candidate for the role, but then again, I was nicknamed 'Jesus,' and he spread the word better than most.

12

The Sport of Kings

Like football, horse racing is in my blood.

I could easily have written a book about the characters around Happy Valley racetrack in the early 1970s; many could have sprung straight out of a Dick Francis novel.

I caught the last season of amateur racing in Hong Kong before it became professional in 1971. The 'White Russian' trainers George Sofronoff and Nick Metrevelli ruled the roost in those days, prior to the era of the great Australian horseman, George Moore.

Racing then was once a week, until night racing was introduced to Happy Valley in 1973. That turned out to be a real money spinner.

The income generated from the Wednesday night meetings – where racing was initially on the sand track – provided enough capital for the Hong Kong Jockey Club to build a second racetrack on reclaimed land in Sha Tin, and this opened in 1978.

The Press Box at Happy Valley racecourse was located on the fourth floor of the Jockey Club Building. In those days the racing press gang consisted of John Hardie, Geoff Somers, Robin Parke, Vova Rodney and Peter Metrevelli, all fine tipsters and writers.

Inside the Box, the punters with typewriters would either scream with joy, or curse, depending on how their selections performed.

My racing habitat in those days was just outside the Press Box, giving me easy access to any late 'mail' floating about.

Race-callers at the track were Terry Butts and fellow Australian Lex Fullarton.

Now the fourth floor also had a handy bar that served cold beer for celebrating or drowning sorrows, depending on how your punting was going. This proved to be a magnet for all types.

I recall one afternoon standing at the bar alongside Lex Fullarton discussing the merits of the day when a bell rang to signal the start of the next race race.

Problem was, Lexy was supposed to be calling that race!

In a flash he shot to the stairs and up two floors to the commentary booth. Fortunately for him it was a distance race, which probably saved his bacon and perhaps his job.

As the horses were coming round the home bend, just about to hit the home straight, a tinkling sound, like a spoon hitting a glass, could be heard over the loudspeaker system, followed by the voice of Lexy: "Sorry about that technical failure." He then described the finish of the race as if nothing had happened!

Lexy could best be described as similar in looks and stature to British sports commentator Harry Carpenter. He was involved in many escapades, but let me say here and now, he had a sharp brain and could call races and write stories with the best of them.

Like a few other sports journalists of that era in Hong Kong he was also a bit of an entrepreneur and liked to have a few schemes on the go to supplement his income.

Not quite in the same league though as Irishman Robin Parke who looms large throughout this book. 'Parky' reminded me of a juggler with four balls in the air each representing a different venture. He made 'Arfur Daley' look like a choir boy.

But Lexy was not far behind Parky in the entrepreneurial stakes. He managed the popular Elbow Bar in the Caravelle Hotel, just two furlongs or so from the Valley racetrack, opposite the Craigengower Cricket Club.

Some great times were had in that bar. It once hosted the legendary Australian jockey Scobie Breasley when he was passing through the city. Scottish pop band, Marmalade, spent an entire afternoon there – I only vaguely remember singing *Ob-la-di Ob-la-da* with them.

What I do recall is their front man Dean Ford telling me how they changed their name from Dean Ford and the Gaylords to Marmalade.

Apparently their new manager, Peter Walsh got the inspiration from sitting at the breakfast table one morning and, you guessed it, staring at a jar of the sugary product in front of him. Talk about being jammy, the name stuck and the hits followed.

One of the scariest stories from the Elbow Bar was told to me by John Hardie, racing editor for *The Star*. It concerned the day one of Lexy's regular customers gave him a deathly fright. That regular was the Philippines Consul.

Lexy decided that the Consul had had enough to drink and tried to send him on his way. The Consul eventually left, only to return a short time later, after going to the Consulate in Causeway Bay and taking a pistol from the safe. He then went back to the bar, plonked the pistol on the counter, and told Lexy to serve him a drink. Lexy went white and bought drinks all round!

My personal favourite Lexy story concerned some fellow footballers.

Lexy was a popular guy with the expat players and we spent many happy hours in his bar. One afternoon there were a few players in the bar drinking and exchanging stories; apparently they were a bit loud and some of their language was not for delicate ears.

Also in the bar that day were a large group of tourists.

After a lot of tut tutting and scowls one of them complained to the barman about the noise. Not knowing what to do the barman phoned Lexy who was at home.

"How many footballers?" asked Lexy.

"Three," said the barman.

"How many tourists?" said Lexy.

"Twelve," said the barman.

"Tell the tourists to leave if they're not happy," said Lexy.

The story was retold many times in the expat football community and Lexy's bar increased in popularity. Lexy knew who his best customers were.

I mentioned the journalist Robin Parke a little earlier. Robin arrived in Hong Kong in 1967 as a young 25-year-old from Northern Ireland to take up a job with the *South China Morning Post*.

Stories centring around him would span the next thirty years and he would be mentioned in dispatches as 'Parky,' 'After Dark', or just simply by his initials: 'RP'.

The tale of why he came to Hong Kong revolved around the legendary steeplechaser Arkle who, at odds of 2/9 on, failed to win the 1966 King George VI Chase at Kempton in late December.

Parky, a keen follower of horse racing, thought it was unbeatable so wagered heavily on it to win. In those days you didn't always have to front up with your stake money if you had a friendly bookmaker on hand.

Sadly for Parky, the great Irish thoroughbred's career – 22 wins from 25 races – came to a shuddering halt that day when it damaged a hoof jumping the 'Open Ditch'. It could only finish second!

Parky quickly hoofed it to Hong Kong to avoid an inquisitive bookmaker looking for payment or perhaps an arm or a leg! But Arkle's loss was Hong Kong's gain, as time would document.

He would become one of my closest friends and I learnt a great deal from him over the years. He was pencil thin when I first met him with light ginger hair, but barrelled out in later years and sported a ginger beard to make up for what he had lost on top.

Parky could think on his feet with the best of them, and proved that time after time.

He would become one of the most prolific sports writers in Asia and cover four football World Cups and European Championships, as well as major cricket and tennis events.

For a considerable number of years, he anchored ATV's horse racing show, initially with Chris Collins and latterly with Lawrence Wadey, and also covered the Epsom Derby.

The list of his accomplishments goes on and on: football manager, bar proprietor, bloodstock agent and, of course, journalist.

A jack-of-all-trades he may have been, but he was also a master at most of them. That said, football and horse racing were the two passions in his life: a man after my own heart.

It was Parky who was instrumental in bringing South African jockey Douglas Whyte to Hong Kong. Whyte, now a leading horse trainer after hanging up his jockey boots, was champion jockey for 13 consecutive years in Hong Kong. The 'Durban Demon', as Whyte was nicknamed during his riding career, would be the first to acknowledge the Irishman's influence.

Parky had plunged into journalism at the tender age of just 17, but benefited hugely by being taken under the wing of legendary Irish journalist, Malcolm Brodie; he was the making of the young Robin Parke.

Parky loved a punt on the horses and a pint with his Irish compatriots, particularly those riding in the off-season in Hong Kong. After race meetings he and the late Pat Eddery were sometimes inseparable, enjoying sessions that lasted way into the early hours of a Sunday morning.

Parky featured in many good punting yarns over the years, but I think the best, and probably most rewarding for him, came quite late in his Hong Kong career when he headed to Australia for the 1993 Melbourne Cup.

His good friend Michael Kinane was riding the Dermot Weld-trained Vintage Crop and it was fancied in some quarters to run well.

Parky went down under with fellow Irishman Ambrose Turnbull – then Circulation Manager of the *South China Morning Post*, and another keen punter, now a fairly successful horse owner currently residing in Madrid with his lovely Spanish wife.

On the day of the race at Flemington the pair approached a leading bookmaker named Peter Coster and asked what odds they could get on Vintage Crop winning the Melbourne Cup.

"16 to one," Coster offered.

Parky turned on his Irish charm.

"Ah, be heavens, we've come all the way from Ireland [they actually came from Hong Kong] to see the great race and no overseas horse has ever won the mighty race [true], surely you can give us better odds than 16/1!"

The bookie sized them up, then told them they could have 20/1. Whereupon Parky and Turnbull hit him with a sizeable bet.

The rest is history: Vintage Crop won, promoting strong rumours that the pair had put bets on elsewhere on the course too.

It was also widely rumoured that a number of plastic carrier bags were grudgingly handed over by local bookies to Parky and Turnbull; they had Aussie dollars coming out of their ears! Parky never told me how much he won that day, nor did Ambrose, but it was a mighty big coup.

Normally the winning jockey celebrates the Melbourne Cup with champagne along with the owners of the winning horse. However Mick Kinane, after his riding duties were finished for the day, headed for the bar and celebrated with his old pals from Hong Kong, capping off an astonishing day.

A piece of international racing history had been created: Vintage Crop becoming the first northern hemisphere-trained runner to win Australia's greatest race. Mind you, quite a few Aussie bookmakers thought it was a day better forgotten!

Talking of bookmakers, another to make his name in Hong Kong racing and then go on to great things was a young Australian, son of a Melbourne bookmaker, who came to the city to try his luck in 1973.

His ambition was to be a race caller, but a dearth of opportunities in his home town led him to Hong Kong. Fellow countryman Terry Butts lured the youngster with the promise that he could kick-start his career in a new land.

Butts was the first English-speaking commentator for the Hong Kong Jockey Club. Although his main job was General Manager of the Carlton Hotel – a small, 23-room establishment in old Tai Po Road that was a popular night time entertainment spot and had wonderful views towards the harbour; before the landscape was modified in later years.

He also had another sideline: Racing Editor of the afternoon *China Mail* tabloid. And that's where Jim McGrath, the young man from Melbourne began his Hong Kong career.

However, he soon felt disappointed. Butts had promised him the chance to call races, but after three months he was still just writing about them. A face-to-face meeting with his boss followed, where the young McGrath demanded that he be allowed to call some races or he would be back on a plane to Melbourne. In December he got his wish: he called his first races at Happy Valley, and never looked back.

Leaving the *China Mail* he went to work on the Sports Desk of the *South China Morning Post* – hired by Robin Parke – and enjoyed more than a decade with the Jockey Club as their chief race caller. He also appeared regularly on ATV television's *Turf Talk*.

After 13 good years in Hong Kong he yearned for a bigger stage, so he took off for England and joined the newly formed racing publication, *The Racing Post*, in 1986. *The Racing Post*'s editor, Graham Rock, knew him from the time Rock worked in Hong Kong as a steward and official handicapper for the Jockey Club.

McGrath would later join the (British) *Daily Telegraph* and write a widely respected column under the name, Hotspur. He would also call races across the UK and Ireland.

In 1997 the legendary race caller Peter O'Sullevan was knighted, and, soon after, decided to retire. Sir Peter had been the BBC's leading horse racing commentator for 50 years, describing some of the greatest moments in equine history.

Before the BBC could even look into possible replacements, O'Sullevan stated publicly that there was only one person who could replace him, that being the man who had been his understudy for many years: Jim McGrath, the young man who had arrived in Hong Kong in 1973 determined to be a race caller.

During the football off-season I would catch up with Jim and Parky when back in the UK as racing in Hong Kong was also in its off-season. We would attend a few race meetings together, especially the annual

July meeting at Newmarket where we would stay in a friendly b&b pub normally arranged by jockey Wally Hood. Wally spent the season riding in Hong Kong and then went back to his home in Newmarket during the break. We would also catch up with Wendyll Woods, another jockey who rode in Hong Kong, for his uncle, Lawrie Fownes.

After racing at Newmarket we would all head to the White Horse pub and talk about the winners we'd backed that day, and those who had let us down. In later years I would frequently stay in Newmarket with Philip Robinson and his wife, Gill who have a lovely house on the Avenue opposite Tattersalls.

I recall one day Jimmy, Parky and I were going to attend a meeting at York, whose racecourse is often referred to as the Knavesmire. We had agreed to meet at a specific time at King's Cross station in London to catch the train to York. Our old racing buddy Brian Rouse was riding a horse we expected to win in one of the feature races – I think it was the Black Duck Stakes, which was an early race on the York card that day. We had high expectations of making a quid on the day.

Unfortunately Parky was held up; by the time he eventually arrived at the station, out of breath, with some lame excuse to Jimmy and me, our train had left the station. We managed to get on the next train, but were cutting it a bit fine to make the race we wanted to punt on. The trip took slightly longer than expected due to disruptions on the line and by the time we got to the Knavesmire 'Brussels,' as we affectionately called Brian Rouse, had passed the post and won at 6/4.

"I'll buy you both a drink to make up for it," Parky said, as Jimmy and I gave him a deathly stare knowing he wasn't the quickest shouting up a drink. As it turned out we didn't do too badly that day, but when we got to the Chase Hotel, our accommodation for the night, we made damn sure Parky lived up to his promise when we hit the bar.

Parky hired a car in York and the next day the three of us headed to Malton to visit horse trainer, Frank Carr. On arrival, we checked into The Green Man hotel where we were met by Stuart Morris, Frank Carr's stepson. Stuart was also riding in Hong Kong during that period and Frank was training there.

Anyone who knows Irish-born Frank Carr will be aware that he was one of the biggest characters in horse racing. From his Whitewall stables in Malton he masterminded some huge racing plunges, including one in the Royal Hunt Cup at Royal Ascot.

He was close friends with Lester Piggott and that night in The Green Man restaurant he entertained us with stories about Lester.

I mentioned Frank had some good winning punts in his time, but the story I'm going to relate concerns one that got away. It was during his six year tenure in Hong Kong. Before I tell the story though let me give you a little of Frank's background.

Frank trained horses in Malton, Yorkshire, with considerable success, before heading to Hong Kong. He was big pals with Liverpool manager Bob Paisley, who, after the end of a football season, would often stay for a week or two at Frank's home – in fact he had just been there prior to our arrival.

Frank told me their friendship started with a chance meeting in a hotel in Dublin in 1963. Liverpool were in town for a game and Bob loved the gee gees. They met and became close friends.

When in 1977 Eamonn Andrews surprised Bob Paisley, on the team bus after a Liverpool away game, with the magic words, *This is Your Life* – the iconic ITV show of that era – he'd brought Frank Carr all the way from Hong Kong just to be on the show. "It cost them a 1,000 quid to fly me over." Frank told me with a smile.

Frank was great company. He swore like a trooper and there was never a dull moment when he was around. But to the tale of the punt that never was...

Frank liked a punt, even more so than most trainers, but he could be very patient waiting for the right moment to strike. One day he had a runner at Sha Tin that was not fancied by the local racing fraternity, but he liked it!

A jockey he was friendly with told Frank he thought one of his horses on the same card that day would win. Both horses were just over double figures in their respective races. This was in the days before online betting could drastically change the odds.

Trainers were allowed to bet in those days, but not jockeys... never, ever.

Rather than use his own cash Frank telephones his punting friend. Why bark yourself when you have a dog, as the old saying goes. So a decent wager is put on for a winning double and hopefully a good collect for all concerned.

Both romped in at good odds, Frank was over the moon. But there was a problem, Frank has not heard from his punter – let's call him Peter – for 24 hours. Surely he hasn't done a runner Frank thinks. Eventually he phones Peter's home and his wife answers tearfully.

"Thanks for calling Frank, Peter died on Saturday afternoon," she says.

Frank passes on his condolences, after he puts the phone down, he thinks: Bloody hell he's got so excited, he's had a fucking heart attack!

Who knows where the winnings went but it wasn't to Frank Carr!

I suppose I was very lucky to witness the ups and downs of the changing face of Hong Kong racing as it went from amateur to professional; and meet many of the colourful jockeys and trainers riding there in the 70s and 80s.

T.C. Cheng, better known as 'Top Cat', was champion jockey in the 1970/71 season, despite tough competition from Johnny Cruz (father of Tony) and Australian, Alan Middleton.

Middleton was married to one of Hong Kong's top cabaret singers of the era, Billie Tan, who performed at the fashionable Club Mocambo in Central District – one of the places for Hong Kong's rich and famous to be seen and heard. I confess to going there myself once or twice after matches, but only as a guest as it was quite pricey for an under-paid footballer.

I daren't go into some of the things that reputedly went on during amateur race days as much was very often hearsay, Much like the jockey who supposedly accidentally fell off his unfancied horse in the last furlong of a race, allowing the favourite to get up to win.

A jockey I got to know quite well was one of the first Australian riders of the professional era, Geoff Lane. Geoff stayed opposite the Happy Valley racecourse with his wife Joanni in Wong Nai Chung Road.

Nicknamed the 'Golden Boy' in his native Australia, Geoff toiled at times making the weight during his riding days in Hong Kong and would often spend a considerable time in a hot bath just hours before racing trying to shed some pounds. After his riding days in Hong Kong were over he became a racing steward before finally securing a trainer's licence for the 1988/89 season.

His training career got of to a flyer; the very first horse he entered in a race won! I was there that day and remember it well. I was standing next to Joanni when the horse came home and we both flung our arms in the air in jubilation. I knew what it meant to Geoff and Joanni. The horse was called Morning Patrol, and despite carrying top weight, it raced home down the straight 1,000 metres under the cool guidance of jockey, Peter Leyshan. And yes, I did have a small wager on it.

After I retired from football I would often meet up with Geoff in Wong Nai Chong Road and go on a run up the hilly Blue Pool Road in Happy Valley, him normally wearing his Collingwood Aussie Rules top. We both agreed it was much easier coming down!

Geoff sadly died of kidney failure in 2019 at the age of 80. He was a real gentleman of the turf and much loved by everyone who knew him. He had been inducted into the Australian Racing Hall of Fame in 2013 and was one of its finest servants.

During the 1970s and 1980s quite a few of the leading lights of the UK racing scene, who normally plied their trade at Newmarket, Epsom or Ascot, would come out to Hong Kong in their off-season to ride.

A who's who of jockeys: Lester Piggott, Bruce Raymond, Pat Eddery, Brian Rouse, Eddie Hide, Joe Mercer, Jimmy Lindley, Brian Taylor,

Tony Ives, Richard Quinn, Walter Swinburn, Greville Starkey and Alan Munro, and many more added lustre to the local scene.

English jockeys Wally Hood, Roger Wernham, Wendyll Woods and Philip Robinson were some who rode in Hong Kong for the full season plus the many Australians, such as Peter Miers and Pat Trotter.

Roger Wernham would often give me a lift to Sha Tin race track as he stayed not far from me in Happy Valley. One morning Roger asked me to pick up jockey Greville Starkey, who was staying in an apartment next to the Excelsior Hotel and bring him to his place in Happy Valley for the drive to Sha Tin.

Starkey, who had Derby success on board Shirley Heights in 1978, didn't know his way around Hong Kong, so I picked him up and that's how I met Greville for the first time. He was actually a very funny man, as well as a great jockey.

After racing one night a group of us were at Landau's Restaurant when it had a branch on the ground floor close to the Excelsior Hotel in Causeway Bay. Brian Rouse, Brian Taylor, Roger Wernham and Wally Hood were there that that night and Grenville was the star attraction.

Suddenly, without warning, he does his party piece, unbeknown to me but not the others. He throws his voice and makes a barking sound.

It's so good the waiters actually think we have a dog under the table and begin peering underneath the white tablecloth. As they couldn't find any sign of a dog they turned their backs and returned to their duties. As soon as they did, Greville barked again. He then innocently asked a waiter, "Is there a dog in here?"

He barked a few more times, and when the waiters saw we were all in stitches, they finally realised what was happening. (It's probably funnier if you have a few glasses of red wine inside you.)

13

The Lawman and the Cranhill sounds

I was just twelve years old when I made the brave decision to take time off school in September 1961 with a fictitious illness. Not sure it would fool anyone though: Scotland were playing Czechoslovakia in a crucial World Cup qualifier at Hampden Park that Tuesday afternoon.

Scotland had to win to force a replay on a neutral ground if they wanted direct entry into the 1962 World Cup finals in Chile the following year.

My Dad gave me his blessing to go, despite my age; but the worry was my Mum, she was kept in the dark and would be working in Marks & Spencer's in Argyle Street. I had to be home before she finished work or it might have been a clip round the ear.

My simple ruse was to plead sickness, go home from school at lunchtime, change into casual clothes, and make the bus trip to Hampden. With a little financial assistance from my Dad I had enough money for entry to the terraces at the east end of the stadium – referred to in the West of Scotland as the 'Celtic' end.

There were 52,000 fans in the stadium that day; there must have been a wave of flu going around, or, more than likely, friendly doctors supplying sick notes.

Scotland were down 2-1, the Czechs had some tasty players including Josef Masopust – voted European footballer of the year in 1962 – but a Denis Law goal levelled the game just after the hour mark. At that time Law was most youngsters' idol.

When I looked at my watch again it was about 10 minutes from time and I feared a Scotland winning goal would never come. I was even more fearful as I realized my plan to be home before my Mum finished work was in peril. It was time to get the bus home, otherwise, it would be hell from Mum, so I left before the end.

Walking down the hill behind Hampden, disappointed by the scoreline, I suddenly heard a tremendous roar, which could only mean one thing: Scotland had scored. I skipped down to the bus stop with a big smile on my face. On the bus home someone had a transistor radio and confirmed to all that Scotland had won 3-2. Denis Law, enhancing his hero status, had scored the winner seven minutes from time.

Some eleven years after my trip to Hampden an opportunity came out of the blue that got me excited. Seiko announced that they had put together a deal for Benfica to play two games in Hong Kong in late May, 1972 – the fee was US$60,000. I had already played against them at the start of that year, but another opportunity to face Eusébio and Nené was a mouthwatering prospect.

Benfica would play Seiko in the first game and Caroline Hill in the second. The Hong Kong clubs would co-sponsor the games, with Seiko handling all the arrangements. But the news that really got me excited was that Seiko were bringing over guest players from the UK through soccer agent Charlie Mitten, and one of them was the Lawman!

You can imagine my delight when a story appeared in the *South China Morning Post* announcing that Denis Law, Rodney Marsh, Don Rogers, Ronnie McKinnon and goalkeeper Bobby Clark would be guesting for Seiko and Caroline Hill in these games. Never in a million years would I have thought, standing on that Hampden terracing as a 12-year-old, that one day I would actually be playing alongside Denis Law. Not only that, but we would be playing together against the mighty Benfica.

Two days prior to the match the *SCMP* ran a sizeable article, the main pictures were of Denis Law and Eusébio, but my picture was also there. To say I was proud would be an understatement. The article was headlined: "The British are all coming," with a subhead that read: "What A Game."

However, sadly for the fans not all did come, and my once-in-a-lifetime dream opportunity to play alongside Denis Law would disappear because of a simple quirk of fate. A bit like losing a poker hand, holding a King flush.

"Law out of the Game," screamed the *SCMP* headline on the morning of the match. The story went on to say that all players, bar Law, had arrived the day before. Charlie Mitten explained that unfortunately Law had to miss the trip: "Denis pulled out the day before we left. His young son hurt himself in an accident and is in hospital. Denis was understandably upset and he and his wife did not think it was right for him to leave his family at that time. He is very disappointed about missing the trip. He was genuinely looking forward to it."

Not half as much as me!

That would be one of my greatest disappointments in football; but understandably Law's family came first. But hey, in another morning preview of the game the *SCMP*'s, Jock Sloan wrote, "It is a shame Denis Law, inimitably, still puckish and a dedicated professional, could not link up with stylish Wu Kwok-hung and widely experienced, Chan Hung-ping. However, top teams in many parts of the world would be hard pressed to field a finer striking force than Don Rogers, Rodney Marsh and Derek Currie."

Jimmy Hagan, the Benfica manager was big on fitness, possibly a legacy of his early army days. In true Hagan style, after clearing customs at Kai Tak Airport, the day before the match and getting to the Lee Gardens Hotel, Hagan informed Seiko officials that he needed facilities for the team to train that evening.

There had been no prior request for such a training session and the Hong Kong Government Stadium was officially closed for the night. Hagan however wanted his players to loosen up after the long flight so, after checking in at the hotel, he took them for a walk up Caroline Hill Road to the Hong Kong Stadium car park, ten minutes from the hotel. For half an hour or so some of the world's most expensive players then exercised on a deserted piece of concrete outside the Hong Kong Government Stadium.

It was late afternoon the next day, the last Sunday in May, when Benfica faced a Seiko Select XI, but the air was still hot, humid and extremely muggy. A little earlier in the day a summer downpour had soaked the turf, the rain appearing to dance on the sun-baked surface, but by the time the sides took to the field the rain had only taken the sting out of the ground.

Seiko had five guest players, including defender Davie Anderson from local club Caroline Hill. The overseas guests included goalkeeper Bobby Clark, who made 425 appearances for Aberdeen and 17 for Scotland, notching up plenty of international experience. Bobby had faced Eusébio and six of his Benfica team-mates when in goal for Scotland in a European Championship qualifying game at the Estádio da Luz stadium two years earlier, losing 2-0 – Eusébio finding the net against him that day.

I had never met Bobby before our game, but got to know him well a few years later when I had a short spell playing alongside him for San Antonio Thunder in the NASL. A top bloke, confident, and always with a cheery grin on his face.

At centre-half, we had Ronnie McKinnon, the former Glasgow Rangers pivot, with 28 caps for Scotland he was also in the national side that became the first country to beat England after they claimed the World Cup in 1966.

Scotland were the new World Champions was the joke doing the rounds after that historic win for the jocks. A game I actually attended in 1967 with my Dad and two older brothers.

McKinnon had been a great servant to Glasgow Rangers and was now coming to the end of his career, which, as it turned out, he would finish playing for a club in Durban, South Africa, a year later.

Up front we had Don Rogers, the hero for Swindon Town when they were in the English third division and beat the mighty Arsenal 3-1 after extra time in the 1969 League Cup Final at Wembley. Rogers scoring the two extra-time goals. Rogers had since moved on to Crystal Palace.

Last of the foursome was the mercurial Rodney Marsh, sometimes described as the 'clown prince' of football because of his cheeky footballing skills and laid-back style; much in the mould of his friend George Best. A wonderful entertainer on the field, he was then with Manchester City, but his great friend Malcolm Allison had resigned as manager just a month or so earlier, so his position at City was far from clear.

I was the other forward in the line-up and it was agreed I would change wing positions with Rogers from time to time during the game as we were both left-sided players.

On paper, we had a decent team, but matches are not won on paper. Manager Hagan had the best Benfica could offer at his disposal.

"We will have eight players in the team who took part in the recent World Cup match between Portugal and Bulgaria. The other three players are also full internationals, so we will have a full strength side for the game," Hagan had said pre-match.

Full strength side! What he omitted to say was that in Benfica's run up to our game his side had won 27 of their last 28 games in the Portuguese league, and drawn the other 2-2 with Porto. For good measure, they had racked up 95 goals and conceded only a meagre fourteen.

Though we had some class players guesting in our side, they were coming to the twilight of their careers. We were huge underdogs, a patchwork team against Portugal's finest.

As to be expected with a Hagan team, they were extremely fit. We lost 6-1.

In truth, despite having some bright moments, we were all over the place: not much understanding in defence and mid-field, leaving us short of options up front. Benfica swamped us in the mid-field, controlled the game, and showed their undoubted class. We never at any stage played with any fluency, but hey, it was an exhibition game and the first time many of us had played together, so despite the scoreline we were not too downbeat.

Don Rogers confessed that he had never felt so tired after a match; clearly the humidity had sapped his energy. McKinnon and Marsh felt much the same, so we had some mitigating factors for the loss. In truth, some of our guests simply ran out of gas.

Don Rogers scored our goal, his shot coming off the crossbar and just bouncing over the line – I had been following up, ready to score if it hadn't – but that was our only reward.

Their next game was against Caroline Hill on the Wednesday evening and it wouldn't be any easier; where was The Lawman when you needed him?

It was an evening game set to kick off at 8pm. All four British guests players had attended a training session with the Caroline Hill squad at So Kon Po military ground, a short hop from the Government Stadium. I was also in attendance as I had been selected to play in the green and white of Caroline Hill against the red shirts from Lisbon.

After the session Rodney Marsh commented that it was good to get the chance to meet the players and get to know them before the game, unlike the previous Sunday.

"We didn't know one another then, or individuals' skills, and it showed! At least with an evening game it shouldn't be so humid," he added.

Showing a degree of optimism a Caroline Hill official commented to the media: "We understand the heat and tiredness were key factors in the first game, but Seiko mixed up defence and that was fatal, their mid-field had no domination whatsoever, leaving Marsh, Rogers and Currie with a thankless task." The same official went on to say, "We are hopeful things will go a lot more smoothly tomorrow night. Certainly, we will not be beaten 6-1... that's a guarantee."

He was absolutely correct: we only lost 5-1! I left the field during the game with what was later diagnosed as a fractured ankle! A rash tackle by their international full-back, José Malta da Silva, more clumsy than premeditated, saw me limp off. My match was over, and, as it turned out, so was my season; I needed a plaster cast. For my efforts, I got a courteous pat on the back from Nené and Eusébio.

Disappointing, but that's part of the game; not the merry month of May for me, but it was great to play with Rogers and Marsh up front while it lasted.

The next time I saw Eusébio was when we happened to be on the same plane going to cover a 1986 World Cup game in Mexico. We were having a brief chat on board prior to take-off, when the next minute, we were all asked to disembark. Apparently unauthorized baggage was on board so we had to identify our own luggage, but finally we got the all clear to fly. Eusébio and I in security scare on the way to Guadalajara, I wrote the next day in my column, a minor scoop.

After the disappointment of not lining up with Denis Law for the Benfica games, I did eventually meet my Scottish boyhood hero in the flesh. But it would be 19 years later.

It was 1992 in a comfortable little hotel in Norrköping, the city in eastern Sweden, 160 kilometres from the capital, Stockholm. I was covering the Euro Championships for a newspaper and he was covering the Scotland games for television. It was a bizarre meeting, I was just leaving my hotel to go for a meal with Robin Parke of the *SCMP* and Denis Law was just checking into the hotel.

"That's Denis Law," I said to Parky.

There were not many people about and it was a smallish reception area so I went up to him and said, with a tinge of humour, "I should have played alongside you."

"With who?" he asked, with that cheeky smile. "Against Benfica," and explained the circumstances.

With typical Denis Law humour, he replied. "We might have beat them if I'd played."

I might never have shared the field with him, but it was a huge pleasure finally meeting him that day.

The year before my trip to Hampden to watch Denis Law as a kid was the beginning of the swinging sixties. After the austerity of the post-war years they would prove to be a breath of fresh air. It was a new age for pop music: jazz and slow ballads were coming to the end of their popularity, so too was the term rock 'n' roll – to be reclassified by the mid-sixties as 'rock music'. New styles in fashion for men and women heralded a more colourful, fun age. The world was finally recovering;

the ashes of the Second World War were slowly being blown into the wind. Bob Dylan was doing his best to remind us not to be complacent, releasing his *Freewheelin'* album in 1963, with *Blowing in the Wind* his timely reminder. Europe was rapidly recovering, though Asia and Africa still had demons to contend with.

This is what I remember as a young boy, just about to be transferred from primary school to senior secondary, as was the norm in the education system in Glasgow in those days.

I had attended Milncroft primary school in the north-east of Glasgow since I was eight years of age. One morning our music teacher introduced us to a new song she had written, which was to become our morning assembly song.

"School that is set on a hill, We Salute You." The song had several verses, but all ending with the powerful line, "We Salute You." Each morning, that song would be sung religiously by all the children. Almost four years or so after I left Milncroft, to attend Cranhill senior secondary school, a couple of young lads would stand to attention in the same Milncroft school and sing that very same song.

Many years later, these same boys would use the words "We Salute You" as the chorus in one of their many hit records; a tip of the hat to their early roots and schooling.

For Those About to Rock, (We Salute You) was the song they penned.

The boys were Malcolm and Angus Young, better known as the two brothers who founded the group AC/DC – despite being Scottish born, they became recognized as adopted Australian heroes, and quite rightly so.

Malcolm would play for the Milncroft school football team and wear the same half-square black and light-blue school colours as I did – although he would not win the Glasgow Primary School Championship for under-12s like me, he would win much bigger accolades in later life, but on a different stage.

Cranhill was a city housing scheme built in the early 50s, chiefly comprising four storey tenements, surrounding a patch of grass. I used to play football after school with the other kids on that grassy patch that separated Strone Road from Skerryvore Road in Cranhill; an older brother of Malcolm and Angus, called George, would sometimes watch us play. The Young family lived in Skerryvore Road.

George would leave Cranhill and Glasgow with his mum and dad and other siblings and emigrate to Australia in 1963. In those days the Australian Government sponsored a £10 'Assisted Passage Migration Scheme', and the Young family took advantage of it to seek pastures new. 'Ten Pound Poms' they would sometimes be called.

A dearth of jobs in Glasgow, combined with dreadful cold weather, forced many Glaswegians, and Scotsmen from other cities to embark on a new life, emigrating to Australia or Canada. There were opportunities in these new developing countries for skilled, and even unskilled labour, and plenty of room for populations to grow. As it turned out, Scotland's loss would be Australia's gain.

Sidetracking slightly, another lad a year earlier in 1962, who stayed in Bridgeton, not far from Cranhill also took the same trip with his family and emigrated to Australia. He would be better known in later years as John Paul Young, and *Love is in the Air* would be an international hit over the airwaves in 1978. I wondered if I had emigrated, would I have become a famous singer? I think not!!!

But back to George Young, when I left Cranhill school at the tender age of fourteen-and-a-half to find employment, George Young was becoming a founder member of a band in Australia called The Easybeats. In 1966 he co-wrote a song with Harry Vanda which would be the first world-wide hit from an Australian band; that song was *Friday on my Mind*, which reached number 6 in the UK charts.

I loved that song, but not having followed George Young's musical career, I never realised at the time that it was the same guy who used to watch us play football on the grassy knoll of Cranhill and who would kick the ball back to us when it went too far.

Friday on my Mind put Australia on the international pop scene; the rest is history.

There was another musician from Cranhill who would go on to great things – not to the same extent as the Young brothers and AC/DC – but a great drummer, nevertheless.

In Cranhill, I lived at 75 Crowlin Crescent, on the top floor of a 4-storey tenement, in a three-bedroom flat. Most of the streets on the Cranhill housing estate were named after lighthouses. (Why lighthouses? The nearest stretch of water was the old Monkland canal, which bordered the estate and is now the M8 motorway. But lighthouses it was!)

As a kid I used to play in the block's communal back gardens, available to the tenants to hang up their washing, but I would use it as a spot to play football. In the building adjacent to our block, which happened to be the end building of Crowlin Crescent, there was constant noise coming from the first floor at all times of the day and night. It came from a chap who was five years older than me called Billy Adamson and his drumming would lead to many complaints from the neighbours When not practising, Billy would play in a band called the Bellrocks, which played at various clubs in Glasgow, and whose vocalist was a young lady called Marie Lawrie: she would later become better known as 'Lulu'.

Funnily enough, my Mum would become good friends with Lulu's mum – they would go to the bingo together as Lulu's mum lived nearby in Dennistoun. I had never met Lulu until she came to Hong Kong in the mid-70s and I had lunch with her in the Lee Gardens coffee shop. She told me her mum had said her friend's son Derek was in Hong Kong so she should try and look him up; and there we finally were, having a good chat and reminiscing about our childhoods. During the conversation she happened to mention Billy Adamson. Lulu told me he had joined The Searchers – who just happened to be another of my favourite bands and very popular at the time. I'm sure a favourite also to many in the same age group as me.

It was not until 1993 or 1994 – the memory is not quite what it was – that I finally met Billy again, some thirty or so years since I had last seen him in Glasgow. The Searchers were playing Hong Kong. They stayed in a hotel in Kowloon and were due to play several gigs, including one at a popular bar in Wan Chai called Joe Bananas, which was the 'in' bar at that time and owned by Laura McAllister, a fellow Glaswegian, and managed by Billy Dock, also from Glasgow.

I was then working for Carlsberg, so I sent a few cases of the Danish brew to The Searchers' hotel, with a message to Billy that I would be at Joe Bananas on their opening night. It was great to see him, slightly nostalgic: we discussed old friends, his family and mine, and all who we remembered from Cranhill as youths. We briefly chatted about the many roads that we had been down before meeting again after all those years. Billy introduced me to his fellow band members, John McNally, Frank Allen and Spencer James.

Founder of the group, John McNally, said, "Billy told us about you and the history between both of you."

To which I replied with a smile, "I know all about you guys, I have been singing and playing your songs for the last thirty years."

I was very proud of what Billy had achieved, remembering all the hours of practice he put into his drumming in a small flat in Cranhill all those years ago, and the shrieks from the neighbours about the noise. Billy had also played with Emile Ford and the Checkmates, prior to joining The Searchers in 1969.

I arranged for The Searchers to play a one-off night at the Hong Kong Football Club in Happy Valley. They were great, playing their golden hits to a packed audience.

Billy would retire from the band in 1998 and move to France to spend more time with his family. I stayed in touch with him periodically, only to learn in mid-November of 2013 that sadly he had faced the final drumroll: Billy had passed away. Many former friends, like Junior Campbell of Marmalade, and members of The Fortunes band, who had toured many times with The Searchers, wrote fitting tributes to Billy.

I still like playing The Searchers' songs, they still sound good and they always remind me of Billy drumming away in his bedroom on the housing estate searching for stardom.

14

Snakes alive, Fast Wullie and a Double Scotch

The bus jolted along a two lane highway, built just above the height of the paddy fields, with makeshift bridges spanning the numerous small *klongs* (canals). It was the beginning of August 1973 and we were heading from Bangkok to Pattaya and a well-deserved break.

The air conditioning system on the bus was fighting a losing battle on the three-and-a-half hour trip to the little resort on Thailand's eastern seaboard, so we were all sweating as if we had just completed a training session.

Alongside me on the bus were Jackie Trainer and Walter Gerrard. The original three amigos were back together again! Jackie had returned from a brief spell in South Africa and signed for Seiko for the 73/74 season.

After a super successful first season in the premier division the club had rewarded the players with five days holiday in Pattaya. Then we were to head along the coast for a two week pre-season training camp in Bangsaen.

Pattaya in 1973 was not the thriving resort it became in later years. Then it was quite serene, a sleepy little fishing village, but a great place for lazing in the sun or taking a boat to one of the many tropical islands just off the coast. It only had a couple of proper hotels. I can't remember if we stayed at the Orchid Lodge or the Nipa Lodge, but I do remember that the hotel had leafy tropical gardens and was only a stone's throw from the beach.

We spent a lot of time sunbathing, but that didn't mean there weren't thrills and spills to be had if you were adventurous. In those days jet-skis were the stand-up type. Once aboard you opened up the throttle and let her rip. As you hit each wave a jolt went through your body.

There were few tourists around, so while we were roaring across the waves Manuel Cuenca, our Spanish right-winger, decided to roar down Beach Road. He hired a motor bike and managed to hit a 'ton' down the straight palm-fringed one and a half mile strip. He then repeated his feat in the other direction, before stopping to ask if anyone wanted to jump on the back and enjoy the thrill with him. There were no takers. Today he'd be lucky to get out of first gear!

There were no takers either for the para-gliding. At that time you took off from the beach and landed back there again a few minutes later; if you were lucky! There were telephone wires running along between the road and the beach and if there was a strong gust of wind there was the very real possibility that you could end up entangled in them; or you could crash into a palm tree! I decided to stick to getting my thrills on the football field.

Our Seiko boss, Keeree Kanjanapas, was no older than many of the players and joined in the fun, taking us out in a junk-like fishing boat one afternoon. He might have held the reins at the club, but he was just one of the boys that day. Now, one of the richest men in Thailand.

We set off from a spot near what is now the infamous 'Walking Street'; back then it was just a dusty road. Once the boat was in deeper water we tried a bit of fishing with makeshift lines, but all we caught were tiddlers. Then it was on to 'Monkey Island'. At that time it had golden sands and tropical palm trees which almost reached the water's edge. If Long John Silver had appeared no one would have been surprised. The monkey population was significantly lower than it is today and they were quite shy. Today they'll be into your picnic basket and steal anything that you don't have a tight grip on.

Our time in Pattaya came to an end far too quickly and it was off to training camp in Bangsaen, where we would endure two hard workouts every day; it was tortuously hot, no matter what time of day we trained! Hardly comparable, but it would give me a very slight inkling of what those brave soldiers must have endured building the Bridge on the River

Kwai in Kanchanaburi. God only knows the suffering they must have endured!

When we arrived in Bangsaen our rooms were not ready. Rather than just sit about and wait, Jackie Trainer and I left our passports with Chan Chik-hung, Seiko's company secretary, so he could handle our hotel registration, while we took a stroll down the beach opposite the hotel. Walter Gerrard declined to join us: "too fuckin' hot outside" he said, sitting under a fan and mopping the sweat off his brow.

If we thought Pattaya was sleepy, Bangsaen was in full slumber; just a smattering of houses along the beach. That said, you couldn't fail to be struck by its untouched beauty; you almost felt like an early explorer landing on a South Sea island. Shady palms lined the beach, but the thing I recall more than any other was the way the locals and their children stared at Jackie and I, as if they had never seen a *farang* (foreigner) before.

While walking on the damp sand that morning, shoes in hand, looking at the sea, I caught sight of what appeared to be long brown, eel-like marine creatures swimming together in large numbers. As I was thinking, "I might just stick to swimming in the pool," Jackie spotted them too. "What the hell are those?" he cried.

"No idea, they look like eels or possibly sea snakes," I replied. Not being a marine expert, brought up a city boy, I had no idea what they were; and I was certainly nor going into the sea to find out. We sauntered back across the road to check into our hotel – amazingly it's still in operation today, renamed Bangsaen Heritage Hotel. They have made various additions over the years, but the central hotel structure still remains as it was over 50 years ago.

There was a makeshift football field only a few minutes walk from the hotel and that apparently was the reason for choosing Bangsaen for our training camp.

It was a lovely hotel in many ways, but us British boys suffered in the days ahead, missing our traditional grub; getting used to the daily spicy Thai cuisine was not easy. They did make a nice scrambled egg on toast for breakfast, but ordering it three times a day was stretching it.

We trained under a relentless sun and would be dripping with sweat as we trudged off the field after each session. But we did have the relief of a cooling dip in the large swimming pool afterwards. The pool however lost its popularity for a short time when an uninvited guest also tried to cool off there.

This was not your run of the mill intruder!

I had gone for a walk along the beach early one afternoon while team-mates frolicked around the pool, making a fair bit of noise. Half an hour later I returned and the pool was deserted and there was an odd, eerie silence.

It was not until meeting up for our 4pm training session that I found out why. The boys had been joined at the pool by an extremely long python, which, as you can imagine, scared the shit out of everyone. Total pandemonium had followed. Fortunately, the hotel staff were more than capable of handling such an emergency. We learned later that it was not uncommon for the snakes to appear by the poolside. Funnily enough they didn't mention that in the brochure! I did say Bangsaen was fairly primitive; snakes and monkeys were probably much greater in number than people.

After the incident the hotel management installed a life guard, or snake guard, by the pool for the remainder of our stay. Never a dull moment in Paradise.

When we eventually left Bangsaen I reflected on the cultural experience: a tad different to living in a teeming city of over 4 million people, as Hong Kong was in those days.

The training camp had been a success and the team members were in good shape physically, ready for the season ahead.

The bus journey back to Bangkok took well over two hours but, thankfully, even though it hummed and vibrated at times, the air-conditioning on board never broke down.

We were scheduled to leave from Bangkok's Don Muang Airport and fly direct to Hong Kong; but, amazingly, we ended up in Tokyo! We had 'Joan' to thank for that.

July and August are the typhoon season in Hong Kong and Joan was the name given by the Joint Typhoon Warning Center to the one that blew us off course. We were relaxing aboard Thai Airways flight TG902 when the captain made the announcement: a typhoon was in the region of Hong Kong causing stormy weather and serious air turbulence, making landing at Kai Tak a safety concern.

A safety concern? Landing at Kai Tak can be bloody scary at the best of times, never mind with a gale force wind blowing!

There were a series of jolts to the aircraft and an element of concern flooded the cabin. Shortly after, we were relieved to hear the captain come on the PA again and announce that after consultation with Hong Kong Air Traffic Control we were not going to attempt a landing at Kai Tak. He followed up by saying that instead we would fly on to Tokyo, assuring us that there was enough fuel in the tanks for the additional miles!

Typhoon Iris had visited the city a week or two earlier, so it was not a great surprise to hear of another storm in the vicinity. Nobody needs to be reminded of what destruction these tropical cyclones can cause: Typhoon Rose hit Hong Kong on August 16, two years earlier, causing 110 fatalities and countless injuries.

I remember during one typhoon, when I was living in the top floor apartment in Tin Hau Temple Road, North Point, I could literally feel the structure swaying slightly from side to side. A building engineer told me that tall buildings in Hong Kong are designed to handle typhoons and sway with the wind, making them more flexible in the face of the elements. But it still scares the devil out of you! So, out of the blue, on to Tokyo it would be, and a first time visit for many of us to the Land of the Rising Sun.

We landed at Haneda Airport feeling a bit weary, but relieved to get our feet on solid ground, and were taken to the 5-star Imperial Hotel for the night.

It was getting late in the evening, but there was enough time to have a stroll round Tokyo's famous Ginza district and to view the magnificent Imperial Palace, artfully lit to enhance its splendour.

As I got into bed that night I reflected on the day: in the morning I was strolling along a pristine beach lined by swaying palms, where luxury costs you nothing; come the evening, I'm walking around Tokyo's elite shopping area, where luxury costs an arm and a leg.

Makes you think, how does one really define luxury?

Sadly, at breakfast the next day, we were informed that we would depart for Hong Kong in the early afternoon as the storm had dissipated; hopes of a full day in Tokyo were dashed.

After returning from the unexpected trip to Japan there was plenty of competitive football in my fourth season in Hong Kong; my second with Seiko. The Hong Kong League XI side, where I had become almost a permanent fixture, had a couple of exciting matches coming up in late 1973.

The first was against a Malaysian International side who had just competed in the President's Cup in Seoul, South Korea. I was selected to line up alongside a chap called Willie Rutherford who was having a short spell in Hong Kong during the off season in Australia, where he played for Sydney club Hakoah.

Willie had signed for local side Kwong Wah and was affectionately known among the local British lads playing in Hong Kong as 'Fast Wullie'. Born in Lochgelly, a former mining town in Fife, Scotland, it was rumoured Fast Wullie had once competed in the famous Powderhall Sprint, a well-known race for professional runners held annually on New Year's Day. Originally run in Powderhall, it now takes place at Musselburgh Racecourse, a few clicks from Edinburgh.

Willie had emigrated to Australia and won some professional sprint races on the Gold Coast, hence the nickname. He had also played for the 'Socceroos', the Australian national side, in six qualifying games during their failed bid to reach the 1970 World Cup finals. I was very much looking forward to playing alongside him, hoping our speed would run the Malaysians ragged.

At a training session prior to the Malaysian game some of the lads suggested Willie and I race off from the halfway line to see who was the faster as we were both considered the fastest wingers in Hong Kong. Willie and I agreed and as we crossed the finishing line the Hong Kong Jockey Club photo-finish camera would not have split us. After the sprint we shook hands and I winked at Willie, our plan to finish neck and neck had succeeded. That was the last time we were asked to run against each other.

Although sometimes quite reserved, 'Oor Wullie' was a great lad.

There was a full house of 28,000 fans at the Government Stadium when we faced the strong Malaysian side. They had a good line-up which included goalkeeper R. Arumugam, nicknamed 'Spiderman' because of his exceptionally long arms and ability to make brilliant saves (he would go on to earn 196 caps for his national side), Wong Choon-wah, a gifted inside-forward, and centre-back Soh Chin-aun who would represent his country on 250 occasions. Even though only 195 of those games were recognized by FIFA as international 'A' games, Soh was FIFA's most capped international player of all time until June 14, 2022 when he was overtaken by Bader Al-Mutawa of Kuwait.

Later that season both Wong and Soh would enjoy a brief loan spell with Seiko; but for the moment I was playing against them.

As it turned out we had a narrow win over Malaysia, mainly due to an uncharacteristic error by Spiderman. For once he allowed a ball to bobble out of his hands straight to our centre-forward Chan Chui-kee, who immediately squared the ball to me and I buried it in the back of the net. Arumugam tried to make up for his mistake by turning away some good efforts from Willie and me later in the game, but it was that costly error that separated the teams at the end of day and we won 1-0.

A month or so later, in mid-December, the League XI side came up against Åtvidaberg, who at the time were the Swedish league champions. Åtvidaberg were a very good side and had beaten Bayern Munich 3-1 at home in their second-leg European Cup match to level the aggregate score at 4-4.

They then, rather unluckily, lost in a penalty shoot-out 4-3 to the German side that included such stars as Maier, Breitner, Schwarzenbeck,

Beckenbauer, Hoeneß and Gerd Müller. Oh, and Bayern Munich would go on to win the European Cup that season. The Swedes were obviously a classy side.

We were all over the place in the opening 15 minutes, like paper on a windy day, and were 1-0 down after just five minutes. Slowly we crept back into the game and Cheung Chi-doy sent some searching long balls through to Willie and me on the flanks so we could try and upset the Swedish rearguard with our pace. It was proving effective, but though we were now an attacking threat we couldn't make the breakthrough for the equalizer as the Swedes tightened their defence

However, a minute from half-time Lady Luck smiled on us. Willie sent a dangerous curving cross over from the right wing. Goalkeeper Ulf Blomberg, who had been between the posts when they had beaten Bayern Munich two months earlier, failed to hold onto it. Before he could retrieve the situation, I had blasted the ball into the top of the net. It was 1-1 at the break.

The Swedes threw everything at us after half-time and got their reward with a second goal 13 minutes into the half; Andersson claiming his second goal. We suddenly had it all to do again.

We came close on a few occasions and about 15 minutes from the end I had a quiet word with Willie: "When they are attacking and their defence are holding a high line, I will drift into the centre. If you get the chance to retrieve the ball in mid-field, knock it over the top of their defenders and I'll be waiting."

A few minutes later Willie gets possession of the ball in midfield, quick as a flash he plays it into the open space behind the Åtvidaberg defence. Their back line lost a second or so in turning to try and stamp out the danger, it was too little too late, I outpaced them, raced forward, and slotted the ball past Blomberg: 2-2. It's great when a plan works; you can't defend against pace... my favourite motto!

That's how it ended. I scored two goals against the Swedish champs, both from passes supplied by Willie Rutherford, I guess you could say the goals were made in Fife.

Needless to say we celebrated with a few restorative ales at the official dinner that night!

Those were the only two occasions I played alongside Fast Wullie. I wish it had been many, many more as we complemented each another on the field and had a natural understanding. Willie went back to his club in Sydney shortly afterwards. He eventually moved to Perth on the west coast of Australia and sadly ran his last race on October 24, 2010 when he passed away at the age of just 65. I wish I had spent more time in Willie's company, on and off the field, but I'm thankful for the short time that I had with the man from Lochgelly.

Australia's Scottish link with Hong Kong didn't end there though.

Who would have thought that a Scot, born in Edinburgh, and set up perfectly by a fellow countryman from Dundee, would score the historic goal for Australia that took them to their first ever World Cup finals in 1974? And what a goal it was!

It was Tuesday evening, November 13, 1973, and a sudden-death play-off game in the neutral venue of Hong Kong between the Aussies and the South Koreans. The first leg in Sydney, on the last Sunday of October, had resulted in a 0-0 draw. The South Koreans had looked to be in pole position with the return leg being played in Seoul on Saturday, November 10.

South Korea held a 2-1 lead at half-time, but Ray Baartz, who had been a youth player for two seasons with Manchester United, scored an equalizer two minutes into the second half. The Aussie, born in Newcastle New South Wales, would never score a more crucial goal for his country. Had the away goal rule been in force at that time, Australia would have progressed, but it wasn't, so a play off was called for.

Hastily arranged, it was decided to play it just three days later in the neutral venue of Hong Kong.

I was writing a football column for the afternoon newspaper *The Star* at that time, so I had a journalistic involvement in the crucial match. I had been at the airport when both sets of players, and the referee, arrived. The ref was an imposing six-footer from the Netherlands who had refereed the 2-2 draw in Seoul. Arie Van Gemert was his name, a very experienced whistler who three weeks earlier had refereed Celtic's second round European Cup tie against Danish part-time side Vejle, when the 'Hoops' were surprisingly held 0-0 by the Danes. A surprise, because Celtic were overwhelming favourites to beat the amateur side from Jutland. They finally did in the second leg through a Bobby Lennox goal in Denmark.

On arrival at Kai Tak, Van Gemert was quoted as saying that he hoped that both teams would play in the same sporting fashion as they had in Seoul.

I went along to the training session for the Australian team the day prior to the match and had a natter afterwards with the two Scottish-born boys, now Aussie nationals. "A couple of pints after the game if you win" was the message I left them with. Jimmy Mackay and Jimmy Rooney raised their thumbs.

Torrential rain an hour before the 8pm kick-off caused worries that the game might have to be postponed, but the rain stopped and the stadium turf dried out quickly. It was a big occasion for both countries: South Korea's only appearance at the World Cup finals had been in Switzerland in 1954; Australia were still hoping to attend one.

Hard work, and many hard matches, had now put these countries 90 minutes away from the finals in West Germany. It would be a night the Socceroos would never forget, thanks to a 'Double Scotch.'

I am not suggesting for a moment that Australian coach Rale Rasic read my preview in *The Star* before the game, but I advised the Aussies to start where they left off in Seoul by attacking from the first minute and getting into top gear quickly, and that's just what they did. It was non-stop attack by the Socceroos, keeping the South Korean defence under constant pressure; although the Koreans were always dangerous on the counter-attack.

Despite the Aussie attacking dominance it was still 0-0 at the break.

South Korea's tall centre-forward Kim Jae-han had a shout for a penalty in the 64th minute when he came down inside the box, but the Dutch referee waved play on. Six minutes later the stadium was in uproar.

Australia were awarded a free kick just inside the South Korean half. Ray Richards floated the ball towards goal, a move that looked harmless as the South Koreans had defensive numbers in the box. However, a headed clearance by one of their defenders went straight to Jimmy Rooney, lurking some 20 metres out from goal. Calm as you like, Rooney opened his body and caught the ball before it had time to bounce, side-footing it in one smooth movement to Jimmy Mackay, a couple of metres away.

Next second the ball was flying off Mackay's boot towards the top left corner of the goal and into the net. Mackay was swamped by his teammates. The World Cup dream was realised by the Aussies, there would be no further goals.

A fitting goal to win any game: the perfect lay-off by Rooney and a wonderful strike by Mackay which sent Australia to West Germany and their first ever World Cup Finals.

When Arie Van Gemert blew his whistle to end the game many of the Australian players knelt down and kissed the Hong Kong turf; four of the side then carried their coach Rale Rasic high on their shoulders off the field. After the game the two Scots-born boys were so overcome they could hardly speak. Jimmy Mackay was over the moon. "Great!" was all I could get out of him. Mind you he had every right to be speechless, it was a stunning goal! In the other changing room silence prevailed, the South Korean boys were feeling the pain.

Although obviously I didn't know it at the time, three of them – goalkeeper Byun Ho-young, defender Kang Kee-wook and centre-forward Kim Jae-han – would be my team-mates at Seiko a few years later. In time, South Korea would go on to become a force in the World Cup and are now regulars at the Finals; but for the players that night it was all gloom.

A lot of drinks were consumed in locations throughout Hong Kong that evening to celebrate the Aussies' historic victory – some even drank beer out of Jimmy Mackay's right football boot, which had suddenly became a treasured article. An historic night for Australia then and for the two Scottish-born players instrumental in creating and scoring the winning goal.

As neither of them was born in Glasgow, *I Belong To Glasgow* might not have been an appropriate song for them to celebrate with, but certainly Hong Kong belonged to them that night.

Sadly, Jimmy Mackay passed away in 1998 at the young age of 54; but the memory of that rocket into the top left corner lives on forever in Australian soccer history and his treasured right football boot is a national heirloom! Or is it still in a bar in Wan Chai?

15

Every shirt tells a story (with apologies to Rod Stewart)

I have a football jersey with green and white hoops; but it's not one you would show off on the wrong side of Glasgow.

"Hey Jimmy, ye shouldna' be waerin' those colours around here," would have been the inevitable greeting had I walked around with it on in the blue part of Govan.

It would have made no difference if I had replied, "It's nae Celtic, it's a Sporting Lisbon top!" Such is the Glasgow rivalry between the Old Firm of Celtic and Rangers.

So I only wore it in cosmopolitan Hong Kong. I got it by swapping shirts with a Sporting Lisbon player after a match during Chinese New Year. I was playing for the Hong Kong League XI at the time. When I was preparing to write this yarn I suddenly remembered that the jersey was still sitting in a suitcase in my condo, along with other prized football shirts I had gathered over the years. I seemed to recall it was their centre-forward who I had made the exchange with after the match, so I checked the old records for the Sporting line-up that day.

My eyes came to rest on the name Yazalde; yes, that's who it was, the number 9. Over the years I had forgotten just how good a player he was, so I did a little research to refresh my memory.

Héctor 'Chirola' Yazalde, born in Avellaneda and raised in the same Villa Fiorito neighbourhood as Diego Maradona, was the sixth of eight children. Like many kids in the poor parts of Argentina he began selling newspapers and bananas on street corners to help provide for his family. As a skinny 13-year-old he would run home at the end of his day with dozens of small coins, known as *chirolas*, and give them to his father, who consequently nicknamed him 'Chirola'. This lovely little story intrigued me, so I continued my research, before climbing the stairs to open my old suitcase to check if that jersey really did have the number 9 on it.

Chirola joined leading Argentine side Club Atlético Independiente in 1967 – not to be confused with their neighbouring club, Racing Club who had that infamous clash with Glasgow Celtic, dubbed 'The Battle of Montevideo', in 1968 when they met for the world club championship; remembered more for the unruly incidents off the ball than on it! He became the inaugural winner of the Argentinian Footballer of the Year award in 1970 while with Atlético Independiente (who won the 'Campeonato Metropolitano', Argentina's premier league that year), and joined Sporting Lisbon in 1971.

During the 1974 season, when I lined up to play against him, he would top the Portuguese scoring tables with 46 goals in just 29 matches; surpassing the previous record. His prolific scoring couldn't even be matched in later years by the legendary Eusébio. Those 46 goals would clinch him the European 'Golden Boot' award that season. As part of his award, he was given a Toyota car, but true to his humble upbringing, he sold the car and shared the money among his teammates.

"Without them I wouldn't have been able to score all those goals," he was quoted as saying afterwards.

The more I read about him the more impressed I was: one of the good guys I thought. Real Madrid tried to sign him, but Sporting Lisbon matched the salary that the Madrid club offered. Chirola was happy in Lisbon, so he stayed. Later he would head to the 1974 World Cup finals in West Germany to represent his country.

I headed upstairs to see if it really was his number 9 jersey that I had in my possession.

I prized open an old canvas suitcase which was full of jerseys I'd gathered in swaps over several decades with players from famous clubs and national teams. Eventually I found the one with the Lion rampant badge and distinctive white SCP lettering on a green background. Excitedly I turned the jersey over. There sewn on a rectangular piece of white cloth was a large black number 9.

Chirola, I've got your jersey! Now back to how I got it.

It was two weeks before my 25th birthday when I faced Sporting Lisbon on the third day of the Chinese New Year. Friday, January 25, 1974 to be exact. On that same day, just under 12,000 kilometres away in Cape Town, Dr Christiaan Barnard would perform the first ever 'heterotopic' twin heart operation.

Much would happen in that year for me: a kick-about with Rod Stewart and Ronnie Wood was just around the corner. I would also walk down the aisle for the first time.

On the other side of the world, Lord Lucan would disappear; and the Terracotta Warriors would be discovered in Xian, China. It was the 'Year of the Tiger' and *Tiger Feet* by Mud was number 1 in the UK charts when I walked onto the field to face the mighty Portuguese side.

My feet seemed to dance to the beat of the song that day and it was probably my best ever overall performance in a Hong Kong jersey, against a side that had just put Sunderland out of the Cup Winners' Cup in the round of 16 two months earlier. A Sunderland side, managed by Bob Stokoe, who had captured the FA Cup, against all odds, beating the great Leeds United 1-0 to earn their place in the 73/74 Cup Winners' Cup. That Sunderland side included some useful players in Dennis Tueart, Dave Watson, Ian Porterfield and Micky Horswill.

Micky Horswill would later have a spell in Hong Kong with Happy Valley in the early 80s – he also guested the odd game for my Sunday morning social team. The social side being the Carlsberg All Stars, an eclectic mix of current players, ex-players, jockeys, football managers and business people. Micky played in the side one Sunday morning when George Best also turned up for a match.

But back to the Sporting Lisbon game.

Let me give you an idea of their strength: they would win the Portuguese title that season and get to the semi-final stage of the Cup Winners' Cup, only losing 3-2 on aggregate to FC Magdeburg.

You might ask, quite rightly, "who are FC Magdeburg?"

They were not a well-known club and had only been in existence for nine years. However, they had a shrewd manager by the name of Heinz Krügel and he had assembled a quality side. They would go on to beat AC Milan 2-0 in the final to become the first, and only, East German side to win the Cup Winners' Cup; so they were a very good outfit.

There were 23,000 fans in the old Government Stadium and though the sun was shining, it was still a traditionally cold Chinese New Year's day.

We had a good League XI side that day: Malaysian international Chow Chee-keong was in goal, guarded by two good central defenders in Scotsmen Davie Anderson and Jim Begbie. A good sprinkling of local players included Wong Man-wai, Chan Kwok-hung and the Cheung brothers, Chi-wai and Chi-doy. My team-mate at Seiko, Manuel Cuenca, was on the right wing and I was on the left.

Sporting Lisbon's attack was led by two Brazilians and the Argentinian, Chirola Yazalde.

The game was barely three minutes old when our keeper made a long clearance, Cheung Chi-doy flicked it over the head of Sporting central defender Alhinho and it was then a race to get to the ball between me and the retreating Alhinho. The ball was still bouncing as I out-sprinted him with my 'Tiger Feet' and reached the ball first, but I was still over thirty-odd yards from goal. I decided to hit it first time with my instep. The ball soared goalwards, arcing into the postage stamp area of the top right corner of the goal.

I could see Damas, the Portugal keeper, leaping high towards the shot, but I was so far out that I wasn't sure if it had found the net. I asked myself: did it go in?

I looked to my right where I knew I would get an answer: the crowd were on their feet cheering in confirmation. What a shot, probably my most spectacular goal ever! Unfortunately it was too quick for the TV news cameras so it still remains a bit of a blur!

Nine minutes later, who else but Yazalde lobbed over our keeper and it was 1-1.

Five minutes after the break, a free kick by Chi-doy was punched away by Damas. Chi-wai, following up, fired into the net, and we were 2-1 up.

Then, in the 66th minute, I collected a ball just inside their half. Racing towards goal I beat their central defender Bastos, veered left, and beat Damas, who was at full stretch, with an angled drive into the corner of the net, we were 3-1 up. The crowd were on their feet again.

My only disappointment in the game came next. Disappointment? Well I was probably thinking a bit selfishly since it was actually another goal for us!

I had worked a move with Chi-doy inside their penalty box. Goalkeeper Damas came off his line to intercept the ball but I reached it first and tried to take it around him to steer it into the net. Damas brought me down, but the ball was still there to be won, I tried desperately, stretching to reach it, all the time Damas restraining me. The whistle went: penalty.

I picked up the ball, but, just as I was about to put it on the spot for my attempt at a hat-trick – which the Damas foul had denied me – it was taken from my grasp by Cheung Chi-wai.

"What are you doing?" I asked.

"I'm the captain. I'm taking it," he said rather arrogantly.

Despite my winning the penalty in the first place, the opportunity of scoring a hat-trick against Sporting Lisbon was thwarted by my own team mate. He did score, but I thought it should have been me!

Yazalde managed to pull a goal back for Sporting, but we ran out 4-2 winners and got a standing ovation from the 23,000 fans inside the stadium.

The *SCMP* report the next day praised Chow Chee-keong and me as the two big heroes of the day. Jock Sloan wrote: "Much of the credit for the victory should go to Currie whose tireless foraging and speed off the mark were constant worries to the Portuguese defence which never quite knew where to find him or how to stop him."

A nice compliment, but it was a team effort and Big Jim Begbie and Davie Anderson were superb at the heart of our defence.

Above: Boxing tip at an early age from big brother Dick – a straight left.

Below: With Motherwell Football Club in 1969.

Motherwell Football Club, 1969. From left to right, back row: J. Wark, J. Goldthorpe, D. Currie, K. MacRae, T. Forsyth, P. McCloy, W. McCallum, R. Campbell, J. Murray. Front row: D. Whiteford, J. Wilson, T. Donnelly, J. Deans, J. McInally, J. Muir.

THE HONG KONG FOOTBALL ASSOCIATION LIMITED

AFFILIATED TO THE FOOTBALL ASSOCIATION
AND FEDERATION INTERNATIONALE DE FOOTBALL ASSOCIATION

Patron:
HIS EXCELLENCY SIR DAVID TRENCH, G.C.M.G., M.C.

President:
MR. HENRY FOK
Vice-Presidents:
MR. D. AKERS-JONES, J.P.
DR. CHIU BUT YORK, PH.D., LL.D., L.H.D., P.E.D., R.B.
LT. COL. J.R. SMITH, R.A.E.C.
MR. CHEUNG KAM TIM, M.B.E.
Chairman:
MR. LIU LIT MO, M.B.E., J.P.
Secretary:
MR. CHAN SHIU KEUNG
Treasurers:
MESSRS. JOHN B. P. BYRNE & CO.

SPORTS ROAD
HAPPY VALLEY.

P. O. BOX 233

TEL. H-764694

CABLE ADDRESS:
"FOOTBALL"

All correspondence to be addressed to the Secretary

Hong Kong, 17th August, 1970.

AGREEMENT.

Whereby it is agreed by Mr. Derek Currie (the player) on the one hand and Mr. Ian Petrie for and on behalf of H.K. Rangers F.C. Ltd., (the club) on the other hand that:-

The player undertakes to play for the club as a professional football player for a contracted period of two (2) years commencing on 1st September, 1970 and terminating on 30th June, 1972, with the club having an option for a further two (2) years period, and further undertakes to maintain a proper standard of fitness and abide by the normal discipline of the club in order to ensure his best playing effort in training and competitive fixtures.

The club, in return for the above services of the player, undertakes to pay to the player a basic salary of £80 sterling per month during the period of the contract with further bonuses of £20 sterling during the playing months of the season as a first division player; £5 sterling for each win in competitive fixtures and £2"10/- for each draw in competitive fixtures.

The club further undertakes to pay the full air passage for the player to travel to Hongkong and the full air passage for the player to travel back to Britain after the completion of his contract. The club will not be responsible for the return air passage if the player is in breach of his contract before or at the termination of same.

A signing-on fee of £50 sterling will be paid to the player on the signing of this Agreement and by the signing of same the player undertakes to depart for Hongkong on the flight designated by the club by 31st August, 1970 or such date thereafter designated by the club. Suitable accommodation will be provided by the club for the player in the club quarters or such other place as decided suitable by the club but the player may request the club to grant a living out allowance and it shall be at the club's discretion whether or not to grant this and if it be granted the allowance shall, in any event, not exceed the sum of £12 sterling per month.

These terms and conditions will be honoured by both parties to this Agreement and will be incorporated in the Hongkong Football Association's Professional Players' Agreement to be signed by both parties in due course.

Signed *Derek Currie* of 7, Aberfoyle St. Glasgow E.1

Signed _____ of 24 Leighton Road, 1st Floor, Hongkong.
for & on behalf of HK Rangers FC Ltd.,

Witness *Veronica Chan* of Villa Calom, 23½ Miles, Castle Peak Rd., N.T. Hong

Occupation of Witness ___ LANDOWNER.

A museum piece: my first contract with Hong Kong Rangers.

*Above: On the way to Hong Kong via London, September 1970, with Petrie's
brother to my left, Walter with the damaged nose, Ian Petrie and Jackie.*

*Below: Farewell to the family at Glasgow Central station – off to Hong Kong.
I am next to my Mum, Maureen the wife of my brother John is alongside her,
my Dad, brother Dick, Petrie and Willie Jorge.*

Above and below: Looking for some goals against Santos, 1970, at the old Hong Kong stadium. I kept the keeper busy with darting runs, but he was up to the task. We were tied at 2-2 but Santos eventually won 5-2 with Pelé scoring a penalty in the dying seconds. The scoreline did not reflect a true picture of the defeat. I would play against Pelé and Santos three more times and once more in the NASL in San Antonio against Pelé's New York Cosmos, beating them 1-0. It's not often Pelé is on the losing side.

With Pelé, 1970. A treasured moment, every schoolboy's dream. Boy, was I lucky!

Above: The first official picture after my arrival in Hong Kong, of Rangers at a friendly game in Sek Kong. Petrie is in the striped shirt and Veronica Chui is far right.

Below: Shaking hands with Geoff Hurst prior to the Viceroy Cup final.

Above: My very first game for the Hong Kong League XI prior to beating the Stockholm side Djurgardens, 1970.
Below: Outnumbered 7-1 by the Djurgardens defenders.

THE WINNING GOAL . . . DEREK CURRIE SLAMS THE BALL PAST CHOW CHEE-KEONG IN THE 55TH MINUTE OF YESTERDAY'S SENIOR SHIELD SEMI-FINAL AGAINST SOUTH CHINA.

Above: Scoring against South China and Chow Chee-keong.

Below: After training at Happy Valley in 1971 – Walter Gerrard, Archie McCuaig, me, Jackie Trainer, Eddie Simpson.

*Above: Our first title with Hong Kong Rangers, the Senior Shield,
and celebrating in the changing room afterwards.*

Below: Sharing a flat with Walter.

居里與杜格利殊曾是隊友，你

his year marks the tenth anniy of the retirement of Derek
from the soccer arena yet still
remembered by this fans
⊃."

rn February 8,1949 in Glasgow,
came from a sporting family.
ther played soccer and my
brother Dick was a Boxing
nwealth Gold Medalist and
Gloves Champion. My middle
John played for Glasgow
" It made sense that Derek
soccer as his ambition in his
dhood and eventually played
e Danny McGrain with
Park and teamed up with
iglish as one of the two

contract with the Hong Kong Rangers.
On September 10,1970, Derek flew in
together with Walter Gerrard and
Jackie Trainer. He was amazed to be
engulfed by a battalion of TV crews
and sports reporters at Kai Tak. During
the press reception, Ian was confident
with his three imports by adding that
he did not go all the way to Scotland
for nothing.

In his much elaborated soccer
career, Derek being a non-resident
was selected to play for the Hong
Kong National side in five international
games. In 1973, he also clinched the
"Top Scorer" title once with a tally of
36 goals in one single season. "I have
been very lucky. The team won

could not resist though
nothing about Hong Kong
and also in other parts of
few players would have t
meet such great player:
reason that lured me to

In 12 years, he had c
than 30 medals and sc
250 goals. It is a rec
player can be proud of.
from soccer, Derek ha
TV commercials and a
Cantonese movies. In
116 crossings on the St
between Hong Kong
during a 20-hour per
$100,000 for the Roun

Above: Cumbernauld United. Kenny Dalglish with the ball, me next to him on his direct left, with a message from Kenny some years afterwards.

Left: Showing Maurice Gibb of the Bee Gees an article about the group in the Hong Kong Music Maker. I sometimes wrote record reviews for the magazine.

Above: Cheung Chi-doy and I getting ready for a match for the Hong Kong League XI. Below: Alongside Rodney Marsh, Don Rogers, Ernie Hannigan and Davie Anderson prior to facing Benfica.

耶穌，安德遜，羅渣士，馬殊合照留念。

Above: Filming 'Afore Ye Go', a Bell's whisky commercial.

Below: Seiko at the old stadium with Henry Fok (dark suit and tie). Next to him is CS Wong. The tall player at the back is Ian McWilliams.

Above: The San Antonio Thunder side in 1976.
Bobby Moore is fourth to my left.

Below: Gus Eadie and I with Tostão.

Above: At Tai Tam Correctional Services for Youths to show off our five-a-side skills – Walter Gerrard, Tommy Hutchison, Alan Dugdale, Sunny Chan (Carlsberg sales manager), me, Hugh McCrory. Below: Somehow getting up from the turf and scoring against Hamburg to win 1-0.

Above: With some young Hong Kong fans in Causeway Bay, 1971.
Below: A game for fun at the Manila Nomads during an off-season break in
the Philippines in the mid-70s. Bernie Poole leans on Parky in the front row,
flanked by Davie Breen in white and Manuel Cuenca on Parky's other side.
I am to Bernie's right with Doug Docherty who arranged the kick-around
next to bare-chested John Charlesworth. Bottom right is Bert Ruers. We won
5-3 with two less players, but San Miguel was the winner that day!

Above: The Eastern boys in my final days. Ronnie Doctrove, Steve Waller, Ricky Heppolette, Norman Sutton, Duncan Waldman and the chairman's son.

Below: 'Auld Lang Syne' – a Hong Kong police piper welcomes former Scotland manager Craig Brown to Hong Kong to make the draw for the Chinese New Year football tournament.

Opposite: SCMP story about Walter and I after 21 years in Hong Kong.

Jardines salute former big guns

By ROBIN PARKE

TWO of Hongkong's sporting heroes of yesteryear celebrated their 21st anniversary with a party yesterday — and it went with a bang.

If the soccer history of Hongkong is ever written, then the names of Derek Currie and Walter Gerrard will start the most glorious chapter in the long, enduring love affair between the local public and the sport.

The newspaper clippings, magazine articles and photographs are yellowing these days and curling up at the corners — but the memories remain green for the two Glaswegians who did more than most to delight the soccer fans who turned up in their thousands to watch a gamble that really paid off.

When manager Ian Petrie recruited three compatriots — the third was Jackie Trainer — back in 1970 for his young Rangers team few believed they would make that big an impact.

But Currie, with experience at Motherwell, was the archetypal flying winger with a deadly eye for goal while Gerrard was superlative in the air and simply impossible for Chinese centre backs to contain.

It was 21 years ago yesterday that the two Scots arrived in Hongkong and, fittingly enough, the strongly Scottish-oriented Jardines concern marked the anniversary by inviting the once deadly duo to fire the Noonday Gun.

"Ironically, when we came here with Rangers the Jardines team were the biggest in town. They'd do everything but within two seasons they were out of the sport," reminisced Currie yesterday.

'Big Walter' as he is known to scores of Hongkong people was in reflective mood before the party got under way.

"The game was very good to me but I don't follow it that closely here any more. But it's funny to think that some of the people I played with, and I'm thinking now of the local Chinese players,

The way they were . . . (from left) Walter Gerrard, Derek Currie and Jackie Trainer as they arrived at Kai Tak Airport 21 years ago to embark on illustrious careers.

C. Y. Yu

The way they are now . . . a little less hair and a little more body, Gerrard and Currie in Causeway Bay yesterday where they fired the Noonday Gun.

are scattered all over the world while I'm still here.

"There's at least a dozen I remember well who are in Canada, America, Australia and even a couple in South America.

"There were a lot of rough patches in the early days but there was tremendous enthusiasm and, of course, being Hongkong if you were prepared to go out and do something, you could get by," said Gerrard whose aerial prowess got him to within one goal of establishing a Hongkong goalscoring record.

Both had their golden days with Seiko while Currie represented Hongkong at national team level as well as playing against some of the best teams in the world for

the highly respected HK League XI side.

He scored the goal that beat the mighty SV Hamburg, two in the 4-2 defeat of Sporting Lisbon, took on Pele and Eusebio when both were at their best and won, probably four times over, every available medal in domestic soccer here.

"The local game I'll never forget was against South China. We were 4-0 down and came back to win 5-4, I got the winner in the last couple of minutes," he said.

Now a public relations executive with a major company, he keeps a weather eye open on the local game.

"There's a new season just started and it should be better than some that have

gone by. It's a positive move bringing back more foreign professionals. The game is all about entertainment and the public don't care what nationality, colour or creed you are — they just want to see good football," he said.

But after the ceremonial firing of the Noonday Gun it was more a case of looking back than forward yesterday.

As the talk and drink flowed, goals and games were gloriously relived, old friends remembered and the odd disaster recalled with laughter.

Was there ever talk of a comeback?

"I think so . . . but it was after one too many. And I don't mean goals," said Big Walter.

Above: Ob-La-Di, an afternoon with Marmalade. Dougie Henderson, Gus Eadie, Dean Ford and me. Below: With Alan Clark of the Hollies at a press conference. Blinded by the flash!

Above: Our first game in Vietnam, 1971. Who would have believed there was a war going on? The love of football can make the darkest of times seem bright.

Below: Winning the 'Governor's Cup' at Boundary Street with my arm around Stan Forster.

With the great Santamaria of Real Madrid at the Lee Gardens Hotel when he visited as manager of Barcelona side Espanyol.

Above: A game at Happy Valley in 1974. Ronnie Wood is kneeling before me with Rod Stewart next to him. 'Fast Wullie' is standing above Rod, and Dave Gilhooly, former manager of the Scene Disco in the basement of the Peninsula Hotel, is sporting a tie.

Below: With Muhammad Ali at a function in Tsim Sha Tsui in 1979.

Above: At the Mocambo Nightclub in Central circa 1971 with horse trainer Vic Mitchell, jockey Alan Middleton and his wife Billy Tam. Below: The Presstuds darts team – Bill McMurdo holding the ball with George Best and me on either side. Colm McFeely is next to me. Parky is at the far left next to footballer Brian Sinclair with two other good lads in the team.

Above: Time to call it a day. Official retirement at half-time against VfB Stuttgart and a lovely presentation by officials of Eastern Football Club. Peter Wong is on the mic.

Left: With Sam Torrance after arriving from Mission Hills golf course in China at the press conference for the Hong Kong Golf Open.

'Marvellous' Marvin doing the rounds

Boxing great "Marvellous" Marvin Hagler slipped quietly into town yesterday for a five-day sightseeing visit. The former world middleweight champion, who outboxed Roberto Duran and Thomas Hearns, flew from Manila where he was making the war movie, *Indio*, which also stars Anthony Quinn's son, Francisco. He is seen here at Kai Tak with his friend, Carlsberg's public relations boss, Derek Currie. Hagler's arrival comes on the heels of a visit by Sugar Ray Leonard, who dethroned Hagler in a controversial decision in the "Fight of the Century" in Las Vegas last year. He leaves for Rome on Friday.

Above: 'I just called to say I love you,' with Marvelous and Stevie Wonder before we sang at the Hong Kong Hotel. Below: Presenting the Carlsberg Cup to Brondby skipper Lars Olsen with chairman of the HKFA Victor Hui and two charming PR girls. A few years later, Lars would be lifting the Euro Championship trophy for Denmark.

Above: With Kevin Livesey, Hong Kong's tennis coach, and two leading players – Patricia Hy and Paulette Moreno of 'Team Carlsberg.'
Below: With Bobby Moore in Mexico City at the World Cup in 1986.

Above: My social football team the day George Best ran the line for me. Tim Bredbury with light hair at the back, Micky Horswill next to me at front left and Billy Semple next to Bill McMurdo with the case of Carlsberg. Others include Jimmy Banks, Wally Hood, Norman Voce, Walter Gerrard, Dave Allen and Clive Saffrey. Below: Making the draw at Old Trafford with 'Great Dane' Peter Schmeichel.

Above: Catching up with Alex Ferguson at the Hyatt Hotel on a Manchester United trip to Hong Kong. Below: In Joe Bananas, the well-known bar in Wan Chai, before a performance by the Searchers. Dave Gilhooly, me, Billy Adamson (Searchers drummer), Mark Giles (SCMP journalist), Davie Anderson and musician Anders Nelson.

Above: A light moment during the 1994 World Cup finals with legendary football journalist Malcolm Brodie. Parky and I are alongside him with 'Benno' who worked for a UK newspaper.
Below: Cesar Menotti, who managed Argentina to their World Cup win on home soil in 1978 was just a journalist at the World Cup in Mexico in 1986. He was still an imposing figure.

Above: In the paddock with the co-owner of Casey's Drum at Sha Tin Racecourse. Below: With Arne 'Papa' Bue of the Viking Jazz Band.

Right: In the press box at the Azteca Stadium for the 1986 World Cup in Mexico.

Below: Casey's Drum in the winners' circle, trained by David Hill and ridden by Paddy Payne.

Above: Getting ready in Hong Kong for another Champions' League show alongside Tim Bredbury for ATV. Below: With coach Bora Milutinovic at the Hong Kong Sports Institute when he brought Nigeria to the Carlsberg Cup. He was the first coach to take five different countries to the World Cup finals. My daughter Claudia is in the picture with our little Maltese terrier, Snowy, as is the leader of the Nigerian delegation.

I should have walked off the park with the ball as a souvenir for a hat-trick, but hey! Two goals against a great side was good enough. As it was, I walked off with Yazalde who also scored two goals.

Sadly he died far too young at just 51 years of age, due to heart failure in Buenos Aires, two weeks before Hong Kong was returned to China on July 1, 1997.

Yazalde's gift to me was his green-and-white jersey.

Which reminds me of someone else who liked sporting a green-and-white top.

The Lee Gardens Hotel, and in particular its Yum Sing Bar, was a popular spot for locals and tourists alike when it first opened its doors in 1971. Situated on Hysan Avenue in Causeway Bay it was owned by the well-heeled Lee family, who also owned the Lee Gardens Theatre, just a hundred metres or so down a slight hill from the hotel.

While the Lee Theatre showed the latest movies and held the odd concert with the likes of Don McLean, warbling his way through *American Pie* and *Vincent*, the hotel hosted some famous guests over the years, including Ronald Reagan, Diana Ross and Tom Jones. The popular theatre also held the Miss Hong Kong pageant and singing stars Teresa Tang and Roman Tam regularly performed there to packed audiences.

The Lee Gardens was the first 5-star hotel to open in Causeway Bay: bearded, white-turbaned Indian doormen in long red cloaks and cream shirts would greet guests at the entrance. Once inside, an escalator would take you up to the first floor where the coffee shop was located; just before that, on the left, was the Yum Sing Bar. The waitresses were decked out in short, lime-green tops, with black hot pants and matching nylons.

The bar opened late afternoon and didn't close until the early hours of the morning. Evening entertainment was supplied by Ollie Delfino and his Filipino band, or the singer Doris Lang, sister of well-known local star Sandra Lang.

I was in there one evening, early 1974, around 5pm, with fellow footballers Gus Eadie and Brian Harvey, brother of former Everton star, Colin. We were just having a chat, relaxing in the comfortable brown leather armchairs and oblivious to what was going on around us, when suddenly two gentlemen loomed over us with hair longer than any of ours.

"We overheard you talking about football and wondered if we could join the conversation?" the light-haired one said. Looking up, we all simultaneously recognized Rod Stewart hovering over us. Before we could turn our attention to the chap with the long dark hair he introduced himself: "Ronnie Wood, lads."

One minute we were having a chat among ourselves; the next Rod Stewart and Ronnie Wood had joined us. That was Hong Kong in the early 1970s. Music hardly came up in the conversation. For the next hour or so the discussion was all about football.

Just before this impromptu gathering broke up Rod asked if we could perhaps have a kickabout together the next day.

"Why not," I replied.

"Make it after 2pm as I have a press conference, but I should be finished around then," he added.

"OK. Meet you outside the hotel at 2.30pm and we can go down to Happy Valley. I'll bring a ball and a couple more of the lads," I said.

Rod Stewart at that time was part of a band called The Faces formed in late 1969. After Rod and Woody had left the Jeff Beck Group they formed this new band with three former members of the original Small Faces. The group regularly toured Britain, Europe and the USA, but although well known in the West, they were fairly anonymous in Asia in the early 70s.

Gus, Brian and I obviously knew who Rod and Woody were as the three of us were into the music of the 60s and early 70s. During the Mods and Rockers era at that time Rod had been known as 'Rod the Mod' due to the dandyish style of clothes he wore. He had played in the same band as Long John Baldry and recorded a best-selling solo album: *Every Picture Tells a Story* in 1971.

Included on that album was his cover of *Reason to Believe*, which became a number 1 hit single in the UK; the B-side was *Maggie May*.

Rod was very much on the way up on the international music scene, but in Hong Kong, Sam Hui and Alan Tam with their Cantopop ruled the airwaves. For now, he was just another face in the crowd.

The next afternoon, Rod and Woody stepped out of their hotel into Hong Kong's chilly February sunshine. Rod was kitted out in a green-and-white Glasgow Celtic top – not a Sporting Lisbon top I might add, but given to him by the late great Celtic winger, Jimmy Johnstone – and, incongruously, dark blue shorts with white trim.

"First time I've seen blue shorts worn with a Celtic top," I said. A cheeky grin appeared on his face. Woody was decked out in a sky blue jersey with white trim similar to Manchester City, but certainly nothing like the West Bromwich Albion colours, the club he claimed to have supported since his youth.

I introduced Rod and Woody to the other lads who joined us for the game: Clive Breen and Willie Rutherford, both 'jocks', and Eric Porgy Abreu and Steve Coetzee, both South Africans. Gus Eadie, who had met the pair the day before was also there. As we set off for Happy Valley I asked Rod how the press conference went.

"Yeah, fine, but might not have pleased everyone," he said without explaining.

When all eight of us arrived at Happy Valley we received a few stares from some young Hong Kong kids who clearly recognized many of us. There was one particular group of boys, who looked around 14 years of age or so, having a game amongst themselves. There must have been about a dozen of them and they stopped playing when I called over to them.

I asked if we could have a game against them, just for fun.

They smiled, they thought I was joking. Then they started asking questions, wanting to know who were the two people they didn't recognize (Rod and Woody). I told them they were new to Hong Kong and we were trying them out to see if they had any potential. That line would never have worked in London, Manchester or Liverpool, but hey, the kids in Happy Valley were hardly likely to recognize Rod or Woody at that time.

Now Rod had a good footballing pedigree as his father had been a very good amateur player and Rod himself had a trial with Brentford when a mere 15-year-old. Although his ambition was originally to become a professional footballer it had been supplanted by his passion for singing; but he still loved the game with a youthful intensity.

Rod was quite dainty on the ball, but provided some neat passes. Woody too had some equally nice touches, he was a bit 'leggy' and someone said, in the nicest possible way of course, that he looked like 'Bambi on ice'!

Both showed great enthusiasm during that little game inside the confines of the Happy Valley racetrack. It might have been many, many years ago, but I have no doubt that they would play with the same passion today, bodies permitting. Their love of the game – particularly Rod's – was clear to see.

As we were walking back to the Lee Gardens Hotel Rod invited me up to his room: "there's something I want you to listen to," he said. A few of the lads came along and as we rode the lift up to his room I was intrigued as to what we were going to listen to: perhaps it was a new song with Hong Kong lyrics and he wanted some feedback.

Rod produced a black portable Sony cassette player – funnily enough, identical to the one I had at home. He pressed the play button and the cassette burst into life, but it wasn't a new song...

"... Morgan flights the ball with the inside of his boot into the box.. Joe Jordan is racing to meet it... It's in the net, Scotland are winning 2-1." It was the voice of STV's distinguished commentator, Arthur Montford, who followed up by screaming "Magnificent Scotland!"

I immediately recognized the game in question, played at Hampden Park in Glasgow roughly four months earlier. It was the commentary on the winning goal in the 2-1 victory against Czechoslovakia in the World Cup qualifier that took Scotland to their first World Cup finals in sixteen years.

"I recorded the whole game in a hotel in America through a telephone link to my dad who put the telephone next to the TV," said Rod proudly. This was said in his London accent, but his old dad was Scottish and Rod supported Scotland and he wore it well.

Rod was in town as part of a Faces tour. They had played in Australia and were due to fly to Japan for two further concerts. Their gig in Hong Kong was at the Hong Kong Football Club in Sports Road. There were about five hundred or so in attendance; most of them expatriates. He came back to do another concert at the Hong Kong Football Club four years later; the crowd was six times larger, by then he had become a household name in Asia.

Two days before Rod was leaving for the Japan leg of the tour he asked me where he could buy silk dressing gowns with the dragon-style logo embossed on the back.

"I know just the place, it's only a five minute walk from the Lee Gardens Hotel," I told him.

The China Products store was situated at the corner of Percival Street and Hennessy Road, so we walked down Lee Gardens Road, which runs parallel to Percival Street, past the fruit shops and tailors. I didn't ask why he wanted the dressing gowns, I assumed they were for himself. We entered the grand old store, closed many years since, but at the time it sold a remarkable array of arts and crafts, all manufactured in mainland China: Chinese calligraphy, brush stroke paintings on rice paper, porcelain pottery, painted bamboo room dividers, the store had it all, including silk dressing gowns! We walked up the steps to the second floor and were soon engulfed in a sea of silk products.

"Perfect," he exclaimed as he looked at the large collection of silk dressing gowns in a multitude of colours; many with traditional Chinese dragons delicately embossed in striking poses across the back. Then he hit me with a question right out of the blue.

He held up a red, a green and a pink dressing gown and asked, "Which colour do you think Britt would like?"

I knew immediately who he was talking about: Britt Ekland, the Swedish actress formerly married to Peter Sellers, and very much the pin-up girl of the seventies.

Trying not to appear stumped by his rather personal question I replied calmly, "I really don't know her that well Rod!" Thinking on my feet, I followed up with, "Why don't you buy her one of each?"

"Great idea," he said.

After selecting gowns in six different shades, and just as he was about to pay, he suddenly realized that he had not come out with enough Hong Kong dollars to cover the extra purchases.

"No problem Rod, your credit's good with me," I laughed, and loaned him an extra hundred dollars. We then headed back to his hotel.

Rod was leaving early afternoon the following day so I popped over with Gus Eadie to wish him and Woody farewell. I took along one of my old Seiko football shirts with my number 11 on the back and presented it to Rod. I wonder if he's still got it?

In return, he produced a yellow top, with flared long sleeves, and a large heraldic red lion rampant on the front. On the reverse side, in black printed lettering, it read: 'Munich 74'.

"I got these specially made for the World Cup in Germany," he told me. He then autographed it: "To Derek, Scotland for Ever, Rod Stewart." For good measure, Ronnie Wood also signed it: "See ya there, Woody", before handing it to me. The yellow top now sits alongside Chirola's.

A lovely gesture, but I was thinking: what about the hundred bucks Rod owed me.

Resigned to not getting it I was thinking to myself, who gives a toss, could be a good yarn over a beer: Rod Stewart owes me a hundred bucks, I quietly chuckled. But, just as we were about to shake hands and wish each other all the best, Rod suddenly said, "I almost forgot, I owe you a hundred bucks." And handed me the money.

There's a postscript to the story about Rod Stewart and the press conference he held at the Lee Gardens Hotel prior to joining us for the kickabout at Happy Valley.

When I had asked him about how the press conference had gone, Rod had replied that he didn't think everybody was happy with it! It was not until years later that I found out just what he meant. Apparently the press conference that afternoon was attended by local Chinese journalists, together with legendary music reporter and D.J. Ray Cordeiro. Ray hosted a nightly show on RTHK, *All the Way with Ray*; and still did until he finally retired at the age of 96 in May 2021. Pictures of Rod were taken and the local journalists asked him some brief questions. Rod then turned to Ray Cordeiro and said: "I'll give you two minutes."

An infuriated Ray Cordeiro, who had interviewed a galaxy of stars over the years including The Beatles, Frank Sinatra, Cliff Richard and Duke Ellington, replied angrily: "I don't need your two minutes, and I don't need you!" He then stood up and walked away, leaving the singer stunned.

Uncle Ray as he was known – a nickname bestowed on him by Anders Nelson, a singer who emerged on the local music scene in the 1960s and went on become a local icon – was so enraged by this episode that he refrained from playing any Rod Stewart songs on his popular radio show for the next six months. Finally he gave in to public demand to play Rod's songs on the airwaves again; his programme was, after all, partly a request show. By then he had also run out of excuses not to play them; but frankly by that time it was all just water under the bridge.

I got to know Ray quite well over the years. At one time we both had racehorses and once they even raced against each other at Sha Tin. Ray owned 'We Know When', trained by John Moore and I had 'Casey's Drum', trained by David Hill.

One day I happened to be in Uncle Ray's company when Rod Stewart's name came up. Ray told me about the press conference and how he had stopped playing Rod's songs for six months. "He was very rude offering me two minutes of his time!" Ray said, obviously still annoyed years later.

"I know why he was in a rush that day," I told him. "It was my fault. He was coming to meet me and some of the boys as he was desperate for a kickabout in Happy Valley and we were meeting at 2:30pm. I guess he didn't want to be late."

"I had no idea you were interviewing him at that time or we could have made it later," I said in my defence.

"My God, what a screw-up," he replied.

Uncle Ray told that story on the airwaves a few times over the years; with the riposte that he never knew the famous rocker was rushing to Happy Valley just to play football with Derek Currie.

I don't think Uncle Ray ever really forgave Rod. On his website he noted the marvellous singers and musicians he had interviewed over the years; household names from different music eras. But one name is missing from that illustrious list: Sir Roderick David Stewart, CBE!

16

Beating the Drum... and a legend with a heart of gold

After the kickabout with Rod and Woody, a more serious game was in prospect when the Uruguayan national team came to town in April. They were preparing for the 1974 World Cup finals in West Germany with an Asian tour that would also take them to Australia.

A smart outfit, they were spearheaded by centre-forward Fernando Morena, a player whose club side Peñarol had paid US$5 million to sign him and he had already scored in the opening Hong Kong game when the South Americans had beaten a HK Select team three days prior to meeting the League XI. Morena would go on to become the Uruguayan premier league all-time record goalscorer with 230 in 244 games.

It's always nice to gauge just how good a name player is by actually competing against them; we soon found out! Despite our best efforts we lost 4-1. Fernando Morena never got on the scoresheet, but another striker, Romeo Corbo, scored a hat-trick. Jim Begbie got our lone goal. Despite losing, it was still an entertaining game for the 16,000 fans who turned up.

One new boy selected to play his first representative game for the League XI that night was Alex Willoughby, although he was hardly a new boy to top class football: a seasoned professional he had already starred in Scotland for both Glasgow Rangers and Aberdeen.

Alex left Rangers in 1969 to join Aberdeen and had recently arrived to play for Hong Kong Rangers. I had been looking forward to linking up with him that night as I had known him since I was eleven years old. He came on as a substitute in the second half to replace Wu Kwok-hung and it was great to be on the same field as someone I had looked up to as a kid.

Alex was one of many famous names to come up through the ranks of the renowned Glasgow amateur nursery club, Drumchapel Amateurs. Others included Sir Alex Ferguson, David Moyes, Andy Gray, Archie Gemmill, Tony Green, Pat Crerand, Jim Forrest, and even Kenny Dalglish.

The club was run by a chap called Douglas Smith, a graduate of Cambridge University, who had the vision in 1950 to implement youth sides for different age groups under the banner of Drumchapel Amateurs; affectionately known as 'The Drum', a name soon identified with the best-known amateur sides in the country. Drumchapel Amateurs would represent Scotland at footballing events all over Europe, playing against youth sides from the likes of AC Milan and Barcelona. Considered to be the leading youth sides in Scotland, if you played for them you took a big step up the ladder in your footballing career.

Alex Willoughby and Jim Forrest had arranged a trial for me to play for The Drum's under-15 side. I thought I had a really good game that day, but the invitation to join never came. The word back to Willoughby was that I was a good player but just too small and lightly built. Where have I heard that before?

Anyway, rewind back to the Scottish Amateur Under-16 Cup Final between Drumchapel Amateurs and Glasgow United in the 1964/65 season. I played in that final and scored a couple of goals for Glasgow United. In a pulsating game we beat The Drum 5-4; I still have the medal to prove it.

After the match Douglas Smith came over to me and said, "Two good players have slipped through my fingers, you and Danny McGrain, you should have been playing for me today. I never realised that you were just 13 years old when you trialled for my under-15 side."

Danny by then was with Queen's Park. I can only assume Smith had the chance to sign him, but he never mentioned why he didn't. I did eventually play alongside Danny when I too was at Queen's Park in their Victoria XI.

Douglas Smith died in 2004 at the age of 67. Ten years after his death a portrait of him was unveiled in the Scottish Football Museum by none other than Sir Alex Ferguson. A poignant quote came from Fergie that day: "We were amateurs, but Douglas Smith always treated us like professionals."

Talking of professionals, more and more were now coming over and Hong Kong Rangers began to look like Glasgow Rangers for the 1974/75 season with four former 'Gers players in their line-up. A bold move by Ian Petrie that would pay dividends in silverware.

Willoughby I have already mentioned. They also added his cousin Jim Forrest, who scored 83 goals in 105 appearances for the Glasgow club before joining Preston North End for a season and then spending 5 years with Aberdeen.

The third member was Billy Semple, a fringe player at Ibrox for four seasons, but still a quality player, who had had two seasons at Dundee. But the star of the foursome was 'Wee Willie' Henderson. An old-fashioned right-winger who played for Glasgow Rangers on 276 occasions, netted 62 goals, and was capped 29 times for Scotland. He would have won considerably more caps had it not been for another great right-winger during that period: 'Jinky' Jimmy Johnstone, who played with city rivals, Glasgow Celtic. They were arguably the two best wingers anywhere in the world in their prime.

Willie had great speed and was very direct down the flanks; Jinky also had pace, and his intricate dribbling skills were amazing. It was Willie who came to Hong Kong.

He had followed my older brother's career as a boxer, and was at Ibrox when my other brother John had a spell there, so he was well acquainted with the Currie clan.

Wee Willie might have been small, just 5'4", but he had the heart of a lion. It would be remiss of me not to mention that he was selected in the World XI to face Sir Stanley Matthews' XI in that great player's testimonial at Stoke's Victoria Ground in 1965.

The forward line that day was Kopa, Di Stéfano, Kubala, Puskás, and Henderson.

They were without doubt the greatest of their time.

They beat the Matthews' XI, that included Sir Stan, Greaves, Haynes and Alan Gilzean, by six goals to four. Although nobody really cared about the result, it was the occasion that counted.

While 35,000 football fans sang *Auld Lang Syne*, Matthews was carried off the field on the shoulders of Lev Yashin and Ferenc Puskás.

I remember attending Wee Willie's first game for his new club in Hong Kong almost ten years later. It was at Boundary Street and I believe Eastern were the opposition. In those days a small basketball court was part of the Police Sports Complex at Boundary Street and it was used as a warm-up area prior to going onto the field. It was the same ground where I had played my first ever game, against Happy Valley back in 1970.

I went along that day to wish Wee Willie well. Also there to welcome Willie was a well-known former Scottish newspaper man, Andrew Rennie, who had worked with the *Scottish Daily Express*. Drew, as he was normally addressed, was in Hong Kong working as Chief Staff Officer for the Hong Kong Police Force and very much the PR mouthpiece of the force, working closely with the Commissioner of Police. Son of a Dundee policeman, Drew was a blunt, but humorous character, who was a good operator at whatever he turned his hand to and damn good company over an ale.

Willie came over to us during his warm up: "what are you two doing here?" he asked.

"To see some of your magic." I quipped. Drew followed up with "To see if you've still got it!"

I think the game ended in a draw. Willie got kicked from pillar to post. Not being familiar with Hong Kong he thought playing at Boundary Street was an away game and that the Hong Kong Stadium was his home ground.

Willie therefore said to one of the opposition defenders, who had tried to rough him up during the game:

"See you son, wait till we get you at our home ground!"

Willie would soon find out, there was no such thing as a home ground in Hong Kong, but nevertheless he showed he had plenty to offer – he clearly still had it!

That season Petrie's Hong Kong Rangers had a good run. Their defence was particularly strong. They had former Greenock Morton goalkeeper Jimmy Liddell, who had signed the season before, and never-say-die defenders Hugh McCrory and Dennis Stanton in front of him. Lee Kwok-wah added the polish in midfield.

We would have great tussles with them that season and they would put us out of both the Senior Shield and the Viceroy Cup in the semi-finals, while going on to win both trophies.

Kwok Ka-ming and Cheung Kai-ming would later claim it was the best Rangers team that they ever played in. Hard to deny on paper, particularly with four ex-Glasgow Rangers players in the ranks.

They did win two cup competitions, but as Ka-ming and Kai-ming would have to concede, the two of them only ever won the 'holy grail' of a league title once, and that was in 1971 when Walter, Jackie and I were in the team. Years later, when people I knew from Hong Kong were back in Scotland and asked Willie if he knew me, he would answer:

"Aye, of course, Puff, a dear old friend, I've known him for many years. I had to go out to Hong Kong in 1974 to stop him winning all those trophies."

Brilliant! Typical 'Wee Willie' rapport. His one liners were almost as good as those of former Manchester United manager, Tommy Docherty.

In a way he was right of course, but he omitted to mention that Seiko won the League title that year! Nor did he mention that, despite Seiko losing 1-0 to Rangers in the first leg of the semi-final of the inaugural FA Cup – which had replaced the Golden Jubilee Trophy – we had beaten them 5-1 in the second leg, and went on to win the final against Yuen Long. (Just reminding you wee man if case you're reading this).

I should clarify, 'Wee Willie' called me 'Puff,' another nickname that would stick with me, courtesy of my non-Asian pals over the years. Puff the Magic Dragon? I think it was more 'Curry Puff,' as in 'comestible'; but definitely 'Puff,' with no double 'o' in the middle I might add.

Alec Willoughby and Jim Forrest would leave for other pastures after the season ended, while Willie would stay for another year with Rangers before joining Caroline Hill for his last season in Hong Kong. Billy Semple would go to the North American Soccer League (NASL) for a season, but, eventually, come back and join me at Seiko.

I had some laughs with Willie during his three years in Hong Kong. He always greeted you with, "Hey Sir." But aside from the joking, William 'Wee Willie' Henderson was a legend with a heart of gold, and despite their football rivalry was a great pal of Celtic's Jimmy Johnstone, who tragically died of motor neurone disease. Willie regularly visited Johnstone during his illness; he was also the last man to call and talk to him before the Celtic great succumbed to the disease in 2006.

Willie had his own personal tragedies, his daughter Michelle died of cervical cancer in 2012 when she was only 28 years of age. During the two years she battled the illness, she set up a trust with the help of her dad to give back to those who had helped her during her treatment. She wanted to raise awareness of the condition and in turn raise funds towards hospital equipment for women suffering from the terrible illness.

The Michelle Henderson Cervical Cancer Trust has, at time of writing, generated in the region of £350,000 and provided life saving devices in hospitals in Glasgow, Edinburgh and Aberdeen.

In 2019, on his 75th birthday, Willie Henderson trekked 100 miles in five days across the Sahara Desert in scorching heat and raised a further £40,000 towards that worthy cause.

The Hendersons can be proud of their legacy, both on and off the field.

17

Interlude: The Yellow Rose of Texas

Like most boys in the late 50s and early 60s I loved a good western. One of my all time favourites was The Alamo – the movie about a tiny group of Texans holding out in a San Antonio fort against an army of 2,000 Mexicans. And it's San Antonio where this chapter of my story takes place.

I had only signed a six month contract with Seiko for the 1975/76 season as a fragile marriage meant my private life was a little unsteady.

At that time Jim Forrest had signed for the San Antonio Thunder, as had former Hong Kong Rangers player Billy Semple, and 1976 was the bicentennial season in the North American Soccer League (the NASL). Forrest phoned me several times, urging me to come over as he thought my goal scoring ability would be a big asset to the Thunder. The money was quite good and perhaps a change would do me good.

I therefore decided to take up the offer, but made a deal with Seiko that if things didn't go to plan I could return and sign for them again – one of the best deals I ever made!

When I left Hong Kong in early March I was the league's top scorer with 17 goals and was hoping my scoring run would continue in America.

I flew to San Francisco, then made the four hour hop to San Antonio, Texas. Halfway into the journey the pilot announced we were flying over Tombstone where the 'Gunfight at the OK Corral' took place. That got my attention: visions of Wyatt Earp and Doc Holliday. The closer we got to San Antonio, the more excited I became. I was going to places I had dreamed about as a kid after watching westerns on TV. I was actually heading for the Alamo! I didn't expect to see John Wayne, but I could soak up the history.

My first few days however were spent mainly on the treatment table, I had picked up a slight knee injury during my last game in Hong Kong. Nothing serious though, it cleared up after a few sessions with the physio.

I visited the Alamo shortly after and was totally caught up in its history. According to my guide book the old church had a backstory much greater than the immortal battle cry, attributed to General Sam Houston: "Remember the Alamo". Jim Bowie, Davy Crockett and William Travis might be the names remembered defending the old Mission, but there were close to another 180 or so who fought valiantly alongside them.

The only fight I had at that time was trying to eat my way through a Chef's Salad in a restaurant which would become a frequent haunt: Reed's Red Derby, just off Loop 33. It was a popular spot for San Antonio Thunder players and was also one of the club's sponsors.

When the waitress put the salad on the table I joked, "I just ordered for one."

"Oh, that's regular," she replied in a lovely Texas drawl.

Naturally I had to say: "I heard everything in Texas is big, but this is ridiculous!"

I couldn't finish it, and I won't even get on to discussing the size of the steaks they served!

When training got under way it was hard graft, but the gym work we did was sensational. Here was I, at 27 years of age, someone who had never done collective gym work with any previous club, but I knuckled down with all the others.

We had a fairly good squad of players at that time: Jim Forrest, Billy Semple, Jim Henry – who had played with Dundee United and Aberdeen, and someone who I had played against at youth level in Scotland – ex-Arsenal star Bob McNab, and, of course, ex-England captain Bobby Moore.

Later we were joined by former Scotland goalkeeper Bobby Clark, Celtic great Harry Hood, and Neil Martin, another former Scottish international – the same guy who played with Ernie Hannigan all those years ago.

We had a big pre-season exhibition game scheduled for March 31 against the mighty New York Cosmos. Pelé was coming to town! But before that we played against an Austin 'select' side and thrashed them 9-0; I managed to get on the score sheet with a goal and an assist.

Of course Bobby Moore was the big star in the team. I recall the night he arrived in San Antonio; there were hundreds of fans at the airport to meet him. He must have stayed there for a good hour after arriving, taking the time to sign autographs for everyone who wanted one, that was gentleman Bobby.

I would first get to meet him later that night and in one way he would help to reshape my life.

We faced the Cosmos at our new home ground, the Alamo Stadium. They had been paid a modest US$25,000 match fee, which seems insignificant even by 1976 standards, but the top-priced tickets were just $5, so that puts the match fee into perspective.

The San Antonio area had many football-loving Mexican descendants, so a good turnout was expected; in the end 15,000 paying fans showed up. It was an evening kick-off, but the sky was still full of light, and the pre-match entertainment, including a Mariachi band from a local restaurant, kept the crowd happy.

I was excited before the match, it wasn't every day you were led out onto the field by two great stars of the game: Bobby Moore and Pelé. Plus, I was playing for the San Antonio Thunder at the Alamo Stadium, even my childhood imagination could never have come up with that one!

I looked up at the sky and thought: Dad, I hope you are watching. My Dad, who had done so much for me, had died two years earlier.

As part of the opening ceremony we were all carrying a yellow rose and had to go into the stands and hand it to one of the many girls attending the match... well you couldn't hand them to a bloke! The band was playing *The Yellow Rose of Texas* as I made my way into the seating area, where an attractive blonde with a smile to die for was waving at me. Clearly, she wanted my rose. But, just as I was about to make my way towards her, I felt someone tugging on my shorts.

I looked down and there was a young girl of about seven years of age who asked me, "Can I have your rose?"

I smiled, shrugged towards the attractive blonde, leaned over, and gave the rose to the little girl – as if I had any choice!

During the brief warm-up before the game I was approached by a big South American guy – who turned out to be Brazilian – obviously wanting a word with me.

"What are you doing here, shouldn't you be in Hong Kong?" he said.

It was Pelé's personal masseur, Mario Américo, who I had met in Hong Kong when he was there on a few occasions with Santos. I told him, "not tonight I'm not." We laughed and shared a few words before he wished me well.

We won the game 1-0, the goal scored by our Canadian international, Victor Kodelja – nice change to be on the winning side against the great Brazilian, probably Bobby Moore felt the same way too!

I recall a funny incident with Pelé during the game. It happened near the halfway line when Pelé and I were going for a ball that was there to be won. As the ball bobbled on the turf we were both thrown off balance, resulting in me lying on top of Pelé, almost exactly simulating a sex act. That picture would have been priceless if there had been a snapper about. As we got up and dusted ourselves off, the referee came over intending to give me a yellow card. Pelé protested, though I didn't, and as he softly patted my head, said to the referee, "No, no, accident." A real sportsman; there was no card given. Mind you, it would have been nice to say in later years, "I got a yellow card against Pelé!"

The Cosmos would play eight friendly matches before the bicentennial season began, the game against Thunder would be their only defeat.

Next up for us was the long hop to Seattle to play a couple of pre-season games against the Sounders. I knew a couple of their players, so was hoping it would not be too 'sleepless'. The flight from San Antonio to Seattle took us over four different states and lasted over four hours. It was a comfortable, pleasant journey; unlike the one hour flight to Spokane we would make the next day which was especially worrying for those who had claustrophobia. Spokane has the Cascade Mountains to its west, and the Rocky Mountains to the east and north. There was no quick, easy access by road from Seattle, so flying it was.

When we arrived at the airfield there were two small planes sitting on the apron; small being the operative word! I believe the aircraft were Twin Otters. We had to split our party into two: twelve in each aircraft. The seats along the inside of the aircraft faced inwards, so we spent the journey looking at one another. After take-off, the planes flew virtually in unison and some of us, like over-grown schoolboys, turned to wave at team-mates in the other plane.

As you awkwardly looked out the window, due to the seat position, there was plenty of magnificent scenery below: Coniferous forests, valleys and mountains, all of which helped to take our minds off the confined space in the cabin. Eventually we landed at Felts Field, Spokane, the same place Charles Lindbergh had touched down some half a century earlier in his iconic *Spirit of St. Louis*. I don't know how Lindbergh felt when he landed, but I couldn't get off the plane quick enough to stretch my legs.

We played that same evening, a Friday night, in front of several thousand fans in the Joe Albi Stadium. The Astroturf surface was not the best, the ball bounced like someone on a trampoline and was difficult to control. But it was just a friendly game and we played out a friendly draw.

Saturday was a free day.

Knowing my penchant for horse racing, Davie Gillett, one of the Sounders central defenders, who played a season in Hong Kong for Caroline Hill in 1973, asked me if I wanted to attend a race meeting with him that afternoon. Apparently the Sounders were sponsoring a race at Yakima Meadows racetrack, a six-furlong sprint named the 'Seattle Sounders Purse'. Davie was going as a representative of the club, along with coach John Best and the player/assistant coach, Jimmy Gabriel. Our coach gave the all clear for me to attend, and team-mates Billy Semple and Jim Henry decided to come along as well.

Jimmy Gabriel, at 35, was still enjoying some game time for the Sounders. A Dundonian, he had spent seven years at Everton during his illustrious career, which included a cup winners medal with the 'Toffees' in their 1966 FA Cup final against Sheffield Wednesday – which, according to Jimmy, was attended by John Lennon and Paul McCartney of the Beatles.

He might have been a good player, but as a tipster he was 'Billy Cotton' – rotten.

Billy Semple, Jim Henry – or 'Shoulders' as we called him due to his well-proportioned upper body muscle mass – and I had decided that we would pool our money and place bets collectively. By the time we reached the track we had missed a couple of the early races and the next one was a 'quarter horse race'. As the name suggests, it originated as a quarter mile dash, a race distance unique to America, although nowadays it can be run over a variety of sprint distances. On this particular day it was an actual quarter mile race: two furlongs: blink, and it's almost over.

I had a fairly good eye for the horses and I particularly liked the look of one, it had a broad chest and strong rounded hindquarters, named Cosmos Folly. We had just beaten the New York Cosmos, so that had to be an omen. It was an outsider so we stood to make a real killing if we backed it.

Step in Jimmy Gabriel.

"I've just had good information from a reliable source on the 5 horse, connections think it will win today," he said. 'Shoulders' and Billy were swayed, and even I know information can be paramount, so our money went on the 5 horse. They pinged out of the starting gates and made their way at a frantic pace to the finishing post. A steely grey horse emerged through the pack to win at odds of 20/1: Cosmos Folly!!!

Jimmy apologized profusely, he was only passing on the hot tip, it's just a pity we believed it. But it was a good day out and a new experience at a new racetrack for me.

The opening game of the new season between us and the St. Louis All Stars was creeping closer, but we still squeezed in a trip to Tampa in Florida for a further couple of tune-up games. We flew from San Antonio to Tampa one morning and trained in the afternoon. The session was on the beach, and could well have been a scene straight out of the TV series, Baywatch. It was only to loosen our legs so we jogged in pairs along the sandy beach near the hotel.

Simple enough. But the beach was specked with bikini-clad Florida lovelies, many of whom waved and smiled as we trotted by. I think that was the best training session any of us ever had; no wonder the Rowdies were a popular team to play for!

The following day we met them in Sarasota and 24 hours later played them again in Tarpon Springs, some 67 miles to the north. The Rowdies might have had both Rodney Marsh, and former West Ham fan-favourite Clyde Best in their side, but we won the first game in Sarasota by one goal to nil and then drew 0-0 in Tarpon Springs.

I had a chat with Rodney Marsh after the games, reminiscing about his Hong Kong trip when we played together against Benfica a couple of years earlier. But it was Clyde Best I got to know quite well and ended up having a few beers with after the game in Tarpon Springs. In his later coaching years Clyde would bring youth teams from the States to Hong Kong and would normally stay with the team at the old Excelsior Hotel in Causeway Bay.

When in town, I would get a call from him and we would have a coffee or lunch at the Dickens Bar in the basement of the hotel. Clyde was a lovely character who at the tender age of just 16 he had moved from Bermuda to play for West Ham United.

As the day approached for the season opener our team was in good shape, but I was getting a little uneasy about my duties on the field. During training sessions and games, prior to Bobby Moore arriving, I had a free role up front. Balls were pinged over defenders for me to run onto and score freely.

One day at training one of Don Batie's assistants, a friendly Mexican by the name of Carlos, even told me Don thought I would be a great asset to the team with my pace and ability to score goals. Unfortunately, that all changed when Bobby arrived.

"Don, what shape have you got for defensive duties?" Bobby wanted to know.

Before I knew it, Bobby was arranging walls for free kicks and telling us where we should all be, including 5 feet 9 inches me. Bobby was not getting any faster as he grew older, so suddenly the emphasis was on defence and breaking out from the back. He and Bob McNab wanted me to drop deep to pick the ball up; might have been good for some orthodox winger, but in truth that was not my game or strength. I was not being lazy, far from it, but I preferred a free role where I could utilize my speed and take advantage of any defensive slips by the opposition. I suddenly felt I was being asked to play contrary to my natural style.

However, I put my fears aside as the opening game of the season against the St, Louis All Stars was upon us. My eldest brother Dick was the first ever Scottish Flyweight boxer to fight in the special American Golden Gloves Tournament between Europe and the USA in 1954 in St. Louis and Chicago. I was hoping I could floor the St. Louis All Stars and create a little bit of history myself. I never put a glove on them, it was my boot that did the damage.

Wednesday, April 14, 1976: the official opening of the American Bicentennial football season. The showpiece game at the Alamo Stadium: San Antonio Thunder versus St. Louis All Stars.

We ran onto the Texas turf wearing our colourful strip, while the band played the Yellow Rose of Texas. Pete Mannos from Chicago was in goal for us that day as the arrival of Scottish international goalkeeper, Bobby Clark, had been slightly delayed.

In front of him we lined up in a 4-3-3 formation: American CJ Carenza at right back, Bob McNab on the left side, and Bobby Moore and Brazilian Jose Berico in the heart of the defence; Kevin Missey, Jim

Henry and Billy Semple in midfield; Jim Forrest, American Dan Counce, and me in attack.

The game was scoreless at half-time, and we made two substitutions: Beriba Santana for Forrest, who was injured, while Kodelja replaced Counce. I had two new partners up front, and it worked out: our first goal came in the 49th minute, the home crowd roared its approval.

Santana got on the end of a harmless looking cross, which actually came off the top of the little Brazilian's shoulder, and the ball broke square across goal towards me. I didn't need an invitation, I quickly outpaced a defender and rattled the ball into the net, and into local history with the first official league goal in the bicentennial year.

From then on we were in total control of the game, until Pete Mannos, who had been faultless up until that moment, was induced into a 'cardinal' sin – excuse the slight pun if you aware of baseball in St. Louis. Al Trost, the St. Louis midfielder, who would play for his country 14 times, took a long throw-in, which was helped on by a strongish Texan wind that had suddenly blown up. As the ball sailed towards our goal it appeared harmless enough. Well, that was until Pete Mannos interfered!

Pete made a grab for the ball which, admittedly, was probably going into the net – but you can't score from a direct throw-in, so it wouldn't have counted. However, our all-American keeper from Northern Illinois University tried to punch the ball clear, but only succeeded in punching it into his own net. Nightmare. If the game had gone to overtime and a penalty shoot-out, I would have been a bit worried about Pete's confidence. (I should mention that draws were unacceptable in the NASL. They liked winners.)

Anyway, Pete's blushes were spared as I got the winner in the 83rd minute.

Victor Kodelja, our Canadian striker, heard me call to square the ball, he complied and from just inside the 18-yard box I slotted it home to give the Thunder a memorable win. Pete Mannos and I became good buddies, our accommodation was in the same complex, and our running joke would be me saying to Pete, just as he went to do something: "Don't touch it!"

I got on well with the US boys in the team, Chuck Carey and Mark Stahl, who also lived in the same complex near Loop 33. I shared a condo with Billy McNicol, a fellow Scot who had been a reserve and youth player with Glasgow Rangers for the prior five years. The complex was comfortable, with a nice swimming pool, and only a ten minute walk to Reed's Red Derby for afternoon tea. Billy came from that famous Scottish resort Dunoon, where if it rained lightly, it was called a good day. That same young boy I remember with the curly dark hair, and with whom I shared quite a few laughs, would go on to become one of the best coaches in America after his playing days came to an end.

He become head coach of the US under-16 national team in 1996 and helped with the growth and tutoring of players such as DaMarcus Beasley and Landon Donovan in their rise to the senior ranks. I believe Billy might still be coaching today Cal Poly.

After that important opening win over St. Louis there was a big party at Reed's Red Derby – for me, the best restaurant bar in the city. It had a large square bar, with a red London telephone box prominently situated nearby; tables were covered with black and white check tablecloths and waitresses were decked out in matching black and white vertically-striped, short-sleeved, open-collared shirts.

Our post-match party had an open bar and plenty of food, all paid for by our generous host and president of the San Antonio Thunder, Ward Lay Jr. Ward was the son of the founder of the Lay company, who merged his company with Frito, bringing the world-famous Frito Lay potato chip brand into existence. He was only 31 years old when he hosted our winning party that night at the 'Derby' and was very much one of the boys at that time in his life.

I earned the award for man of the match, which was presented at the party.

The San Antonio newspapers gave us a good write-up the next day, including a couple of nice lines about me: "Slender Derek Currie, the little Scot with the burr accent, got the two goals." The *San Antonio Express* led with, "Left-winger Derek Currie slammed home two goals and narrowly missed the hat-trick with a header just going wide near the end."

In press comments before the game, it was mentioned that my 138 pounds were spread sparingly over a slender frame, and that I was a fascinating little guy, quick moving, with a mind to match. Made me feel like a character from the fictional island of Lilliput in Jonathan Swift's classic Gulliver's Travels. Was I really that small? By Texas standards, I probably was!

Three days later we made our first NASL road trip to play San Diego – the 'Jaws,' as they were known. (I say road trip, but most of the time we flew.) We had a dress code for away games: a nice red jacket and, wait for it, a Stetson. Mind you, they were quality hats, fashioned from beaver pelts and a symbol of Western pride and bravado.

When we fronted up for a trip, we looked more like 'Pinkerton Agents' than 'The Wild Bunch.'

Our team shirts were equally 'stylish'. Our coach had been instrumental in their design, ensuring that they were in line with the Bicentennial Year theme. The jersey was a lurid tricolour of red, white and blue, with lightning bolts and stars and stripes. How American was that?

We were meant to relax on board a flight, but we had a lot of jokers in our midst. For instance, Billy Semple once took his shoes off while having a quiet snooze as we were returning to San Antonio after a game. They were hijacked. Upon waking, Billy saw they were missing, but rather than bother the air hostess, who he knew wouldn't have a clue where they were, just asked out loud: 'Has anyone seen my shoes?' Stony silence. Billy walked off the plane in his socks. However, while waiting to collect his sports bag, what should he spy but his shoes going round on the baggage carousel! Never a dull moment on the road for 'Pinkerton's Agents.'

When we arrived on the Friday night before the game we were put up in a splendid hotel in the San Diego Marina; I think it might have been the Hyatt. However, we were soon brought down to earth when we saw the venue for the game the next day.

It was a cramped old stadium on the campus of San Diego State University. The field looked as if it hadn't seen water for a month, and there were no changing rooms on site. Hardly a fitting venue to promote soccer in the USA in the Bicentennial Year!

There was a high school nearby which provided changing facilities; and that was where we also went at half-time, being bussed there and back. It was a total shambles to say the least, and the game was no better.

I was asked to play on the right-wing, but never felt relaxed on the tight field. What's more, their full-back appeared to have been told to stick to me like glue – if I had walked off to relieve myself he would probably have followed. My two goals against St. Louis had made me a marked man. To make matters worse we lost 1-0 to a goal in extra time.

Bobby Moore's influence on how we played was becoming more evident. Under his captaincy we adopted a style of play that meant more possession football and slow build-up from the back. I was on the bench for our next game against Dallas, the city synonymous with the assassination of JFK.

Dallas Tornado had a fair side, with All-American Kyle Rote Jr. playing for them. Midway through the second half we were 1-0 down, I was introduced to add some firepower to the attack, or so I thought. I hoped I would have free rein to roam, Jamie Vardy style, in search of an equalizer; utilize my talents to best advantage.

No sooner had I come on the field, than Bobby Moore was signalling me to come deep and collect the ball out of defence. Fine, I did, but going backwards to collect the ball seemed like moving one space backward on a chess board, perhaps it was 'Bobby's Sicilian Defence'. Hey, not Bobby's fault; but my skills weren't as an orthodox winger, nor would they ever be, as much as he tried to change me.

I had to be at the sharp end of proceedings, a free roaming spirit, use my quick acceleration to upset hesitant defenders, and pounce on opportunities to score, or set up a fellow team-mate, like a foil for a target man in a 4-4-2 system. Or even the 'big man – little man' combo, where a big striker is the target man for long balls and crosses, ready to knock the ball behind the defence or down into the box for someone like me and with my quick pace and acceleration to latch onto.

Near the end of the game, we had a corner on the right, the ball came over and there was a bit of a scramble in the Dallas 6-yard box. One of our players looked as if he was about to have a shot at goal, I screamed at him to play the ball square to me, confident I would burst the net from 5 yards or so... I was good at that. I can't recall who the player was, but he shot and it was blocked.

In hindsight, it was probably better that he didn't pass to me. Had I scored, it could possibly have meant me staying in San Antonio for the whole year and being used as a super-sub, coming on only when we were in desperate need of a goal. Clearly I was not going to fit into the team under Bobby's style of play. To be honest, I didn't want to and they were certainly not going to change that style of play to accommodate me. Don Batie might have been the coach, but when Bobby was on the field he ran the show.

I should say however that socially, off the field, we all got on great together.

On May 19 I was again on the bench, for what would turn out to be the last time with the Thunder. The game was against the Portland Timbers. We lost by one goal to nil and I warmed the bench for 90 minutes, like a man on death row with no last minute reprieve.

It proved a point though, to me at least, the team were not conceding many goals, which must have pleased Bobby, but they were not scoring goals, and that's what wins games. Even if defending is historically synonymous with the Alamo, it wouldn't be my problem for much longer.

During the 1976 NASL season clubs could only have a roster of 18 players and obviously American-born players were very much encouraged to join the ranks. It was with a heavy heart, I felt, that Don Batie summoned me one morning to tell me that we had too many players and that I would have to drop off the roster. I was free to go.

To make it easy for him I said, "No problem Don, I understand the situation." I think he was surprised by my reaction. I told him that I knew my style was not suited to the way the team were operating. With a shrug, he nodded soberly, as if it was out of his hands.

I had once been his ace in the hole, quietly mentioned as a possible 'Team America' player after the opening game when I scored the two goals; but my status within the club seemed to have fallen in quite a short time. I felt through no fault of my own. In one way, I knew he was reluctant to let me go as he liked my speed, approach to the game and goal-scoring ability. However the squad had to be trimmed, there were too many on the roster, and keeping the big-name players was paramount.

Bobby Calder, a reputable Scottish scout, had brought some of those big name players to the club; I was only 'wee' Derek Currie from Hong Kong (I say with tongue in cheek). So, the Thunder's number 11 jersey was officially retired for the season. In fact, I still have that very jersey in all its sartorial elegance, which, for a short time, I wore with pride. I'm sure the founding fathers would have approved when I scored that first goal in the bicentennial year.

Bobby Clark would go on to say that the club should have kept me on being a prolific goalscorer, but in a way I was relieved to go. It would be the best thing to happen as my heart was really in Hong Kong, not San Francisco, or any other American city. It had been a nice change and a great experience, but America was only a detour for me, as it was for many foreign players in the NASL.

San Antonio would win 12 games and lose 12 in 1976; finish fourth out of five teams in the Southern Conference; and miss the play-offs by one place. Harry Hood would be top scorer with 10 goals in 20 appearances; Dan Counce would be next with 6 goals, also in 20 appearances; and Neil Martin would be third with 5 goals in 19 games. I had scored two goals in my two and a bit games. I got the Thunder out of the blocks fast and I like to think that had I been given a free role, I could have eclipsed all of them in the final goal tally. I bade farewell to my team-mates with drinks at Reed's Red Derby, where else?

San Antonio Thunder would fold at the end of that season. I returned to Hong Kong and helped Seiko win the FA Cup, beating old rivals South China. Texas steak knives were replaced by chopsticks; the Yellow Rose by the Bauhinia. I was home again.

So, in a roundabout way, I have to thank Bobby Moore for not fitting me into his system, it allowed me to get back to my roots in Hong Kong quicker than I thought possible. Despite our differences on the field I became good friends with Bobby over the years. Everyone has a path in life, we just never see it.

Bobby's path would ultimately take him to Hong Kong in company with his old 1966 World Cup-winning buddy, Alan Ball. You never know what's around that corner. It's a funny old game but I was back in my happy stomping ground with plenty of goals yet to be scored.

18

Sweet and Sour

In the same year that America reached their Bicentennial, China mourned the loss of 'the Great Helmsman'.

"A soldier, classical poet, historian and Marxist philosopher who placed his faith in China's peasants, passed away on September 9, to the distress of a grieving population."

The man in question was of course Mao Tse-tung; the description was by journalist John Roderick in a well-written obituary in the *SCMP*. While Mao was proclaiming the founding of the People's Republic of China in 1949, I was being born in a Glasgow hospital in Duke Street on the east side of the city. A gypsy lady telling fortunes at a carnival on the Glasgow Green once told me I would go on a long journey; how could she see that in the tea leaves?

Some two months after the solemnity of Mao's passing things got back to normal, from a sporting point of view at least, and one of the most exciting matches ever to be seen at the old Hong Kong stadium took place. The name 'El Classico' might be reserved for Real Madrid versus Barcelona, but in Hong Kong it meant Seiko against South China – El Classico, Cantonese style.

It was the last Sunday in November. A full house of just over 28,000 were inside the stadium to see the two local giants lock horns once again, fighting for precious points in the race for the league title. Tickets for the match changed hands at double face value. There was even a story floating about the changing room that two prominent figures had made a friendly six-figure wager on the game. Everyone however expected it to be a close encounter and felt it too close to call.

Who would have imagined then, with the stadium clock showing we were just 30 minutes into the game, South China were already leading 4-0?

Fung Chi-ming had just lashed South China's fourth goal into the net from the penalty spot, after a handball by our defender, Au Wing-hung. I recall my displeasure as we regrouped, but shouted encouragement to my team-mates to get back into the game. There was still well over half the match left to play, we could reduce the damage and not be totally humiliated. I was ready to fight for goals, and expected no less from my team-mates.

Three minutes later, I flighted a ball from the left and our Korean centre-forward, Kim Jae-han headed home, 4-1. Manuel Cuenca, our Spanish winger, then squared the ball to Kim Jae-han who sold a lovely dummy and Wu Kwok-hung slotted home in the 39th minute, 4-2. Game on.

There was an air of optimism in the changing room at half-time, which was carried onto the field for the second half.

In the 64th minute Cheung Chi-wai, now a Seiko player, flighted over a cross and again our tall South Korean striker got his head on the end of it and banged it home: 4-3 and the South China fans were dumbstruck by what was happening. Barely a minute later we were all square: a moment of magic from Wu Kwok-hung.

Nicknamed *dai tow jai* (translated as big head boy, due to his large cranium) he beat three South China players inside the box turned in the space of a 10 cent piece, and fired home a glorious equalizer: 4-4.

The final goal of the game came in the 72nd minute.

Which way did it go? To the team with the momentum of course.

Wu Kwok-hung sent a sweeping cross to the far post, Cheung Chi-wai got his head on the ball, and sent it towards goal. At full stretch the South China keeper got his hands to the ball, but couldn't hold it. I gleefully fired it high into the net: 5-4 to Seiko! I was still razor sharp around goal! I think I even got a kiss from our defender Hugh McCrory after it flew across the line.

An amazing comeback. Even today fans recall that game, though it was over 45 years ago, and talk about it as if it was yesterday.

We did get a sizeable bonus after the game, so perhaps there was some merit to the pre-match rumour about the wager! A memorable victory for Seiko, a bleak day for South China. El Classico Cantonese style had been 'sweet' for us and 'sour' for our old rivals.

On the international scene however, things weren't quite so sweet.

The German side Hertha Berlin arrived in Hong Kong a few days before the advent of New Year 1977. Affectionately known as '*Die Alte Dame*' (The Old Lady) due to their rich history in the Bundesliga, they played the Hong Kong national team on December 30, and the League XI were due to play them on the second day of the New Year.

Hertha Berlin were your typical strong Bundesliga side, coached by Georg Kessler. They finished second to Borussia Mönchengladbach in the Bundesliga in the 74/75 season and were captained by Erick Beers, who would win 24 caps for West Germany. There were no 'old ladies' in the side, but one of their players flew higher than 'Mary Poppins' the day we played them.

Our League XI side had plenty of experience, but perhaps was lacking a little in youth and height; it included ex-Glasgow Rangers and Scotland star Willie Henderson and former Heart of Midlothian star, Tommy Murray. However, Willie was weeks away from his 33rd birthday, Tommy was almost 34, and Cheung Chi-doy was well into his 30s. Willie and Tommy were both under 5 feet 8 inches tall. Perhaps we were '*Der Alte Herr*'.

But we did have some young faces in the team: Davie Anderson, Hugh McCrory and Colm McFeely in defence; Bernie Poole, Manuel Cuenca and the Koreans Byun Ho-young and Kim Jae-han in midfield and attack. Willie was on one wing, I was on the other, and Korean Kim Jae-han lead the line.

Rod Stewart was at number one on the Billboard Hot 100 chart that week with *Tonight's the Night (Gonna Be Alright)*. It might have been alright for football-mad Rod, it wouldn't be for us! We got hammered at set pieces and our night would be like one on Elm Street.

I mentioned earlier that they were a big strong side, but they had one player in particular who we just could not deal with: we called him 'Tiny'. He could have stacked 8 foot shelves in a supermarket. He was 1.95 metres tall – if you prefer in feet and inches: 6' 5" – almost a foot taller than some of our lads! Uwe Kliemann was his name and he was a defender, but, also, paradoxically, their best attacker.

On match day he controlled the air better than the Red Baron and got on the end of every corner or free kick Hertha were awarded. He was either scoring, or heading the ball down for a team-mate to score. He was our Achilles heel; we lost 5-1.

"The Towering Inferno" could easily have been the headline on the sports pages the next day!

Late in the game, two of our lads decided to playfully draw everyone's attention to his height advantage. We were awarded a corner on the right side of the field, at the changing room end of the ground. As the ball was being placed Bernie Poole bent down and lifted Tommy Murray onto his shoulders. They then moved up close to 'Tiny.' It was the first time he had been overshadowed all day.

The packed crowd were quick to see the humour, and the significance; even the referee saw the funny side, as indeed, did the rest of the Hertha defence It was just one of those moments in a game, perhaps a poignant compliment to Kliemann.

The game finished shortly afterwards; we were well beaten. But it might have been a slightly different outcome without 'Tiny,' who well deserved his man of the match award. It may sound like a tall tale, but to our team, he was the height of frustration!

Talking of international frustration reminds me of one of my favourite stories about my old team-mate Walter Gerrard. A few years earlier he had been in a team to play Santos, who had the legendary Pelé in their side. The Big Man had just come back from Australia to play for a spell with Caroline Hill.

Santos had already played two games during their visit to Hong Kong and I had played for a South China select in one of those games, losing 4-2. I was due to also guest for Caroline Hill in the last match of the tour, but Petrie blocked my participation – rightly or wrongly, he claimed to be worried about me getting injured. I was therefore restricted to watching the game from the fourth row of Section 27 at the old stadium; which happened to be right on the halfway line.

It was late in the game, Santos and Caroline Hill were each making substitutions. Walter was coming off for Caroline Hill at the same time as Pelé for Santos. As they were leaving the field together, Walter put his arm around Pelé and whispered something to him. After the game I asked Walter what he had said?

He answered with a shrug, "I just told him: these coaches don't know a good player when they see one!" Absolutely priceless!

A year later we forgot all about the loss to Hertha Berlin when in December 1977 we won a quadrangular tournament that featured Yugoslavia's Dinamo Zagreb, Göteborg from Sweden, and the HK National and League XI sides. Quality European opposition against the best that Hong Kong could offer. It would be two days of double-headers for the fans to enjoy.

Our National side lost 3-1 to Göteborg in the first game, two of the Swedes' goals scored by Olle Nordin, the same player, after retirement, who managed the Swedish national side at the Italia '90 World Cup finals. We played the Slavs in the other game, drawing 0-0, but beat them in a sudden death shoot-out, NASL style to enter the final against Göteborg.

A few days later, we were down 1-0 in the final but I pulled a goal back with an overhead kick that Ronaldo would have been proud of. Four minutes from time Bernie Poole, from a long free kick by Davie Anderson, headed the ball on to me; I prodded the ball on to Lai Yue-shue who hit the roof of the net to the delight of the home crowd giving us a 2-1 win.

At full-time Hugh McCrory and I proudly lifted Lai, and carried our diminutive Seiko team-mate shoulder-high off the field. The League XI boys picked up $ 40,000 first prize, which earned the boys in the squad about $3,000 each. It made for a very happy Christmas and Hertha Berlin and 'Tiny' were well and truly forgotten.

19

Hall of Fame... or should that be infamy?

By the end of 1976 a flood of players had come through passport control at Kai Tak Airport, far too many to mention them all individually.

Some left with an exit stamp as fast as they came: approval by the local fans could soon determine the length of your stay.

Off the field there were not many quiet moments in Hong Kong, which was the beauty and the elixir of the place.

Returning from my brief stint in the USA I found Seiko had signed four South Koreans: goalkeeper Byun Ho-young, defender Kang Kee-wook and tall centre-forward, Kim Jae-han – all had faced Australia in the 1974 World Cup play-off match. The fourth was an attacking mid-fielder named Park Soo-duck.

Byun and Kim had over 90 international caps between them so they brought good footballing credentials with them.

Unfortunately, they also brought *kimchi*. Its pungent smell seemed to be permanently on their breath – a smell not unlike a dozen rotten eggs. This did not sit well with the other players on the team bus that took us to training.

"Open the bloody windows!" was Hugh McCrory's daily cry before we set off.

Looking back through the mists of time there are plenty of characters who deserve a mention here.

John McGunnigle, whom I knew from my Glasgow playing days, was a skilful midfielder and my pal when going to the races at Happy Valley; we both loved the excitement of horse racing.

In later years John would open an aptly-named bar called 'Traps' in Happy Valley. It was in the basement of the site that used to be occupied by the old Caravelle Hotel and became very popular with the sporting and advertising crowd; some – possibly after a few drinks – even claiming that it was the best bar in Asia.

Ben Balboa, the Filipino singer / guitarist from the Dickens often guested there on the small stage and was sometimes joined by some of the punters.

Bobby Moore had the honour of cutting the ribbon on opening day for the 'Wee Man' – as John was affectionately known.

It will come as no surprise to those who knew the Wee Man, that he now resides in Newmarket, headquarters of horse racing in the UK.

Colm McFeely was another who displayed his many talents in Hong Kong. An Irish defender, Colm had his fair share of injuries, although these were not always incurred on the football field.

I recall one such injury being sustained at Kai Tak airport. A group of us were seeing off a fellow player who was flying home. We were grouped around the old airport bar. Colm, for reasons known only to himself, decided to do his 'Superman' act, without the cape, diving from the top of the four foot high bar and out into space… crashing in a heap on the floor. A broken nose resulted.

Admittedly it was in the days when 'bar diving' was a popular pastime, the idea being that you had a group of friends ready to catch you, but Colm had omitted to tell anyone what he intended to do!

Plagued by injuries, mostly sustained on the field, he retired and began a successful coaching career.

Colm now resides in LA, holds a FIFA coaching licence, and has been instrumental in developing the high standards of men and women's football at Occidental College in LA.

He had a notable football career himself, being in the team that won a Division 1 championship in his native Northern Ireland, before enjoying spells in Hong Kong and Australia.

At this point I should mention that despite the high jinks performed by many in those days, most subsequently went on to build good careers, either in football or commerce – Alan Devlin, Jim Savage, Andy Savage (not related) and Alan Venables, to name just a few.

Seiko signed two Brazilians: João Regiva Filho and Roberto – it was the only name we knew him by.

Chan Fai-hung, the Seiko coach, asked me to look after them, neither of whom spoke English any better than I spoke Portuguese.

However, with a deft use of hand signs we managed to make some progress understanding one another.

I took them along to the Hong Kong Football Club one day and could not get them to leave, particularly 'Joe' as we called him. It had nothing to do with a breakdown in communication, rather it could be summed up in two words: San Miguel.

"San Miguel, *bueno!*" was all Joe could say after downing his fifth pint.

He and Roberto were not bad players, but their limited English was a big drawback and largely contributed to their staying for less than a full season; but they were two nice lads.

Then there was Willie Coulson. Who could not like Willie! A cheery red face and long hair, reminiscent of General George Custer. That he was a native of Newcastle was obvious as soon as he opened his mouth. He played two seasons for Newcastle United and then several seasons at Southend United.

Willie only seemed to use one leg on the field, his left, but it made up for the other in spades. He moved to Australia after Hong Kong and I believe he's been in Melbourne for over 20 years now.

Willie was straight as a die and a very good player, but he had a major problem getting up for morning training, especially during his early months in Hong Kong – nothing to do with a liking for his customary brown ale, of course.

"This jet-lag really gets me," he said to me one day, "I can't wake up in the morning like, even the alarm clock doesn't work."

"Did you put batteries in it Willie, you've been here for over a month!" I said in jest.

"Why aye man," said Willie, "before I went to bed I got a plastic coat hanger, like, twisted it round my neck, and even hung another small alarm clock on it, next to the big one."

"Did it work?"

"Naw, I still slept in," he said with a cheeky grin.

Mind you, with Willie, you wouldn't know if he was taking the piss or not; but David Allison, his team-mate at the Urban Services Department club (USD) told me he wasn't sighted on quite a few mornings.

'Ali', as we called David, was the eldest son of flamboyant former Manchester City manager, Malcolm Allison.

Ali left England in 1972 to play football in Oz and was signed for USD in 1974 for just under £10,000 from Safeway United in Sydney. He would spend six years playing in Hong Kong for USD and Eastern.

A strong mid-fielder he knew how to distribute a ball and took his defensive duties very seriously, not unlike his famous dad in his playing days at West Ham.

After retiring from football Ali would spend almost two decades in Hong Kong managing bars and eventually working for local brewer San Miguel in a managerial position.

Now back in Manchester he spends alternate weekends at the Etihad Stadium watching his beloved Manchester City, sitting alongside greats like Mike Summerbee.

His dad, Malcolm, was not only a great manager and player, but also a well known social animal, often referred to as 'Champagne Mal'.

I think Ali was a bit of a chip off the old block; in fact I know he was.

I recall one night seeing him and Willie Coulson singing and dancing in the rain on the top of a bus shelter outside the Godown Restaurant and Bar in Central. The bus shelter was 8 foot high!

Eddie Loyden, or Ted as we would call him, joined Caroline Hill in the mid-70s. He was a good footballer and fitted easily into the Hong Kong scene.

Ted brought with him a team-mate who had played alongside him during his spell with Highlands Park in South Africa. His name was Tommy Henderson.

As a 16 year old schoolboy Tommy had joined Leeds United, and, after spells with Celtic, Hearts and St Mirren, Don Revie brought him back to Leeds in 1962. Tommy played another couple of seasons for them, but ultimately lost his place in the side to Johnny Giles.

Unlike the 6 foot tall Ted, Tommy was a mere five foot something, but in the same mould as Willie Henderson – no relation, except in height.

Ted and Tommy were inseparable when not training with the club and team-mate Bernie Poole dubbed them 'Little' and 'Large'.

Unfortunately Tommy was 34 years old and did not take well to the ruthless tackling from some of the local lads, so his stay was fairly brief. He would go on to play for the Ottawa Tigers and manage the Canadian club side at the culmination of his great career.

Ted on the other hand was around for about four seasons and I loved playing alongside him in League XI games against quality opposition from Europe.

He was a clever, gifted centre-forward who could score goals; even against the toughest opposition.

It was 1973 and Ted's side, Third Division Tranmere Rovers, were in a second round League Cup match against First Division side Arsenal at Highbury. They were not given a hope against the side that had done the League and Cup double just two years earlier.

The iconic Highbury clock was showing 29 minutes past three when Ted smashed the ball into the back of the net: Tranmere were 1-0 up against the mighty Arsenal.

Marshalled by an ageing Ron Yeats and a young Mark Palios, Tranmere man-marked danger man Alan Ball out of the game. Despite late pressure, Rovers held on, causing a major upset and dumping the mighty Gunners out of the Cup. A magical, historic day for the Merseyside club.

I understand that a few sherbets were consumed on the train back from London to Lime Street Station in Liverpool that night.

Funnily enough, former Gunner, Bob McNab also played in that match, but he never mentioned it when we were together in San Antonio.

"That was a great night," Ted, who sported a Freddie Mercury-style 'tash in those days, told me over beers in the Dickens Bar one evening. Ted was a big fan of the Dickens and often used to go there in his tracksuit, "so I'll be ready for training in the morning," he used to say.

One of Ted's team-mates in that game, Mark Palios, would go on to have a spell as Chief Executive of the English Football Association and, at time of writing, is the owner of Tranmere Rovers.

Not sure what became of Ted, but someone told me he became a Jehovah's Witness. 'Big Ted' was good at whatever he put his hand to and lit up football during his stint in Hong Kong.

Another I really enjoyed playing with in the League XI was my old flat mate Bernie Poole. Bernie was a scouser who spent his early years playing for Skelmersdale United before moving to South Africa and eventually to Hong Kong where he joined Caroline Hill.

He was a strong, skilful midfield playmaker with an eye for a good long ball; and we had some good times in the flat watching classic Sherlock Holmes episodes starring Basil Rathbone – it wasn't all wine, women and song in those days.

The third member of the flat was Charlie (John Charlesworth), who kindly helped me assemble this book. His claim to footballing fame was being in the Hong Kong Football Club team who once beat Rangers in the First Division, I hasten to add this was well after I had left for Seiko.

Veronica Chiu, or Chan Yiu-kam as she was known when she became the boss of Caroline Hill, was the lady who came with her husband, Dr Chiu But-york, to Glasgow when I signed for Hong Kong Rangers.

She signed a very good player herself called Lucas Moripe, whom she brought to Hong Kong from South Africa.

Unfortunately, Lucas was somewhat moody and appeared very unhappy at times. So Veronica, full of good intentions, decided to sign another fellow South African so they could room together and be company for each other. But she forgot to do her due diligence.

A second South African player was duly signed, his first name was James and his surname was Mthombeni (I hope I've spelt that correctly).

I asked Bernie Poole how things were going with Lucas and James.

Bernie smiled, "they're staying in different rooms; it's not working out."

"What's wrong?" I asked.

"Nothing really, they're just from two different tribes in South Africa – one Zulu, the other Tswana – and the tribes are not very fond of one another!" Bernie said with a straight face.

So, tribal enemies then. Lucas stayed for the season, James left. But here's an interesting postscript to that story.

I mentioned that Lucas was a good player, and although he might have been a footnote in Hong Kong football, playing just 33 times for Caroline Hill, he was revered back home in his township.

In his youth he was prevented from playing at the highest level by the sports restrictions put in place by the then apartheid government in South Africa.

Lucas played for the Pretoria Callies, before moving to the Soweto Giants, but his roots remained with the Callies where he had been a cult hero.

In 2010 the stadium in Atteridgeville, a township in Pretoria where the Callies played, was renamed the Lucas "Masterpiece" Moripe Stadium, in his honour. Every match day the club sent a car to fetch Lucas to come and watch the club play their home games at the 30,000 capacity stadium.

I know of no other player in Hong Kong history ever to have a stadium named after him.

20

Cordoba Revenge and one night in Bangkok

My dear old Mum died a day before her 103rd birthday. She got a card from the Queen but never saw Scotland win the World Cup, despite being led to believe they would in 1978.

She was one of 30,000 brave souls alongside her sister Martha, who paid 50p to be at Hampden Park in Glasgow to see the team off as they headed to Argentina. It was meant to be the precursor to the victory parade they would take a month or so later; the kind of party normally reserved for returning champions.

Scottish comedian Andy Cameron, who once did a gig for the Hong Kong St Andrew's Society at their annual Burns Supper in the Hilton Hotel, released a record that got to number 6 in the charts. *Ally's Tartan Army* was the song, with the lines:

"We're going tae the Argentine,
and we'll really shake them up,
when we win the World Cup,
cos' Scotland is the greatest football team."

Optimism was at its highest around the hills and glens. Girls, some in tartan, others in white pleated skirts like majorettes, waved lion rampart flags as they welcomed team manager Ally MacLeod and the players onto the Hampden turf. It was sheer pantomime. My Mum said it was the best 50p she'd ever spent.

It was 'Saturday Night Fever' as the bus that had taken the team around Hampden continued on to Prestwick airport in South Ayrshire, some 32 miles from Glasgow. The roads were lined with thousands more well-wishers. The team eventually boarded a chartered British Caledonian plane for the flight to Argentina to collect the Jules Rimet Trophy.

Ally's Tartan Army never got to number one; and Scotland never won the trophy.

Three weeks later, after a dismal 3-1 opening defeat to Peru, followed by an awful 1-1 draw with Iran, the jocks were returning to Glasgow by the proverbial back door. A spirited 3-2 victory over the Netherlands in their last group game was not enough to lift the gloom.

The damage was done in Cordoba, losing to Peru. A disastrous day for Scotland and Andy Cameron's lyrics. I recall having a drink with Andy in Wan Chai after his gig at the Burns Supper at the Hilton. He never sang *Ally's Tartan Army* for me that night despite my urgings but he did sing a chorus of *Goodnight for me Argentina* as he slipped into his taxi.

Well, he was a comedian. You might well wonder where I am going with this yarn?

Well, going back to that calamitous World Cup for Scotland, just five months later, the leading club side in Peru arrived in Hong Kong on tour. They had eight players in their squad who had beaten Scotland including their captain, Héctor Chumpitaz and flamboyant goalkeeper, Ramón Quiroga.

Five of the Hong Kong League XI that would face Sporting Cristal on that Halloween night of October 31, were Scottish. How spooky was that!

Cordoba revenge? Damn right we hoped and a packed stadium waited with bated breath. I wish my old Mum had been there that night. Dad had passed away in 1974.

Sporting Cristal had already disposed of the Hong Kong National side 3-0 the Sunday before they faced us on a very muggy Tuesday evening. Rubén Toribio Díaz, Roberto Mosquera, Julio César Uribe and the brilliant left-winger Juan Carlos Oblitas – who between them would go on to have over 200 caps for Peru – were just some of the other stars we faced that night.

Rather than give my take on the game I'll let Jim McGhee, who wrote a report on it for the *Glasgow Evening Times*, give you his thoughts from a Scottish perspective.

Under a banner headline: "CORDOBA REVENGE... or almost, thanks to the Hong Kong Exiles!" McGhee wrote.

"The venue was Hong Kong's National Stadium, the crowd capacity was 30,000. Officially it was a tour friendly between a Hong Kong League XI side and FC Sporting Cristal, the pride of Peru. But unofficially it was Cordoba revenge night for five Scots selected in the Hong Kong side. The South Americans boasted eight of the World Cup squad who beat Scotland 3-1 and had the fans laughing in Lima and greetin' in Glasgow... and the five, Derek Currie, Billy Semple, Ian McWilliams, Hugh McCrory, Davie Anderson, did their country proud in belittling the distinguished visitors, albeit with a little help from their friends, three Englishmen and three Chinese. The result was 0-0 but the Hong Kong League XI were unlucky not to win, and they left the field with sky-blue Cristal jerseys thrown over their shoulders as if they were trophies."

We did as well; but mine just happened to be a green goalkeeper's jersey worn by their goalkeeper, Ramón Quiroga. True, we were unlucky, I had a shot that came off the post and Billy Semple had a shot headed off the line by defender Carlos Carbonell in the closing minutes. But our defence had to take a lot of credit for restricting the firepower of the Peruvians. Hugh McCrory had an outstanding game in containing the threat of Cristal's brilliant winger, Oblitas.

We jocks in the team were proud of our efforts; it might not have been in Cordoba, but we felt we got a little bit of pride back that night, perhaps not enough to hire a bus around Hampden, but Ally's Tartan Army would have been proud.

When things quietened down after the game, a few of our boys took some of the Peruvians down to the Dickens Bar after the game. Well we had to cheer them up for not winning. There was a question I wanted to ask Ramón Quiroga out of earshot pertaining to the World Cup earlier that year when Peru lost their last game to Argentina. Brazil had beaten Poland 3-0 and Argentina had to beat Peru by four clear goals to meet the Netherlands in the final. They beat them by six. I had watched that game on numerous occasions and had some doubts about dodgy defending, debatable to say the least.

"Ramón" I said with a smile on my face, "it's okay to tell me, how hard did your side try against Argentina?"

"No, No we try our best," he answered, looking slightly hurt. I knew not to pursue the subject, I respected his answer and that was that.

Controversy reigned supreme during the game: for instance, Peru substituted their best mid-fielder José Velásquez, early in the second half, itself a head scratcher. In fairness I suppose Peru could not qualify for the final, so apart from pride, the game was of no real importance for them. However, my new pal Ramón, who scribbled his contact details on the back of a beer mat for me to visit him if I was ever in Lima told me they tried their best that night against Argentina. That was good enough for me, you don't disagree with someone who has just bought you a beer... *¡Salud!*

1979 started with a bang, not the fireworks sort, rather a big bang in the face from an opponent. It left me on the turf at the Hong Kong Stadium like a boxer flattened by a left hook. In great pain, I lay there seeing stars, there could have been a dozen fans for all I knew instead of the 30,000 spectators with god knows how many more watching live on local TV. It was the worst pain I have ever endured from an injury and it came about at the worst time: the final of the Senior Shield against arch-rivals South China on Sunday, January 7.

Happy New Year, I thought!

They say Sunday is a day of rest, well from then on it was for me, sleeping in a hospital bed in nearby St. Paul's Hospital. It had all come about when we were 2-0 down and into the 55th minute of the game. I had risen to head a ball from a good cross and with the right connection would pull a goal back for my club, Seiko.

Wrong.

A young inexperienced South China central defender, Tsui Hoi-wan, with shoulders and a head like the Incredible Hulk (slight exaggeration) thought he could beat me to the ball. Suddenly, realizing that he might not, he threw his sizeable head back in my direction and cracked me full in the face. I'm sure it was accidental, but I crashed to the turf as if hit by a passing train. Pain severe, damage unknown.

I was attended to on the field by our team doctor and medics from the St. John Ambulance Service. The game came to an abrupt stop, silence descended inside the stadium. I can't recall much about being stretchered off and the ten minute trip to St Paul's Hospital, except a doctor looking at me as I lay flat on a medical table. But I do remember whispering one word to him: "painkillers."

"Later," I faintly heard him say, "we need to X-ray you to see the extent of the damage." Shortly afterwards, I passed out. It must have been an hour or so later when I woke up. I raised my head when a nurse put on the overhead television; in hindsight it must have been to cheer me up. The hospital staff knew what had happened, as did many in the hospital – those not performing duties had been glued to the match live on television.

As I focused on the screen, I thought I saw my Seiko team-mates parading around the perimeter of the field with the trophy. Still under the weather and drowsy, I thought I must be dreaming. I wasn't! '

I soon found out the boys had come back into the game, scoring a last-minute equalizer, then going on to win 4-2 in extra time. What a tonic! I tried to smile as the nurse turned up the sound to let me hear the Cantonese commentary. Half an hour later, the entire Seiko team were in my hospital room, and so was the Senior Shield – a first for the hospital.

When things in the hospital returned to normal the surgeon came along and told me the extent of my injury: a depressed cheekbone and a fractured nose. It could have been a lot worse.

"Derek's finding it hard to smile" was also the caption on the front page headline in the *SCMP* the next day. Someone had sneaked in and taken a picture of me with my intravenous drip whilst sleeping and under painkillers. The accompanying story mentioned that I had been selected to be the first full-time European professional to be play for the Hong Kong National side at the Asian Cup in Bangkok, beginning May 1, 1979. To be honest I was not sure at the time if I would be able to make it.

I was visited in hospital by Mike Fleming, a Scottish doctor who had his own practice in Hong Kong. He suggested a colleague, and specialist in facial surgery, so a day later I had the operation. Now, I can honestly say I have never taken drugs of any kind (beer does not count,) no 'hippy hallucinations' or 'magic mushrooms'; but when they gave me morphine for the pre-med, I was the happiest patient in the hospital. I was lying there in Nirvana land, if you'd pinched me I would have laughed; on reflection a bit scary as I felt little control of my body.

Mike Fleming was the anaesthetist, he gave me my final injection asking me to count to ten before Dr Nicholson performed surgery. Half giggling I started counting in Cantonese. *Yat, Yee, Sam*, I got to *Baat* (8) and conked out. The operation proved a success. The procedure was to make an incision, then use a blunt instrument to push the depressed cheekbone back into place.

It worked. Bangkok and the Asian Cup was a go.

It was a great honour for me to be part of the squad: you had to have lived in Hong Kong for seven years to be eligible for the national side; my time had come, though much later than I would have liked. Davie Anderson had later been introduced to the squad, which was also a great honour for him.

Our first game was an annual interport against Guangzhou (formerly Canton) across the border on the Pearl River, about 120 kilometres north-west of Hong Kong. We played out a dreary 0-0 draw in a dreary old stadium, not the ultra modern stadium they have today in the city. A shower after the game would have been nice, instead it was two large plastic drums filled with water and small plastic tubs with handles to scoop out water. Oh the glamour of international football!

Before we left for Bangkok the national side played a friendly against a visiting British Combined Services Military side and we drew 1-1 at the Government Stadium.

Finally, we went to Bangkok for the Asian Cup qualifiers, held from May 1 to May 14.

Following a Cathay Pacific flight to the 'Big Mango' we were put up at the Rajah Hotel in Nana, Soi 4, just off Sukhumvit. Now, anybody who knows Soi 4 today, will be aware it has a somewhat seedy reputation having wall-to-wall bars and friendly female bar staff. However, back then there were no bars whatsoever except a German restaurant called 'Heidelberg'.

In mid-1979 the traffic from our hotel to the old National stadium was fairly light by today's Bangkok standards. Our team bus drove straight straight up Sukhumvit, past the Erawan Shrine at Ratchaprasong to the stadium in Pathum Wan – at the right time of day it could be done in 20 minutes or so.

During the tournament we lost our final group game to hosts, Thailand by 1-0 through a poor defensive error. This meant we were second in the group and had to face Malaysia in the semi-final; a win against them would qualify us for the overall Asian Cup finals in Kuwait.

I had scored my first national goal for Hong Kong – believe it or not with my head, proving my old noggin had fully recovered from injury – in a 5-0 drubbing of Sri Lanka.

Malaysia would be a much trickier opponent.

In that crucial game we were left to rue missed chances in the early stages of the match. One of which came after I dummied the ball to Wu Kwok-hung who went for power and blasted just over the crossbar with the goal gaping.

Ultimately, we lost 5-4 in a penalty shoot-out and our dream of going to the Asian finals, disappeared in the still air of the Thai capital. There's nothing worse than losing that way and by the slimmest of margins. I believe our side was good enough; but things just never went our way against the Malaysians. As the song goes: One night in Bangkok can make a poor man humble; it did for us.

John Charlesworth was also based in Bangkok at that time. I had previously shared a flat with him and Caroline Hill player Bernie Poole in the mid- to late-70s in Hoi Ping Road, Causeway Bay. Both were at the Malaysia game that night and afterwards 'Charlie' as we called him, tried to cheer Davie and I up by showing us a little of Bangkok's infamous nightlife – hoping it would make up for the pain of losing.

Some years later, while discussing that tournament with well-known Bangkok hack, Roger Crutchley, he asked if Charlie had taken us to the Thermae coffee shop after the game. "Indeed he did," I said.

'Old Crutch,' as he is known by his pen name when writing a wonderful, colourful column in the *Bangkok Post* can, even to this day, recall every nook and cranny of Bangkok during that period, when the city lived up to the lyrics in the song made famous by Murray Head. The same Murray Head who tapped me on the shoulder in the Professional Musician's Union bar in Hong Kong some years earlier asking me what time the place closed. It was just after I had played an evening game, I told him it was open all night and he bought me a beer.

Bangkok was no different. The Thermae was an after-hours magnet for everyone from bar staff looking for a drink after work to gentlemen in tuxedos and ladies in their finest coming from a society ball, and anyone in between who wasn't ready to go home. With a jukebox blasting away, it was just the place to drown your sorrows after a penalty shoot-out defeat.

By the end of the tournament I was 30 years of age and there would be no more campaigns for me with the national side; time for new blood, But it was a great honour to be the first European professional nominated to represent Hong Kong at football. Just a pity it had come so late in my career.

It was the middle of May when we arrived back in Hong Kong, the following month I would spend a whole day going back and forward on ferries – all in the name of charity – well it made a change from running up and down a football field!

I should also mention that just five days after returning from Bangkok I would face South China again (couldn't resist that) for the first time since my facial injury. It was in a President's Cup match – a Cup donated by tycoon, Henry Fok. We were down 2-1 in the match and lo and behold from an excellent cross by Hugh McCrory, I headed home from a slightly acute angle; then scored two more with my feet to accomplish a hat-trick.

We won 4-2, which was a very sweet victory for me after being laid out flat on my back the last time I played against them several months earlier.

No visits to St. Paul's Hospital this time, but I might have tasted some medicine at the Dickens Bar.

21

A helping hand... or three

I somehow managed to get involved in a surprising number of activities that had nothing whatever to do with football.

Among the more memorable: riding the cross-harbour Star Ferry 116 times in just 20 hours; being hauled out of the stands to play in a rugby shield semi-final – although I'd never played rugby in my life – and recording an album (well a tape actually) with a group of very average singers.

The Star Ferry escapade was the brainchild of two English gentlemen after a relaxing Sunday lunch with friends and family in a flat in the Mid-Levels on Hong Kong Island. Retiring to the balcony which overlooked the harbour, each with glass of wine in hand, they watched the iconic Star Ferry chug to and fro. Suddenly, an idea suddenly emerged. It was early 1979 and they were both members of the Association of Round Tables, an organization which encourages fellowship, while doing sterling work in raising money for charity.

Always on the lookout for suitable fund raising vehicles the pair came up with their idea, just before the wine dulled the grey cells. It was quite simple: a competition to see who could make the most crossings in a day on the Star Ferry. A great idea they thought; just as long it wasn't them participating.

At their next Round Table meeting it was rubber stamped, and subsequently put to the other nine Round Tables for approval. They agreed and the idea was adopted.

Individual Tables were then asked to nominate a representative to participate in the gruelling 20-hour-long competition, or 'Ferrython' as it was named. A flyer was printed outlining ways to sponsor individuals and the event was scheduled for Saturday, June 9, 1979. It had the full co-operation of the Star Ferry owners.

Companies could sponsor individuals to wear their T-shirts and hats, or any branded product, so long as they donated a fixed amount per item. Funds were also raised by contestants getting sponsorship pledges for each individual ferry crossing.

Ex-Round Table presidents would act as umpires throughout the event which would start at 6am, when the first ferry sailed from Central Pier, and finish at 2am, when the last departed Kowloon. Television, radio, and the print media would cover the event, providing awareness for sponsors and giving updates throughout the day. John Norman, Vice-President of the National Association of the Hong Kong Round Tables, even promised that an official statement recording the event would be sent to the The Guinness Book of World Records. It was hoped that $100,000 could be raised, which would go to various children's charities in Hong Kong.

Competitors would travel on the ferry in the normal manner, paying cash for each trip and queuing when necessary before entering the ferry concourse. Once onboard, a journey could take anything from 9 to 10 minutes for the single trip across the harbour. There was a choice of going first class, which was the upper deck, or second class on the lower deck. After payment and passing through the turnstiles there was a walk of about 80 metres or so to reach the boarding area. A green light meant you could board, but if a red light appeared you had to wait for the next ferry.

So if you heard the whistle which accompanied the red light as staff were closing the barrier you had to sprint to get through, or duck under, the barrier; meaning the faster competitors could gain an advantage – it became quite competitive, despite the charitable nature. Being a member of Round Table 2, and fairly high profile through my sporting achievements, I was nominated to represent our Table for this historic event.

It was just after 5am, and daybreak was still 45 minutes away, when all ten Table representatives arrived at the designated meeting place beneath the iconic Star Ferry clock tower. A fenced area had been set up for helpers from other Tables acting as scorekeepers, collators and signature collectors, to verify each individual's crossing. Despite the early hour there was a buzz of excitement as the helpers went about their business, setting up tables and chairs, and a scoreboard to keep track of the race. Being early June, the air was very muggy, though light rain was doing its best to drop the humidity as we sheltered under the clock tower before the start of the race.

Those who visited Hong Kong prior to 2006 might remember that magnificent clock tower that dwarfed the Star Ferry concourse. The 'turret clock' was a gift from John Keswick (the tai-pan of Jardine Matheson), who in turn had received it from the Prince of Belgium. It was very much the focus of attention on completion of the ferry pier in 1957, and would chime every quarter of an hour. The actual mechanism was manufactured by the same British company that provided the mechanical signature for 'Big Ben' in London. Sadly, the old pier was knocked down and then relocated in 2006. Hong Kong lost a bit of its character that day. And, unfortunately, it certainly wasn't the last of Hong Kong's historic buildings to feel the weight of the wrecker's ball. All in the name of progress.

Each representative in the Ferrython secured their own sponsors: I had Cathay Pacific, the Hong Kong Hilton hotel, and many individuals. This meant I had to wear a dozen or so different caps over the 20 hours ahead of me, with many changes of sponsors T-shirts. I was probably one of the fittest of the ten contestants, but, unbeknownst to my rivals, I almost had to pull out of the event 48 hours before it started.

I had played in a football match a few days earlier and suffered an injury which resulted in two fractured ribs; leaving me with a fair bit of discomfort and a trip to the doc. I explained to the doctor that there was so much riding on this charity event that I could not pull out; so he strapped bandages tightly across my chest and said I was good to go.

Nowadays, that would certainly not be the protocol for such an injury; but that's how it was back then.

I also asked him for some sea sickness tablets for the 20 hour journey ahead of me.

When I got the pills the nurse said to me, "Are you going on a long sea journey, Mr Currie?"

"No, I'm going on the Star Ferry!" I said. At this she burst out laughing. I never told her it was for 20 hours!

I believe I had one big advantage: my right-hand man. Without him I might never had made it. His name was Alan Railton, a character in his own right, but Mr Dependable for me that muggy day in June. Even thought heat and humidity were at their highest during that month he came through.

Alan was a fellow Round Table No. 2 member and a handy sportsman, playing hockey and tennis at quite a high level. In fact he was pretty much a dab hand at most sports, but most importantly for me, he was a good runner. One of his jobs was to help me change sponsors' T-shirts and hats – which he kept tucked inside a Cathay Pacific carry-on bag; advising when to make those changes and photographing me to satisfy our sponsors.

While I would be sprinting to the designated area to sign my name to verify each crossing, Alan would be checking the quickest way to get on the next ferry: sometimes suggesting we go second class if there was a long queue for first. He would also carry the coins we needed to put into the turnstiles in payment to get on the ferry; no smart cards in those days.

Bearing in mind he was carrying a bag, Alan would sometimes encourage me to race ahead of him if we heard the whistle for the barrier ahead to be closed. But amazingly we never got separated; there was a side gate for staff, which Alan was allowed to use to join me on the ferry. After all, he was not a competitor. We made a good team.

As lunchtime approached we had the luxury of silver service, courtesy of the Hong Kong Hilton, one of our main sponsors. In full uniform, a waiter came on board the ferry with a well-stocked trolley of food and drinks; which had to be consumed a lot quicker than we would have liked. We even had a glass of champagne, but that was all the alcohol we consumed that day.

I recall John Norman, who was also a senior policeman in Hong Kong before he joined Interpol, was representing his Table, and also received his lunch on board the same ferry. One of his sponsors just happened to be the famous Kowloon bar 'Bottoms Up'. The Tsim Sha Tsui establishment, managed by that wonderful lady Pat Sephton and briefly featured in the James Bond movie *The Man With The Golden Gun*, was famous for its sexy female bar staff.

Unfortunately John only got sandwiches, while Alan and I devoured our juicy steaks; but his waitress was a lovely lady wearing a traditional Bottoms Up uniform, which covered considerably less of her body than the white-shirted uniform worn by our Hilton Hotel waiter.

Quite a few of those on board the ferry that Saturday lunchtime became very inquisitive, wondering what was going on and many asked if we were making a movie as the scenario was very different from the regular crossing on an early Saturday afternoon. The only people missing were William Holden and Nancy Kwan (Suzy Wong)!

Radio and television crews boarded the ferry throughout the day conducting interviews for the early news, so there was never any real boredom; that would come late in the evening, and in the early hours of the next morning when the crowds dwindled and the ferry schedule was more drawn out.

When planning the event it had been estimated that each competitor would make around 70 to 100 crossings within the 20-hour period. By 6 in the evening, I had already done 70, and there were 8 hours still to go. However, as we got into the wee small hours after midnight, the time between ferries increased. Sometimes we would sit waiting for 15 minutes or so until another ferry would depart. More crossings could I'm sure have been made, but the final number was dictated by the ferry timetable.

Nevertheless, it was very satisfying to know that I had caught every ferry available in those 20 hours, thanks to the speed I still had in my 30-year-old body, and a little help from Alan. It was a long slog and two of the 10 contestants dropped out due to leg cramps.

When I got off the last available ferry I had completed 116 crossings, two clear of my nearest rival, John Maloney, an accountant, but a handy amateur runner. It was just after 2am the next morning. A picture was taken as I was hoisted high on the shoulders of two ladies, wives of fellow tablers. Quite a few people had come down to show their appreciation for our efforts; not just Alan and I, but all the contestants. That picture was sent by wire service across the globe.

I only know this because my eldest brother, working for the *Daily Record* in Glasgow, was shown the photo by his news editor a day or so later. My brother took a copy of the picture and showed it to our Mum. Her reply apparently, as Dick recounted it, was, "He looks dopey with his eyes, has he been on drugs?" On reflection, I suppose that when she looked at the picture she had no idea what I had endured, or indeed what the picture related to, but my sea sickness pills probably didn't help!

My feet were swollen and I had blisters, but willpower and a desire to raise funds for the needy had kept me going; as I'm sure it did for all the contestants who had slogged it out to the end. We actually raised over $100,000, a sizeable chunk in those days, of which a large portion went to the Sai Kung Children's Home, which was not a normally well-supported government charity.

My 'Team Manager' Alan Railton was an enormous help and his companionship throughout made all the difference. In the following year Alan himself competed in the event, but had to carry his own bag, and came up just short of my record number of crossings. A great achievement nevertheless.

Sadly, for all those involved in making the Ferrython a charitable success – publicity-wise, logistics-wise, and in terms of the large amount raised – Guinness never put the record into their sacred Book of Records. It had been raining on and off throughout the day of the event, and a couple of my signatures were slightly smudged, either through my own sweat or perhaps in handling by one of the judges, who knows, it was a sweaty old day. Because of this however, Guinness refused to acknowledge the veracity of the event.

Con Conway – a well-respected man in the Hong Kong community, Vice-President of the Hong Kong Sports Federation, an Olympic Committee Vice-President, and Chairman of Round Table No. 2 – was one of the judges during the Ferrython and was pissed off, to put it mildly. He actually sent a letter to Norris McWhirter, who produced the Guinness Book of Records, expressing his great disappointment and asked them to reconsider. From his lofty office McWhirter did not. The Guinness went flat that day for the many who gave their honest time and effort for such a worthwhile and record-breaking cause. After all, wasn't that the idea behind McWhirter's publication?

It actually mattered little to me, the money we raised was the important factor, McWhirter's record book was a side issue. What's more, my record would never be surpassed using the same rules and format. Hardly climbing the Alps, but even with two fractured ribs, I raised money to help kids in need, and that was as good as conquering Everest. But, I can honestly say, it took me some time before I rode the Star Ferry again.

Despite the ferry pier relocation, and although not exhibiting all its former glory, I would still urge anyone who has never ridden on the iconic Star Ferry to do so if ever you visit Hong Kong.

It is never too late, and the green and white boats will always be an endearing part of Hong Kong history, well, I hope they will despite economic times being hard for the grand old company. I might suggest however that one crossing might just be enough!

As you might have noticed, I seemed to be a sucker for punishment. But my next noble gesture came out of the blue, and ended up with me being black and blue!

I was sitting comfortably, I say comfortably, but the old stand that encircled the Hong Kong Football Club pitch was anything but pleasant on the rear end, just pure, rock hard concrete, unless you had a cushion, but who carries a cushion?

The Blarney Stone 7's Shield was being played at the old ground. There was just a handful of spectators, of which I was one, but that was about to change. I could never really call myself a rugby aficionado, but I liked watching most sports, rugby included. The old rugby hands who propped up the bar in the Football Club would often rib me, saying I should be playing a man's game, the ball I kicked was the wrong shape. Even to this day former Welsh rugby captain Mike 'Spikey' Watkins now residing in Bangkok tells me the same thing when we occasionally meet for an ale.

The rugby lads at the HKFC were a great bunch of characters in those days, particularly the older crowd. Two of whom were Jack Moran and Ray Bruce who both worked for the Fire Services in senior positions. I was at the HK Sevens in 1980 when the Hong Kong Football Club ground was flooded during the tournament and the Fire Services were called in to help drain the field. But it wasn't Jack or Brucey pumping out the water or taking control of the situation, they were busy helping to drain pints in the Club bar. "Delegation" was their answer to questioning looks.

Back in the stands at the Blarney Stone 7's I was minding my own business when I was approached by Paul Ogolther, skipper of one of the Club sides who were due to play their semi-final tie in a half-hour's time. Oggie, as he was known, was a quality player. He had been a member of Hong Kong's first international Sevens squad and also played against Wales, when they jetted into Hong Kong for a one-off match in 1975. A Welsh side that contained Gareth Edwards and Mervyn Davies with John Dawes as their coach was not a bad team! Wales managed to scrape home by 57 points to three. Ian Duncan, a hotelier with the Hong Kong Hilton got the three points for the home side.

"A couple of our lads are injured, so we're short of a player for the semi-final Derek," Oggie said, "do you fancy playing for us?"

"You're kidding," I said. "I've never played rugby in my life, and if I got injured I hate to think what Seiko might have to say."

Ten minutes later he came back, "I've spoken to the opposition and they know the situation, nobody will manhandle you." On that basis I agreed to play.

I changed and started to warm up. It felt very weird throwing a strange oval ball to team-mates rather than kicking it. Although I did take the opportunity to practice some four or five conversion kicks to get my eye in, just in case I was called on to stick the ball over the bar and between the posts – again, something alien to me as I normally tried to keep it under the bar!

The game had barely started and there was a line-out in our favour. We won it, and as I was standing at the end of the line the ball was passed to me. I had barely caught it when the wind was knocked out of me; I was pole-axed by Will Layfield, a six-footer who worked for HSBC and was the Club rugby section captain that year. I thought it was meant to be a semi-friendly game as it was two Football Club sides against each other. Evidently not!

Layfield got an ear bashing from Oggie and some of my team-mates, but in reality, the big fella was only playing to the code and tackles were part and parcel of the game. However he did apologize for the hefty challenge as I struggled to my feet. There was no way I was going to show any sign of weakness and continued the game.

Now I was fast, probably faster than anyone on the field, but one thing I learnt that day playing rugby, is that when you make tackles it saps your energy and strength. It was my first experience of actually playing rugby, but I soon realised that as the flying Scot, I was a lot faster with a round shaped ball to chase. The match ended in a draw, I think 7-7, so it was to be decided by sudden-death conversions from a designated point in the field.

I fancied myself to take the kicks for our side, despite the oval shape; I had been sending them sailing over the bar in the pre-match warm-up. I urged Oggie to let me have a go, but he overruled me, he was the captain and he took them, probably rightly so, but I had offered. After converting his first kick, his second unfortunately scraped the outside of the post. The opposition converted both theirs.

I was a little disappointed: one minute I was sitting in the stand as a spectator, the next I was one game away from playing in a Blarney Stone 7's Shield final. A grand old competition which was first played at the Club ground in the early 1930s. But my budding rugby career was over. I might never have played rugby again, but that's not to say I couldn't still sing the songs.

During a few beers with the lads at the Hong Kong Football Club someone mentioned that people were recording albums of rugby songs and making money out of selling them. Peter Trace, a rather tall well-spoken elegant Englishman, or 'The Commander' as he was known in certain circles, decided it was time the boys from Hong Kong got in on the act. He therefore took it upon himself to bring together a group of fellow rugby players and friends to make a demo recording.

Naming them 'The Dogs' he took his pack of Hong Kong's finest to House Records studio in Aberdeen and set about taking the music world by storm. Lionel Richie, Stevie Wonder, Paul Simon, Kenny Rogers and others were successful just under 10 years later with *We are the World*, but we were the pioneers. Unfortunately, we were just not very good singers. Although, to be fair, the Welsh boys in 'The Dogs' were more than passable and a few others could harmonize reasonably well.

Following in the footsteps of some well-known bands from the sixties we got well stocked up with cases of beer; much of which was consumed before we even arrived at the recording studio. It could have been the Magnificent Seven, the Dirty Dozen, but there were thirteen of us including 'Charlie', our very own sound engineer, who during the day masqueraded as an advertising copywriter and amateur footballer.

'The Commander' had as his sub-lieutenant, ginger-haired Taff Reel, nicknamed the 'Singing Policeman' because he was actually a policeman and he could sing a bit. Three others were also in the Old Bill: South African Bill Baillie; Scotsman Norrie Rae; and Englishman Mike Horner, who would rise to the dizzy height of Assistant Commissioner of Police (Crime) in Hong Kong.

Geoff Prichard, an Englishman who flew with Cathay Pacific, was another Dog; and in truth we were all flying after that session in the Aberdeen studio. Doctor Mike Fleming, who had assisted me in the past, and, was often the doc on call at the famous Hong Kong Sevens was also there, more to do the drinking than to administer medicine, unless of course someone fell down.

Also there was Ian Findley, a London boy who claimed *Ready Steady Go!*'s Cathy McGowan and singer Georgie Fame were his pals before he arrived in Hong Kong. Unfortunately he didn't have a voice like Georgie, but, to be fair, he did play football like Cathy McGowan, said the sound engineer – rather harsh, but good banter.

And then there was adman Barry Arnold. He was the sponsor paying for the recording studio and the ale, of which he supped more than anybody else, until he remembered he was the man paying the bills! Bernie Poole and I were the only professional footballers. Bernie, being a true Scouser, did a great rendition of *In My Liverpool Home*, one of the few songs sung that day without any foul language. I just joined in the chorus.

Last, but not least, was Welshman Colin James, with his trademark 'tash' as thick as the one Tom Selleck sported in Magnum P.I. who, when I first met him at the Football Club, told me he was the best rugby player in the bar. Other players later emphatically told me he was far from it. However what they didn't realize was that, at the time he made this claim, it was only him and I in the bar! Taff, the singing policeman – also known as the Welsh Mario Lanza – insisted that the first song to be sung was the Hong Kong Rugby national anthem. Many will know the words:

"Me no likey Blitish sailor,
Yankee sailor I adore.
Me no likey Blitish sailor,
Yankee pay five dollar more.
Yankee call me honey darling,

Blitish call me bloody whore.
Yankee stay one night and leave me,
Blitish here for evermore!"

That was followed by another fairly polite local classic:

"If you ever go across the sea to Kowloon,
on a bright or foggy day.
You can watch the barflies crawling over Wan Chai,
or you can watch the sun go down on Causeway Bay,
on Causeway Bay."
(To the tune of *Galway Bay*)

Most of the other songs are unprintable, but that Saturday was one of the funniest days we ever had together. We were all young – well, reasonably – and took the day for granted. The trouble is, you don't appreciate it at the time, it becomes a memory that can never be replicated. But that's what memories are made of. They may not be Dean Martin's lyrics, but the message is the same.

Sadly a couple of 'The Dogs' are no longer with us and a few have lost a bit of their bite.

I still have the cassette tape we recorded that day, when we were all just young pups, although it never made vinyl, it was a barking success for 'The Dogs'.

22

The long goodbye

After eight good seasons with Seiko, countless trophies, and netting around 200 goals in their colours, it was time to think about the world outside football.

Seiko had plans to bring new blood into their ranks and my time with them had run its course. In the season 1979/80 I had helped the 'Watchmen' win the First Division title, the FA Cup and the Senior Shield. I was 31 years old, Hong Kong was my home, and I was well known publicly, so, I'm pleased to say, opportunities outside football came knocking.

I knew I could get some football commentary work on TV, and it was time to move away from the playing field and enter the field of business, albeit very slowly. My mate Walter Gerrard had already done this, working in the wine and spirits department of the East Asiatic Company or EAC for short. He suggested that I try out a part-time job with the company. A wage that would supplement playing football part-time would certainly be welcome so I decided to give it a go.

EAC had some interesting wines, including the popular Portuguese Mateus Rose on their list, so with contacts made over the years, I was able to flog quite a few cases. At this time I also joined a rather exclusive group called the 'Monday Club', made up of jockeys and horse trainers in Hong Kong. As the name suggests, after a weekend at the race course they liked to let off steam by having a big day out on the Monday. Suffice it to say, they were very good customers and helped my wine sales immensely!

In our early days in Hong Kong I mentioned Walter and I had a very good relationship with John Madsen and Eric Bøgh Christensen of EAC. The pair were already working in Hong Kong when we arrived in 1970 and over the years strong friendships were forged with both of them.

In fact, they were instrumental in Walter and I getting into the wine business, and later, for me, the beer industry. Walter and I owe a lot to both these amicable Danes.

As it turned out, when I was looking to increase my workload Carlsberg were looking to open a brewery in Hong Kong as part of a joint venture with EAC. An office was set up in Mongkok in preparation for the opening on April 28, 1981, when Her Royal Highness Queen Margrethe II of Denmark would officially open the Carlsberg Brewery in Hong Kong. My Danish friends arranged a meeting for me with the recently appointed GM of Carlsberg HK, Stig Poulsen. at his office in Pioneer Centre, Mongkok. A handshake sufficed and I was soon working part-time as a representative for probably the best beer in the world – originally brewed by JC Jacobson in 1847.

But I wasn't ready to stop playing football entirely.

You lose your sharpness and fitness with age – particularly when reverting to playing part-time and not training every day. But you never lose your football brain, so I decided to look at my options. Peter Wong, a flamboyant character very much in love with the game, wanted me to play for Eastern, the team that used to kick lumps out of me in my early years with Hong Kong Rangers. But they were a different side from those early years and a very different team in the early 80s, with an emphasis on playing good solid football. So I joined Eastern, but before that I played a for a short while with Seiko's sister club, Bulova.

Bernie Poole had left Caroline Hill and was enjoying a good spell with Bulova and he convinced me to join the 'Junior watchmen' as they were called. But being part-time, Cheung Chi-doy who had become coach of Bulova gave me little game time, much to the annoyance of Bernie Poole, their captain who had lured me there. I decided not to continue my short spell by mutual consent with Bulova after a game against South China in the second round of the Senior Shield. Bulova were down 2-0 at half-time and then they introduced Juan Carlos to their side. Eventually Chi-doy brought me on for the last 15 minutes; Bulova were still behind by the same scoreline. There was a roar of approval from the crowd; they anticipated an exciting finale, and they were not disappointed. Nine minutes later I scored to make it 2-1, but despite coming close again, South China held on by the skin of their teeth.

The *SCMP* the next day questioned why Juan Carlos, an influential player was left on the bench at the start of the game and why a prolific goalscorer like myself, who came on only fifteen minutes from time to score, did not start earlier. The report said "The decision not to use Currie until this stage was impossible to understand and Bulova paid for it... if the Scot had come on for the whole second half this game would surely have gone to extra time."

I had a loose contract with Bulova, and did not expect a lot of game time with them due to my new circumstances, but I decided not to play under Chi-doy any more and left for Eastern and a delighted Peter Wong, their coach. Chi-doy was a wonderful football player but his coaching career only lasted a season.

Tung Fong as Eastern were called locally had a group of players who blended together like a good malt whisky; after joining them football was good again, even being part-time. They had a core of experienced local players including my former Hong Kong team-mate, Tang Hung-cheong. Also in the side were Tsui Kwok-on and Hung Wai-ping. They were joined by some battle-hardened expatriates: former Hong Kong Football club keeper, Scotsman Duncan Waldman – better known as 'Waldo' not the tallest but as brave as a Lion, ex-Crystal Palace, Preston North End and Leyton Orient mid-fielder Ricky Heppolette, and wee Norman Sutton, an excellent dribbler who would ably assist me up front. Steve Waller and Ronnie Doctrove were later added to the squad; both handy forwards.

The side had great chemistry and that's what won us the Viceroy Cup that year, taking big scalps along the way. I suddenly had a new lease of life. Much of that filtered through the enthusiasm of the coach, Peter Wong who encouraged and energized the players. Peter was always positive, despite suffering tragedies in his early life. His father was a Hong Kong tycoon who was kidnapped and killed in 1959 in a case known as the 'Three Wolves', a violent crime which was made into a movie. He lost his wife in a plane crash in the USA but battled adversity admirably. Today he is a well-known football and TV pundit. If anybody deserved a break in life it was Peter Wong Hing-kwei.

I fitted quickly into Eastern and we beat Happy Valley in the first round of the Viceroy Cup. Our next game was against my old club Seiko in the next round of the cup. It was March 1981 at the Hong Kong Stadium – the Hong Kong Rugby Sevens was also being played, but at the Hong Kong Football Club. How times have changed! Wu Kwok-hung was still playing for Seiko as was Billy Semple and Hugh McCrory and other former team-mates. They also had added a central defender, Dave Jones.

If he sounds familiar, he was, Jones had five years with Everton, then moved to Coventry, before Seiko. He would also manage several big English clubs, including a three year spell at Wolverhampton Wanderers.

But that night everything went right for Eastern and I had a hand in one of our first two goals and were leading 2-0 at half-time, a shock was on the cards. I scored with a penalty in the second half and later a perfectly weighted cross of mine found the head of Ricky Heppolette and he made it four. It was a solemn-looking Seiko team who trooped off the field that night and a few of my old team-mates had their heads bowed low, including my old boss Wong Chong-san and coach Chan Fai-hung. But that's the ups and downs of football.

Sea Bee were our opponents in the semi-final as they had knocked out Bulova in a penalty shoot-out in the previous round. Mind you I would have enjoyed playing against Bulova in the semi, but Sea Bee it would be. I scored one and Ricky Heppolette got the other for a 2-1 win and were in the final. I thought to myself; the old dog still has some life in him, what's more Seiko and Bulova are both out.

The final was an epic against Caroline Hill and after extra time and a scoreline 2-2 we beat them 5-4 on penalties with Waldo the hero saving the deciding spot kick. As Captain, Waldo was presented the trophy by the then manager of England, Ron Greenwood, who was flown out as guest of honour It would be my last appearance in a Hong Kong final but every bit as good as my first with a great bunch of guys.

We ended that season with a friendly game against Arsenal, who had finished their season in third place behind Aston Villa in the English league, for the Po Leung Kuk Cup at the Hong Kong stadium. Big Pat Jennings thwarted me from scoring against them with a great save, but it wouldn't have mattered as The Gunners ran out 3-0 winners and it would be Frank Stapleton's last performance for the club before joining Manchester United.

We all went for a meal at the Jumbo Floating Restaurant in Aberdeen harbour after the game. I had a good night and a good blether with their centre-half, fellow Scot, Willie Young but it was tough trying to find a pair of chopsticks to fit into big Pat Jennings's hands.

I could never have imagined having being kicked off the park in my first game at Boundary Street against Eastern I would be sharing joy with them ten years later. Old Father Time can create anything. So much so I was asked to compete in the Super Sportsman heat in Hong Kong which TVB covered on local TV. An event that would be popular for a while in the UK, I think dubbed as 'Superstars'. Famed swimming coach Dave Haller was one of the judges as he was working at the Jubilee Sports Centre in Hong Kong at that time. In the swimming event I was lying second with ten metres to go and finished sixth of eight. Dave told me jokingly he held little hope for me as a swimmer! Having swum at the Tokyo Olympics and coached at ten Olympic Games he could spot a good swimmer, which obviously wasn't me! I bumped into him not so long ago at the Hong Kong Golf Open at Fanling and he asked if my swimming had improved. We both had a laugh at that.

Funnily enough, at the Super Sportsman my best points were in the basketball challenge, so perhaps I should have played for the San Antonio Spurs instead of the San Antonio Thunder.

I also competed in another Charity event for Round Table. It was an event called the Rickshaw Derby held on a course at Victoria Park. We had to pull a rickshaw with a passenger as part of the event, thankfully my team which comprised Ian McWilliams and Alan Railton had a petite Cathay Pacific hostess as our passenger, which made the load a tad lighter. Another long and tiring day but raising money for the needy is always worth the sweat. Which takes me to my last football season in Hong Kong, the 1981/82 season.

It would only be bit appearances for me as the legs were telling me time to slow down, but I still went off on the pre-season training tour with Eastern to the US and Hawaii. Why not?

I had visited Hawaii several times and had fond memories of lying on the beach in Waikiki listening to Jackson Browne pounding out *The Pretender* on my cassette while watching outriggers sailing past and surfers riding the waves. Funnily enough it was through an American guy trying to flog sunset cruises that I met a fellow Jock on one trip, who just happened to be a bit of a musical idol.

The chap handed me a flyer on the beach and when he heard my accent said, "You should meet Eric, he's on his own and he'd probably like to meet a fellow Scot for a drink." I told him I'd be in the Outrigger Bar on the beach for a sundowner at 6pm the next evening. Next night in walks Eric Faulkner of the Bay City Rollers, part of the tartan-clad group who were teen idols across the States from California to Maine, not far behind the Beatles in popularity. We talked about music and a song he recorded called *Shanghai'd in Love* which had lyrics that included:

"In search of love down Wan Chai way I did run… into a sanpan world the night seems so young…"

I told Eric it wasn't love you found in Wan Chai, you had to pay for it! He had a laugh at that. We had a couple of Molokai Mules and a few other cocktails over the next few days.

So I flew off to Hawaii with Eastern then on to Los Angeles and we stayed in the City of Dreams at the Hyatt Sunset on Hollywood Boulevard where you can see all the stars, as the Kinks had aptly sung on their *Celluloid Heroes* hit.

We did actually, Ray Davies was staying in the hotel as was Richie Havens, the man who was the opening act for Woodstock in 1969 and we were fortunate to have a brief chat with Richie, much to the delight of Ricky Heppolette who was a big fan.

Coach Peter Wong went to university in Los Angeles and knew the streets of LA well, so he had us running to the Hollywood Bowl and back to the hotel on Sunset. Some injuries and cortisone injections on the ankles had taken their toll over the years so after a few days of running on concrete, my legs waved the white flag and it was just the swimming pool for me. Where's Dave Haller when you need him?

When I returned to Hong Kong I resigned myself to playing only cameo roles for Eastern in the 1981/82 season and concentrated on my job with Carlsberg.

I officially retired from professional football three weeks after my 33rd birthday in February 1982, but my last game would be against a crack German side.

A pitch invasion, a penalty shoot-out and a farewell lap of honour, seemed an appropriate way to sign off and hang up my professional football boots.

It was Sunday, February 21, 1982. I bumped into a neighbour that day as I was leaving my flat in Paterson Street to go to the game and she wished me well. Her name was Anita Mui. She lived a few floors above me and I would occasionally meet her in the lift as she was on her way to sing in a night club in North Point.

She was not ultra famous in those days, but I knew who she was, and she recognised me: in time she would be dubbed the 'Madonna' of the East and would go on to become one of Asia's best loved singers; until sadly cervical cancer took her young life away at the tender age of just 40. I should have been the one wishing her well! 'Ah Mui' as she was known to music lovers in Hong Kong ultimately became one of their musical treasures.

I walked from Causeway Bay to the stadium, crossing Yee Wo Street onto Pennington Street and finally up Caroline Hill Road. The occasion for my retirement game was the visit of VfB Stuttgart, a founding member of the Bundesliga and one of the leading club sides in West Germany.

I had got myself in shape as best I could and it was agreed I would play the opening 20 minutes; then at half-time receive an award to mark my official retirement.

On that same date 10 years earlier Nixon was shaking hands with Mao Tse-Tung; I would be shaking hands with Hansi Müller. Whereas countless millions had watched Air Force One land in China in 1972, just over 21,000 were inside the Government stadium for my last game.

Former Norwich City goalkeeper Roger Hansbury was now the custodian for Eastern and the club had invited three Norwich City players to guest in the game – Phil Hoadley, Mark Nightingale and Graham Paddon – putting them on short playing contracts. Many of you might remember Paddon from his West Ham United days.

Norman Sutton and Duncan Waldman had moved to Australia to continue their football journey, while Eastern had brought former Peterborough forward Jackie Gallagher into their lineup and had made several personnel changes through the season, although many of the local Hong Kong lads were still in the squad. The evergreen Ricky Heppolette was still around and my old Motherwell buddy from my playing days there, Jim 'Jumbo' Muir had joined Eastern for the season, as had 23 times capped Australian, winger Peter Sharne.

I was flying about like paper on a windy day during my 20 cameo minutes, looking to finish my career with a goal. It almost came. Just before my time was up we were awarded a free kick just outside the box for an infringement against me. Graham Paddon, who was a bit of an expert from free kicks at that range, came over and said to me, "I'll take it, Derek."

"Sorry Graham, it's my last game and I am off shortly, so I'm going to take it, mate."

Now most German footballers are pretty tall, particularly defenders, and Stuttgart had plenty in that category. So getting the ball over their heads and down within the distance I was out from goal was not going to be easy, and their goalkeeper Helmut Roleder was over six feet tall. I needed pace and some swerve. I hit the ball with the inside of my right foot and it sailed over the wall of German defenders. It was dipping just beneath the crossbar, until Roleder rose and tipped it over the bar for a corner.

"Ai ya!" (a Cantonese expression of dismay) roared the crowd, but that was my chance to score gone. I left the field shortly afterwards.

When I came out of the changing rooms during the half-time break the Stuttgart players waited as I headed towards the presentation area. It's not every day Karl Heinz Forster and his brother Bernd, along with Karl Algöwer, Dieter Müller and Hansi Müller (no relation) – with a collection of 178 caps between them for West Germany – bid you "Auf Wiedersehen" for your last day on the professional football field. There was also a Frenchman amongst them, a left-winger like me, Didier Six. He had played in two World Cups and would be part of the squad that would win the 1984 European Championships for France at the Bernabéu Stadium in Madrid.

It was a proud day for me as I collected a lovely silver salver from Lam Kin-ming and his brother Peter alongside fellow officials Lee Leung-han, Tong Yee and coach Peter Wong. As I ran round the stadium carrying the silver salver above my head, inscribed with the words "For his tremendous contribution to the game", the crowd gave me a lovely send-off.

Inside the changing room shortly afterwards I sat for a while after I had taken my boots off and quietly reflected on my career. Then I went back into the stadium and watched the end of the game. There was no score after 90 minutes and just before the penalty shoot-out there was a crowd invasion, catching the police and stewards totally unprepared. They swarmed around players of both sides and I got quite a few pats on the back, but eventually the boys in blue got the fans back to their seats in the stadium.

I don't know what started it, I can only say it was a friendly invasion; perhaps someone thought it was a good idea and thousands just followed. It made front page news and TV coverage. Maybe they thought it was the fans' way of saying goodbye to me on my retirement; although I swear the invasion had nothing to do with me! When the dust had settled

Eastern beat Stuttgart 4-2 in the penalty shootout. There was no further excitement in the stadium; the fans left happy.

I did too, clutching the lovely souvenir given to me by Eastern A.A. for my services to them and Hong Kong football. They were a good, caring club and I enjoyed my swansong with them. As I walked down Caroline Hill Road for the last time, with my football boots in my bag, I again reflected on memories of having played against some of the best players in the world at the Government Stadium. Pelé, Eusébio, Tostão, Carlos Alberto, Manny Kaltz, Yazalde, Clodoaldo, Beckenbauer, Neeskens and so many, many more.

Around thirty trophies; 250 goals; representing my adopted home Hong Kong at international level. I had a lot to be proud of. All due I suppose to a Mr Ian Petrie and a game at Douglas Park in Hamilton one Sunday afternoon almost 12 years earlier.

Despite our differences, Petrie opened the door to Asia and I was lucky to be one of the first through and will always be eternally grateful for that; thanks also go to Pelé who lured me there in the first place.

Not long after I left Eastern, Peter Wong left the club to coach South China and they brought in a new coach who would last eight months with the club. His name was Bobby Moore. Things were not going great for the club and Bobby brought in Northern Ireland winger Terry Cochrane and his former World Cup teammate Alan Ball to try and change their fortunes. Many won't recall, but he also brought in Trevor Brooking for a couple of games. But, like all of us, age had caught up with him, and he failed to make any impact.

I would bump into Bobby now and again at the Hong Kong Football Club where he was given a temporary special guest membership. He would, as usual, call me 'Del Boy' and over his favourite tipple, a gin and tonic, we would beat the gums about life in general or share the latest Hong Kong gossip.

One night, near the end of Bobby's stay, I was sitting in Rumours wine bar, a ten-minute walk from the Government Stadium in Hoi Ping Road and owned by yet another former footballer, Billy Semple and his wife Annie. I had been at the Eastern game that night and half an hour after the game had finished was nursing a half-pint at the bar. Suddenly the door burst open and an unmistakable high-pitched voice cried out, "I won't be fucking needing them again," as a pair of boots were hurled into the furthest corner of the bar. The voice was that of Alan Ball and he wasn't happy. He was pissed off that Bobby, his former World Cup pal, had given him the hook during the game, despite Alan having 72 caps for England. 'Bally' was 37 years of age at the time.

Five minutes later he had cooled down somewhat and was in deep conversation with Bobby mere metres from where I was sitting. I couldn't hear the conversation, but obviously some soothing words were being said by Bobby. Eventually there was a warm embrace and everything was OK again. Why wouldn't it be, these were two of the finest players England ever produced on a football field, and a game at the old Hong Kong Stadium and a substitution wasn't going to change all that.

Bobby Moore, the only Englishman and British player to captain a World Cup winning side, left Hong Kong in March 1983. I would bump into him in later years in Mexico, Italy and Sweden when we were both covering the Euro Championships or the World Cup finals. The last time I saw Bobby was in Gothenburg in Sweden during the 1992 Euro Championship finals.

I had heard Bobby was undergoing therapy for cancer, but that was not common knowledge. Bobby kept it to himself, never mentioned it, so neither had I. He was that type of character, he never wanted any sympathy and fought life's challenges on his own terms. It was surprising to think of his condition because he looked great and was in such a buoyant mood.

"See you in America (for the 1994 World Cup) unless I come to Hong Kong for a holiday before," were the last words I heard from him. I bade him farewell not realizing that would be the last time I would ever have the pleasure of his company. In mid-February 1993 there was a report published that mentioned Bobby's colon cancer problems. A week later while driving to work, I heard his name mentioned on the car radio. As

I turned up the sound I feared the worst. It was to announce the hero of 1966 was dead. A part of me felt the same.

I can still picture him after a gruelling 4,500-mile flight from London to San Antonio in 1976, besieged by soccer fans of all ages at the airport, still signing autographs at least a full hour after landing, with the same cheery grin on his face. He and I might never have been on the same page or been the perfect match to play football together, though we did play under the same colours and beat a side captained by Pelé.

However, what I treasured most was his genuine friendship. He was sadly taken away from the sporting world at just 51 years of age, but Bobby will be remembered for ever as will his heroics in 1966, winning the World Cup and that iconic picture of him holding it aloft.

PART TWO: Life after football

23

Probably the best beer in the world

I suppose you might say that the Jacobsen family were, in a way, responsible for the direction of my life after football. Particularly Jacob Christian Jacobsen that is, better known as J.C. Jacobsen.

Around the time that Louis Pasteur was discovering the mysteries of fermentation, the young Jacobsen was on his way by stagecoach to acquire two pots of yeast from a brewer in Munich; in the mid 19th century it was a long tedious journey from Denmark that took several weeks.

On his return, he used the yeast to produce Denmark's first bottom-fermented beer which he kept in storage cellars around Copenhagen. (Lager is a bottom-fermented beer.)

With money he inherited after the death of his mother he bought land and built a brewery on a hill, or *berg* in the Danish language. At the time, he had a son called Carl, aged five, so he put the two names together and christened his new brewery Carlsberg; literally, 'Carl's Hill' in English.

The first lager beer brewed by Carlsberg emerged on November 10, 1847.

Just under 150 years later I began working for that proud Danish company which boasted that it had 'probably the best lager in the world.' Words delivered in the sonorous tones of Orson Welles during the 1973 advertising campaign certainly gave it gravitas. It was 'probably' the right job for me when I retired from professional football.

A general manager had been appointed for the brewery. His name was Flemming With-Seidelin and he would prove to be the best guy I ever worked under. Kind and considerate, he knew how to get the best out of his staff. My official title was PR manager, but I was a bit of a jack of all trades, turning my hand to sponsorship and brand building, acting as ambassador for the brand and regularly visiting outlets.

When we started producing draught Carlsberg in the early days it was part of my job to persuade outlets to stock it. One of the early problems I encountered was bar space. San Miguel, who had a 70% market share at the time, had bulky draught beer machines which dominated bar counters. However we managed to squeeze our compact machines into outlets to such a degree that San Miguel were forced to purchase new compact machines themselves.

As our presence in the market increased we perceived a niche in the premium beer market for a higher alcohol product. It was decided that we would therefore also produce our stronger beer, Special Brew, which we started selling in cans. Now, put simply, Special Brew is twice as strong as the regular pilsner brew, and is a fairly full-bodied dark golden beer with a good bitterness. It was first brewed in 1950 to commemorate the visit of Winston Churchill to Copenhagen.

It's a strong lager, to be drunk in moderation, but one night, there was an unfortunate event: the brewery mistakenly filled twenty kegs of Carlsberg with Special Brew.

I hasten to add this was a one-off, as quality control is essential in brewing and packaging and was normally scrupulously controlled.

We managed to track down 18 of the 30-litre kegs and had them returned to the brewery unopened. However, two were missing. We eventually discovered that they had been delivered to the Kangaroo Club bar in Chatham Road, Tsimshatsui.

Now I knew the owners of the bar, John McDougall and Ross Way, but I didn't have time to ask for them when we arrived as the manager Stephen Anderson knew exactly what we were there for.

"Sorry they're gone Derek, empty. Last night was one of the best nights we've ever had in the pub, everybody was buzzing. Can we order some more?" said Stephen with a big grin.

He wasn't the only one ordering Carlsberg.

We were beer sponsors of the 1995 Hong Kong Golf Open and I had a request from one of the golfers participating who I knew rather well. He was taking a limousine trip from Mission Hills Golf Course in Shenzhen to his hotel on Hong Kong Island. I asked him if he needed anything?

"Refreshments," he answered.

He had just played in the Heineken-sponsored World Cup of Golf alongside Andrew Coltart finishing in third place. So I arranged a case of Carlsberg, suitably chilled for the trip to Hong Kong. Just as he was settling himself in the car, a leading executive from Heineken stuck his head inside the car to wish him well. He was apparently somewhat aghast to see the ice chest of Carlsberg sitting inside the roomy limousine.

"Different competition, different sponsor," was Sam Torrance's reply. Always cool under pressure, was Sam!

Another day I was standing on a staircase overlooking the playing area at the Kowloon Cricket Club as a Worcestershire Cricket Club touring side were playing a Hong Kong President's select side. Not a huge cricket fan, I had only played the game once and that was for a China Fleet side against the Navy boys stationed at Stonecutters Island, where they kept their ammunition. Hardly the Oval.

But I was here for two reasons: one to check our beer sales, and two to watch Ian Botham in action.

Botham hits two sixes in a row and then hit another screamer, only problem was, it was coming straight for three of us standing together on the staircase! The impact from that hard leather ball could cause considerable damage if it hit any of us.

As it got closer, and I made ready to duck or swerve, a pair of hands appeared and took the catch of the day for me. "Got it, you're out Botham," a voice jokingly mocked. Thank God I thought. Our hero on the stairway threw the ball back onto the field like an experienced fielder. He wasn't though, he was a newscaster: Mark Austin, working that day for ITV sports.

I had met Mark before at the 1988 Euro championships, introduced to me by the late great football commentator, Brian Moore.

"Thanks Mark," I said in relief and offered to buy him a beer, which he duly enjoyed after he did his interviews.

Ian Botham also came into the KCC bar and I offered to buy him one as well. He had recently done an ad for Dansk LA a new Carlsberg low-alcohol product for the UK market.

"Carlsberg or Dansk LA?" I asked straight-faced. Botham laughed and said, "I'll have the real one."

I bumped into Mark Austin in later years at the Foreign Correspondents' Club when he was based for a period in Hong Kong.

"Is that the man who caught Ian Botham at the KCC?" I said to him across the bar. "Do you remember that?" he shot back.

Many might remember Mark for his nightly news programme on ITV and subsequently later with Sky News, but I'll always remember him catching a Botham crowd-threatening six on a staircase and saving my bacon!

The next tales happened in two of the most popular pubs in Hong Kong, sadly both long gone.

The earliest one was the Bull & Bear where one of the most famous footballers of all time made an appearance in the fine old British style pub, without even having a drink. Located on the ground floor of Hutchison House, Central, it first opened its doors in 1974 and became the drinking den that catered to both rich and poor – lawyers and footballers.

Tudor beams dominated the dark interior. There was a small bar on the right as you entered, but the main bar area was up half a dozen steps, followed by a short walk down a corridor. It was the first traditional British pub in Hong Kong and had carpets on the floor, two dartboards and there was even a piano for any budding Liberace. Imported ales from the UK sat alongside local Carlsberg and San Miguel. For a Hong Kong pub it covered quite a large area; but the two toilets were only slightly bigger than a telephone box.

Mine hosts were two larger than life characters: Jack and Phyllis Rodgers – better known as Mr Bull and Mrs Bear. Phyllis was a no-nonsense lady, tall and strongly built – she had formally been one of the famous Tiller Girls in London.

Someone told her one night that a couple were having it away in the ladies toilet; how they managed that I don't know! Phyllis stormed to the toilets, but unbeknownst to her the couple had already departed and an innocent girl had entered the toilet shortly afterwards. The girl was yanked down the stairs and thrown out the door being told, in strong language, never to return. Apologies came later when Phyllis discovered the truth.

Some of the more rebellious footballers who frequented the Bull & Bear used to take delight in a little Bear-baiting. Phyllis couldn't abide bad language or rowdy behaviour so they too were often banned, only to return a few weeks later. Some famous players felt the sharpness of Mrs Bear's tongue in their time.

The Pub also had an Assistant Manager when Mr Bull and Mrs Bear needed time off and he was a larger than life character himself called Jack Holloway. The same Jack Holloway who played the part of Ralph Bellamy the 'Squire' in the long running BBC radio show, The Archers. The Squire had been written out of the show, so was now in Hong Kong. He had also occasionally read out the football scores on BBC sports report at 5pm on a Saturday night, before the days of James Alexander Gordon, and would amuse us sometimes fictionally with the scores.

East Fife 4 Forfar 5 using the high and low tones of his voice when necessary.

A great old character who, if I recall, was in Hong Kong because his daughter was living and working there. Tom Smith was another custodian of the bar when Jack and Phyllis were not around and would eventually part own the bar.

Anyway, one Sunday night in January 1982 I was sitting in the pub having a beer with journalist David Price. Earlier that day my old club, Seiko, had played against Argentinian side Boca Juniors at the Hong

Kong Stadium. In those days Seiko had quite a few former Dutch internationals in their side, including Gerrie Mühren and Theo de Jong. Germany's Gerd Müller had also guested for Seiko that day, but Boca proved too strong and won 2-0.

As we were discussing the game Sonya – spiky hair and red lipstick – who was the bar manager on duty that night, came over to me with a request: "Derek, there are three guys here, they look like foreign footballers, and they want to know some good spots for nightlife, can I get you to talk to them?" I was happy to oblige and as David didn't mind, off I went to meet the 'foreign footballers'.

I didn't recognize two of them, but it took just a fraction of a second to see the third was, amazingly, Diego Maradona. (If they were looking for nightlife I'm not sure how they ended up in the Bull & Bear?)

I'd like to say I spent the rest of the evening talking football with Maradona, but in reality, him and his friends were looking for somewhere a little more exciting than the Bull & Bear, and football was the last thing on their minds. I wrote down a few places that I thought might appeal, and went with them to get a taxi.

I told the driver: "Wan Chai, Lockhart Road". Diego and his friends got in; I went back into the pub.

The famous 'Hand of God' gave me a wave as they sped off. It might have been a different story had I gone with them! Hard to imagine that I would see that same hand famously in use four years later at the Aztec Stadium in Mexico City!

Most cities around the world have a bar synonymous with sport. I'm not talking about sports bars with lots of TVs showing sport, but rather places where sportsmen and sports enthusiasts gather for a drink and a chat. The name certainly doesn't suggest it, but the Dickens Bar in the Excelsior Hotel was Hong Kong's version, with a sporting heritage going back over 40 years. Mind you, Dickens himself was fond of a drink, and there was always plenty flowing in the downstairs bar that bore his name, so in a way, there was a common thread linking the two. The hotel basement was originally a disco of sorts, but it never hit the high notes, and in 1974 the Dickens Bar moved down from the third floor to take its place; much to the delight of the regulars.

The walls in those days were adorned with pictures of Dickens characters – the Artful Dodger was particularly appropriate considering some of the characters that were attracted to the bar – but over the years these were replaced with sporting icons such as Mark Spitz, Tiger Woods, Pelé and Jonah Lomu. I was fortunate to be at the opening of the 'new' Dickens Bar and a year later had the honour to cut the cake on its first anniversary, along with the then manager of the hotel, Peter Daetwiler.

Although British Airways crews frequented the bar when staying in the hotel during stopovers, the hard core regulars were from the local sporting ranks. Footballers, rugby and hockey players would head there after matches to unwind, usually entertained by resident Filipino singer, Ben Balboa. Small in stature, but big on entertainment, Ben was incredibly popular and married to a strong English lady – Ann, I think it was – who liked to sit in the bar and keep an eye on him.

Late one night, after Ben has finished his set and had had a couple of beers, and was eyeing another, I saw her literally pick him up, throw him across her shoulder, and walk out, telling him along the way that it was time to go.

From the 1980s onwards the Dickens became the unofficial bar of the Rugby Sevens for locals and tourists alike. Over the years many a sporting great had an ale and a beat of the gums in the fine old establishment. I recall once sitting with a young Graeme Souness – he was around 19 or 20 years of age at the time – after he had played in Hong Kong with Middlesbrough. As we sipped our beers, he casually remarked, "I like it here, perhaps you could get me fixed up." He was probably joking, but I told him that I thought he would be going on to bigger things in his career, and I was proved correct.

One of the best nights I had in the Dickens was in the company of the legendary John Charles, arguably one of the best of Britain's footballing exports, who went from small star in Swansea to a big hero in Turin with Juventus. Charles could play centre-half or centre-forward, and became

Serie A's top goalscorer at the time. A true legend who the younger generation might never have heard of.

I met this gentle giant one afternoon, purely by accident, during a race day at Sha Tin. He just happened to be sitting with friends in a Loge box in front of mine in the members enclosure. By coincidence, he and his friends had backed the same horse as me in one race and we were all cheering it home, which led to one of his friends talking to me.

He asked me what I was doing in Hong Kong, so I told him I was a professional footballer. He pointed at a tall man in his party and said, "Do you recognize him?" "That's not John Charles is it?" I said. "It is," he replied with a smile.

I ended up taking them all to the Dickens Bar that night; and, yes, they just happened to be staying at the Excelsior. One of the 'Gentle Giant's' friends was a semi-professional singer, so I got him on stage with Ben Balboa and we had a hoot of a night. I might even have sung *Rhinestone Cowboy* myself that night, it wouldn't have been the first time I'd done a duet with Ben.

Peter McParland, who coached the Hong Kong national football team for a year in 1980, would often phone and suggest a drink in the Dickens. The excuse being, he wanted to know the answer to a sporting question, but to give me time to think, he'd wait until we met in the bar before I gave him the answer. Peter was on his own in Hong Kong and didn't know a lot of people, so as he stayed near me, and that was close to the Dickens, it was a natural meeting place.

Old timers will recall McParland helped take Northern Ireland to the quarter-finals of the 1958 World Cup, scoring five goals in the competition before losing out to France. Frenchman Just Fontaine scored 13 goals, which is still a record tally for an individual in a single World Cup final tournament, but McParland's five goals was only one behind a young 17-year-old called Pelé. McParland also scored both goals for Aston Villa when they beat Manchester United 2-1 in the 1957 FA Cup Final. Was it that long ago?

Dutch legend, Johan Neeskens was another to grace the Dickens Bar, and also my couch! My club side Seiko had drawn 3-3 in an evening game against the New York Cosmos, a team which included two World Cup winning captains, Carlos Alberto of Brazil and West Germany's Franz Beckenbauer, plus famed Italian striker Georgio Chinaglia.

The game was part of a Cosmos Asian tour in September 1979.

We were leading 3-2, before Beckenbauer took a dive in the last minute to earn them a penalty and the equalizer. I jest. It was a clear penalty and Chinaglia converted. It would have been nice to say that I was on the winning side against those three famous names, but a draw it was.

Late in evening after the game a few of the players headed to the Dickens Bar and after last orders Johan came back to my place for a nightcap. When my wife got up the next morning, she soon ran back into the bedroom saying there was a man asleep on our couch. I told her he was a very famous footballer and not to wake him as he was very tired.

George Best, Bobby Moore, Willie Henderson and numerous others drank in the Dickens, and even Peter Sellers visited during the making of the *Revenge of the Pink Panther*.

Emlyn Hughes and champion flat jockey Keiren Fallon, who did the Carlsberg Cup draw for me one year, joined me for beer there after the draw. Kieran was riding in Hong Kong at that time; Emlyn just happened to be in town. I remember Emlyn had a smile as wide as the Grand Canyon, and he had me in stitches with some of his footballing tales. Particularly the one about playing one day for England against Scotland at Hampden Park in Glasgow. "This Jock wearing a kilt came and head-butted our bus just after we arrived at the ground, I've never seen anything like it," he told me with a laugh.

Snooker players, Stephen Hendry and Steve Davis also had a tipple at the bar, as did rugby greats Gavin Hastings and Sean Fitzpatrick. Even the 'Big Yin', Billy Connolly, visited. The latter caused me embarrassment meeting him there one day and the conversation went like this: "Billy, we met many moons ago in the Scotia Inn in Glasgow, you might not remember me, but might my older brother, Dick Currie."

"The Scrap Merchant?"

"No, he was a boxer," I said, and felt a right twat.

It was a sad day in 2019 when The Dickens closed its doors for the last time, along with the Excelsior Hotel itself.

It will be sorely missed, especially by those who visited every year during the Hong Kong Rugby Sevens. Dickens may have written Bleak House, but his namesake bar was quite the opposite! Had Dickens still been around he might have written: It was the best of times when it opened; it was the worst of times when it closed!

Mind you, it saved a few of us a bit of money and fewer hangovers.

All That Jazz

My two big brothers got me hooked on traditional jazz at an early age. The record player would boom out the Dutch Swing College Band, Chris Barber, Humphrey Lyttelton and even Scotland's own, The Clyde Valley Stompers. My brothers were a bit older than me, but they also let me listen to the records of Bill Haley and Lonnie Donegan.

Eldest brother Dick got to be great pals with members of the Stompers and even went on a busman's holiday with them in the 50s to Spain. He told me he had a great time, particularly in Sitges, which he recommended to my parents as a great spot for a holiday – we went there five years running!

Despite having a great time, Dick's suitcase, perched on the car rack, broke free somewhere in Catalonia and he had to borrow clothes in Barcelona from his friend, famed Spanish boxer Luis Romero – going home in shorts was not an option.

I was fortunate enough to watch the Dutch Swing College Band live in Manila in February 1986. I remember it well because returning to my hotel in Roxas Boulevard I turned on the radio and Ferdinand Marcos was giving his farewell speech as he fled his beloved country to exile in Hawaii.

But it was none of the above-mentioned jazz bands that I would become extremely friendly with. It was a jazz band from Denmark, who were almost an institution in that country: Papa Bue's Viking Jazz Band.

Led by Arne 'Papa' Bue Jensen, who delighted in strolling about the stage with his trombone, they included Jørgen Svare on clarinet, Jørn Jensen (piano), Ole Stolle (trumpet), Jens Sølund (double bass) and Søren Houlind on the drums.

The Excelsior Hotel brought them out to Hong Kong in the late 80s to play for a week in the Dickens Bar. Carlsberg was the sponsor and I was given the role of looking after them. As it turned out that meant I needed a couple of pints of milk to line the stomach.

I had never heard their music before, but after listening to them perform I believe that there were few better Dixieland jazz bands around at that time and they all became dear friends of mine.

I recall one afternoon taking them for lunch at the Lamma Hilton Seafood Restaurant, which some readers may have dined in as it was (and still is) a well known spot on the isle south-west of Hong Kong Island.

Upon returning to the hotel, I asked Ole Stolle what he was going to do before he went on stage that night.

"I'm going to talk to Johnnie," he told me.

"Johnnie?" I said.

"Yes, Johnnie Walker, I like to loosen my lips before I go on stage!"

All I could do was laugh.

They came to Hong Kong several years running and I visited them in Denmark in 1988 when I made a trip to Copenhagen to visit the Carlsberg Brewery, before going on to Germany for the Euro Championships.

I quietly sneaked into the Tivoli Gardens one night and caught them by surprise; they had no inkling of my visit. Papa, as usual, was strutting across the stage, but came to an abrupt halt when he spotted me. When they finished playing, Papa insisted on taking me to his regular spot for a nightcap or three. I can't remember the name of the bar, but it reminded me of the Mos Eisley Cantina in Star Wars.

I didn't get home too late, my third night in Copenhagen, but the next evening I got no sleep at all. Well, when you're youngish, you can get away with it.

Søren Houlind, the drummer, took me for a couple of drinks after their show and then we went back to his apartment for a nightcap and a good chat. It must have been close to 6am when he suggested we go for a drink after we had drained a few cups of coffee.

"A drink?" I said, amazed.

"Just follow me," he said.

We went to Nyhavn and I was utterly astonished. The bar was three deep with customers – it could have been a Saturday night in a Glasgow pub – yet it was close to 7am in Copenhagen. Søren explained that the bars are open for the fishermen who have been working all night and like a drink or two before they go home to sleep.

I felt like a fisherman, I was flat out at 11am!

The trip to Odense the next day to visit Hans Christian Andersen's house, followed by Denmark's last friendly game before the Euro Championships, was a bit of a blur. I could easily have slept in Hans Christian Andersen's bed but Danny Kaye, who portrayed the famed storyteller in a movie, had tried that in 1963 and felt the wrath of the Danish public, so it was not an option.

Arne 'Papa' Bue died in 2011 at the ripe old age of 81.

Fortunately good old traditional jazz music never dies and I often listen to the band on YouTube and think of the Star Wars bar and going for a pint at 6.30am.

Not even Hans Christian Andersen could make that one up!

24

The Carlsberg Cup

The first time the Chinese New Year football tournament was named the Carlsberg Cup it proved popular with local fans. It was played in 1986 as a triangular tournament between a Hong Kong select side and national teams from South Korea and Paraguay.

The final resulted in a 3-1 victory for the South Americans over South Korea.

I presented the trophy, alongside the Chairman of the HKFA, Victor Hui, to their captain, Rogelio Delgado, and wished him all the best for the upcoming World Cup, to be played in Mexico a few months later.

The following year we added another international side to make it a quadrangular competition. This time the teams were: Hong Kong select, Beijing select, Dalian select, and the Brøndby club side from Denmark. This would be the first time Hong Kong fans caught a glimpse of a young goalkeeper who would go on to become a bit of a legend. Five of his teammates would also be part of the side that won Denmark the European Championship five years later.

The goalkeeper was Peter Schmeichel, the Great Dane!

Brøndby were a young side, managed by Ebbe Skovdahl, an uncle of the Laudrup brothers, Michael and Brian, two of the very best to grace the red and white of Denmark. I got to know the team quite well, we had billeted them at the Excelsior Hotel and aside from the football we had a few laughs during their stay over the Lunar New Year holidays.

The day they arrived Carlsberg hosted a traditional dinner for them in the hotel's Chinese restaurant. The two Danes to my left at that dinner were John Jensen, who Arsenal fans will recall, and Kim Vilfort. Who would have thought that in 1992 they would score the goals that defeated West Germany 2-0 in the European Championship final, and that I would be sitting in the Ullevi Stadium in Stockholm watching them? But for now they were sitting next to me. The chap to my right was a young 23-year-old in his first season with the club, Peter Schmeichel.

With the help of an elastic band I tried to show them how to master chopsticks, but I was not sure that they were enjoying the local delicacies. My doubts were confirmed a little later. Schmeichel asked if I'd played football myself. One of the other guests quickly informed him that I was a bit of an old legend in local football. I was now almost 38 years of age.

I told Peter I used to take the penalty kicks. He smiled at me and said: "Derek, you can take five penalties against me; you will be lucky to score one!" Next day at training in Happy Valley, I took five, scored four, and hit the inside of the post with the other.

All Peter said was "Not bad."

Over the years I have never let him forget that.

As the dinner ended and we were leaving Peter said to me, "Derek, do you know if there's a McDonald's near here?"

"Did you not enjoy the dinner, Peter?" I said, knowing full well some of the dishes were a little too exotic for most of the team.

"Oh, it was fine, but we Danish boys are not used to Chinese food, it's not as filling as we would like."

I took Peter and four of his team mates round the corner to the McDonald's in Paterson Street, which, incidentally, was the first in Hong Kong, having opened in January two years earlier. As we walked back to the hotel they were busy scoffing burgers and fries. The extra calories must have helped, Brøndby won the tournament that year.

I mentioned that Ebbe Skovdahl was the Brøndby manager, he was a flamboyant character, who in later years would have a season managing Benfica and four seasons as manager of Scottish club, Aberdeen.

Taking me aside one day Ebbe asked if I knew any place near the hotel where we could have a quiet beer; he didn't want the players to see, so he was avoiding the popular Dickens Bar. I took him to the Shakespeare Bar, a nice little hideaway, two minutes walk from the hotel run by Ying and her Scottish husband Bill. We sat there on several nights, chewing the fat as it were. Ebbe thought it was a perfect little spot, near the hotel, but far enough away from prying eyes. Well that's what he thought.

Peter asked me one day, "Has Ebbe asked you to take him to any little bars yet? He thinks we don't know, but the players all know he likes a drink."

I got to know Peter Schmeichel quite well and he would do me a big favour for the Carlsberg Cup in 1994, showing what the gentleman he was, on and off the field.

It was midway through the first week in January 1994 when I telephoned Alex Ferguson at his office in Old Trafford. I asked if it would be okay for me to fly to England to make the draw for the upcoming Carlsberg Cup at Old Trafford with Peter Schmeichel.

"No problem Derek," said Fergie, "as long as Peter is happy to do it." He was.

Four days later I flew to the UK. I had a film crew arranged, thanks to Keith D'Arcy of international football agency, Kam Sports International. Keith, a director of the company, had impeccable contacts with many national Football Associations; he was responsible for bringing many of the top club and international sides to our competition over the years. I arrived in Heathrow on a bleak Sunday, then took a shuttle flight to Manchester.

Early the next morning it was bitterly cold and misty as I made my way to Old Trafford; the icy air making it uncomfortable to even breathe – reminded me of when I was sixteen and trudging through the sleet and rain to work in Glasgow in the middle of winter. No wonder people emigrate abroad for some vitamin D. Foolishly I had forgotten to bring suitable clothing. I was just wearing a jacket and tie, but thankfully at least I had a scarf. You forget these things when you live in the tropics.

I arrived at Old Trafford by taxi (with a heater) and was guided to one of their main hospitality suites. Everything was set up nicely: the backdrop was perfect, the film crew were ready, all we needed was the Great Dane. He arrived 5 minutes later.

The idea was to film Peter making the draw. The four competing teams in the hat were national sides from Romania, the USA, and Denmark, plus the HK League XI. A pretty good line-up considering this was only months away from the 1994 World Cup finals in America.

The US side had Thomas Dooley and Alexi Lalas, who had both scored in the 2-0 US Cup victory over England the previous June, and would be coached by Bora Milutinovic. Bora went on to become the only man to take five different countries to the World Cup finals. He would also take three of them to the Carlsberg Cup.

Romania had defender Daniel Prodan and mid-fielder Ilie Dumitrescu in a side which had clinched their place in the World Cup finals by defeating Wales 2-1. Funnily enough, the US and Romania were in the same group for the Finals that year. Would they be paired together in the opening game of the Carlsberg Cup?

I flew back to Hong Kong with the tape and we had a full scale press conference at the Hong Kong Jockey Club auditorium at Sha Tin race track on the Thursday. We showed the draw, plus an interview with Schmeichel, on the auditorium's large screen. Everything went smoothly and the event drew a large gathering of TV stations and journalists. Next day it made the front page of every newspaper in Hong Kong.

All done within a week; it's great when a plan comes together! But let me rewind a few days back to Old Trafford.

Peter did the draw, it paired Hong Kong with Romania, and the US to face Denmark; winners meeting in the final, losers in a play-off for third. After filming, everyone was sworn to secrecy as this would only be officially announced on Thursday, so no loose tongues. I interviewed Peter after the draw and one of the first things he said was that he thought Denmark would win the competition.

"We are a young side and we like touring, I remember winning the Carlsberg Cup with Brøndby back in 1987. I can guarantee we will play good positive football, just as we did in winning the 1992 European Championship."

We briefly discussed individual players and then he wished everybody watching *Gung Hei Fat Choy* – Happy New Year in Cantonese. Excellent interview, I thought. I collected the tape from the production team and continued to chat with Peter. I thanked him for making the time after training to conduct the draw for us. I then pulled out a bundle of pounds and said to Peter, "This is the fee for making the draw, thanks big fella."

"I don't want it, Derek," he said

"Well, can I give you at least £100 to at least take the wife for a meal?"

"No Derek, I am happy to do it for you and the Danish Football Association."

To be honest, I don't know many footballers who would not have stuck the money into their 'sky rocket'. But not the Great Dane, a man of integrity.

As I left I jokingly said, "Can I not give you money to take Kasper to McDonald's?" His son Kasper, now with Nice, was six years of age at that time. Peter just laughed, I think he remembered our little excursion back in 1987.

This time, due to club commitments with Manchester United, Peter could not make the trip to Hong Kong himself, but his national team-mates did him proud. They beat the USA in a penalty shoot-out 4-2 after drawing 0-0 in regulation. The other game also ended in a draw, with Hong Kong eventually winning 5-4 on penalties, to the howls of delight from the local crowd; well it was the Chinese Year of the Dog!

The Danes then went on to beat the Hong Kong League XI 2-0 in the final at the Mongkok Stadium, with a performance that was fit for royalty. Which was just as well, as Prince Joachim of Denmark was in the crowd. What's more, the young prince had really entered into the spirit of the occasion as he and his friends were all decked out in red and white and regaled the crowd with a few choruses of: "We are red, we are white, we are Danish dynamite!" – the battle cry from the successful campaign at the 1992 Euros in Sweden.

I didn't see Peter Schmeichel again until the 1998 World Cup finals in France. It was after Denmark had defeated Nigeria 4-1 in the Stade de France in Paris. Peter seemed happy to see me, but one of the main Nigerian officials tried his best to avoid me. I'll tell you why!

Agatha Christie might have titled it *The Case of the Missing Suitcase* which happened at the official teams dinner on the night before the 1998 Carlsberg Cup tournament was due to kick off. We were entering the Year of the Tiger; but this concerned eagles, not tigers.

The 'Super Eagles' was the nickname for Nigeria and they would be participating in the tournament, alongside Iran and Chile, plus the local Hong Kong League XI. The welcome dinner, hosted by the HKFA, was in the Chinese restaurant at the Ramada Renaissance hotel on Peking Road, Tsim Sha Tsui. As we were getting to the end of proceedings it was time for the visiting team managers to exchange souvenirs with the HKFA, a traditional ritual for any tournament.

The stocky gentleman in the seat next to me began looking somewhat uncomfortable. Eventually he whispered to me, "Derek, we forgot to bring souvenirs! What should I do?" Despite having a couple of Carlsberg's inside me the little grey cells, as Poirot would say, were still working. To calm his anxiety I simply said, "When it's time for you to receive your souvenirs, just apologize and tell them that the suitcase with your football gifts was lost in transit."

The gentleman in question was Head of the Nigerian Delegation and very happy to take my suggestion on board. When invited up to the small stage to receive his souvenir, he apologized profusely to the assembled audience, saying that two of the team's suitcases were lost in transit, one of which held their souvenirs. Great I thought, that sorts that out.

But instead of leaving it at that, he went on to say that he would make sure that each Association received their Nigerian souvenir at a later date. Mm, we'll see about that I thought.

When my burly friend arrived back at our table, he solemnly whispered to me, "Thanks for that Derek, I will definitely send the souvenirs, and I'll include one for you too." Keith D'Arcy, who had arranged the visiting sides for the tournament, was sitting near me during the dinner and was aware of our conversation. Over the course of the next few months, Keith and I would joke about when the souvenirs might arrive. They never did.

Five months later I was in the Stade de France press room for the post-match conference after Denmark had just beaten Nigeria 4-1 to reach the quarter-finals of the World Cup. I was there to have a chat with Peter Schmeichel, and anyone else I might know from the Danish FA.

Suddenly, who caught my eye, but the gentleman from the 'Super Eagles' who was going to post the souvenirs five months earlier. I think he must have remembered his promise, as he took flight when he saw me! He was never seen again, nor were the souvenirs!

The Lunar New Year tournament in Hong Kong got mileage from Alaska to Zambia, with highlight clips shown on CNN and other news channels across the globe. Sometimes I would get useful feedback or advice along the way as the tournament progressed, no more so than in 1995 when the new 40,000-seater Hong Kong stadium hosted the event for the first time.

There was an exciting line-up that year featuring Yugoslavia, South Korea, Colombia and the Hong Kong League XI. Three years in the football wilderness during the political upheaval in the Balkans, Yugoslavia had been allowed back by UEFA, now being the Federal Republic consisting simply of Serbia and Montenegro. Their first officially recognized tournament would be the Carlsberg Cup.

FR Yugoslavia had played two friendly games in South America over the Christmas period to warm up for the event, losing by narrow margins: 2-0 to Brazil in Porto Alegre, and 1-0 to Argentina in Buenos Aires. They had some great players in their side. Dragan Stojković, their captain, has long been considered one of the best players in the history of Yugoslav and Serbian football. Aston Villa fans will remember striker, Savo Milošević, who later would be Assistant Manager for Montenegro, as an exceptional goalscorer.

Strangely enough, it was the President of the Yugoslav Football Association who would give me advice after the tournament that year. South Korea faced Colombia in the opening tie, the first day in the Chinese Year of the Pig. The second match therefore was the local League XI against Yugoslavia. Just like Yugoslavia, Colombia had to put some bad 'joss' behind them. I am referring to the untimely murder of their national player, Andrés Escobar, six months earlier, following the World Cup finals in the USA. They included some new players in their side, but the man Hong Kong fans wanted to see was their ultra-flamboyant goalkeeper René Higuita, famous for his 'Scorpion Kick', and for coming out of his 18-yard box to link up play with his team-mates, or at least try to.

He didn't disappoint on either count! However, his side still lost 1-0 to a goal by Korean talisman Choi Yong-soo in front of 30,000 excitable fans. The South Koreans, who had played so well at the World Cup in the US, were into the final.

Milošević then scored two goals for Yugoslavia to help them beat the local League XI 3-1 in the second match of the day. Ricky Cheng Siu-chung getting the solitary goal for the hosts. A few days later the local League XI lost again, going down 3-1 to Colombia. Dale Tempest getting a consolation goal for the home side.

Despite the disappointment, the home fans were again kept entertained by Higuita. He even managed to produce a scorpion kick that had 30,000 people shouting *"Wah!"* as with one voice (an exclamation of exuberance in the local dialect).

The final proved to be a tense affair; scrappy fouling and few good passages of interlinking play, but just after the break a near-post header by Darko Kovačević, from a wonderful cross by Savo Milošević, broke the deadlock. The goal was enough for Yugoslavia to win the Carlsberg Cup, historically, probably the last cup success under that flag.

Shortly after the game I received the few words of advice in the VIP room. They came from the legendary Miljan Miljanić. He had a suggestion as to how to improve the tournament. Miljanić had coached

Real Madrid from 1974 to 1977, winning double La Liga titles and he was the all-powerful President of FR Yugoslavia. Such was his status that he was awarded the highest order in football, the FIFA Order of Merit. I was all ears!

"Derek," he said, "you have a wonderful tournament, only one thing is missing, you need international referees." He was right of course, the local referees did their best, but fell just below the international standards really required for the calibre of tournament, particularly with the world coverage it was now receiving.

Incidentally, Carlsberg in Copenhagen were loving it: free advertising for all their markets, without Head Office spending a penny. Perhaps they might like to help cover the costs I thought; but sadly no, I still had to arrange everything myself!

I took Miljanić's advice and tried to convince the HKFA to allow international referees to handle games. I thought it through, and then approached the FA with my suggestion: if we bring out international referees to officiate, then during their stay they can give seminars, passing on their unrivalled knowledge and experience to local officials. The international referees would officiate the HK League XI games, while other games might be allocated to a local referee, if the circumstances were right. I also emphasized that the referees I had in mind had a wealth of experience handling European and international matches, so they would not be intimidated by players or crowds.

Good sense prevailed, they agreed.

One problem I had was getting the referees: remember in those days they were not full-time professionals, they had day jobs. The first one I secured had been voted 'referee of the year' in both 1991 and 1993. He was also one of the youngest ever appointed to officiate at the World Cup finals: Italia '90. His name was Peter Mikkelsen. Peter, a Dane, was also working at the time in human resources for a Danish company, which explains how we met, and led to the following little yarn.

I introduced myself on meeting him and innocently asked: "Aren't you the man who launched David Platt's career?" Platt would go on to play for big-money clubs Juventus and Sampdoria after two years at Aston Villa. He didn't seem to understand quite where I was coming from so I followed up with: "You were the man who gave England a free kick in the last minute of extra time and David Platt became an instant hero by scoring the winner against Belgium in Bologna."

Gascoigne had floated the free kick over, and Platt, on the half-turn, had blasted the ball into the net for victory, and a place in the last eight of the World Cup finals at Italia '90. I remembered it well, I had been covering the match. "Yes" he said with a smile, "perhaps you could say that."

Okay, fast forward. I'm sitting in the Star Sports studio in Singapore with former Liverpool and England player, Steve McMahon. It's the wee small hours of the morning and we're off air before watching live Champions League matches on a split screen – we were both pundits that night.

Not sure how it came up, I think it was while discussing Italia '90, but I told Steve the story about my first meeting with Peter Mikkelsen. With a dead-pan face, McMahon said to me, "He wasn't the one who made Platt famous, it was me!"

"How do you mean?"

"I was the one who got substituted in that game so he could come on!" Steve said.

Brilliant, I thought with tears in my eyes. "Sorry Steve."

"No problem, it's a fact, not Mikkelsen, me!"

Well, you learn something every day.

After meeting Peter Mikkelsen I was able to sign him up for the Carlsberg Cup. I then managed to get another international referee; this time from the USA. His name was Esfandiar Baharmast, but better known as Esse. He was an Iranian-American and well respected having refereed at the Olympic Games and in CONCACAF Gold Cup matches. He would go on to officiate at the 1998 World Cup finals.

I'm pleased to say both referees lived up to our high expectations. The 1996 event featured Japan, Poland, Sweden and the League XI and was played before 30,000 fans, with Sweden beating Japan 5-4 in a penalty shoot-out in the final. The tournament was flourishing and with our international referees on board, the players now had full respect for the officials.

In subsequent years, Hugh Dallas, Anders Frisk, Leif Sundell, Willie Young and even Kim Milton-Nielsen – who many will recall for sending David Beckham off in a World Cup tie against Argentina – officiated at the tournament.

However, things changed in 2002.

The HKFA were quite insistent that from then onwards we should only use Asian officials as the tournament was being played in Asia. By then, there were lots of good referees in Asia, so we gave it a try, going back to local referees. But what happened in 2003 would make news all over the football world.

It was perhaps fitting, after spending seven years in Glasgow with club side Celtic, that Denmark's captain Morten Wieghorst should stride out of Chek Lap Kok airport carrying a copy of Pamela Stephenson's book about her husband, simply entitled *Billy*.

"Any good?" I asked him, nodding at the book.

"Aye, great," he replied, in an accent more Glaswegian than Danish.

Wieghorst was in town for the Carlsberg Cup. But little did he know the fun in store for him: he would play the leading role in a sketch that even Billy Connolly couldn't have dreamed up. The tournament was to be played from February 1 to 4, and featured teams from Denmark, Iran, Uruguay and the League XI. It was to herald the Year of the Rooster, which seemed appropriate as it almost ended up as a major cock-up!

The Asian Football Confederation had been leaning on the HKFA to get them to appoint either local or regional referees for tournaments such as the Carlsberg Cup. In the previous year there were two referees from the region: one from Japan, the other a South Korean; both had World Cup experience. The winds of change however were being dictated by the AFC and this year local refs were chosen.

For the opening game between Denmark and Iran the HKFA appointed Hong Kong's Chiu Sin-chuen to officiate. Things seemed to be going well and approaching half-time the game was still goalless. Suddenly a piecing whistle sounded.

Everybody in the stadium, bar one, assumed it was the half-time whistle. I stood up ready to look after the VIP guests. When the whistle blew an Iranian defender had the ball at his feet, nobody was near him except his goalkeeper. He flicked the ball to his keeper, who passed it back to him and he picked it up, then drop-kicked a short pass to the referee, assuming they were all about to walk off for half-time. Wrong.

It was not the referee who had blown for half-time, it was someone in the crowd! That's when the fun started.

This time it was the referee who blew his whistle and pointed to the penalty spot. The Iranian players went crazy! I quickly jumped out of my seat and headed for the Danish bench and their coach, Morten Olsen. It was pandemonium. The Iranians were about to stage a walk-off, the whole event was in jeopardy.

Eventually everybody realized what had happened and, to be honest, any referee with a modicum of common sense would have picked up the ball and signalled to both teams to walk off for the half-time break. End of! At the very least he could have used FIFA rules to award a dropped ball at the edge of the penalty area. But the local referee stubbornly insisted it was a penalty.

Morten Olsen was in discussion with his captain Morten Wieghorst who was to take the spot kick. Olsen saw me coming and signalled not to worry, he had the situation in hand.

He spoke quickly with Iran's coach, Homayoun Shahrokhi who began to smile. I figured out what was going to happen, but did the fans in the stadium?

Wieghorst walked up to the penalty spot and put the ball down. He took a few steps back, and then calmly side-footed the ball three yards wide of the goal. The stadium erupted in cheers.

The Dane got a standing ovation; even the Iranian defenders high-fived him as he ran back to his own half. This time the referee did blow, it was half-time.

Suffice it to say that when Iran got a penalty of their own, four minutes or so into the second-half, there was no stroking the ball casually wide of the mark, it was buried in the corner of the net. Iran were 1-0 up.

Denmark had claims for a penalty near the end, which I thought should have been given, but the referee disagreed and Iran won 1-0. The victory proved to be a side issue, the main story, which was covered by print and TV across the world, was Wieghorst's act of 'Fair Play' – which just happened to be the FIFA motto. Just a pity the local referee never considered that. CNN called it the 'Play of the Day,' while other print media described it as a supreme act of sportsmanship and fair play. On this occasion football was the winner. After the game I had a talk with Wieghorst.

"Can you imagine," he said, "if I was playing for Celtic against Rangers at Parkhead in front of 60,000 fans and was asked to do the same thing?"

"Not in a million years!" I replied

Next up was the final between Iran and Uruguay. The South Americans having beaten the League XI 3-0 in the other match. On paper it looked a highly charged game.

Despite that high probability, it was given to another local referee, Fong Yau-fat; and in fairness to him, someone with SAS training might have struggled to control the match! A bad tackle, just five minutes into the final, left Iran's up-and-coming 18-year-old star, Hossein Kaebi with a six-inch-long stud mark just above his knee. Amazingly, Uruguay's captain, Martín Ligüera, who was responsible for the challenge, never received a card.

Certain players took this as an indication that they had a weak referee and that was a recipe for disaster. The football equivalent of the Gunfight at the OK Corral was on the cards.

The *South China Morning Post* took up most of the back page with the story of the game, but there was little mention of who had won and how the game had gone, it was mainly devoted to off-the-ball incidents. It would be fair to say that the local referee was somewhat out of his depth. I genuinely felt sorry for him, the behaviour of both teams would have pushed a vastly experienced referee to the limits.

A real free-for-all took place in the 89th minute of normal time after Uruguay's Horacio Peralta kicked Iran's Alireza Vahedi Nikbakht as he was lying on the turf. Both benches emptied onto the pitch, with a posse of security staff right behind them. In the ensuing brawl punches were thrown. Eventually things calmed down and Peralta was sent off. As for the actual match itself: it ended 1-1 and was decided on penalty kicks, with Uruguay winning 4-2. But football was not the winner that day.

I met a lot of good football men over the years through the tournament, who I still like to count as friends. Roy Hodgson, who came over coaching Malmö; Roy gave me a Malmö tracksuit for my 40th birthday and came back twice later with the Swiss national side. Morten Olsen, Steen Dahrup and Simon Rasmussen of the DBU (the Danish Football Union) and Frits Ahlstrøm who later joined UEFA as their Media Director are just some of many.

My last involvement with the tournament was the year following Uruguay's win, when the teams involved were Sweden, Norway, Honduras and the League XI. Suggestions from certain quarters to bring Uruguay and Iran back for 'Rambo 2' were quickly dismissed.

25

The Jockeys Dash

In the popularity stakes, two sports were neck and neck in Hong Kong: football and horse racing.

Followers of both were very much target audiences for Carlsberg.

In horse racing, San Miguel were a shoo-in with the Jockey Club after sponsoring the first ever commercially backed race in 1980: The San Miguel Silver Tankard for horses in classes 1 and 2. It became a very popular event on the racing calendar.

I spoke to Flemming With-Seidelin, Carlsberg GM, telling him that I thought we too should get involved more closely with the Jockey Club; both to lift the Carlsberg profile and increase beer sales – after all, finding winners was thirsty work.

Flemming ruled out sponsoring a race, he didn't want to be seen to follow the same path as San Miguel, so he asked me to come up with something more original.

My solution: the annual Carlsberg Jockeys Dash, to be held a week before the racing season started.

The idea was simple: instead of a jockey riding a horse to the finish, they would take part in a foot race to usher in the new season.

I approached Noel McCaffrey, the racecourse manger, with my idea; he gave me an initial green light, but said he needed to run it past a few people 'upstairs' to get final approval.

This was granted, but on the condition that the race would be run on the inside circular sand track at Happy Valley, rather than on the turf!

I tried my best to persuade Noel to let us use the turf; a 50kg or so jockey was hardly likely to damage the pristine grass surface, they were hardly rugby prop forwards.

But no, Noel would not budge on the issue, their turf was as sacred as that at Wembley Stadium. It would therefore be a race on the sand, over 1200 metres – hardly a dash! – at the beginning of September, 1983.

There was 10 entries for the first ever Carlsberg Jockeys Dash that warm, muggy Saturday morning.

Three Australians: Peter Leyshan, Pat Trotter and Rod Staples; a lone Englishman, Wally Hood; and six local boys: Samson Lau, K.L. Tsui, Y.P. Chan, Y.S. Wong, M.C. Tam and W.T. Leung – I had spent a lot of time myself at early morning track work the week before encouraging them to run.

As a reward for participating, all entries were given a case of Carlsberg, along with a cash voucher for a meal at the famed Jimmy's Kitchen.

The winner of the Dash received a voucher for the Peninsula Hotel, with second and third receiving cash vouchers for meals at the hotel.

Everyone was happy.

That was, until they started running on the sand! There was an awful lot of huffin' and puffin' going on during the race; in the old days running on the sand track at Happy Valley was like pushing through a snow drift; a few were under the 'whip' from quite early on.

During the race the field stretched out 'Red Indian' style, with large gaps between runners.

In the last furlong Australian Peter Leyshan stormed home down the straight to be the inaugural winner.

Some of the others however came home on one leg, breathing heavily, like tailed-off runners in the Grand National.

I shouted out that they ran as bad as their tips. It was good banter, and Carlsberg had good press coverage, which was what really counted.

The following year Y.S. Wong became the first local jockey to win.

After five years we moved across the harbour to Sha Tin racecourse and then the event really gained momentum.

Australian John Jeffs, nicknamed 'the Gardner', was the racecourse manager at Sha Tin and had no problem with holding the race on the turf – J.J. as everybody called him could turn a rhubarb patch into a putting surface.

The Dash became a race from the starting stalls – yes we even had starting stalls by this time – and to make it more competitive the distance was reduced to 130 metres, with some of the older jockeys getting a modest handicap start. It was now a true dash!

Television news channels covered the event in 1988, as did the local press, and I had Carlsberg branding on top of the starting stalls and along the race fence.

Carlsberg PR girls held Carlsberg bunting across the finishing line, which ran across the track to the towering horseshoe-shaped finishing post.

Local jockey P.H. Chan won the first ever Sha Tin event, with Philip Robinson winning the following year.

The event went from strength to strength. It was now the unofficial opening event for the horse racing season.

A case of Carlsberg, or Jolly Shandy – another of our products – plus a $700 voucher for Jimmy's Kitchen or Maxim's Chinese Restaurant was given to all participants.

Third place won a $2,000 dinner voucher at the Kowloon Shangri-La Hotel, second $2,500 at the Grand Hyatt Hotel.

Different hotels supplied prizes over the years, but the first prize of $3,500 was always either dinner at Gaddi's, or the Spring Moon Chinese restaurant, both in the 'Old Lady' of Hong Kong, the Peninsula Hotel.

It grew in popularity and was a fun morning out; always held on a Saturday morning, about an hour after track work had finished.

Director of Racing, Philip Johnston, and other leading officials at the Jockey Club, such as Mike Tibbatts or Geoff Lane would go out of their way to attend.

I even had the chief of security for the Jockey Club regularly at the event, Bob Brewer. Not that we expected any illegal activities, but Bob was partial to the odd glass of Danish nectar as his name suggests. A top bloke and always a delight to be in his company.

We would have 16 to 20 jockeys taking part and over the years international participants included Tony Cruz, Paddy Payne, Lance O'Sullivan, Paul Eddery, Steven King, Douglas Whyte, and many, many more.

Thankfully none of the jockeys ever pulled up lame. Mind you, that might not have been the case if we had had a Dash for horse trainers, as was once suggested.

Because it enjoyed good publicity, and was a light-hearted way to start the season, the Jockey Club eventually decided to make the event into a carnival family day, to usher in the new racing season.

They wanted a piece of the action and saw an opportunity.

I had a call from Maisy Chan, who was part of a relatively new line up in the Marketing Department of the Jockey Club, asking if they could incorporate the Carlsberg Jockeys Dash into their plans.

Of course, I told Maisy. I had worked hand-in-hand with the Club over the years, and though we had good cooperation, I was still the one actually inviting the jockeys to run and making it all work!

It was at this time that Lawrence Wong, former Chief Executive of Ford Motor Company in Taiwan, become the first ethnic Chinese to become Chief Executive of the Jockey Club.

In essence, he was a business man, as I would soon find out.

The next year, 1997, the Club Family Day started with barrier trials down the 1,000 metre chute, with pony rides for kids and sideshows; but the Carlsberg Jockeys Dash was still an integral part of the festivities.

A year later, Maisy phoned to ask for a $50,000 sponsorship fee!

I'm sure Lawrence Wong sniffed a money-making opportunity and Maisy was just the messenger.

I could hardly call it my event, or Carlsberg's for that matter, despite handling all the logistics involved over the years and despite it being my baby in the first place.

I told her: "No!"

We had had a good run (excuse the pun) – 15 years. Time to move on. I had no regrets, Carlsberg now had a permanent place on the drinks menu in Jockey Club outlets. No need to spoil the relationship; I wished her well.

One final note...

At every Carlsberg Jockeys Dash I had a photographer to snap the contestants before the race.

I made sure every jockey received a nice framed print of the group wearing their specially-designed tank tops, ranging in colour from pastel pink to yellow to light blue.

They might not have fully appreciated it at the time, but as the years fly by such pictures remind you of happy days when you get older.

Philip Robinson told me recently that he still has his framed photos in his home in Newmarket. Every time he looks at them he's reminded of his wonderful time in Hong Kong.

Memories are made of this, as Dean Martin once sang, backed by The Easy Riders.

26

Rugby shorts

The original Carlsberg office was near where Kowloon Rugby Club played their weekend matches, just a ten minute walk away adjoining the Police Recreation Ground in Boundary Street. At a Friday curry lunch in the Kowloon Police HQ mess, Tony Wolfe, a Kowloon rugby official and player, asked if Carlsberg might be interested in sponsoring a club event.

Now Kowloon Rugby Club were preparing to hold the first ever ten-a-side rugby tournament in Hong Kong, the only other one in Asia, being the Cobra 10s in Malaysia. Rugby and beer, a match made in heaven.

My first sports sponsorship deal for my new employer would therefore be the Kowloon/Carlsberg Ten-a-Side tournament. It turned out to be a great success. Carlsberg provided a nice trophy and silver tankards for the winning team. And who were the first winners?

Well, they just happened to be the Hong Kong Football Club Select, captained by Jim Rowark, who went on to become a local legend in Hong Kong rugby. He would become national coach for both the Hong Kong 15's and 7's sides and was inducted into the local rugby Hall of Fame in 2015. Jim sadly passed away recently in 2021, aged 73. But on that day back in late 1980 with his trademark bushy moustache, Jim was still just a happy 33-year-old enjoying the game he loved.

I recall the day well and still have the picture taken on the roof of the changing rooms overlooking the ground. I was the only one in the presentation picture without a tankard filled with beer. How did I get that one wrong?

Kowloon RFC were a relatively young club, formed in 1976 and our sponsorship of the event continued for close to a decade. I am happy to say that Kowloon RFC still keep up a fine tradition to this day and their major event is now the Rugbyfest which is open to 24 men's teams and 8 women's teams and played just prior to the HK Sevens with sides coming from all over the world. Even travelling fans know they can put 'boots in the bag' as they can make up teams to play in the event, which is followed by a grand dinner with over 600 regularly in attendance.

Changed days since a few hundred spectators lined the field in the days of the inaugural Tens at Boundary Street. But it's great that some things never change: the fun and friendship that rugby seems to bring is still there, certainly at Kowloon Rugby Club.

Carlsberg Tens

With the popularity of Tens rugby growing in the local rugby fraternity, the Hong Kong Football Club decided to hold a Tens tournament to mark their 100th anniversary in 1986. The tournament was a success and became an annual event. In 1988 the Club obtained a major sponsor in Steinlager – a well known beer if you were a Kiwi – who decided to sponsor the HKFC Tens as part of their launch marketing. It made good sense advertising wise and worked well for two years until I came into the picture; then it all changed.

My involvement started with a phone call from fellow Scot, Jimmy Gibson to my office at the Carlsberg Brewery in Tai Po. He wanted a meeting with me at the Hong Kong Football Club and insisted it was important, so could we meet the next day. It was late 1989 and Jimmy had recently become Chairman of the Hong Kong Football Club Rugby Section, and his problem had significant ramifications as he would soon explain to me.

Steinlager wanted to move the goalposts. The boss of the Kiwi company had insisted that if Steinlager were to continue to sponsor the Tens, then during the period of the competition at the HKFC the only beer that could be served in any part of the club would be Steinlager. Being an HKFC member myself, I replied, "That can't happen. A member of the Club cannot be dictated to as to what beer he or she drinks at any of the outlets within the Club premises."

Jimmy concurred, "That's my problem!"

He then asked me openly if Carlsberg could take over sponsorship of the Tens, and emphasized that the Committee were desperate to solve the problem. They badly wanted the event to continue, but anarchy would have reigned supreme in the club if regular drinkers of Carlsberg, San Miguel, Fosters or Heineken were told they could only order New Zealand's finest. The tournament was not that far away and they needed the sponsorship money for the event to continue without any financial disruptions.

"What do you need?" I asked Jimmy.

"50,000 dollars and you would be getting us out of jail and seen as a friend to the local rugby community," Jimmy answered. "Leave it with me for 24 hours," I said.

I had told Jimmy that my sponsorship budget had already been allocated for the year, but I would talk with the then General Manager at Carlsberg, Flemming With-Seidelin and hopefully I could give Jimmy a positive reply the following day.

I explained the situation to Flemming and emphasized that taking over the event would foster, excuse the beer pun, a good relationship for us within the Hong Kong rugby community and certainly with all those that drank at the HKFC. I also mentioned the fact that as the Tens was played on the Wednesday and Thursday, prior to the Sevens at the weekend, many people, including a great number of tourists, would be flocking to the ground at Sports Road. It was a high profile opportunity for Carlsberg that could only enhance our sales at the 30,000-seater Government Stadium, home to the Hong Kong Rugby Sevens.

Flemming knew I had a good eye for opportunities and agreed to find the sponsorship money from another budget, giving me the green light to inform Jimmy Gibson that we would take over the sponsorship of the Tens at the HKFC.

"You've really saved my bacon," said a relieved Jimmy when I relayed the good news. We decided to mark the occasion with a cold Danish lager or three. And that's how the Carlsberg Tens came into existence.

As we got into our second beer I casually told him that Carlsberg also wanted to be the exclusive beer at other club outlets during the two day competition; a horrified Jimmy almost choked on his beer, until he saw the grin on my face and realised that I was pulling his leg!

"Jesus saved Hong Kong" ran a headline on the football pages not long after my arrival in Hong Kong a decade previously; well 'Jesus' saved the HKFC Tens that day, but it was hardly a miracle, just common sense. Suddenly I was involved with the rugby crowd, well I had played the code, if one game counts... okay better not go there. I made a long distance call to my Mum in Glasgow one late Saturday night. It just happened to be St. Patrick's Day, March 17, but there was nothing Irish about the call.

It took her a few more rings than usual to pick up the phone: "Oh sorry Derek" she said, "I had the telly turned up loud as Scotland have just won the Grand Slam!" Even I knew that didn't happen too often. She sounded as excited as any young rugby fan as she described how the TV cameras had gone into the Scotland team changing room at Murrayfield and all the players were caught dancing around and singing *Flower of Scotland*. "It was really lovely," she said "and I had a wee bubble."

"That's lovely Mum," I said, "nice to win something for a change."

It was a phone call I'll never forget because almost two weeks later I was singing the very same song with four of the very same players from that Five Nations winning team.

1990 was an unbelievable year for Scottish rugby and to clinch the Grand Slam with a win against old rivals England 13-7 in the final round of the tournament made it even sweeter. Scotland have always been a proud sporting nation; we just never had enough success to satisfy the hungry supporters. Even the national football team have never progressed beyond the first group stages of a Finals tournament. Not good enough for a country who share the title of joint oldest national football team in the world. (if you were wondering, the other team is England).

That day the Irish might have been celebrating St Patrick by downing pints of Guinness, but it was us jocks who were doing all the singing, with a little help from a few wee drams of whisky. Jimmy Gibson had told me before the Five Nations that Gavin Hastings would be coming out afterwards to play in the Tens that year with a side called E.A.T.S – I can only assume it stood for Edinburgh Athletic Touring Side. I was therefore soon on the blower to Jimmy to see if Gavin and his team would be still coming over; I was worried they might still be celebrating in the pubs of Rose Street in Edinburgh, which they would certainly have been entitled to do.

"Nae problem, the boys are coming and thoroughly looking forward to it," Jimmy said. "As a matter of fact, four of the boys will be staying with me at my flat in Shouson Hill."

The four being Gavin, his younger brother Scott, winger Iwan Tukalo and flanker Derek Turnbull. That first year Carlsberg sponsored the Tens has many cherished memories for me; and I'm sure for many others as well. For the record books, the Cup event at the Tens that year was won by Hong Kong who beat Royal Marines (UK) 20-10.

But let me take you to the Carlsberg International Rugby Tens dinner, arranged by the Hong Kong Football Club Rugby section at the Hilton Hotel in the evening after all the finals. I arrived early to make sure everything was in order. I had carefully rehearsed my speech but, as it turned out, that would soon go out the window. The banquet hall of the Hilton was a popular spot for many such functions. It was the venue for the St Andrews Society annual Burns Supper so was certainly no stranger to convivial eating, drinking and bouts of spontaneous singing.

As I approached the head table I saw what I can only describe as a giant of a man easily over 6' 5". By his looks, demeanour and stature he was obviously someone with a rugby heritage. However, not knowing him from a bar of soap, we exchanged pleasantries, without exchanging names. I then moved along the head table looking at the names on the printed place-cards to see who was sitting where.

My eye came to rest on a famous name that I recognized and it suddenly dawned on me who I had been talking to former All Black captain, Andy Haden, lock for the Kiwis from 1972 until 1986. Who, in the sporting world at that time, had not heard of him? He was to be guest speaker.

I made a quick decision, if he wanted to drink Steinlager, rather than Carlsberg, I was not going to argue; after all he was about a foot taller than me! Thankfully it never came to that. He was happy to enjoy plenty of the sponsor's product, as good rugby boys tend to do.

I approached him again and, looking up, said: "We never really introduced ourselves." We shook hands. "Andy Haden," he said. "I thought so" I said, "Derek Currie, from the sponsors, Carlsberg." He handed me a copy of his book about the controversies in rugby at that time entitled *Lock, Stock 'n Barrel*. If it's still in print it's a good read if you're a rugby enthusiast.

As the evening progressed, and the amber liquid flowed, I made my way over to Gavin Hastings' table. Next minute I'm in full flow singing *Flower of Scotland* with Gavin and Scott Hastings, along with Iwan Tukalo and Derek Turnbull. Arms swaying in the air, voices belting out the lyrics. It might not have been the changing rooms at Murrayfield, with the Calcutta Cup and the Five Nations Trophy being passed around, but I wish my old Mum could have seen us that night. She might have had another wee bubble!

The Carlsberg Tens attracted some famous names over the years; some of them slightly past their prime, but they were still a big enough attraction to bring the world media and many spectators to the old ground at Sports Road. In combination with the Hong Kong Sevens, which was beginning to dominate seven-a-side world rugby, it meant that Hong Kong was the place to be at the end of March and early April.

Sevens party

I grew up with the Sevens, watching and eventually working at the event, making sure fans were kept well lubricated. Here are some of my memories with a little bit of history.

The HK Sevens was first played in the all-concrete stadium of the Hong Kong Football Club in Sports Road. A stadium built back in 1954, with floodlighting added in 1955. The Club's football team played their local amateur first division games in the stadium during the late fifties.

Tokkie Smith, one of the leading lights in the formation of the Hong Kong Sevens, had captained the Club's first rugby XV, winning trophies alongside his team-mate, a young Trevor Bedford who would go on to be chairman of the Hong Kong Land conglomerate. Gerry Forsgate took over the presidency of the HKFC in 1977 from Vernon Roberts and in the same year became president of the Hong Kong Rugby Union, again taking over from Roberts. Both were instrumental in the success of both the Sevens and the growth of rugby in the city.

I attended the first HK Sevens in 1976, more out of curiosity than anything else. Being a Club member I knew quite a few of the players representing Hong Kong that day including Ian Duncan, Drew Lamont and Paul Ogolther. Almost three thousand other people half-filled the Club stadium for the Rothmans/Cathay Pacific one-day tournament that day.

Now over 40,000 people cram into the Hong Kong Stadium with countless millions viewing live television coverage. Being inside the stadium back on that Sunday, March 28, 1976, who could have suspected it would now become one the best social and sporting events in the world.

The Sevens moved to the Hong Kong Government Stadium in So Kon Po in 1982 as it had outgrown the Football Club stadium. A packed Football Club stadium created a great atmosphere; would the wide seating and open spaces of the new venue with its capacity of just under 30,000 do the same? Well they needed have worried because spectators arrived in big numbers, many from overseas, particularly New Zealand, Australia and Fiji.

Initially San Miguel was the only beer featured for sale at the Sevens; but now that I was working for Carlsberg who were supporting local rugby, plus good relations and contacts within the Rugby Union, Carlsberg made its first appearance for sale at the new venue in 1982. Initially we only sold cans but a couple of years later they were not allowed so we produced jugs with a Sevens logo and served draught beer only. A percentage of the profits (in the region of 20%) was given to the HKRU and sales flourished.

Back in the early 80s the price for a jug of Carlsberg was around $20 with a refill of around $14. Nowadays a jug can cost in the region of $200, but with catering contracts and franchises, that's to be expected.

Everybody wanted to be at the Sevens, whether it was a passion for rugby, or just to share in the carnival atmosphere that began as soon as one walked up Caroline Hill Road. Tickets were like gold dust. Eventually even the Government stadium became too small for the Sevens and so it was enlarged and officially reopened in 1994 accommodating 40,000 spectators.

Bypassing the actual playing side of the tournament, which has been well documented elsewhere, I'd like to highlight some of the social aspects over the early years at the Government Stadium.

The South Stand seemed to host one long party: beer flowed and outfits of sartorial elegance and the downright exotic could always be seen. The Bull & Bear, the great old pub then located in Hutchison House in Central, had a Sevens drinks stall located at the top of Section 28 in the East Stand: one of the premier locations. There were plenty of girls from different companies hawking beers, but if you wanted a tipple of something else, the Bull & Bear stall was the place to be. Particularly on a Sunday, when they made jugs and jugs of Blood Mary! The custodians of the bar, Tom Smith and Norman Voce, could not make them fast enough.

Nowadays every worldwide Sevens event plays music in between games; some of it modern, but a lot is old classic hits where fans sing along and dance, *Hey Baby (Uhh, Ahh)* being a particular favourite. I like to think it was an idea of mine that helped contribute to the musical fun we see around the world Sevens today.

When the new Hong Kong stadium opened for the 1994 Sevens, it came with a spectacular new addition to entertain fans: a Diamond Vision screen high above the South Stand where for over 40 years the stately old scoreboard had been. A company called Prism, formed by

Des McGahan and Marlene Lee – business and social friends – were responsible for much of the PR and management for the Sevens. They knew the Hong Kong scene pretty well and from humble beginnings in 1989 the company went on to become very successful. They sold 30 second slots on the Diamond screen, which was a great advertising vehicle for companies to display their products to the 40,000 crowd.

Naturally it was also used as the scoreboard, but over the years many a marriage proposal appeared on the screen, to the delight of the crowd, who would scream "yes, yes, marry him!" When I got a brochure outlining the Diamond screen advertising rates in the year the huge screen was introduced, a little clock in my brain started ticking. You have to be quick to take opportunities in life I have found, so I marched into the office of the then Marketing Manager of Carlsberg, Edwin Lam.

"Edwin," I said, "I have a great idea for the Sevens at the new stadium."

I then outlined it to him: "The Carlsberg ad made in Singapore with that vivacious lady stepping down a white staircase singing, 'I love you, I need you, simply the best, better than all the rest'. It's just what the Sevens crowd need: music! I guarantee they will be singing along: Carlsberg, Simply the Best! I know a winner when I see one and it will boost sales, big time," I emphasized. "We have to do it now!"

"We can't," he answered.

I was crestfallen. "Why not?"

"It's from Singapore; it's not part of our Hong Kong advertising strategy; and our agency here would not like it."

"Bollocks to that and them, it's an international Sevens with fans from all over the world and I dare say even the international TV audience might see it, particularly with thousands singing and screaming, 'Simply the Best' at the top of their voices." Now I knew that if he shared the idea with our local ad agency they would have sung from the same hymn sheet as Edwin. Partly because it was not their idea, and partly because it infringed on the advertising campaign they were running.

I got all that, but for a two-day international event before an international audience, that was just bollocks to me. To say I was pissed off was an understatement. Now, Edwin and I were good friends and have remained so over the years, but he left me fuming that day. I never mentioned this to anyone who might have been a potential advertiser, for fear of their jumping the gun, as you only get one bite of the cherry.

Not long after the Sevens finished that year I was having a chat with Marlene Lee and told her about my idea and my discussion with Edwin Lam; and how pissed off I was that they never followed through with it. Marlene turned to me and said, "Derek, that's a great idea," and, the genuine character she is, said "You don't mind if I do that next year?"

"Go ahead, let them see the opportunity they missed." I said.

Well, Marlene did just that and played music, now there is not a Sevens anywhere in the world that does not play music with catchy lyrics and choruses that fans love, dance and sing along to. It's now an integral part of the Sevens. Well done, Marlene, you gave music to the Sevens, and I like to think I contributed to make it simply the BEST.

Sevens characters

One of my most cherished memories of the Sevens came from two members of the Hong Kong Welsh Male Voice Choir; but first, a little bit about the choir.

They would often form together and sing underneath the East Stand on a Sunday afternoon; entertaining the many who flocked around them with *Calon Lân* or *Men of Harlech*. Music from the heart of a choir, whose second patron, after Sir Harry Secombe CBE, was Jack Edwards OBE, a campaigner for the rights and welfare of war veterans and their families. He was a grand old character I used to regularly meet at the Sedan Chair Race around the Peak on Hong Kong Island where we both acted as judges for the charity event in aid of the Matilda Hospital.

Just before Hong Kong was returned to China in 1997 the choir sang for the last governor, Chris Patten, at Government House. I am told there were not many dry eyes that day.

But for me, the picture of the Sevens indelibly ingrained in my memory is that of two Welshmen every year running into the middle of the field and planting a large plastic leek dead centre, then bowing as if to pay homage to Wales and the Sevens. They would then run off the field carrying their leek to the full approval of the crowd. It was the unofficial opening of the Hong Kong Sevens for a number of years. This was before the new stadium was built. The two wonderful characters, who would open a bar in the New Territories and call it the 'Prince of Wales', were Terry Brewster and Bill Hawes.

I was happy to be at the pub when Welsh comedian and singer Max Boyce parachuted onto the field adjacent to the bar for the grand opening. A lovely gesture to Bill and Terry, but nothing was normal when around these two Welshman. I gave Max a tankard for the occasion, filled to the top with lager of course, him being hot and sweaty after the jump; the beer never touched the sides!

In 1995, when *Rockin' All Over the World* was blaring out at the Sevens in the Hong Kong Stadium, the only thing rockin' at the Football Club were the bulldozers. The HKFC was going through a redevelopment programme in conjunction with the HK Jockey Club to extend the race track and, without going too deeply into the architectural details, the Club made do with a temporary stadium and stands built for them by the Jockey Club.

The 1995 Tens were held a few days before the Sevens at this makeshift stadium right smack in the middle of Happy Valley racetrack. It might have been subdued, slightly, noise-wise, without the echo bouncing of the walls at the old concrete stadium, but plenty of good Tens rugby was still played and lots of fun was still to be had in the temporary stands.

The sponsor's box was smack in line with the halfway line, in prime position, seating twelve and a magnet for invites. Big Walter Gerrard collared me and asked if two of his guests could spend an afternoon in the box. Walter was working for Hiram Walker at that time, the company who also had the agency for Steinlager beer.

"Steinlager have got a couple of VIPs coming in, can I get them in your box? Don't worry, they won't be drinking my stuff, they know the Hampden Roar [rhyming slang for score]," he added.

I told him, "Anything for you big man, just get them to come to the entrance and ask for me; I'll reserve two places for them." So, on the Thursday afternoon of the Tens Finals I get a message: two gentlemen are waiting for me at the entrance. Rising from my seat and avoiding tipping or tripping over any jugs, I wandered down to the entrance to collect the pair and escort them to the box. Now, I might not have recognized Andy Haden when I first met him, but I immediately recognized one of the two big 'fellas' waiting for me, both with smiles on their faces.

Sean Fitzpatrick was captain of the All Blacks at that time; he needs no fanfare to describe him, so I won't. The other fella looked vaguely familiar. He put out his hand and said, "Robin Brooke, [brother of Zinzan] nice to meet you." So, there I am, taking two current All Blacks into the box and we are soon drinking and chatting away, having a good time.

A little later in the afternoon my GM at Carlsberg, Flemming With-Seidelin, turns up as he is doing the honours for the presentation later in the day. He sits down and looks to where I am sitting with the two All Blacks wedged to the right of me. Flemming is of course Danish, a very smart man, but he would know more about Danish bacon than rugby. In fact he was not great generally with sport, unless it was perhaps sailing. It could have been Pelé and Maradona sitting next to me and he still would have asked me who they were.

Suddenly, he loudly asks, "Derek, who are these two people next to you, and why are they wearing Steinlager caps?"

For God's sake, a bloody privilege to have two of the finest rugby players on the planet gracing the box and Flemming is asking me who they are?

"They are two very famous sportsmen from New Zealand and they are drinking Carlsberg," was all I gave him back. Flemming got the hint. Sean and Robin just laughed and, eventually, so did Flemming after I introduced them to him and provided a little background on the pair; it was then that the penny finally dropped.

Sandy Carmichael, the first Scotland player to get 50 caps was also in attendance, as was the legendary Bill McLaren, generally regarded as the best rugby commentator ever. It might have been a makeshift stadium with makeshift stands, but there was plenty of quality rugby personalities watching, past and present, which made the surroundings insignificant.

The Pieman

I should also mention another colourful character who came to the box on the first day of those Tens, someone not known for his rugby prowess.

Tens Tournament Director Simon Earles thought it would be good to invite him, as did I, because apart from the good standard of rugby played the fans always played a big part. So we invited the 'Pieman', who became a cult hero of the Sevens for a couple of years, and yes, two seats were reserved for him!

Fans are a big part of any sporting event and the Sevens and Tens in Hong Kong certainly had their fair share. The gentleman in question loved his rugby but was also a 32-year-old football fan from Northumberland, who supported "Sunderland till I die." He attended his first ever Sevens and Tens in 1993.

He recalls that his oversize, expansive posterior was somewhat sore from sitting in the half-finished Hong Kong Stadium that year, where slabs of concrete were the only form of seating. A forex trader in London, he was back again the year after. Sitting in the South Stand his expansive beer gut was covered by an XXXL T-shirt with the wording: "Who ate all the pies?"

It was not long before he was picked out by TV cameras and soon his frame was filling the large overhead screen behind him. As he saw himself on the screen he stood up proudly displaying the message emblazoned on his T-shirt: "Who ate all the pies?" Voices in the stadium, quick off the mark, erupted with a chorus of: "You Fat Bastard, You Fat Bastard."

The 'Pieman' was born.

The following year, after a long two days at the Tens and trips to Wan Chai for curry and numerous beers at a smattering of water holes, the Pieman would retire at 10pm to get some sleep. When the mornings of the Sevens arrived he would spring out of bed (is that the right word?) at 5am and head to the Stadium to be one of the first in line. Gates opened at 7.30am and once inside he would make his way to his usual spot in the middle of the South Stand where, as the day progressed, a multitude of pies and jugs of lager were consumed by the Pieman. Nothing too heavy: just a dozen pies and perhaps somewhere in the region of 20 pints or so of Carlsberg, but only if he was really thirsty.

Again he would be picked out by the TV cameras between games and would give another academy award performance to the crowd: standing tall and wide with his T-shirt off and his belly hanging like a hippo's chin. He would raise his plastic cup of beer in salute, like Nero might have done had it been the Colosseum, only this time the citizens from all corners of the arena would mock back once more: "You Fat Bastard, You Fat Bastard." No T-shirt was needed, the crowd knew who ate all the pies, Martin Hollis was now, officially, the Pieman.

So at the 1995 Tens, held within the confines of Happy Valley racetrack, Martin Hollis was invited as a VIP guest on the first day. Simon Earles and I presented Martin with two jugs of beer upon arrival to whet his appetite; the pies came later.

Martin had, unwittingly, become a Sevens icon, a character, a part of the story of the Sevens, an infamous part of the Sevens, call it what you may. While he might not have flashed down the wing at the Stadium wearing a team's colours to score a try, he represented the other part of the Sevens, the fans, the ones that made you smile. We made sure Martin had a good day with us and even my Carlsberg G.M. Flemming With-Seidelin, seemed to recognize him as he entered the box a little later.

"Is that the Pieman?" he asked. "Indeed it is, Flemming," I replied. There is a nice footnote to this story. As I was writing this piece I wondered where in the world the Pieman might be now. Using my investigative abilities I managed to find an email for one Martin Hollis.

I pinged out an email and twenty minutes later a reply came back; the Pieman was still around. What's more, like me, he too was living in Bangkok! As he remarked: it's a small world. Martin has now shed many kilos and pies are now off the menu but he still has a drop of lager.

Google Hong Kong Pieman, it's well worth a look and still a classic.

Mrs Fixit

As I finish writing about these early tournaments it would be remiss not to mention a guiding light at the Sevens, known as 'Mrs Fixit'. If anything went wrong and you needed help – or advice on how to get an extra ticket for the sold-out event – there was Beth Coalter.

Beth worked for almost 20 years at the HK Sevens and was a much-loved HKRU executive. She always managed to solve a problem and was a joy to work with. She finally left her position in Hong Kong in 2005 and joined the IRB, later becoming World Sevens' Operations Manager.

Sadly this 'Grand Old Dame of the Hong Kong Sevens' passed away in Belfast at the relatively young age of 59 in 2015, suffering a brain haemorrhage. The Sevens has had many heroes and heroines, on and off the field, and Beth was one of the best.

27

Four World Cups and four European Championships

I'd been writing sports columns for various newspapers for a while, but my writing career really took off when I was sent to Mexico to cover the World Cup Finals in June 1986. However, a few years before, a brief exchange with a great writer had given me a lot of confidence.

One day in the summer of 1982 Flemming With-Seidelin, my boss, asked me if I could arrange a lunch with someone he would dearly love to meet. A few phone calls and it was arranged; Flemming was over the moon.

The lunch was with Richard Hughes, a doyen of journalism and a permanent fixture at the Foreign Correspondents' Club on Lower Albert Road. Richard regularly dined at his own table inside the main club restaurant on the first floor. After some 12 years in Sutherland House the Club had recently moved to its current premises just up from Queen's Road Central, and Dick Hughes had wasted no time in settling in.

Most people took a taxi to the entrance of the new premises, the other main access being via a narrow alley, with 50 steep steps up from Wyndham Street to Ice House Street causing more than a pant or two before you reached the top. Flemming and I took a taxi.

Built at the end of the 19th century the Club's new premises were once owned by the Dairy Farm Group and were steeped in history, in keeping with the man we were about to have lunch with.

As we entered the restaurant Richard, or Dick as he was referred to by friends, was sitting at his table down in the far right hand corner. Now I had never before been officially introduced to him, but my reputation was enough for him to accept the request made through the General Manager of the FCC, Heinz Grabner, and a journalist friend, Kevin

Sinclair. Kevin was also a bit of a writing legend in his time: among his books were the history of the Hong Kong Police Force and one of the Hong Kong Rugby Sevens.

We were about to have lunch with the man who worked for Ian Fleming as his foreign editor on the *Sunday Times* and who Fleming later used as his inspiration for the fictional character 'Dikko', in his James Bond novel, *You Only Live Twice*.

John Le Carré, another friend of Dick Hughes, was so intrigued by the larger than life, flamboyant character that he portrayed him as his fictional character Old Craw in his spy novel *The Honourable Schoolboy*. Had Dick Hughes himself actually moved in the murky world of espionage?

There are plenty of dossiers on his life, so you can form your own opinion, but he was certainly one interesting character. I therefore totally understood my GM's desire to meet the man who was one of only two Western journalists summoned to meet fugitive British spies, Maclean and Burgess in 1956 in Moscow and bring their exploits to world attention. With his huge frame he could have been 'The Third Man', a young Orson Welles walking down an alley in a trenchcoat, but today he was sitting at his usual table.

"Young Currie," he said as we met. Flemming greeted him warmly and was soon engrossed with the legendary writer and perhaps master spy. Oops, did I say that?

Hughes was known to deliver ecclesiastical benedictions before lunch, which to some might seen slightly eccentric, but not to those who knew him well, and this led to him affectionately being referred to as 'Monsignor'.

"Your Lordships!" he toasted us before the first course arrived, and there were more than a few more toasts over the next hour and a half. It was an enlightening lunch and a privilege for me; although at the time I never knew the true depth of the man; had it been ten years later, I would have had a list of questions to grill him under a low wattage light bulb! Instead, shortly before lunch ended, he asked a question of me; well it was more of a suggestion.

At that time I had begun writing a daily column on the back page of *The Standard* covering the World Cup finals in Spain.

"Can I give you a suggestion, your grace," he said, touching the monocle over his right eye, "when you make a statement, there is no need to finish with dot, dot, dot. Everybody knows what you mean!"

There I was, getting writing tips from the man who wrote *Hong Kong: Borrowed Place – Borrowed Time*. But more importantly for me, it meant Dick Hughes actually read my daily newspaper reports! That sent a shiver down my spine, it was a compliment of the highest order... from someone who knew a thing or two about dots being in the wrong place.

Just under two years later, in 1984, Richard Hughes had a liver ailment and died at the Queen Elizabeth hospital in Hong Kong at the age of 77. Journalism lost a legend.

———

Going to the Mexico World Cup meant I would be working alongside the first division of journalists – McIlvanney, Lawton and Glanville – striking a typewriter key instead of a ball.

Writing for *The Standard* my column was entitled: "What's brewing in Mexico" – prominently supported by a Carlsberg logo – and once there I wrote a daily piece under the sub-head: "Special report from Mexico". I also wrote daily snippets for the *Oriental Daily News*, the best-selling Chinese language newspaper in Hong Kong, in return for *gratis* Carlsberg advertising space.

It would be just the beginning: I eventually covered, live, four World Cup finals and four European Championships.

I arrived in Mexico several days before the event got under way; securing accommodation at the Romano Diana hotel in Mexico City. It was centrally located just a short distance from the '*Monumento a la Indepencia*' – better known as '*El Ángel*' – a victory column situated at a roundabout on the busy thoroughfare of the Paseo de la Reforma and built for the centenary of Mexico's independence.

Incidentally, Mexico was not the original choice for the 1986 World Cup, that had been Colombia, but for economic reasons they had to forgo the rights.

You could feel the excitement building in the city as the opening game drew near. The densely-populated, high-altitude capital was replete with baroque cathedrals, but now it was ready to pay homage to the world of football. I was just as excited.

The Media Centre was situated in the Aztec Stadium and travelling there was fairly easy on non-playing days. A small Volkswagen beetle taxi, with the front passenger seat removed, was the popular mode of transport and would take 20 minutes or so. But not so on match days.

The atmosphere during the pre-match opening ceremony was electric, the locals appreciating the fact that it was based on Aztec history. They also had Charro horseman, wearing wide-brimmed sombreros, sitting aloft magnificent steeds and trotting around the stadium. There was 95,000 spectators inside the stadium; virtually every one of them expecting a comfortable victory for the Italians, the reigning world champions.

But Bulgaria, after going behind to a goal by Altobelli, shocked the Italians with a dramatic late equalizer. 56 million fans, from Milan to Palermo, must have choked on their pasta. The World Cup was up for grabs for anyone who had the appetite to win it.

Eleven cities and twelve venues hosted matches; the farthest from Mexico City being Monterrey, the place Frank Sinatra once crooned about.

Travellers' tales

I won't go into many detail of the matches, rather I'll tell you a few tales of our travels, starting with our visit to León. The city in the state of Guanajuato was never actually on our original itinerary. It was my travelling companion, Mr Robin Parke, Sports Editor of the *SCMP* who was responsible for this little side trip and it came after a three hour journey by private car from Mexico City to Querétaro to cover the vital Scotland versus West Germany group match. Fellow Scot John Crean, a sports writer who also worked for the *SCMP*, had travelled to Mexico as a fan and joined up with Parky and me for the trip.

Despite taking the lead through a Gordon Strachan goal, the jocks lost 2-1 in extremely hot and draining conditions. Conditions that we too found hot and draining, so after filing our reports we found a wonderful little oasis that served ice cold beer. The melancholic mood that had descended as we discussed the 2-1 defeat was broken in an instant when a booming voice roared: "Parky, Derek, wonderful to see you, what do you want to drink?" Decked out in a black, red and yellow scarf it was an old friend from Hong Kong – he was German, but I'm sure you already guessed that.

Herbie Schwartzer, Airfreight Manager for Schenker (HK), and born in Cologne, had followed West Germany at the World Cups since 1966. His best mate since childhood was Wolfgang Weber. The same Wolfgang Weber who had scored the dramatic equalizer against England that took the 1966 World Cup final into extra time. With a sincere look on his cheery red face he gave us our beers and said "sorry about the result boys."

Our gloomy mood evaporated with the larger than life Herbie around and as the night progressed we sang a few Bavarian songs, while Herbie joined in for a few choruses of *Flower of Scotland*. Then, through the fumes of alcohol, Parky, the sweet talking Irishman, convinced us that instead of heading back to Mexico City as planned, we should go to León to cover the France versus Hungary game the next day. Parky was a huge fan of the French national side, hence his keenness to go to León. Knowing him, he probably had it all planned in advance and was just waiting for the right moment to spring it on us.

"You won't be disappointed, lads," he said.

Little did we know at the time that going to León to watch 'Les Bleus' would almost wreck Parky's World Cup campaign.

We arrived early next day at the press centre in León, after an 80 minute hop by car from Querétaro. First thing, was to get accreditation tickets for the match, and buy a match ticket for Creano. Next, was to book three air tickets for the one hour flight back to Mexico City after the game.

Blow number one: all flights back to Mexico City were fully booked.

"Thanks Parky!" we said in unison.

"Is there a bus service from León to Mexico City?" I asked one of the girls working on the travel service counter inside the press centre.

"*Si*," she answered and gave me the details of where to get tickets for the bus.

Knowing we now had a way back to Mexico City we settled in to watch the France versus Hungary match – France controlled the game with a cheeky arrogance, but were only 1-0 up at half-time. However in the second half they slipped into top gear and the *Carre Magique* – magic square – comprising Platini, Giresse, Tigana and Fernandez cut through the Hungarian defence and it finished 3-0. Should have been five or six, but the front pairing of Stopyra and Papin contrived to miss some easy chances.

It had been worth the trip. Watching the elegant French side with Platini, playmaker supreme, strolling about like a modern day Napoleon was a great experience.

Little did I imagine that eight years later I would share a three-hour flight from New York to Dallas with the maestro during the 1994 World Cup Finals; and then be introduced to Giresse on landing at Forth Worth airport. But I digress; back to León.

The match had been a lunchtime kick-off, so we got to the *Estación de Autobuses* – the bus terminal – late in the afternoon, around 5pm local time.

"Sorry *Señor*, the first available bus is at 10pm and will get into Mexico City around 5 am," the lady at the ticket counter informed me. Blow number two!

I shrugged and booked three seats for the overnight journey back to the capital. How to kill five hours?

Trust the Irishman to come up with the solution.

"Why don't we just have a good bevvy somewhere, at least that will make us sleep on the journey back," said Parky. Was that also planned in advance I wondered?

Opposite the bus terminal was a string of marquees, and judging by the noise it appeared a mini fiesta was taking place. Towns across Mexico embraced the World Cup and León was no exception. We ambled across the road and ventured into a marquee.

The place was alive with music and before we knew it we were seated and surrounded by a local mariachi band. We quickly got into the swing of things. Soon, out of the blue, we were joined by two Mexicans who spoke hardly a word of English; but the international language of drinking beer, supplemented by the odd "Cheers!" or "¡Salud!", meant we got on well. Our two new friends were apparently farmers who had come to León to sell their livestock and were awash with pesos. They were up for a good time before heading home, more *cerveza* was ordered. As the evening wore on, we exchanged contact details with our new friends, promising to stay in touch; such are the promises made through alcohol. Funnily enough, I still have the scrap of paper with the details they gave us, along with a photo of the 'team' taken that night: Efram Rios was one of farmers.

Half an hour before our bus was due to depart for Mexico City, I called an end to the proceedings. Although we had had quite a few beers the three of us were still fairly *compos mentis*. Well, I certainly was, as my reaction to what happened next will attest.

I boarded the bus and found a seat halfway up the aisle. Creano then appeared, and plonked himself in the window seat next to me. Parky finally came aboard, weaving his way up the aisle. As he moved unsteadily along, a rather stout Mexican bellowed something in Spanish, rose from his seat, and brushed past Parky. Not fluent by any means in Spanish, but grateful that many holiday trips to Spain had given me a slight grasp of the language, I could make out him saying something like "*me bus equivocado.*" Call it a sixth sense, but something did not seem right. With no announcement from the bus driver, why would he suddenly say he was on the wrong bus?

"Parky," I shouted, "You got your passport?" He felt his back pocket, but there was nothing there.

"It's gone!" he cried

"The fat Mexican, let's go!" I yelled.

I leapt out of my seat, tore off the bus, and looked around. I saw the Mexican bandit walking briskly up ahead. I was convinced Parky had not lost his passport while supping beer in the marquee, nor indeed when he went to the toilet before boarding the bus. I knew instinctively the answer lay up ahead of me. As I got closer to our erstwhile fellow passenger, he turned to run, but he couldn't get away from me, I was still capable of running fast.

I caught up with him and, screaming "*policía, policía,*" I used all my strength to push him to the floor, much to the bemusement of the waiting throng in the bus terminal. But no police arrived, only Creano and a wheezing Parky gasping for air. I shouted at the fat Mexican, who was now looking somewhat guilty and frightened with three big foreigners surrounding him, "*Donde passporte?*"

He sullenly jerked his head towards the rows of seats next to us. There, lying underneath, was a passport. He had thrown it under the seat when he knew the chase was up. Parky scrambled over and picked it up. Thank God it was his!

What I didn't know at the time, was that Parky had all his traveller's cheques inside the passport wallet! Worse still: they were all already signed by Parky! Had the Mexican escaped, Parky's World Cup plans could, and probably would, have been in tatters. Remember this was 1986, not the twenty-first century when lost credit cards can be readily replaced by a telephone call. They could have easily been spent by anyone who found them.

I kept calling for *policía*, but none were forthcoming. I asked Parky what we should do with the Mexican; Creano and I were still standing over him as he sat on the ground.

"Let him go, I've got everything," said Parky, who was clearly shaken by the ordeal, but had sobered up very quickly.

I let the guy go and watched him stumble away; I was still fairly angry at the attempt to rob my friend. Then my brain clicked into gear: what if he was carrying a knife, or a gun, and no police around? Sense prevailed and we again boarded the bus, amid cheers from some of our fellow passengers; clearly word of what had happened had got around.

That was the only encounter of a criminal nature during our whole sortie across Mexico – an isolated incident. If anything, the Mexican people were over generous with their hospitality. Hey, who knows if the Spanish-speaking thief was even Mexican? I just hoped Parky would refrain in future from keeping his passport in his back pocket! And I told him so in no uncertain terms.

After watching England brush aside Paraguay in the Aztec Stadium by three goals to nil, thereby reaching the quarter-finals, I hopped on a late-night Aeroméxico flight to Acapulco.

I was on my own. Parky and Creano had decided to sidestep the game and head to Belize for a short break, intending to savour the history of Georgetown, in what was formerly British Honduras. Normally Parky and I followed the same match schedule, but earlier in the competition he had covered a different match, and afterwards spent a day and a night in Acapulco; later informing me of the delights that the Acapulco Princess Hotel had to offer: "It's palatial, and so cheap!" Fortunately I was carrying US dollars, so a 5-star hotel was now affordable, even in Acapulco, so off I went.

The hotel resembled an ancient Aztec pyramid – a third tower was added in 1982 – and had over 150 acres of gardens with towering palms framing the view of the Sierra Madre mountains. With three magnificent swimming pools the hotel reeked of Hollywood opulence – the room I stayed in was enormous, with cane furniture and pastel prints on the walls; although not facing the ocean, I found it pleasingly quiet and serene in the evening. I did take advantage of poolside Happy Hours, enjoying the sunset and the entertainment provided by a trio of mariachi musicians.

Comfortably seated in a lounger one evening, with the sounds of *Guantanamera* drifting on the air, I noticed three youngsters with Scottish accents sitting close by. At the end of the song I went over and asked if they were enjoying the World Cup.

"Aye, it's great," one of them said.

"Where you boys from?" I asked, I knew from the accents it wasn't Glasgow.

"Edinburgh," was the reply.

"Enjoying the hotel?"

"We're no staying here, but we heard the Happy Hour was great."

I asked what games they had been to see?

"We went to all three group games and loved every venue," said one.

Deciding to get a regular supporter's view as to how they thought Scotland had performed, I asked "how do you think Scotland played?"

The response was totally unexpected, but summed up their trip:

"To be honest, we hav'nae really seen the games, though we were in the stadiums. The wine and drink is so cheap over here, it's all been a bit of a blur, we cannae really remember much aboot the matches."

Then one of the three followed up with the final *coup de grâce*.

"Nae problem, we have a mate back in Edinburgh taping the games for us, we'll watch them when we get back hame!"

I had no answer to that.

Visiting the World Cup media centres dotted around Mexico I bumped into leading sports journalists from across the globe, representing newspapers from Italy's *La Gazzeta dello Sport* to *The Times* of London; there was even someone from the *Penguin News* in the Falklands.

I also met the great Malcolm Brodie. Born in Glasgow, but evacuated before World War II to Northern Ireland, he was one of the world's most recognized football and sports writers. Parky had worked under him at the *Belfast Telegraph* and introduced us.

"You're young Currie, are you?" Brodie said. "Your older brother Dick and I are old pals." After only talking to him for 10 minutes I felt as if I'd known him for donkey's years. Brodie covered his first World Cup in 1954. He would eventually cover another thirteen, a record for any journalist, and one more than famed English writer Brian Glanville.

Parky called Brodie 'the Legend'. He certainly was. He knew everybody worth knowing in the world of sport, and they knew him. His telephone book was as priceless as the Mona Lisa. I often wondered if he kept a back-up somewhere. My brother Dick once told me of a good story attributed to Malky, when covering the 1970 World Cup finals in Mexico.

Brazil had just beaten Italy 4-1 in the final and Malky called the *Belfast Telegraph* to give his story to the copy-taker over the phone.

"*Magnifico, magnifico, magnifico*," said Brodie.

"It's okay, I heard you the first time," replied the copy-taker.

Years later, 1998 to be exact, I had a wonderful afternoon with Malky, Parky and Sir Bobby Robson outside the media centre in Paris during the World Cup. Countless stories unfurled that day far too many to repeat and I would meet Sir Bobby a few times over the years, once even in Bangkok in a golf competition in his honour. I even took him shopping to the famed Patpong market.

I had my first overseas holiday in Sitges in the late fifties and Sir Bobby told me that was where he stayed during his managerial days with Barcelona. We both agreed it was a wonderful spot and exchanged a few memories.

Another wonderful writer I got to know along the way was the great Hugh McIlvanney. I first met him with some hard-core journalist pals of his during the 1988 Euro Championships in West Germany.

Introducing myself as Derek Currie, youngest brother of Dick Currie, I was welcomed with open arms by Hugh – it's fair to say eldest brother Dick opened a lot of doors for me! Dick and Hugh sat together ringside while covering major title fights in many of the great theatres of boxing. The young Currie was therefore accepted into his illustrious company.

One night during the Championships McIlvanney invited me for a drink. Memory fails me somewhat who was all there, but I do recall Ken Jones of *The Independent* was among those assembled at the German pub that night. I had telephoned my eldest brother Dick earlier to tell him that I was going to have a drink with McIlvanney and Jones and a few others. I remember him saying, "You're in serious trouble son."

I'm going to sidetrack briefly when Dick himself might have got into serious bother, the story came from him. It was during the 1953 European boxing championships held in Warsaw and the city was still a sea of ruins in many parts following the end of World War II. Resplendent in blazers with a large British crest emblazoned on the top pocket Dick went for a walk not long after arriving in Poland with two of his compatriots, Len Mullen and John Smillie, together with English boxers Bruce Wells and Henry Cooper. The smallish group looking way too smart for the background of rubble surrounding them were suddenly attacked by a gang of stone-throwing thugs. During the attack Henry Cooper approached a giant of a man who was the main protagonist.

With the left hook which would be known in later years as 'Henry's Hammer' he floored him and the gang quickly scarpered. Dick approached Henry: "We were outnumbered three to one, I'm only a Flyweight," he joked.

"I was always taught if you are attacked in numbers, go for the leader, if he goes down they will scarper," said Henry.

"What if he doesn't go down?" queried Dick.

"You run like fuck," said Henry.

So back to my night with the doyens of Fleet Street: it was just great to be accepted and to listen to their yarns. As the night progressed trivia questions were thrown about like confetti at a wedding. What was the Real Madrid forward line at Hampden in 1960? How many times did Rocky Marciano defend his title? And so on. It was late in the night when I brought up my Lester Piggott poser: name Piggott's Epsom Derby winners. The question cut through the smoke from the Romeo y Julieta cigars, which by this time was hanging in the air like a cloud.

There was however no quick riposte, which surprised me as I thought McIlvanney would have no problem naming them; he was a fountain of knowledge on the subject, but he could only come up with eight horses. Mind you, we had been hard at it for several hours in that Dusseldorf bar.

As I was heading for a taxi, he asked me, "what was the one I missed?"

"It will come to you," I said, "if not, I'll tell you tomorrow." Next day a voice rang out across the media centre: "Empery, 1976; bloody Empery! Annoyed me all night."

For me, it had been a night to remember with some of the stars of Fleet Street; but for my liver, it was probably not one it would want me to repeat in a hurry.

Eastern Express

In February 1994 a new English language newspaper – the *Eastern Express* – debuted in Hong Kong, backed by money from the Chairman of the *Oriental Daily News*, Ma Ching-kwan. The belief was that they could capture market share from the *SCMP* and gain a good chunk of advertising revenue.

An able crew was assembled, led by Chief Editor Steven Vines, comprising journalists from rival publications, including the *Far Eastern Economic Review*. That year the World Cup was to be held in the USA. So, with backing from my employer Carlsberg, I did a deal with the *Eastern Express* to let me cover the tournament for them. A prominent Carlsberg logo was displayed under my mug shot and the column was called 'World Cup Diary'. Flying against the clock to Chicago however left me with the worst jet-lag I have ever endured.

When I finally got myself together enough to go to the media centre for accreditation the first person I met was commentator Martin Tyler. It was uncanny, at almost every World Cup we both attended he was always the first person I would meet, and I'd jokingly say: "We have to stop meeting like this, Martin."

The Windy City lived up to its name, but at least the breeze blew away the cobwebs in my head. My hotel was a hundred metres or so from the Sheraton, where the media centre was located. But the story I am about to relate happened almost 1,300 kilometres east, in New York.

"Enjoying the World Cup?" I said to the figure waiting for flight AA 1383 from Newark to Dallas.

"Yes, up to now," he replied, drawing on a French cigarette and blowing smoke slowly into the air.

"Did you watch the game yesterday?" I asked.

"Yes, I was at the Mexico game; but I watched the other match on television."

Before I could say another word he continued, "I thought the refereeing at both games was really terrible; inexperienced referees in important games; made it more like basketball."

"Yes, they turned the games into non-contact sports contests," I concurred.

He had been referring in particular to the Mexico versus Bulgaria match at the Giants Stadium, where the performance of the Syrian official, widely criticized by many, spoilt a potentially exciting match by continually blowing for negligible fouls.

"Where are you from?" he asked.

"Hong Kong, but originally Scotland."

"Let's have a drink," he said.

"Coffee?" I asked.

He settled for a Diet Coke.

"My shout," I said as I handed the money to the cashier. "But I invited you," he said.

I just smiled. And that's how I met the great Michel Platini.

We were both on the same flight to Dallas, so as we boarded I was thinking of asking him if we could sit together; but he beat me to it, and the air hostess agreed. We then spent the next three hours chatting about everything from football, to golf, to life in general, and back to football again; like two old friends who hadn't seen each other for years. At that time Platini was joint President, with Fernand Sastre, of the organizing committee for the next World Cup to be held in France. He was running an eye over the USA event to get pointers as to how they might manage, and improve it, four years later. I asked him what he thought of the opening ceremony at Soldier Field?

"It was OK, they had Diana Ross and some other stars, but you could hardly see them from your seat. It only looked good for television," he said. "With the country being so big I also think the fans are finding it expensive to follow their team in America. In France, it will only take two to three hours from Paris to reach most venues by car or train." Somewhere over Tennessee we started talking about his career and Mexico in 1986 came up.

I had attended the classic quarter-final encounter between France and Brazil in Guadalajara, that had been after my brief stay in Acapulco. It was close to being one of the finest games I have ever watched – France defeating Brazil on penalties – a game neither side deserved to lose.

"Just like 1982 perhaps, we should have won the World Cup then. I got the equalizer in the 1-1 draw against Brazil. I also missed my penalty in the shoot-out, I put it down to tiredness, it just sailed over the bar in the high altitude."

I knew what he meant about the altitude affecting the ball. I had joined a European journalists team in a little tournament played at the stadium adjoining the Aztec Stadium. Losing 1-0, I came on and scored an equalizer. It went to penalties. I slotted mine home, but for some reason they wanted it retaken. I hardly touched the ball the second time around, but it flew up, up and away, over the crossbar, so I could certainly sympathize with Platini on his miss.

France got to the semi-finals in Mexico. Platini claimed they should have beaten the Germans in that game, somewhat upset that the goal scored by Andreas Brehme was never a free kick in the first place. He confided to me that at the time he and Alain Giresse were carrying injuries. It was kept secret from the Germans for obvious reasons, but they needed pain-killing injections to get through the game. His injury was to the tendon in his foot; they had to slightly cut open one of his boots to make it more comfortable for him in the game. Those injuries to key players certainly didn't help their cause with the Germans.

Just before we landed I mentioned to Michel that my friend Parky would be gutted to have missed the flight, and the chance to meet one of his heroes. I told him that Parky raved about the French team, so much so that it was like a schoolgirl crush. He especially adored Giresse. After landing at Fort Worth we bade each other *au revoir*.

But a minute or so later I got a shout from Michel who by then was some 50 metres away. He pointed at the person next to him and shouted: "Giresse."

I quickly walked over to them and was introduced to another member of the greatest midfield I have ever seen. It was time for the camera to come out from my bag. I said in jest to them: I will be Fernandez, let's take a picture. We did. And then went our separate ways; me with a big smile on my face. When I told Parky the story later that night he was like a man who had missed winning the lottery by one number.

My writing career at the *Eastern Express* was short-lived. The paper was aptly named: it set off like an express train, but in less than two years it hit the buffers.

Before then however I had covered the Euros for *The Standard*.

I remember a rainy night at the Volksparkstadion in Hamburg; I was there to watch a semi-final tie between the Netherlands and West Germany in the 1988 Euros. I'd arrived in Hamburg the day before and ran into Herbie Schwartzer, a German friend who worked in Hong Kong; as usual, he was following his beloved country's progress. (The same guy I bumped into during the World Cup finals in Mexico.)

I had been supping a quiet beer in a quiet bar on a quiet Monday night, just off the Reeperbahn, amusing myself watching a lady of the night, sadly with her best days behind her, attempting to solicit a customer in the drizzling rain outside, with little joy.

"Rainy days and Mondays always get me down," sprang to mind.

After quaffing two beers and a delicious dish of Grünkohl – kale served with sides of pork and sausage – I was about to hail a taxi back to my hotel when larger than life Herbie emerged out of the blue.

"You can't go home yet, I'll show you around the Reeperbahn," he insisted.

Well, I was no stranger to seeing the seedier sides of Manila or Bangkok, or even Wan Chai, but the Reeperbahn, with ladies dancing behind glass windows, with chains dangling, was a little too much, even for me. I therefore suggested to Herbie that we just go for a drink in a bar and forget the scenery. Which we did. Unfortunately we didn't stop at just one, and I was still feeling a little ropey when watching the semi-final tie the following evening.

It was a pulsating game, but my main memory is of what happened after the final whistle.

The Netherlands and West Germany were huge football rivals; the Dutch still touchy about losing 2-1 in the 1974 World Cup final in Munich. After going a goal behind, Ronald Koeman put the Dutch level from the penalty spot. Then, with just two minutes to go, van Basten slid along the wet turf like a duck to water to hit the winner. It was the Netherlands' first win over the Germans in 32 years. Wild celebrations followed from Dutch players all over the field.

Then they ran to the side of the stadium to celebrate with their delighted fans.

Not so many in the press box noticed, but my eagle eye spotted Ronald Koeman pretending to wipe his arse with the German jersey he had in his hand after swapping with Olaf Thon. Two days later I am at the press conference for the Dutch side, prior to the Saturday night final against the Soviet Union, who had beaten Italy 2-0 in the other semi final. It was a relaxed atmosphere and you could talk freely with the Dutch players. I had a word with van Basten, who I admired immensely, but it was really Ronald Koeman I wanted to talk to. I had not read any reports of his 'jersey transgression' after the Germany game.

When I got him one-on-one I said, "You must have been very, very happy with the win in Hamburg."

"Yes, it was great to beat them, so happy," he said.

"Incidentally," I said, with a smile on my face, "I saw what you did with that German jersey after the game."

"Oh no! Please don't mention that. It was just a bit of fun, I was over-excited at the time. I probably shouldn't have done it," he added.

I laughed, shook his hand and wished him all the best in the final. In fact, I had used it in a story I had filed to *The Standard* the day before, but downplayed the incident. I never mentioned that to Koeman.

28

Live at the Hong Kong Hotel with Stevie Wonder and Marvelous Marvin Hagler

There was a nice old bar on Ermita's M.H. Del Pilar street in Manila called the Boomerang Club. The area itself was full of bars and very rowdy by night, but during daylight hours it was as sleepy as a ghost town. The club, located above a tailor's shop, had a couple of pool tables, with a well-lit aquarium behind the bar brightening the dark interior.

One early afternoon in mid-1988 I was playing pool there with Dave Gilhooly when I was interrupted by a telephone call.

"Hodges here," said the distinctive cockney voice. "I want you to get your ass over here, Steve Ball is having a barbecue." Hodges was a professional English photographer based in Manila with a real dry sense of humour.

"I'm playing pool with Gilhooly," I told him.

His reply was quite a surprise: "Marvin Hagler is here."

I thought he was having me on, so to call his bluff I said, "Yeah, yeah, ha ha, get him on the phone."

A few seconds later an American voice came on the line, "Who am I talking to?"

"Are you Marvin Hagler?" I asked cheekily.

"Marvelous Marvin Hagler," was the reply.

I still thought I was being conned so, feeling cocky, and conscious that if it was Hagler he was a long way away, I replied, "Well, you're not that marvellous because you've never beaten a Scottish boxer!"

"Just get over here and I'll show you," was all he said.

Hodges got back on the line and suddenly doubt set in: could it really be Hagler? I decided not to take any risks, so I said to Hodges: "Tell Marvin I was only joking!"

I told Gilhooly, who was a big boxing fan, and we set off to, hopefully, meet arguably one of the greatest middleweight boxers of all time. It was only a small gathering, just six people, so when we arrived at the house I quickly recognised the familiar face and well-muscled body of Marvin Hagler as he approached Gilhooly and me alongside Dave Hodges. Thankfully, he had a smile on his face; obviously Hodges had passed on my earlier apology regarding my Scottish boxing wind-up.

After introductions we learned that Marvelous had just completed a movie called *Indio*, filmed in the Philippines and starring Hagler, Francesco Quinn, son of the legendary actor Anthony, and well-known American character actor Brian Dennehy.

Gilhooly, a diminutive 5'4" fellow Scotsman from Bathgate who had refereed Asian title fights and was very knowledgeable about boxing matters, poked a question at Hagler: "Why did you not box the early rounds as a southpaw against Sugar Ray Leonard?"

Hagler, who boxed those opening rounds in orthodox fashion in that famous, well-documented fight instead of his usual southpaw stance just laughed, without giving an answer, clearly realising Gilhooly knew his boxing. A southpaw is normally a left-handed boxer who leads with his right hand and right foot forward.

Steve Ball, who entertained us well – being very generous with both food and drink – had produced T-shirts promoting the movie *Indio* and that's how he came in contact with Hagler, which led to us all meeting up that day. Just as we were leaving Steve's house, after a long enjoyable afternoon, Marvelous asked me, "Are you living in Hong Kong?"

I said yes. He then told me that he was going to be there the following week and asked, "Would you look after me when I arrive?"

"Delighted to," I said, and gave him my home telephone number, not in the least expecting that he would call.

But a week later he did, and I'm really glad that he did, for what followed was undoubtedly one of the most amazing things to happen in my life. It was a Sunday morning, May 1, 1988 to be exact, when the phone rang in my flat in Causeway Bay.

The call would signal the beginning of a remarkable six days and culminate with me having dinner and singing alongside one of the most successful songwriters and musicians in the history of music – and for good measure, the best middleweight boxer of the last century was also singing with me.

The phone rang six times before I picked it up.

"Is that Derek?" an American voice at the other end of the line asked.

"Yes," I answered.

"It's Marvelous here. You said I should call you. I'm arriving in Hong Kong this afternoon."

I took down his flight number and arrival time and said I would be at Kai Tak airport to meet him. In those days, apart from my role as PR manager for Carlsberg, I was also doing some work for *The Standard* so I quietly tipped them off that Hagler would be in town, but refrained from mentioning my scoop to friends on the Sports Desk at the *SCMP*.

A quick telephone call and arrangements were made for a photographer from *The Standard* to meet me at Kai Tak. Hagler arrived at the airport resplendent in the latest edition, dark blue Adidas tracksuit. I got the obligatory snap: my left hand in a tight fist under his chin, while he gave a thumbs up. The picture appeared in *The Standard* the next morning under the apt heading: "Marvellous Marvin doing the rounds".

The only mistake was whoever wrote the banner headline spelt 'Marvelous' with two l's instead of one, but what the L.

Next stop was the Nikko Hotel in Tsim Sha Tsui East, Kowloon, where Marvelous was staying. After he checked in we had a few drinks at the hotel bar and I told him I would catch up with him the next day and arrange a few sightseeing trips.

The following evening I took him to the California Restaurant and Bar in Lan Kwai Fong for dinner. Quite a few people recognized him, one of them being well-known horse trainer John Moore, and I took pleasure in introducing them to each other. I also introduced Marvelous to the manager of the California, Dick Kaufman, who guided us to a cosy table.

The restaurant was five years old at that time and considered one of the trendiest places on Hong Kong Island. It was opened by Allan Zeman in 1983, but I don't recall Allan, or Mr Lan Kwai Fong as he is popularly known, being around that night – he is credited as being the man who turned the narrow street into the most fashionable night-time area in Hong Kong's Central District.

It was during dinner that I casually told Marvelous that Sugar Ray Leonard had been in town a month or so earlier. Marvelous was taken aback, but got straight to the point: "What did he say?"

"He said he beat you fair and square," I told him honestly.

"He said what!" Marvelous was looking more than a bit agitated.

"I'm only telling you what he said," I added.

"You know, after the fight, he put his hands round my neck and whispered, 'You got me, babe'," revealed Marvelous.

"You know what that means?" he asked.

"Of course, he thought you had beaten him."

"Can you organize a press conference?" he asked.

"I certainly can," I said, "Give me a day or so."

The press conference was held two days later at the Hong Kong Football Club in Happy Valley. The then Hong Kong Football Club manager, Malcolm Davis, was delighted to help me host the impromptu event. There was a good turnout, much of it achieved by word of mouth through my contacts in the press. I had also told a few friends so they could get a picture with Hagler for posterity. One was the then Clerk of the Course for the Hong Kong Jockey Club, and a big fight fan, Noel McCaffrey. I think Noel was happy to get away from the daily horse race chatter and he and Marvelous discussed the merits of boxing – fists were raised, but I assume this was to emphasize some pugilistic point.

The conference went well, Marvelous giving his account of the fight, held a year earlier on April 6 at Caesar's Palace in Nevada, and billed as the 'Super Fight.' It was a controversial fight in many ways, involving two of the greatest boxers to grace the ring, pride very much at stake. In the end, the official judges gave a split decision to Leonard, but any good judge will tell you Hagler won that fight. By his own admission at the final bell, Leonard had told Hagler, "You got me babe," so he really thought he had lost the fight.

Key elements were not in Hagler's favour: before the fight took place Leonard insisted on three conditions being met and these were ultimately crucial to his strategy.

The ring size was to be 20 x 20 feet, instead of the standard 18 x 18 feet; the gloves had to be 10 ounces, rather than 8 ounces; and the fight was to be over 12 rounds, rather than the 15 rounds favoured by Hagler. Without those conditions I think Hagler would have beaten Leonard within the distance. The gloves made a huge difference: Hagler being a big hitter can exercise more power using an 8-ounce glove. A bigger ring also allowed Leonard more space to keep his distance from the big hitting Hagler.

People still debate the fight to this day, but both boxers earned a lot of money from it. Figures quoted were Hagler US$20 million, Leonard US$12 million. It was clearly evident during the press conference at the Football Club that Hagler was still bitter about the verdict, but I'm pleased to say his mood would get better as the day progressed.

Marvelous and I left the Hong Kong Football Club and I reckoned he could afford to buy me a beer, but it was not what you might call a quiet beer!

As I walked out of the Hong Kong Football Club with Marvelous I asked him what he wanted to do next.

"I need to go to a tailor in Austin Road, Kowloon for a fitting," he said.

My car was in the Club car park, but I decided not to drive through the cross-harbour tunnel to Kowloon as traffic would be very busy. As it panned out, a wise decision.

"What about taking one of those little boats that go across the harbour?" he suggested.

"You mean the Star Ferry," I said. "Okay, I'll drive to the Park Lane Hotel and leave the car there and we'll take the ferry." I stayed on Paterson

Street in Causeway Bay and had a monthly parking ticket for the hotel car park. We took a taxi from the hotel to the Star Ferry in Central and I bought two first class tickets for the short ride across Victoria Harbour to Tsim Sha Tsui on the Kowloon peninsula. The flaps, which cover the sides of the boat during foul weather, were open so a nice cooling breeze flowed over us. It was a very relaxing, scenic ride; until Marvelous threw me a 'curve ball'.

We were seated on the port side and Marvelous was enjoying the panoramic view – a trip on the Star Ferry is the best way to appreciate the sights of Hong Kong.

Suddenly, he pointed across the water and said to me: "Is that the Hong Kong Hotel over there?"

I nodded.

"That's where Stevie is staying," he said, "Let's go and see him."

Shrugging my shoulders, I said, "Okay." I had no idea who this Stevie was, but if he was a friend of Marvin's then who was I to say no. As we reached Kowloon pier, the Star Ferry sailors, dressed in their smart blue cotton uniforms, dragged the mooring lines of the Celestial Star – our iconic green and white liveried ferry – onto the bollards and we disembarked.

I guided Marvelous to the Hong Kong Hotel via the shortest route, turning a sharp left from the ferry pier and using the side entrance just behind the Star House building next to Ocean Terminal. We pushed through the swing doors and walked briskly to the check-in desk – Marvelous looking smart in his open necked greyish-blue shirt and dark jacket. We were welcomed by a young European desk clerk who asked if he could help.

"Can you put me through to Mr Stevie Wonder's room please," Marvelous said.

Well, when he spoke those words, I said to myself: "Gimme a break, I don't believe this!"

Obviously playing for time, the young clerk started shuffling papers around – I think he was Swiss, although he had a German accent.

Eventually he said, "I'm sorry, he does not appear to be staying here, sir." At that point, the local hotel security guard, who had recognized me, pointed upwards, indicating that Mr Wonder was indeed upstairs in his room. However, before Marvelous could further question the young clerk, a loud voice called out: "Marvelous!"

Next minute, Marvelous is in a welcome embrace with Stevie Wonder's tour promoter.

Exit the hotel clerk!

After high fives with members of the Stevie Wonder entourage, Hagler introduced me to the tour promoter and we shook hands. His name was Zev Eizik and he had arranged Stevie Wonder's tour of Japan – just concluded – and a one-night concert to be held at the Hong Kong Coliseum. He asked Marvelous if he had received the message, sent to his hotel, inviting him to the birthday dinner that night for one of Stevie's backing girls. It was due to be held in a private room on the hotel's 6th floor, beginning at 7.30pm.

Apparently, the tour of Japan was so hectic that they had decided to delay her party and hold it in Hong Kong as they only had one concert lined up here, and that was not for a couple of days. Marvelous and Stevie had been in touch throughout and knew they would both be in Hong Kong at the same time – I wasn't privy to the comings and goings of these superstars, I was just the local travel advisor. But, if Marvelous was going to the party that meant I had a free evening, or so I thought. After confirming his attendance, more high fives followed and then we set off again for Austin Road and his fitting at the tailors.

Marvelous had given me the name card of the tailor and with some difficulty we managed to find it – how he found it in the first place I cannot imagine, unless it was a recommendation from his hotel concierge. It was a 15 minute walk up crowded Nathan Road, the main thoroughfare in Kowloon, then a right at Hillwood Road, left at Pine Tree Hill Road, and there was the tailor's shop, almost directly opposite Cox's Road and the Kowloon Bowling Green Club.

Fitting done, we took a leisurely stroll back to the Nikko Hotel for a drink, then headed to the Hong Kong Hotel so Marvelous could attend the birthday dinner. This time we went through the front entrance into the elegant lobby of the hotel – there have been quite a few name changes over the years and it is currently rebranded as the Marco Polo Hong Kong Hotel.

It was a little early for the party so Marvelous suggested we have another drink and we seated ourselves in a couple of comfortable chairs in the lobby bar. When the waiter arrived Marvelous ordered two Carlsbergs, which I thought was 'probably' a good choice bearing in mind my job at the time. We people-watched for a while, spoke a little about how the day had gone, and when we finished our drinks Marvelous said to me:

"Okay, let's go upstairs and see Stevie."

I was quite shocked. "I don't know Stevie," I said, "and it's a private party. I haven't been invited."

"You wanna' fight?" he asked with a straight face. "No," I stammered, "let's go." We took the elevator to the sixth floor and there was a ping as we exited, just like the bell sounding to end a boxing round.

There was a great deal of trepidation on my part as I walked into the hotel room, and unknown company; Hagler on the other hand was totally at ease as his name echoed around, he could have been walking into the ring in Vegas. Suddenly a figure appeared, elegantly dressed in what appeared to be a loose fitting white kaftan and wearing dark glasses: it was the great man himself.

"Marvelous," he called out, as Hagler walked over and embraced him in a friendly bear-hug. Fair play to Marvelous, he then immediately said to Stevie, "This is my good friend Derek, he's been looking after me in Hong Kong." The musical genius put his hand out and I shook it. "A real pleasure to meet you," I said. Could the day get any better, I thought?

Shortly afterwards I introduced myself to some of the assembled entourage, including Keith John, one of the male backing singers and a quality singer in his own right. I also met the two female singers, one of whose birthday we were celebrating. There were four circular tables in the room set for dinner. Three were quite full, so I was seated at the remaining one. On this table there were only three people: Marvin Hagler, Stevie Wonder and me.

Since my early footballing days I have always been relatively well known in Hong Kong, but sitting next to these two greats for the very first time, I felt totally overawed and somewhat anonymous. But hey, before I knew it the singing superstar next to me started chatting away, asking me about Hong Kong and my background. Soon we could have been mistaken for the 'three amigos' as we laughed and chatted through dinner. Stevie talked about his recent tour of Japan and Marvin described some of the amusing moments he'd had during the shooting of his movie in the Philippines. As we were enjoying the meal I was blown away thinking how much the man sitting next to me had achieved in his life, despite being born blind. What he had accomplished was an inspiration to all.

A true champion, just like the man sitting on the other side of him.

As we were finishing dinner, there was a lot of laughter coming from the other tables and the sound of glasses clinking. A toast to the birthday girl. Before I knew it, the other tables could be heard singing *I just called to say I love you*, one of Stevie's classic hits.

Next thing I know, Marvelous joins in, so does Stevie, and I think, what the hell, and belted out, "And I mean it from the bottom of my heart!" Marvelous, Stevie and I linked hands as we sang several extra choruses: it was surreal, just surreal!

We all clapped when the impromptu performance had finished: Derek Currie, live at the Hong Kong Hotel with Stevie Wonder and Marvin Hagler. What a billing, but what sounded like a fantasy had actually happened!

Amazing, truly amazing, and it all came about because of a telephone call from my old mate, professional photographer Dave Hodges to a bar in Manila. Talking of photography, Marvelous had his camera with him and so did I; after all we were supposed to be sightseeing. I still have in my possession a few of the pictures we took that evening, including one of the three of us at the table together, before our singing act. It comes in handy.

On a few occasions, when the beer has been flowing, I've mentioned the episode to mates in the pub. Their response has always gone something like this: "Singing with Stevie Wonder and Marvin Hagler, yeah right! Sounds like a porky pie to me." Then, after looking deliberately sheepish, I produce the photo on my phone app and with a big grin on my face exclaim "Voila!"

Every time I hear that song, I think of that wonderful day and how good days can banish the bad. As we were leaving the party, Marvelous told me that everybody was going to the Hot Gossip discotheque a little later. I knew Hot Gossip very well and its manager, Bob Teasdale. Carlsberg did regular business with the club, so it was very tempting to go along. But I suddenly became very brave; it might have been the beer and wine I'd consumed. Anyway, I turned to Marvelous and said, "Sorry, it's been a long day, I'm going home... and I'm ready to fight if you insist."

He just laughed and said, "See you tomorrow."

I'm sure it would have continued to be a good night, but I had had enough fun that day, it was time to go home. When I arrived back I was greeted by my Filipino maid. (My second wife worked with Cathay Pacific, so as we had a two-year-old daughter we needed extra hands.)

The maid's name was Loida.

She said, "Sir, you are home late, where have you been?"

"I've been singing with Stevie Wonder," I replied.

Shaking her head knowingly she said, "You're drunk sir, you better go to bed."

I accompanied Marvelous to Kai Tak Airport on the Friday evening. After the excitement that had gone before it was quite a sombre occasion. He was flying to Rome, where he was based, and would miss Stevie's concert the following evening at the Hong Kong Coliseum. After he checked in we walked slowly towards the departure gate. Suddenly he stopped and said, "Wait here a minute." He then dashed off to one of the shops.

He returned carrying a bulging carrier bag. "I almost forgot," he said, "this is for you, thanks for everything."

He handed me the present, then we shook hands and promised to stay in touch. I watched him go through passport control and disappear out of sight; I wondered if I would ever see him again. I began to walk away, then stopped and opened the carrier bag. Inside was a rather smart Cam-Fis sleeveless photographer's vest.

It was a thoughtful touch. I had been his chief 'snapper' for the past six days – taking rolls of film to the camera shop to be developed and then collecting it. Even using my own camera on most occasions. I still have that vest hanging on a rack in my home in Bangkok. I've never really worn it: too much sentimental value.

A few days after Marvelous had left, my Filipino maid got a huge surprise when I showed her my pictures with Marvelous and Stevie Wonder. She put her hands over her mouth in astonishment, then said, "My god, I thought you were joking, sir."

Three days before Christmas 1988 I returned to the Carlsberg offices in the late afternoon and the receptionist handed me a few telephone messages. I walked upstairs to my first floor office, sat down and scanned the messages. One stuck out, it was from Marvelous. I looked at it and smiled; I could just imagine him dictating the wording to the telephone receptionist at the brewery. It was received at 2.14pm, Hong Kong time, and this is how it was spelt out by the receptionist:

"Marvelus Marvin Hagler, World Boxing Champion (USA)," was the heading, then there was a nine digit telephone number and the message "Just to say 'Merry Xmas' to you and please call me back."

It was Christmas, lines were busy, and I never did manage to get through to him; perhaps a digit in the number was wrong. I was very disappointed that I hadn't been in the office to receive his call; but how nice and thoughtful of him to telephone me. It was typical of the gentler side of Marvelous. He may have displayed a ruthless fighting image inside the boxing ring, with his frightening looks and barrage of punches, but he was a real gentleman away from the ring.

I did see Marvelous again, but it would be 27 years later.

I have to thank PC Robbie McRobbie for re-connecting me with Marvelous. (I jest when I call Robbie a PC, although he did spend 11 years in Hong Kong's finest). He became CEO of the Hong Kong Rugby Union and was a worthy recipient of an MBE for Philanthropy and UK Relations in the 2019 UK New Year's Honours list. A top bloke, a fellow Scot from East Lothian, and a director of 'Operation Breakthrough' which was set up by current and former police officers in Hong Kong to help at-risk youngsters find a meaningful life through sport.

Robbie and I are both members of the Carbine Club (Hong Kong Branch) – Robbie is on the committee, while I am a former president (1998-2000) and now an honorary overseas member. Primarily a luncheon, networking and charitable group, whose members have a strong affiliation with sport, there is a Carbine Club branch in every state in Australia, with further branches in New Zealand, Singapore and London, as well as Hong Kong.

Operation Breakthrough was apparently having a fundraising function in conjunction with the widely known Laureus 'Sport for Good' Foundation, which supports many charitable events.

Laureus have International Ambassadors such as former All Blacks rugby great, Sean Fitzpatrick, and former athletic and Olympic champion Dr Edwin ('Ed')Moses was the then Chairman. Boxing is one of the sports Operation Breakthrough supports and a planned sponsorship night to raise funds was scheduled for Friday, March 6, 2015 at the newly built Kai Tak Cruise Terminal, the site of the old Hong Kong airport. Guest of Honour was to be another Laureus Sport for Good Ambassador... you guessed it, Marvelous Marvin Hagler.

Now Robbie knew I had met Marvelous all those years ago, so he told me about the planned event and asked if I would like to come along. His idea being that as I knew Marvelous I would be someone he could relate to and make him feel at home. I offered to MC the whole event, but Robbie already had someone lined up, so I simply accepted his invitation.

I made arrangements to fly up for the event from my base in Bangkok and was excited at the thought of seeing my old friend from nearly three decades ago. Mal Thomson, another director of Operation Breakthrough, as well as being the Hong Kong consultant for Laureus Sport for Good, helped organise the event and was instrumental in getting Marvelous and his wife Kay to Hong Kong. I knew Mal from my time in Hong Kong and suggested to him and Robbie that a night at the Happy Valley horse racing might be an option for Marvelous and Kay on their first full night in Hong Kong. Wheels were put in motion through former Chairman of the Hong Kong Jockey Club, Brian Stevenson – another jock – and a table for ten in a VIP box was arranged for the evening.

It was great to see the champ again when we caught up at the iconic racetrack in the middle of Happy Valley. "I recognize that face," was his opening line. I gave him a friendly hug and he introduced me to his lovely wife Kay. He hadn't changed much, slightly heavier, but the same classy individual.

I never really had the chance to reminisce with Marvelous about his last visit, except to show him that old snap with Stevie Wonder, as everybody at the table was keen to meet and talk to him. "Man that was a while ago, let me have another look at that," he said grinning and taking the photo from me. We backed a few winners that night and several people tried to explain the intricacies of horse racing to our guests as Marvelous and Kay had never attended a race meeting before. Marvelous was not too interested in having a bet, but Kay got the bug and had a few flutters during the course of the night. Luckily some of my tips paid dividends.

Just before the last race finished, Marvelous and Kay left to avoid the race night traffic and headed back to their hotel. I bade them farewell saying I would see them on Friday at the boxing charity night, billed as: 'Cruising for a Bruising'. As it was being held at the Kai Tak Cruise Centre, I thought that was quite apt.

On the day before the event Marvelous gave a boxing clinic to youngsters involved in the Operation Breakthrough boxing project. The event itself was black-tie with over 400 people in attendance; the biggest fund-raising night Operation Breakthrough had ever hosted. There were great auction prizes, including autographed pictures of Dr Edwin Moses and Marvelous from their sporting days, together with autographed treasures of other sporting legends.

Four amateur bouts would take place with Police/Breakthrough boxers against local Hong Kong pugilists. The final fight of the night would be a professional bout between one of the most successful Breakthrough boxers and a leading Filipino fighter. I met Kay and Marvelous on their arrival at the Cruise Centre.

Kay was wearing a classic little black dress, while Marvelous was resplendent in dark dinner suit and a gold stud in his shirt rather than a bow tie.

(My dinner suit had been to the tailor for alterations; it had been a while since I'd worn it.)

As we walked together to our ringside table, Marvelous got side-tracked by autograph hunters and fans who wanted pictures with him, so I walked ahead with Kay to our designated table. Now all the tables had a table card in the centre featuring the name of a boxing great. Ours, unfortunately, had the name: Sugar Ray Leonard!

Kay looked at me aghast and said, "Marvelous won't like that!" It might have been a wind-up, who knows? but I quickly removed the card and deposited it at the table behind! Fortunately Marvelous never saw it. It was a good night's boxing and great to see the enthusiasm shown by the young boxers, cheered on by an equally enthusiastic audience who really got into the spirit of things.

Just before the last fight, the MC announced that they were going to show the classic three rounds of the Marvelous Marvin Hagler versus Thomas 'The Hit Man' Hearns encounter in Las Vegas in 1985. All eyes went to the screens that circled the room.

Billed as a 'Fight', it was later renamed the 'War'. Three rounds of constant action, drama and brutality – and that's putting it mildly – but considered by many to be one of the best, most gruelling fights of all time. Kay was sitting to my left, Marvelous next to her, as we looked up at the action. On the screen, Hearns hit Marvelous with a vicious blow. I leaned towards Marvelous and whispered to him:

"How did you feel when Hearns caught you with that punch?"

Expecting him to say "it was painful", or words to that effect, he just said:

"I was angry!"

I smiled: that was Marvelous.

The fight lasted two minutes and one second into the third round: the referee deciding Thomas Hearns could not take further punishment and stopped the fight. The contest might have taken place thirty years before, but when the recording on the screen came to an end, there was a thunderous roar from the audience inside the hall. Many stood, looked in the direction of Marvelous, clapping wildly in appreciation of what they had just watched; paying homage to an all time great boxer.

Marvelous stood and acknowledged the crowd with a wave.

I almost felt a tear coming to my eye, such was the emotion of the moment. Marvelous must have been the proudest man in the hall as he took salutes from every corner of the packed room. Shortly afterwards, he entered the ring and gave a speech to the assembled audience, talking of the great work being done to help underprivileged youngsters in Hong Kong and around the world.

Dr Edwin Moses, the Laureus Academy chairman, also said a few well chosen words. The night raised a whopping $700,000 for Operation Breakthrough. Valuable money to support sports coaching projects for young people from disadvantaged backgrounds or low income.

Kay and Marvelous were flying back to Rome early the next day, so when the function came to a close, I escorted them to their hotel car and bade farewell, telling them that if they ever came to Bangkok I would look after them.

A few emails would pass between us, particularly at Christmas time, but that night was the last time I would ever see Marvelous. It came as a huge shock to me when I heard the news that he had passed away at the relatively young age of 66 in his home in New Hampshire. His wife Kay, who was at his bedside, reportedly told the media that he died with his usual smile on his face.

A warrior in the ring but one of the kindest when the gloves were off – and not a bad singer as well.

29

The Hong Lok Yuen All-Stars

Hong Lok Yuen is an upmarket housing estate situated beneath Cloudy Hill in the New Territories northeast of Hong Kong, and where I once resided for sixteen years. It was only a 10-minute drive by car, if the traffic lights were with you, to my Carlsberg office in Tai Po.

That said, when driving to work you had to be cautious around the last bend in the road that brought the towering silos of the brewery into sight because the 'old bill' used to ambush you there with speed cameras.

The speed limit was a mere 30mph – even cyclists could get nicked – and many felt the long arm of the law. Saturday morning was their favourite for conducting their modus operandi.

One Saturday, close to Christmas, I received a telephone call from a senior officer who I was acquainted with at Tai Po Police station. The station was roughly two minutes drive before 'ambush pass' in the direction of my office. He asked if I could donate some beer for their Christmas bash in the mess.

Yo ho ho. In good spirits I drove to the station and gave them several cases of beer, plus some goodies for their Christmas raffle; all delivered personally.

When I left the police station I drove across an opening which gave me access to turn right, and headed back towards the brewery still feeling the joys of Christmas approaching. That was until the arm of the law waved me down... I had been ambushed again! Despite pleading that I had just been Santa Claus delivering goodies for their Christmas party, I still got a ticket.

The joys of Christmas quickly vanished; but a telephone call to one in authority put a smile back on my face and I can't recall getting nicked again.

Hong Lok Yuen, which translates as 'happy healthy garden' was originally an orchard owned by Li Fulin, a former Chinese general. Approved for development in 1977, it was completed three years later. The area is reputed to have good *fung shui* – a wind and water expression which translated in English, meant the area had good energy and was a good place to be.

It certainly had a lot of energy as many lively characters lived in the 1,000-odd properties scattered across the hillside.

Hong Lok Yuen also had a kindergarten and primary school within its boundaries. There was a fashionable clubhouse, with a European-style coffee shop on the ground floor, and an excellent Chinese restaurant on the floor above. An angular swimming pool was a short step away from the coffee shop terrace and a further 50 metres down a slight slope was the gym and tennis court, sitting above the aptly named Generals Arms.

The GAs, as it became known, was the entertainment hub where many of the characters who resided within the estate congregated. None of whom, I might add, would have often looked out of place in the sandpit of the kindergarten!

A Scottish-based newspaper once came out to interview Scots who had made Hong Kong their home, and I was one of them. I told the female journalist interviewing me that I had made it 'big' in Hong Kong.

"How do you mean?" she said, looking for an explanation.

"I own a lawnmower!"

She doubled up with laughter, knowing full well that 98% of the population in Hong Kong resided in flats, whereas Hong Lok Yuen, being primarily detached or semi-detached villas, had nice garden areas and the grass needed cutting from time to time.

I was nicknamed the 'Lawnmower Man' in the article that was published in the weekend edition of their newspaper a few weeks later.

In what went on in the GAs – in addition to serious drinking – I can lay some claim to being the Minister of Fun, or guilty party for want of another term.

One of the 'entertainments' I dreamed up was creating an obstacle course in the bar by moving around chairs and other pieces of furniture, including the dart board mat which would be our very own Becher's Brook.

There were normally ten or twelve bodies left in the bar near last orders time – which could really be any time if you tipped the bar staff enough.

When the fun started on the obstacle course – with a substantial liquid inducement to the winner – the participants would crawl under tables or jump the rows of chairs that I had carefully arranged. The fastest over the makeshift course would be declared the winner of the GAs Grand National.

I never participated, I was the chief stipendiary steward and would disqualify anyone who broke the rules.

Bubbles, a tallish West Ham fan, and a largish square-shouldered yank called Carl, would frequently have problems at the Foinavon fence – the space between the chairs was often too tight for them to squeeze or crawl through so they would need assistance.

Many limped out of the GAs with bruises or carpet burns that would only surface the following day.

We also formed a Golf Society and named it GAGS – Generals Arms Golf Society. Most of our outings were across the border to golf courses in Guangdong as the border crossing was not that far on four or six wheels. If we didn't stay there overnight we would head back to the GAs for the presentation of prizes, and that could play out to well past the 19th or even 20th hole.

One of our GAGS boys was Robert, an Irishman, who some years later – 2009 to be exact – would be the one to hand over the Irish Open Golf trophy at County Louth golf club to a young 22-year-old amateur golfer called Shane Lowry; which heralded the young Lowry's entrance onto the sporting world stage. He was destined to become one of Ireland's great golfers.

I remember watching live on TV, the driving rain pouring down, as hundreds of fans at the 18th hole surrounded Lowry being interviewed before Robert handed him the Crystal Trophy. I will always recall how Lowry described the brave fans who had followed him round the golf course that day in horribly wet conditions: "The fans were my 15th club in the bag." Great words.

Robert had left Hong Kong to take up a job as CEO of 3 Ireland, the telecommunications and internet service provider. In 2005 his new company were the sponsors of the Irish Open, hence Robert doing the presentation duties. It was nice to see a former GAGS boy doing the golf honours at such a prestigious event.

Robert, I believe, is now the CEO of 3 UK as well as Ireland, but my last memory of Rob in the flesh wasn't him presenting any trophies, rather it was him helping his pal Bubbles squeeze through the Foinavon fence one boozy night during the GAs Grand National!

We had a great mix of nationalities and many of the golf group were local Hong Kongers – one of them had the initials 'KC' so we called him and his friends KC and the Sunshine Band; in fact KC was actually a good guitarist.

This meant we would often have impromptu jam sessions in the GAs. We also had the 'Doc', an Indian doctor who played a mean guitar and liked to sing and play the blues, when he was not singing *Knockin' on Heaven's Door*.

I used to say to the Doc, give us a song, but not Dylan again! Mind you, he did sing it well.

We were not short of singers in the bar either. There were two Welsh lads who could sing like Harry Secombe and be good in any choir, Goody and Jonno. Unfortunately they tended to hog the mic and I could never get a note in myself.

We also had Sam the Tailor, not the famous one in Tsim Sha Tsui, our Sam was born in Brighton, and was responsible for our tour shirts on trips around Asia. He claimed he was also a good singer, but there were only two bad singers in the club, and Sam was both of them.

We had Aussies in our crew. Rosey was responsible for the Sunday 'barbies'. In his back garden of course. A fun social gathering under the sun, cooking slabs of meat and sausages, washed down by ice-cold beer.

Rosey had a fellow Aussie workmate, Lowey, who used to assist with the barbie. He was a chap who found it difficult to compose a sentence without a swear word or three. A good bloke, though, but the only man I ever heard mentioning the F-word twice describing New South Wales in a conversation. But he cooked a f.......n good barbie.

It would be remiss of me not to mention Ronnie and Johnny, the two barmen who kept the GAs ticking along. If either of them decided to write about the sights they'd witnessed over the years, *War and Peace* would seem like a short story.

They batted off calls from wives looking for their husbands; took car keys away from those not capable of driving – or drove them home; and kept unsigned bar bills for another day.

Dickie, another barman. worked for a short time, but decided driving a taxi was a lot easier.

Then there was 'Georgie Boy'. Nothing to do with a slightly similar title song by the Seekers, he was a Scotsman from Kilmarnock, the former home of Johnnie Walker whisky. Georgie had been in the merchant navy before landing a job with Swire Shipping in Hong Kong, and was happy to wax lyrical about his wartime exploits delivering water to the Falklands during the conflict. Georgie would say that he never feared his ship getting sunk during the conflict, his biggest worry was the cooking. Meal times were a welcome break, but alone on a ship for a month made some of the shipmates on board a bit randy, particularly those in the kitchen. There was even a nasty rumour that a rogue cook on board took great delight in doing something unmentionable into the mashed potato. Georgie told us it put him off mashed potato for life.

We also had a chap called 'Wild Thing' – a play on his name – but he was nothing like his sobriquet; he was one of the most peaceful chaps you could ever meet. Wild Thing worked for the MTR in Hong Kong and also turned out in GAGS golf events. Easily recognizable with his ginger side whiskers and pipe dangling from his lips he had the best golf clubs available on the market, which was great, if only he managed to make contact with the ball.

I recall him on a tour to Thailand where, after we had completed a round at Phoenix golf course in Pattaya, he told me: "Derek, Stocksy has just given me some great advice. He told me I should cut six inches off my grips."

"Will that help you?" I asked Wild Thing.

"No, but Stocksy told me, when I put the clubs in the rubbish bin, I'll be able to close the lid." It was said with a straight face.

We also had a football team on the estate named the Hong Lok Yuen All Stars; the name might have been slightly over the top, but it helped scare the opposition. It involved some of the guys I have already mentioned and others yet to be introduced.

The boys in the GA drank a lot of Carlsberg, so the least I could do was get the company to pay for their jerseys, and I had good contacts at Adidas so the shirts cost next to nothing.

We would play occasional games on a Sunday morning, mainly against army teams in the area, often at Sek Kong army camp. We had a couple of useful players in the team and a few of limited ability who just loved a game.

Step up Brooksy, a Nottingham Forest fanatical supporter, who worked as an aircraft engineer at Kai Tak airport. His love for the game was only superseded by his lack of ability. But he always won the drinking challenge after the game. Brooksy, as I write this, passed away in Manila a short time ago, perhaps not remembered for his football ability, but certainly for the buckets of fun he gave to those around him.

We had the 'Cat', who, when born, must have been dragged out of his mum's womb by his hands, they were so enormous; needless to say he was our goalkeeper. I once anchored a Champions League game on ATV live in the early hours as the regular anchor, Tim Bredbury, was under the weather, so I invited the Cat to replace him on the show. First thing I said as we came on live was that the guest with me that night had bigger hands than Pat Jennings, and on cue, the camera panned in on them.

Then we had a Dutchman called Bert, who I had first met in Manila when he played for the Manila Nomads. Bert had relocated to Hong Kong with his family and although he carried a few extra pounds, still retained a football brain from his Manila days.

The Dutchman also fancied himself as a bit of an ornithologist and claimed to have books on the subject. I assumed he meant that was a fancy way of saying he had copies of *Playboy* or *Penthouse*. But no, one day he told his next-door neighbour Kev, an Aussie boy who put away two packs of fags a day, that he was having a problem with his budgies, and asked if Kev knew anything about the species as he was trying to mate them, but to no avail.

"Listen, mate, I was brought up in Oz and we know all about birds and lizards, let me have a look."

The Dutchman explained he had put mirrors, egg shells and even prepared a nest site to make the birds comfortable, but nothing had happened.

Kev had a look at the budgies and said to the Dutchman: "You have six birds here, right. I know what the problem is. They're all fuckin' male, you stupid bastard!"

'The Birdman of 18th Street' we called the Dutchman for a while and used to whistle when he walked into the pub.

As a matter of fact, Bert the Dutchman was one of my closest pals, but now, another gone to his maker.

Sadly, Bert met Scotty in Hong Lok Yuen. Scotty was a Geordie who worked for a commercial printer that printed the banknotes for the Hong Kong Government. I say sadly because, although they had a love of football, they both had abandoned training.

For instance, just before we were going on a tour to Manila to play in a Carlsberg-sponsored, Manila Nomads six-a-side, I called Scotty's wife, only to be told that Scotty had gone out for a run with the Dutchman.

I ran around the estate looking for them and then wised up. I walked into the GA a half-hour or so later and there were Scotty and the Dutchman sitting with large glasses of beer in front of them, not their first!

"I thought you had both gone for a run, to get some fitness into the pair of you," I chided them.

"We did," was the reply, "to the pub!"

I just had to laugh, well, it was hardly the World Cup finals we were heading to in Manila.

Scotty had a next-door neighbour called Carson who was a flyer, not down the wing, but in the air, a captain with the local airline. He just happened to be on the same flight as Gascoigne and company making their way back to London after the famous 'dentist's chair' incident in Hong Kong, heading back for Euro '96.

Carson was not flying the plane, but on as a passenger in Business Class, but rumour has it he was passing out more drink to the English players than the air hostesses.

Scotty was such a Newcastle United fanatic that he would watch repeats of Jackie Milburn's funeral on his DVD on a Sunday morning while his Filipino wife attended church. Scotty was over six feet tall and well built; occasionally he would go on a diet, telling me he was limiting his breakfast to only poached eggs... but his wife leaked it was eight portions!

Being a man of appetite, I told him the Bostonian Restaurant in Tsim Sha Tsui's Ramada Renaissance Hotel had a 46-ounce prime rib of beef offer on its menu: the incentive to order it was that if anybody could finish it, the hotel would tear up the bill. I told Scotty that one person had actually finished the meal; but it had taken them one and a half hours.

"Get away, that's ridiculous," said the 190cm tall, 89kg printer, who promptly took up the challenge one evening.

In an astonishing display, Scotty not only downed the gigantic prime rib, but did it in a mind-boggling seven minutes. "There was no charge so I rounded the meal off with a salad," he told me.

A couple of days later, Scotty's exploits appeared in the *SCMP* which had a much-read daily column entitled, 'Keeping Posted'. I had leaked the information to my old friend, John Dykes, who was covering the column for regular writer Simon Beck while he was on annual leave.

I gave Dykesy Scotty's telephone number at work and he called the big Geordie for confirmation and to get some quotes for the story.

"It wasn't that hard, I hadn't had any lunch that day and it went down well with my beer," he said.

"I asked the waiter for some sauce while I was eating, but he was too slow and when he came back I had scoffed it; he started looking under the table to see what I had done with the steak."

The postscript was that when I next met Scotty's missus, she gave me an earful, saying people would think she never fed her husband properly. She didn't speak to me for a month, although she eventually relented and saw the funny side.

Scotty is now residing in Malta and still working in the 'paper money' business; his hobby is keeping old classic cars in his garage, but claims it eats up a lot of petrol when he takes one out for a spin. If anybody knows about eating up, it would be him.

At that time, a lot of Cathay Pacific pilots and flight engineers lived on the estate, as well as quite a few jockeys, such as multiple champion jockey Basil Marcus, Wendyll Woods, Dean McKeown, Geoff Allendorf and Philip Robinson, so there was always the odd tip flying about, excuse the pun.

Georgie Boy's next-door neighbour was Sam Hui, star of TV, music and movies in Hong Kong. Even former Manchester United and Leeds United star Gordon McQueen lived there for almost two years during a stint with my former club, Seiko.

His next-door neighbour was Brooksy, who would cheekily hang his Nottingham Forest scarf out the window, just to annoy big Gordon.

I might have played against some of best players in the world, but my Hong Lok Yuen days were as memorable as any playing against Pelé or Eusébio.

30

Going to the dogs

Another unconventional character was Rex Joseph, alias 'The Witness'.

Rex resided in Macau, the 'Monte Carlo of the East', where the gambling empires of businessmen Henry Fok and Stanley Ho had taken root.

Sadly the The Witness never joined them in the multi-millionaire category, quite the opposite in fact, but he was one of the best liked characters around.

In the early 70s the tiny Portuguese enclave had four divisions of gambling: casino games; greyhound racing; sports betting; and lotteries. Rex's forte was greyhound racing – or the 'dish lickers' as it was called by many, including me.

The sport was popular around that time and Macau had the biggest dog track in Asia; for many years it was also the only dog track in Asia, opening in the mid 60s. The dogs would be brought over from Australia and the kennels housed over 600 dogs at any given time; the track was owned by the Ho family.

The Canidrome had two grandstands, with a football ground in the middle where Macau played their home fixtures. On various occasions I played on the rock-hard surface there during my early Seiko days when we would have friendly fixtures against Macau. More like training sessions if truth be told as, for good measure, multi-millionaire Henry Fok, a capable footballer himself, used to guest for our team.

Fok, a keen sportsman who loved playing tennis and football, was President of the Hong Kong Football Association; a legacy passed down to his son, Timothy, who, I believe, is still president today.

But back to The Witness.

Although you could bet on the dogs at the track, or in the Lisboa Casino, which had betting booths with a live feed link-up to the course, it was not quite legal in Hong Kong. Back in those days, willing bookies were not too difficult to find if you fancied a wager on our four-legged friends.

Dog racing was four nights a week: 16 races at 15 minute intervals – though some races were delayed slightly in order to accept bets pouring in to supplement the tote. Races were staged over 350 or 510 yards.

Bearing in mind horse racing was limited to one meeting a week, prior to the establishment of night racing, then dog racing was another option for many gamblers… and there were plenty of them about. So because of the popularity in Hong Kong of racing in the Canidrome *The Star* newspaper published the fields for the meetings, as did many local Chinese newspapers.

Step up Rex Joseph, the top dog tipster in Macau: Rex featured in the sports section of *The Star* providing expert advice and selections. A job he was ably suited to.

His problem however was coming over from Macau to Hong Kong once a month to pick up his pay packet.

Just opposite the newspaper office in Pennington Street, in the heart of Causeway Bay, was Keswick Street, which was only 150 metres long. It had a nice little bar, tucked away halfway down, called the Moonlight – perhaps it should have been called 'Twilight' since it had a dark, murky interior and was populated by somewhat shady characters.

It was owned by a Hong Kong native going by the English name of 'Henry', who invariably had a cigarette dangling from his lips and a glass of Scotch in his hand.

It was also the spot where the predominantly Aussie sports journos from *The Star* had their piss-up at the end of the month when payday arrived.

Copious cans of Fosters and San Miguel were downed, before slipping up to the room above the bar for the all-night poker game; interspersed with betting on a toy set of electric horses the boys had somehow acquired.

Although he had a lot of fun on these nights, regular as clockwork, The Witness invariably went back to Macau broke most months. Losing his entire earnings at the card table or on the electronic horses.

Sometimes he even had to borrow money for the ferry ride back to Macau.

For many, it was a social – not to mention financial – tragedy the day his wife announced that The Witness was banned from going to Hong Kong to get his pay packet... she found other means of obtaining his monthly earnings.

Sadly, The Witness was never seen in Hong Kong again.

31

The Currie stable

Ever since I asked my old Dad to put a shilling each way on Lester Piggott's mount St. Paddy – which romped home by three lengths to win the 1960 Epsom Derby at 7/1 – I'd always hoped, but never thought it possible, that I might own a racehorse myself.

I remember the lyrics of Peter Sarstedt's 1969 number one hit, *Where Do You Go To My Lovely.*

"Your name is heard in high places
You know the Aga Khan
He sent you a racehorse for Xmas."

The Aga Khan: a name synonymous with horse racing and wealth.

Well, 25 years after that Sarstedt hit I owned a horse that would race against one carrying the Aga Khan's famous racing colours: green with red epaulettes. The boy who had a shilling each way had upped his stakes. Let me tell you how it came about.

Owning a racehorse is a costly business, but I thought in Hong Kong it might be possible. So one day I asked my colleague at Carlsberg, Marketing Manager Edwin Lam, if he would like to apply alongside me for a permit to buy a horse and race it there. We were both racing members of the Hong Kong Jockey Club and therefore allowed to jointly apply in the annual ballot to obtain such a permit. Thankfully, Edwin agreed, so our joint names went into the ballot and we were lucky enough to be successful.

Next thing: find a suitable horse.

I turned to my friend Parky. He had a lot of good connections when it came to buying horses; or so he told me.

There were two types of permit given for importing a horse into Hong Kong: one was for bringing in a previously raced horse, or PP (Pre-import

Performance) as it was known; the other was for a Privately Purchased Griffin, an unraced horse, otherwise knows as a PPG.

Edwin and I had applied for a PP rather than go the unraced route. Parky didn't let us down. Ever the optimist, he had been sure that Edwin and I would get a PP permit in the draw, so was ahead of the game. He had already contacted a friend of his in Ireland called Bobby O'Ryan, a bloodstock agent, asking him to be on the lookout for a suitable horse for Hong Kong.

Bobby told him that eleven-time Irish amateur champion jockey, Ted Walsh, now turned trainer, had a nice two-year-old sired by Faustus. Before retiring to stud in 1987 Faustus had won listed Group 3 races, including the Lanson Champagne stakes at Goodwood. His breeding lines went back to his paternal racing grandfather, Roberto, who won the Epsom Derby in 1972, ridden by none other than the great man himself, Lester Piggott, my 1960 Derby hero (was this an omen?).

In 1972 Roberto also won the inaugural Benson and Hedges Gold Cup over a mile and a quarter at York, handing the legendary Brigadier Gerard his only defeat in 18 starts. (Brigadier Gerard was considered by many to be the best horse of the 20th century.)

Bobby O'Ryan had already mentioned to Ted Walsh that Parky, who Ted knew, was looking for a horse for a friend in Hong Kong. He offered to give Parky first call on the steely grey gelding son of Faustus and a nominal fee was agreed, subject to agreement from the potential owners.

Parky often went back to the UK during the racing off season in Hong Kong to see old racing buddies, and could be seen regularly at Newmarket, Ascot and York, plus Killarney in his native Ireland. When he went back this time, his first port of call was County Kildare to see Ted Walsh.

Parky called me from Ireland to tell me that according to Bobby O'Ryan the steely grey had recently done an impressive gallop at the Curragh racetrack, so Ted might be reconsidering his decision to sell. "But don't worry," Parky said confidently, "Ted's an old friend, and he's promised me first call on the horse."

A day later an excited Parky was on the phone again: "You've got a horse, my boy, I told you Ted was as good as his word." Ecstatic, I passed on the good news to Edwin.

The next step was to find a suitable race for him in Ireland as he needed a race rating to be eligible for import to Hong Kong. The grace period for a PP is 18 months, but I was keen to get the horse in early to ensure that he was suitably acclimatized before the racing season started. After all, Hong Kong is a tad hotter and more humid than any heat wave County Kildare has to offer.

The Hong Kong Jockey Club required rating (a score derived from the horse's performance overseas) was 68 for two-, three-, and four-year-old PP horses; five-year-olds and above are prohibited in order to preserve a good standard of racing in Hong Kong. I checked with Parky and he told me that Ted Walsh had entered the horse to run at Fairyhouse on the third of September in the Woodpark Stud Maiden for two-year-olds. The year was 1994.

The horse would race under the name I had given him, Casey's Drum – as managing partner I had naming rights – but would race in Ted's wife Helen's colours; although technically now the horse belonged to me and Edwin. We would pay the entry fee and jockey fee, and any winnings would come to us.

Let me briefly explain the choice of name, it had nothing to do with it being foaled in Ireland.

My dear old Dad often used to take me to Hamilton Park racetrack just outside Glasgow in the late 1950s. The crowds were enormous; people flocked to the track to enjoy a good family day out and, if they were lucky, supplement their income. My Dad used to sit me on his shoulders so I could see the thoroughbreds flashing past on their way to the uphill finishing post. "It couldn't beat Casey's Drum," he would often utter if his selection trailed home behind the leading pack, using an old Irish expression. That's what I'll name my horse I thought, if I'm ever lucky enough to get one! Sadly, my Dad died in 1974. He would never see the mighty Casey's Drum race.

In 1994, September 3 fell on a Saturday. I would not be at Fairyhouse to watch Casey's Drum make his first race appearance, though I had made arrangements to listen to live commentary on the race from my home in Hong Lok Yuen. Parky, as enterprising as ever, had promised to give me a direct line to Tony O'Hehir, the famed voice of Irish racing, who was calling the race at Fairyhouse that day.

"Inside connections my boy," said Parky.

As race time approached, I supped a cold Danish lager to lessen the tension, worried as to how the horse would perform – well we were seven hours ahead of Ireland, so it was almost ten thirty in the evening in Hong Kong. I dialled the number Parky had given me from my house phone and, amazingly, Tony O'Hehir answered after a couple of rings.

"Hello Tony, it's Derek Currie here," I said, "many thanks for letting me listen to your commentary."

"Derek, no problems, happy to do so," he replied. "Any thoughts on how he might run?" I asked.

"He looked good in the paddock, and if he runs anywhere near the even-money favourite in the race, you have a horse."

"Who's the favourite?" I asked.

"Manashar, ridden by Johnny Murtagh and owned by the Aga Khan," he answered.

'The Aga Khan!' I echoed in disbelief; my mind going back to the Sarstedt song.

"Derek", he said, "it looks like the race has been delayed five minutes or so, why not call me back in four minutes; no sense in wasting money on the long distance call." We both hung up. More tension.

"The Aga Khan," I kept repeating, as I headed to the fridge for another can of lager. As a young boy from the east end of Glasgow, never did I imagine that I would one day own a horse that would race against one of the Aga Khan's. A sense of pride rippled through me. The lager initially helped ease my nerves, but when I again phoned the race caller's box in Fairyhouse I was tingling all over.

"The white flag is up... and they're off." The familiar Irish lilt of O'Hehir crackled through the ether all the way to Hong Kong. As the race progressed I became more and more excited.

The horses galloped round the right-handed bend into the straight... two and a half furlongs to go... Casey's Drum hit the front. My heart was pumping, hoping he would still be there at the business end of proceedings. Not far to go now I thought.

Tony O'Hehir's voice rose several decibels: "It's Casey's Drum with a furlong to go; Tirolean on the outside and Manashar just behind looking for a split between the two."

Argh! It sounded like the Aga Khan's horse was ready to pounce; with no picture to look at I could only go by O'Hehir's rising voice.

"As they race towards the line it's Casey's Drum with Willie Supple on board from Manashar and Johnny Murtagh," O'Hehir roared.

"A hundred yards to go and Manashar has got past Casey's Drum. As they race up to the line, it's Manashar by a length from Casey's Drum, with a fast finishing Mister Positive in third."

The next thing I heard over the phone was Tony O'Hehir saying to me: "You've got a horse!" I thanked Tony profusely and the line went dead.

I held the phone in my hand for a few seconds, then called Parky, who by now was back to Hong Kong.

"It ran second to the favourite, Manashar," I told him excitedly, "the one owned by the Aga Khan."

"My boy, I told you I had an eye for a horse, as, of course, does Bobby O'Ryan, between us we have got you and Edwin a real racehorse." Ted Walsh, had truly prepared the horse well, although I never really had any doubts. Ted was part of the fabric of Irish racing, as were his family. I called co-owner Edwin Lam and told him the good news: the Drum was coming to Hong Kong on a rating of 74. So far, so good.

Parky had done a great job, so when Casey's Drum arrived in Hong Kong I took his advice again and stabled the horse in David Hill's yard. David was a youngish trainer who started his career in India in 1969 under the guidance of his father. In 14 years training there he was

Champion Trainer in both Madras and Bangalore. On leaving India David was granted a licence to train in Hong Kong and wasted no time building up a successful stable. He had in his care probably one of Hong Kong's greatest equine heroes, the magnificent River Verdon.

To local racing fans River Verdon was a superstar. He was the first, and so far only, horse to win the local Triple Crown in a season, achieving it in 1993/94. His effigy has pride of place in the Hong Kong Racing Museum. Being in the same stable, I was hoping River Verdon might inspire my young steely grey; they could at least nod to one another each day – if horses talked like 'Mr Ed', I hoped the Drum would listen to him!

At 1,140 kilos Casey's Drum was a big horse and the often fast tracks in Hong Kong were a slight concern for his fragile legs. We were therefore careful in picking his races.

He made his Hong Kong debut on May 13, 1995 over 1200m on a good to yielding track. His dam's sire was Kenmare, so any cut in the ground would favour the big fella. He was to be ridden by John Marshall, who, incidentally, went on to win the 1999 Melbourne Cup on Rogan Josh. A quietly spoken man who shunned publicity, John was a real gentleman who made his name riding for Bart Cummings in Sydney. In later years, John would sadly lose a battle with pancreatic cancer, leaving behind Debbie, and two young sons. I'm sure they must be immensely proud of their father's accomplishments.

On that afternoon in May our racing colours saw the light of day for the first time: John wore blue silks with white cross-belts, paying homage to the St. Andrew's Cross (the national flag of Scotland), and a matching cap. Edwin and I wished him well in the Paddock and Parky even left his duties in the press room to come down and offer words of encouragement. Now it was up to the big steely grey.

Anyone who has ever owned a horse, and I don't mean just for the first time, will tell you how nervous they feel just before the starting gates open. I was never nervous before a football match as it was all in my own hands. Now I was relying on somebody else's hands, literally; John's judgement of the pace of the race, his positioning in the field, and the release of the Drum's speed at just the right moment were things I could do nothing about. All you want is for your horse is to get a clean break at the start, give his best, hope he suffers no injury, and, most of all, get that little bit of luck in running to give him a sporting chance. John Marshall gave Casey's Drum every chance.

He ran a gallant second, finishing a length and a quarter behind the 3/1 favourite, Green Supreme, ridden by Tony Cruz, a jockey I'd known since he was a lad of fourteen. I was absolutely delighted with his performance, as was Edwin. I had backed the Drum each way, and at 5/1 enjoyed a reasonable payout as I also had him in the quinella with the winner.

Training fees in Hong Kong were quite high, but prize money was really good, so a second place was a good result all round. The higher the class your horse raced in, the bigger prize money; this had been a Class 2 race. The big fella would get plenty of carrots from my nine-year-old daughter Claudia the next day.

Casey had a big heart, but he would have leg problems because of his size, so would need to be sparingly raced. Although he would run again just two weeks later. This time over 1400m on a good track. Again he was ridden very well by John Marshall, and again he finished second, beaten by the same margin as before. I was delighted by his efforts; surely a win would come soon.

But I had to wait a long time before that day came.

Due to leg problems he wouldn't race again for another 16 months. Finally, in late November 1996, he was fit enough to run. This time he would be ridden by Frenchman, Eric Legrix as John Marshall had moved on to become stable jockey for trainer John Moore.

It was a 1,000 metre race, which was considered way too short for him, but we wanted to see how his legs would hold up after he had recovered from an operation he had undergone earlier in the year. The operation had come about thanks to the generosity of trainer Bruce Hutchison.

Hutchie had one of the best Australian equine surgeons, Alistair McLean, in town performing operations on some of his injured horses.

He kindly let Alistair take X-rays of the Drum to try and locate the cause of his problems. As a result of these, Alistair performed a minor operation on him – I might add, at a fraction of the cost that I understand would normally be charged.

I thanked Hutchie and Alistair for their kindness. Believe me, they were very generous! To my great relief the Drum came through the operation in good shape. It was now time to see if he could still perform, hence the run down the straight 1,000 metres at Sha Tin. I remember the day well.

I had been at Fanling watching the Hong Kong Golf Open a few days earlier. One of the young amateurs competing was only 18 years old and had just missed the cut, leaving him and his caddie with a free weekend. I think it was local golfer Dominique Boulet who suggested that I cheer them up by taking them to the racing on Sunday; the caddie in particular was a keen horse racing fan.

As I had Casey's Drum running, it would be fun for them to sample the thrill of Sha Tin and being in the paddock. The golfer was young Graeme Storm, who went on to have a great amateur career before joining the professional circuit. So, I'm in the paddock with the pair of them and Casey is at 25/1 on the tote board.

"I can't really tell you to back my horse, he's had a few leg issues," I lamented. They were just happy to be there, they told me. I then had a few words with Eric before he jumped aboard Casey and I shouted "*Allez les bleus!*" as he left the parade ring.

As I stood with my guests in the owner's stand watching the race, I started to get more and more excited. Eric was suddenly coming with a late surge. He was threading his way through the field: fifth... fourth... third... second... but eventually he was beaten two lengths! Second again! Unbelievable! Eric leapt off him shouting, "*Allez les bleus!*"

I was over the moon with the run, but had to apologize to my two guests who had not backed the Drum. I had given them little encouragement. I had not expected him to run so well, although I did have an owner's modest each-way bet on him, just in case. Not enough for a bottle of Lanson bubbly, but I did buy my guests a few ales.

Casey's Drum had now had three starts, with three second places. He went on to finish fourth and second in subsequent starts. But we never got the best out of him until we upped the race distance; something his breeding indicated he needed as he got older.

In a Class 3 race at Sha Tin, in the hands of Aussie jockey, Paddy Payne, he again finished second, this time over a mile. Another second! That made five in all. But, despite that, there was a new feeling of optimism.

On March 11, 1998 he was entered into an 1800m race. Brian Rouse had ridden him in a dirt trial for me several days before the race and told me he was in fine fettle. Brian was a good judge.

He won by a length and a quarter at odds of 9/1 carrying almost top weight in another Class 3 contest. 35,000 people on course watched him that day and we celebrated with more than a few glasses of bubbly.

"Patience has been rewarded, the steely grey wins his first race. Derek Currie and his partner Edwin Lam deserve the plaudits for their trust in the horse," were the words of commentator Richard Hoiles after Casey had passed the finishing post.

The next day the *SCMP* carried the following headline in their racing pages: "Casey's Drum and Jesus, the perfect pair for Easter Saturday." Suggesting it was the omen bet of the day. Mind you, 'Holy Grail' also won that day. I should have backed the double!

Three weeks later, over 1900m on a yielding track, and up in Class 2, he won again. This time by a head at 11/2. "Happy Days" said Hoiles after Casey passed the post.

Casey's Drum would race in further class 1 and 2 events, but in 1999 Edwin and I decided to retire him. He had done us proud, but we knew his large frame was putting undue pressure on his legs so it was time to call it a day. He had brought a lot of joy and pleasure, not only to us, but to many of our friends who had enjoyed the race day outings and excitement whenever he ran. I even had Archie Knox (who had been

Alex Ferguson's assistant at Old Trafford and Walter Smith's at Ibrox) and goalkeeper Andy Goram with me one afternoon in the paddock.

As to the Drum's retirement. well, David Hayes was training in Hong Kong at the time and his family had the wonderful Lindsay Park stable in Victoria, Australia. David offered to accommodate Casey's Drum at his beautiful complex after Casey had spent a short time at Beas River, the home for retired racehorses next to Fanling golf course and run by the Jockey Club. David said he would be happy to look after Casey's Drum at no cost; who said you don't have friends in horse racing! It was a long way from where he was born in Ireland, but the steely grey deserved a pleasant retirement and Lindsay Park certainly provided him with that.

———————

I had another horse two years later, he might not have had the same pedigree as Casey's Drum, but supplied just as much joy. He also lived up to his name, winning a race by a head.

His name: Glasgow Kiss.

Both my horses had 11 letters or apostrophes in their name, no coincidence as I always wore number 11 on the football field.

Anyway, trainer David Hill showed me a video of a nice two-year-old going through its paces in Australia. I had applied successfully for another horse permit – a PPG for an unraced horse – this time on my own. Hill was bullish about the one cantering in the video. It was sired by Keltrice which had breeding links to Kenmare, who had sired Kenmara, Casey's Drum's mother. The lineage was good and the price seemed reasonable. However, just prior to making arrangements for the young horse to be flown to Hong Kong I got a call from David Hill informing me that the horse had had a bad accident in training. The deal was off!

That's the ups and downs of racing.

On the bright side, Hill told me the agent would try and get a good replacement for me. To cut a long story short, an unraced horse sired by Magic Ring out of Quiet Little Drink became available. The Keltrice progeny had looked a good prospect, but since I was still working for

Carlsberg, perhaps the replacement's dam being Quiet Little Drink was an omen.

The brown gelding would turn out to be no superstar. In his first season as a griffin – an unraced horse that has been imported – he ran against similarly classified two-year-olds, but the best he could do were a couple of fifth place finishes, although that meant I got some minor prize money.

During his career he would win just over a million dollars in prize money, so the 'Kiss' paid his way.

The racing colours were almost identical to those of Casey's Drum: blue with white cross-belts, the only difference being a red and white cap. As I was born and brought up in Glasgow I had decided to name him Glasgow Kiss. I thought the name had a pleasing ring to it. Mind you, Glasgow is probably not the place for a 'Quiet Little Drink!' To me it was a fun name for a horse, but a steward in the Jockey Club didn't agree.

Winfried Engelbrecht-Bresges was the Executive Director of Racing at the time; he became CEO in 2007. Winfried, who often chatted to me about football, him being a former German youth footballer, stopped me at the track one day and asked if I could explain, by letter, why I sought to name my horse Glasgow Kiss. He told me Sir Gordon McWhinnie, a fellow Scot who I knew fairly well, had queried approval of the name, saying he believed that it meant 'head butt' in Glasgow slang.

In my letter I pointed out that the term was now culturally accepted; it was simply a humorous allusion to Glasgow being a tough city. I pointed out that the BBC even had a popular TV series titled Glasgow Kiss and that the show had received no complaints about the name. I concluded by saying that if I had wanted to call it 'Head Butt' I would have done so. I was tempted to sign with a few xx's. The name was accepted.

After his first season, Glasgow Kiss was graded into Class 4, one above the bottom grade. He did later drop into Class 5, but midway through the season, jockeys Douglas Whyte and Eddie Lai each managed to coax second placings out of him over 1400m. But it was his run near the end of the season that caught me and almost everyone else out.

The date was Saturday, May 25, 2002.

Portugal, featuring an all star line-up that included Real Madrid's Luís Figo and AC Milan's Rui Costa, were playing in Macau against the Chinese national team. It was a friendly game on Taipa Island with an 8pm kick-off, and it was a sell-out. I was doing part-time TV work with ATV in Hong Kong and they were covering the game live; Tim Bredbury and I were to provide the English commentary. I wanted to get over to Macau early for the game, but there was one slight problem: Glasgow Kiss was running in the third race at Sha Tin.

It was a muggy afternoon. I was wearing my white jacket and tie at the track and carrying my football notes in a folder, ready for a quick exit. Suffice to say, I didn't expect a win.

South African jockey, Anton Marcus, brother of champion jockey Basil, was riding Glasgow Kiss over 1400m but had been badly drawn in gate 12 of 14. The track was good to yielding. The Kiss was 13/1 in the betting, but I had no great confidence in him; I was just hoping for a top five finish and a bit of prize money.

From his poor gate he was near the tail of the field as they headed to the turn. Suddenly there was considerable buffeting between the leading horses as they began rounding the long bend going into the home straight. Anton quickly took advantage. Despite already being four or five off the fence he pushed the 'Kiss' even wider coming off the bend and hit the front.

I remember watching the race on the TV just inside the weighing room with a couple of trainers. One of whom was Lawrie Fownes. Watching Marcus take the horse wide, and then trying to make him lead down the straight, Lawrie remarked: "Currie, you giving your horse a run today?" – meaning running it into the ground so it would ultimately fold and be better handicapped for its next run. I didn't reply, I was glued to the TV.

There were 300m to go and he was still in the lead, Marcus urging him on.

100m to go. He was still in the lead.

Lawrie Fownes glancing at me, somewhat shocked, said: "he might win!"

Frenchman, Eric Saint-Martin on board Handsome Man threw everything he could at the Kiss, closing rapidly right up to the line. They finished neck and neck. A photo was called for.

I was suddenly nervous, the photo seemed to take forever and I also had a taxi to catch. Eventually the result went up: Glasgow Kiss by a nose – I suppose you could say he stuck his head out and butted the line first! I didn't know whether to laugh or cry.

I had to wait to get the victory picture taken of me and the Kiss, then rush to pick up winnings – I had placed a few hundred dollars on him each way, just in case. (He won at 13/1, which was very handy; but the prize money was even handier.)

After a hair-raising taxi ride I just made the ferry and was relieved, but very happy, when I eventually landed in Macau. I had an hour or so before I had to be at the stadium, so stopped at a hotel where I knew some friends were having a drink before they went to the match. David Allison, son of 'Big Mal', and Ambrose Turnbull, circulation manager of the *SCMP*, were in good spirits. They had both had a little bet on the 'Kiss' and offered to buy me a celebration drink. I desperately wanted a drink to celebrate, but since I was working on TV it was only a soda water!

For the record, Portugal beat China 2-0.

Jiang Jin, in goal for China, saved a penalty in the first half, but two second half goals by Fiorentina's Nuno Gomez and Bordeaux's Pauleta sealed the win.

At 11.45pm, in the Macau Mandarin Oriental Hotel bar, I finally had a beer to celebrate Glasgow Kiss's win. It had been one heck of a long day I can tell you. It was well 'after midnight' when Tim and I left the bar, Clapton could have been there for all I knew, but it wasn't a 'Quiet Little Drink!'

In the late afternoon of the following day I made the trip to Sha Tin stables with my daughter, Claudia. She gave the Kiss his much deserved carrots. I was still a little dazed: where did that amazing run come from?

Early the following season Australian Craig Williams, a 25-year-old jockey very much on the way up, managed to coax Glasgow Kiss to a couple of minor placings. Sadly, like Casey's Drum, the Kiss had his fair share of injuries, mostly back related. However, four days before Xmas he was to race on a good to yielding surface over 1400m from a good barrier draw in gate 2.

It was a funny old time in the paddock that day. I had a few pals with me, Sam Perry, Kevin Boorer, but it was Martyn Goodchild's father-in-law, Len Jones, who stole the show. Martyn had brought Len along. He was a Welshman who loved the horses and he and his wife Margaret were visiting their daughter and son-in-law over the festive season. Len was genuinely excited, it was his first time in the paddock before a race, so I asked him, "Did you bring a camera to take some pictures Len?" Ah, he didn't.

"Martyn, did you bring a camera?" Len asked. No, he didn't either.

In fact, none of our group had a camera – mobile phones with built-in cameras had yet to be invented.

"There is one chance Len," I said with a big smile, "if Glasgow Kiss wins today, they'll take an official picture of us all with the horse and I can get you a copy."

Craig Williams then joined the group to discuss our winning chances, prior to getting ready to mount up for the race. Before I could even introduce Craig to everyone, Len piped up: "I've travelled over 6,000 miles to be here, you better win today!"

Craig took it in his stride:"I'll certainly do my best." Happily, his best was good enough: he won by a length at 9/1. Len got his photograph.

While the cameras snapped away as we all stood under the winning arch, a beaming Len whispered to me: "This has been the best day of my life!"

"Do you want me to tell Margaret that?" I joked.

"I mean second best day," he quickly replied guiltily.

Such moments are what make owning a racehorse so rewarding. Len was over the moon with his framed photograph and Martyn told me he gave it pride of place in his home back in Wrexham. He also told me that, unbeknownst to me, Len had had a good bet on Glasgow Kiss that day, winning enough to buy a new suite for his sitting room! Apparently he even named it the 'Glasgow Kiss Suite' and hung the photograph on the wall above. Thank goodness the Kiss won that day!

In the second half of the season the Kiss suffered more back problems. He was well cared for however and did manage to race again, although placing fourth was the best he could manage. On May 18, 2003 he was actually backed into favouritism, after running on well for sixth in his previous race. Champion jockey Douglas Whyte elected to ride him on a yielding track, and there was a great deal of optimism. However, taking him down to the start Whyte felt something was amiss and decided to jump off him. He was subsequently declared a non-runner. The favourite was out of the race.

An X-ray clearly illustrated further back problems; it was time for the Kiss to retire.

Stuart Mitchell, a racing buddy who was in charge of equestrian affairs at the Jockey Club, had family connections at a racing farm in Australia's Hunter Valley and that is where Glasgow Kiss saw out his days.

Being the son of a Quiet Little Drink, the major wine area north of Sydney, seemed the perfect place for him.

32

Lasting impressions

Over the years I've met some amazing people. With some it was just for a chat; others became great friends. All have contributed to a lifetime of memories.

Robin Parke

My old friend Parky features so often throughout this book it's a wonder nobody has written an epic about him. Mind you, would it be fact or fiction?

I'm going tell you how I sadly put my dear old friend to rest in August 2001; but first, a classic Parky story.

He was responsible for bringing Glasgow Celtic to Hong Kong to play a one-off match on Sunday, March 7, 1982.

Parky thought it would be a financial blockbuster because their opposition was to be Hong Kong Rangers – not quite the other half of the Glasgow 'Old Firm', but interesting enough to attract spectators, or so he thought.

He was as proud as punch when two days before the game, he welcomed manager Billy McNeill and his team at Kai Tak airport. The side included captain Roy Aitken, Tommy Burns, Murdo MacLeod, Packie Bonner and Danny McGrain. I had played alongside Danny as a teenager with Queen's Park so it was nice to catch up with him.

There was also a young fresh-faced 19-year-old in the Celtic team, who would eventually go on to replace Alex Ferguson as manager of Manchester United. His name: David Moyes.

Albert Yeung – a wealthy gentleman who, then as now, was chairman of the Emperor Group in Hong Kong – was chairman of Hong Kong Rangers at the time and on hand to greet the visitors. He may even have been Parky's financial backer in this little venture as they were good friends.

Celtic were to be paid £20,000 as a match fee, plus airfares and accommodation at the Park Lane Hotel in Causeway Bay.

The team were also on a goal bonus of £500 for the first goal and £200 for each subsequent goal.

However, the canny Irishman put a clause in the contract that if Celtic lost to Hong Kong Rangers they would forfeit half the match fee. This was inserted to ensure that Celtic took the game seriously, rather than just treating it as a leisurely exhibition. All this information was leaked to the media to help boost the gate.

Hong Kong Rangers had former St Mirren, Norwich and Partick Thistle player Jimmy Bone in their side. Bone had also had a short spell at Celtic.

Steve Paterson, who would go on to manage Inverness Caledonian Thistle and Aberdeen, was also in the line-up, as was former Scottish international Tommy Hutchison – at the time he was playing for local side Bulova but they had consented to him guesting for Rangers.

It all looked good on paper. Then the rains came.

It poured so heavily that at one stage the match going ahead was in the balance.

I had helped Parky arrange a friendly game before the main match between a team of jockeys against a team comprising local TV celebrities, just to add a bit of colour to the occasion and bring in the crowds.

But as it turned out, the only colour were the grey skies up above.

The torrential downpour meant our 30 minutes each way game became 30 minutes in total and we had to wear soft shoes instead of boots to preserve the turf for the main match.

The rain did stop eventually, but it had been enough to keep the fans away. The 28,000-seater stadium had only five and a half thousand spectators that day.

Celtic turned on the style and won by five goals to nil.

It certainly wasn't the financial blockbuster Parky had been hoping for.

After the game he remarked sadly: "I brought them from Glasgow, but I never expected them to bring the bloody weather with them!"

However, over the years the unflappable Irishman would be involved in many schemes that were profitable; he wore more hats than Tommy Cooper in one of his hat sketches.

Born in Limavady, County Derry in 1942 he showed an early aptitude for writing and started in journalism at the tender age of 17 with the *Tyrone Courier*. He soon moved to the *Belfast Telegraph* where his mentor in those early years was the legendary Irish scribe, Malcolm Brodie.

The final Parky story I am about to recount took place in 2001, the year the flamboyant Irishman died of a brain tumour

His passing was a sad day for all who knew him through his exploits in journalism, horse racing, dog racing, football, television, radio, or just knew him as a good mate.

Tributes poured in from the sporting world, especially the racing fraternity:

> *"He was up there with the best racing journalists I've come across. He lived racing, really understood the sport, and was a very good friend."* – Mick Kinane, Irish racing legend

> *"He was a top-class journalist and a real expert on racing. His comments have always been beneficial to the development of racing in Hong Kong."* – Winfried Engelbrecht-Bresges, Director of Racing (currently CEO) of the Hong Kong Jockey Club

Parky had undergone an operation to remove a brain tumour in March 2000. He returned to work at the *SCMP* but had a relapse and was forced to retire in December that year.

One day in early March of the following year I went to visit him at his home in Happy Valley. There was another visitor sitting in his bedroom,

Australian horse trainer, David Hayes, then having his first training stint in Hong Kong. We talked with Parky as best we could, and then left as he tired easily.

As we stood waiting for the elevator David turned to me and said in a sombre tone, "It looks like the last furlong for our old pal." I just nodded.

David's words that day will always stay with me, not because it would eventually be the final furlong for Parky – he remained for a while – but because sadly, out of the blue, it was to be David's brother who would pass away unexpectedly just a week later.

Peter, a leading trainer in Australia, died when his light aircraft suffered mechanical problems and plunged to the ground.

Instead of passing my condolences on to Parky's wife, I was passing them on to David Hayes. One just never knows what's round the corner.

Anyone familiar with the southern hemisphere racing scene would know Peter and David were the sons of the renowned horse trainer, Colin Hayes who won the Melbourne Trainers' Premiership thirteen times.

Just before I headed back to the UK in mid-July 2001, to visit my old Mum in Glasgow, I sat with Parky, telling him I would see him again soon and to stay strong in the meantime.

The dreaded call came while I was still in Scotland: my dear old friend had finally passed away. I returned to Hong Kong somewhat earlier than planned and, being very close friends, took it upon myself to make the funeral arrangements.

Parky had married a local Chinese girl in 1970, Bobbie was her name, and I had attended the wedding along with Walter Gerrard and Jackie Trainer. They had two sons, but eventually the marriage fell apart. He subsequently remarried, to a Filipino lady named Juvette, and had another son and daughter.

Parky and I never discussed religion. He was a staunch Celtic fan so I automatically assumed he was a Catholic. I telephoned Juvette to try and verify this before going to visit St. Joseph's Catholic Church in Garden Road, Central.

"Of course Robin was a Catholic," she said, as if I had asked a dumb question.

By this time Parky's brother and sister-in-law had flown out to Hong Kong to help with the arrangements. His brother Davie was a sea captain, but fortunately he was not sailing on some far off ocean and was on home leave, so could attend the funeral.

When I met the Bishop in charge of the Catholic diocese I explained that Parky was not a regular practising Catholic. I assumed therefore that the service would not be too lengthy. I was quickly put in my place.

I was told firmly, that the Catholic funeral mass is the same service and procedure for everyone, regardless of how often they came to church.

I got busy with the arrangements. I hired a harpist to perform during and after the mass and bought appropriate CDs to be played later at his wake.

The mass at St. Joseph's Church was very well attended and was actually a very lovely service.

When it concluded the coffin was wheeled out of the church by close friends, including horse trainers, Lawrie Fownes and David Hill.

The next day Parky's body was taken to Cape Collinson Crematorium in Chai Wan on Hong Kong Island.

Brian Murphy a fellow Irishman and brother of famous Irish actor Gerard, gave a moving rendition of *Danny Boy*. Tears fell like raindrops as Parky was finally put to rest.

A wake was then held at the Hong Kong Football Club.

Day turned into night and after the official wake ended four of us took a taxi to Delaney's Irish Bar in Wan Chai. The four being Davie and Elaine, racing writer Jim McGrath and me.

So there we were, drinking and telling stories about Parky's exploits.

I was keen to learn a little of Parky's early life so I said to Davie: "I know your father was Catholic; did Robin have a strict Catholic upbringing? "

Davie almost choked on his beer.

"Our father a Catholic? He was a Presbyterian minister! Robin was a Protestant, and you sent him off with a Catholic mass!" he spluttered.

Now it was my turn to choke on my beer. The look on both Jimbo's face and mine was one of sheer astonishment.

We soon learned from Davie that if you said something was black, Robin would say it was white, that was the way he was. Davie gave us a few family stories to illustrate this contrariness and after a while we all eventually saw the funny side of what I'd done.

When it came time to say goodbye at the end of a long day, Davie turned to me and said, "You did a wonderful job arranging everything, thanks for all the effort. But when I die, please don't arrange my funeral; God only knows what religion you might choose for me!" Then, with tears welling in his eyes, he broke into a huge grin.

Big Jack

Scotland had played Uruguay in the Estadio Neza, just outside Mexico City, in the 1986 World Cup. The match was brutal. Had it been a movie it would have been X-rated; with the South Americans playing the part of the villains. If you weren't in your seat at kick-off you would have missed the first 'mistimed' tackle. It happened after just 56 seconds to be exact.

José Batista viciously scythed down Gordon Strachan from behind and subsequently went into the record books for being the fastest ever sending off in a World Cup finals game. That set the tone for the rest of the game which finished 0-0. Scotland had needed a win to qualify to the next round.

I wandered out of the stadium with Parky, who was covering it for the *SCMP*, slightly disappointed with the outcome of the match. Though not as depressed as Rod Stewart who was certainly not 'wearing it well' in the stand that day. In the strong late afternoon sunshine, we were walking to the media bus for the trip back to Mexico City. Up ahead there were some trees, which provided a partial shade, and standing alone under one of them was Jack Charlton – I found out later he was waiting for his wife Pat. Jack was then manager of the Republic of Ireland.

Although I'd never met him before, I knew he had a reputation for being very approachable, so I walked over to him and said, "What did you think of the game, Jack?" Briefly, without recounting the full conversation, he said: "They should be banned from World Cup tournaments, they think they have God's right to do anything they want. I hate to think what I might have done to some of them if I had been playing today!"

I had little doubt what he meant, it certainly lightened our mood. No half measures with Big Jack.

I would meet Jack again a few years later, when he came to Hong Kong, and I invited him to attend a Hamilton Accies Supporters Club luncheon at the Hong Kong Hilton. The Accies were a bunch of businessmen led by Roger Perrin who entertained visiting sportsmen over the years, such as Jimmy Greaves, Tommy Docherty, Bryan Robson, Gavin Hastings to name a few.

Subsequently, I got to know Jack well. So much so that he gave me his home telephone number. I remember him telling me one day: "If anybody from a newspaper calls me at my home, the first thing I ask is: are you football or news? if they say news, I put the phone down!" Jack told me he had no time for that side of the coin, he was only interested in talking football, nothing outside the realms of the game. Quite right too.

Of all the times that I met him, one I'll never forget is when I visited him at the Republic of Ireland's team camp near Lake Nemi, just before they played Italy in the quarter-finals of the Italia '90 World Cup in Rome. And yes, he had me laughing again.

I had been hoping I might bump into Jack at some stage during Italia '90, but to be honest, I hardly expected it to be two days before the Republic of Ireland's quarter-final against home nation Italy in Rome. Jack's boys had been on a remarkable run, they were now only two wins away from a spot in the final. Before the tournament this would have been thought as much a fantasy as the film *Darby O'Gill and the Little People*. Parts of the Republic's football adventure have been well documented by those in the Irish squad, but my tale is from the horse's mouth – if I can be excused for saying that about Jack – on the day it actually happened.

Picture the scene: there is to be a press conference at the Irish hotel after their final training session. The Media Centre had laid on a coach to get us there and it was packed to the rafters. There must have been every sports writer from Dundalk to Cork on board, as well as many from the Italian and foreign media. Security was tight. There was a roped-off area around the hotel guarded by the local Polizia. We arrived before the Irish team, but 10 minutes later their bus came into view.

One of the first off was Big Jack; he looked a bit weary as he trudged up the grassy knoll to the hotel. As he was getting nearer to where I was standing behind the rope I shouted out to catch his attention: "Jack, it's Derek." I was hoping to have a quick chat. Hearing me he looked over; next minute he's telling the security to let me through, shouting "C'mere." As I ducked under the rope a journalist next to me said in a lilting Irish accent, "Who the hell is he?" I was obviously Jack's pal! "I'm knackered," said Jack, "what a day it's been. What are you doing here?"

"Here to see you big man and wish you well."

"Let's have a drink," he said, and once inside the hotel ordered two pints of Tuborg from a pretty Italian waitress at the bar just inside the door.

"Come on, let's sit outside on the patio, it's cooler," he said. It was 7.30 in the evening. I am now in the enviable position of being alone with the man everybody wants to talk to, two days before the big game in Rome. Did we discuss, the upcoming game? Not initially. It was the early part of his day that he wanted to talk about. Jack had been to Rome to see Pope John Paul II in the Vatican's Sistine Chapel. What he said to me, as closely as I can remember, was:

"We had to get up before 5am this morning, but I promised the lads before the tournament that if we made it to Rome, we would have an audience with the Pope. You know he speaks in over four different languages, it takes forever, and being up so early I nodded off during the Mass. When I woke up, the Pope was looking in my direction and waving his hands, so, only half awake, I thought he was waving at me. I stood up and waved back. I was quickly pulled down by one of my staff who whispered, 'sit down Jack, he's giving the holy blessing!' Eventually, when the service was over we went forward to be introduced to his Holiness. He looked at me, and said: 'I know you, you are the Big Man.' What a day! The players and staff were over the moon. Still it's been a tiring day, what with all the travelling and then our training session, I'm dying of thirst, let's have another pint."

We then briefly talked about the game against Italy, just as some Irish and English accredited journalists were allowed into the hotel and came towards our table. "Give me ten minutes lads," Jack said, "just having a beer and a chat with a friend." It's not everyday that Big Jack gets an audience with both the Pope and *Ye So*, I jest. As I left a horde of journalists descended on him like locusts with the all too familiar questions: Do you know your line-up? Any injuries? Will Whelan play? The day had just got longer for Jack.

Next time I saw Jack it was in Hong Kong.

In January 1995 I brought him out to Hong Kong to make the draw for the Carlsberg Cup Chinese New Year football tournament. The trip was also a little holiday for Jack and he brought his wife Pat along for the 10-day visit.

I took him along to meet the Hong Kong League XI players – the team was also in the tournament – at their training session in So Kon Po. I also even took him to meet the Governor of Hong Kong, Chris Patten who was another keen to meet him. Jack was popular. Walking in the street with Jack there was no shortage of people wanting to greet him; Jack would reciprocate with a cheery greeting of his own.

Jack's big passion away from football was fishing. He liked nothing better than to go to Galway and cast his line alongside friends and he told me about one such trip which involved a few hours driving, they stopped at a pub, an hour from their destination, just for a pint. As he and his friends entered the pub they discovered that it was some old fella's birthday. "The pub was rocking more than Bill Haley," he told me. Before he knew it, the old fella came over to Jack and said, "I knew you would come to my party Jack." He firmly believed that that was why they were there.

"I hadn't the heart to tell him otherwise," said Jack. "Just as well we had a driver that day. We never got to the fishing either!" That was Jack, loved the Irish people and they loved him, both during, and after, his tenure as Ireland's manager. Anyone who got to know Jack Charlton was a lucky man.

On the day of his funeral in 2020 the national flag was flown at half-mast in Dublin for an Englishman, the son of a miner. What a tribute! At 12.30 that day everyone was asked to raise a glass to coincide with his funeral. I also did in an Irish pub in Bangkok. As we were six hours ahead of the UK I carried on and raised more than a few more glasses to the Big Man as the night wore on. I'm sure they did in Dublin as well.

Craig Brown and Jimmy Armfield

It was meant to be dinner for three in a popular restaurant on the Champs-Elysées, a short walk from the Arc de Triomphe. I was staying just around the corner at the Royal Hotel on Avenue de Friedland. I was in Paris for the 1998 World Cup final only five days away. My dinner partners were to be Craig Brown, or 'Broon' as he is affectionately known, who managed Scotland during their campaign in France, and referee Hugh Dallas, who oversaw the quarter-final between France and Italy. But there would be a fourth!

Craig Brown had asked to bring a pal along. He claimed this person didn't have a lot of friends in Paris and would appreciate the company. I said, "No problem, I'll book for four, what's your pals name?"

"Jimmy Armfield," he replied.

"Jimmy Armfield!" I spluttered, "the same Jimmy Armfield who was in the England 1966 World Cup squad, but unfortunately never played a match? Be a real pleasure to meet him."

Jimmy had played right-back for England during their four World Cup games in Chile in 1962. He had 43 caps for his country, and captained them 15 times. He was now commentating on games for the BBC. Jimmy spent his entire footballing career – all 17 years of it – with Blackpool and played alongside the legendary Stanley Matthews. That was in the days when players caught the same bus to the game as the fans!

Broon introduced us and we soon got chatting. I told Jimmy we had someone in common from our playing days – no, not Stanley Matthews – we had both played alongside Cheung Chi-doy! Chi-doy was the first ethnic Chinese to play in the top flight of English football, turning out as a youngster for Blackpool in 1960. I played alongside Chi-doy against both Santos and Hamburg as well as other sides with the Hong Kong League XI.

"He was a talented, skilful ball player, but I felt a bit sorry for him because he was on the end of some nasty tackles; his skills were not suited to the tough tackling English game at that time," Jimmy said of Chi-doy.

The dinner was *par excellence* and the full-bodied Chardonnay slipped down a treat. But for me, the conversation and stories were just as tasty as the food. At some stage the topic of football technology came up. Obviously this was before the days of VAR and refereeing top games was a big job for an individual, trying to see everything that happened on the field. The suggestion from those supporting the use of technology was that referees needed more help, with some pundits even suggesting a referee in each half of the field. This was something Hugh Dallas quickly shot down, saying referees have their own interpretation of the flow of a game so two refs was a non-starter. Did the ball cross the line or not had often been the catalyst for the introduction of technology, remember this was 1998. I need hardly mention the often debated affair of 1966.

But I remember that night for what Jimmy Armfield said on goal-line technology: "It's simple, I've been saying it for years on the radio, but nobody listens to me, and it would hardly cost a penny."

"What's that Jimmy?" I asked as the waiter poured us another glass of white.

"All you need is somebody sitting in a seat behind the goal with a flag. If he raises it over his head it's a goal. Simple as that." Many might think that old fashioned, but in reality, it would have been a good start. But far too spartan and simple for FIFA to implement. That particular debate would continue until VAR came in twenty years later at the World Cup finals in Russia – at a considerably greater cost than a man on a chair with a flag I can tell you.

George Best and Bill McMurdo

"Do you want to play on the right wing?" I asked one Sunday morning on the military football pitch situated a short stroll from the Government Stadium.

"Better not, I have a game in a couple of days, and if the club hear about it they could be pissed off, but I'll run the line for you," said the 1968 European Footballer of the Year, George Best.

George had come to Hong Kong with his agent, the one and only Bill McMurdo. Whereas George refrained from playing, McMurdo was our centre-forward against the Senior Rates' Mess from HMS Tamar that morning. Our team was the Carlsberg All Stars, a side I put together for friendly games against military or social clubs.

The team were a motley crew: a senior policeman, jockeys, former FA Cup winners, English Division One managers, ex-players, and some of the best-known characters who roamed the streets of Hong Kong and Kowloon. Micky Horswill, who won the FA Cup with Sunderland in 1973; Ron Wylie, who managed at Aston Villa and West Bromwich Albion; and jockey Wally Hood, were just some of the stars.

That Sunday morning, George ran the line and seemed to enjoy it. It was 1982 and he was in Hong Kong to play a couple of games with Sea Bee, followed by a brief stint with Hong Kong Rangers. We won 8-2 and Bill McMurdo scored five. He could have scored twenty five – slight exaggeration – but George was having fun and disallowed a few for offside, when clearly they weren't. After the game we headed to the Senior Rates' Mess in the Prince of Wales Building at HMS Tamar. The mess situated high in the 28-storey building afforded great views of the harbour.

The Navy boys put on a lovely buffet for us and I had laid on a couple of kegs of beer to be quaffed after the exertions on the field. It was all going great, George was signing autographs left, right and centre and posing for photographs. After all, it was not every Sunday that the mercurial George Best was in the mess. We had been there for 25 minutes when a member of the Senior Rates' team asked to have a quiet word with me. I was taken aback when he said to me, "George will have to leave the mess, someone's complained. He's wearing tracksuit bottoms and flip-flops, they are not allowed in the mess. I'm sorry, but there's nothing we can do Derek."

George – who had been drinking only orange juice – left without a word of complaint, and we followed in a show of solidarity. George could easily have sat in a quiet area, or worn borrowed trousers or shoes as the rest of us were hardly dressed for a civic reception, but some sanctimonious twat wanted to make a name for himself and no doubt boast he got George Best kicked out of his mess. Many of the lads in the Senior Rates' team apologized, but army/navy rules and regulations are paramount, even in messes, so we accepted it.

Bill McMurdo was George Best's agent and personal adviser for 15 years. In later years he would manage many stars, including Andrés Iniesta of Barcelona. One day Bill said to me during George's stay "Derek, can you arrange some trips to keep George occupied? He's got a lot of spare time on his hands and I don't want him getting bored and going to the pub if he's got nothing to do." So, I arranged some ports of call that didn't involve alcohol: trips to Macau, Stanley Market and the beach at Repulse Bay. I knew George had a penchant for the horses, so I also arranged a Wednesday night at Happy Valley racing.

We had a prime location on the fifth floor of the members' stand, in a box reserved for members of the Hong Kong Football Club, Kowloon Cricket Club and Hong Kong Cricket Club. After 10 minutes or so that Wednesday night, Joanni Lane, the wife of then horse trainer and former Jockey Club steward Geoff Lane, cried out "That can't be George Best, he's drinking tea!"

"It is, and yes, Joanni, he is drinking tea!" I replied.

Despite being offered something stronger, George stuck to tea. He backed three winners that night.

I played in a darts team in Hong Kong called the 'Presstuds', so named because it comprised journalists and footballers. Carlsberg sponsored the team shirts and I got George and Bill to play for us during their stint in Hong Kong. It never ceased to amuse me when an opponent would observe disbelievingly that he was about to contest a match with the legendary George Best.

Under the watchful eye of Bill McMurdo, George refrained from drinking alcohol; but it was too good to last. I was in Rumours Bar in Causeway Bay with custodian Billy Semple having a half-pint and discussing business. In walked George with McMurdo nowhere in sight, "make it three half-pints Billy" and we stayed there for another four hours. Needless to say, McMurdo was not too pleased with me and Billy! But only for a little while, I'm happy to say.

The last time I saw George was a number of years later inside a bookies shop in London; he was a keen punter and good at it too. (Mind you, he wasn't a bad linesman either.) There's a short postscript to the story concerning Bill McMurdo, who I still stay in contact with today.

It must have been six or seven years after the Hong Kong visit by George and Bill. I had just arrived back in Glasgow to visit my dear old Mum in Dennistoun. I like to contact old pals when I'm back, so on Saturday morning, July 8, I picked up the phone and gave Bill a call.

"Nice to hear from you Derek, back to see your wee mum?" he said.

We made small talk and then I asked him how things were going with his soccer management and agency business; I'll never forget the answer he gave me. "There will be a story in a couple of days which will shake the foundations of Scottish football."

"C'mon Bill, you can trust me, what's going to happen?"

"Sorry, Derek, your big brother writes for the *Daily Record*, so it's not fair to put you in an awkward position, it's such a big story you might be tempted to tell him."

I left it there, and to be honest I was not up to date with the local football scene so had no idea what type of story was about to explode. The story broke on Monday, July 10, and it wasn't the one about Tommy Trinder dying at the age of 90. It was Mo Johnston, becoming the first high profile Catholic player to sign for Glasgow Rangers!

You would need to live on the moon not to know of the awful religious divide between supporters of Celtic and Rangers in Scotland; so much so that even the Church of Scotland and the Roman Catholic Church in Scotland, were asked to comment on the news after it broke.

McMurdo had brokered the deal; no wonder he had kept mum.

Kenny Dalglish

Another chap I met on a trip back home had also done rather well since we last met. I bumped into him at Anfield during the 1996 European Championship. We had spoken over the years, but had never managed to meet in the flesh. Ships in the night and all that, but let me take you back to the 1967/68 season in Scotland.

They say you can't put an old head on young shoulders, but Kenny Dalglish turned that adage on its head. As an 18-year-old I played alongside him when he was farmed out from Celtic to Cumbernauld United Juniors.

For those not familiar with Scotland's grading of football Cumbernauld United were a Scottish junior side, the Scottish Junior Football Association is an affiliate of the National Association and is the governing body for the 'Junior' grade of football in Scotland. The term 'Junior' refers to the level of football played, not the age of the players. It means that experienced professionals, getting close to their sell-by-date, can drop down to this level, still play a good standard of football, and continue to earn some money from the game. At the opposite end of the scale, it's a grade where young players can develop and, if they're good enough, be snapped up by big professional clubs. Finally, it's a grade where young professionals from the top clubs can be sent to play for a year to allow them more regular playing time; which is what Celtic did with Kenny.

He was a mere 16 years of age, but what I recall, more than anything, was how mature he was on the field – as we were both forwards I got to enjoy a close-up view. A few of our team were over thirty years of age, some with years of professional experience. Did that faze Kenny? No, quite the opposite, he used to shout out instructions as if he was the captain of the side, demanding where the ball should be played and moaning when poor passes went astray. Confidence he had in spades! Little wonder he went on to win 102 caps for Scotland.

However, off the park he was more prone to act his age. We shared some good laughs together as well as some tough times on the field. There's a great picture of us taken to promote Miss Cumbernauld after she won the title. Holding up the beauty queen were Abe Monaghan, Ian McEwan, our club captain, Kenny and I. That picture is still floating about on the internet – one of the few still around of me minus the beard and with short hair – but some might not even recognize the young Dalglish standing next to me.

I recall a Scottish Junior Cup quarter-final tie we played against Johnstone Burgh, away from home one Saturday afternoon in 1967. They were a good side, with a great cup reputation, but Kenny's skill and my speed that day were causing the Burgh defence all sorts of problems and it looked only a matter of time until we scored. Step up David Chisholm, the Burgh centre-half, to change all that.

I was on a run through the middle when he crudely pulled me down. For good measure he stamped on my nose for afters, with the accompanying message: "That will slow you down, you little bastard!" With blood streaming down my face, I was taken off for treatment and played no further part. The game ended in a scoreless draw.

That night our team captain Jackie McKenna was having a party at his home and we were all invited; we had been hoping it would be a victory celebration to get into the semi-final of the Scottish Junior Cup. There was no real medical treatment within the club, so I decided to go to the Glasgow Ear, Nose and Throat hospital after the game to see if my nose was broken or needed further medical treatment.

Up piped Kenny: "I'll come along with you to the hospital and we can go to the party together afterwards." I should mention at this stage that Kenny's father, along with mine, used to come and watch us playing together. Kenny's father had also asked my Dad if I could keep an eye on him; me being 18, two years older than his son.

I told Kenny he could come to the hospital with me, but I had a date to pick up afterwards, before we went to the party. "Any problem?" he asked.

"No, better you come with me, I know where the party is."

Kenny waited patiently at the hospital. My prognosis: nothing broken, but the bone in my nose was slightly misshapen, but that could be rectified later if need be. With two cotton wool pellets stuck up my nose and some bruising, I looked more like Lon Chaney than Robert Redford! Kenny and I walked to the rendezvous point where I was to meet my date. Kenny spotted a girl standing alone and, by way of a compliment, said, "She looks nice."

"She's with me," I said sternly. Then we both laughed, all good fun.

On seeing the look of horror on my date's face I quickly explained to her what had happened; then the three of us took a Glasgow Corporation bus to the party. On arrival at the party Kenny looked at me sheepishly and asked, "Can I have a shandy?"

I said, "No, you can have a Coca-Cola, I told your dad I'd watch you."

"Okay," he grumbled.

When the party ended I put my date onto her bus home and Kenny and I caught our bus; no flash cars in those days. That cup tie quarter-final against Johnstone Burgh eventually went to a third replay. In the coldest conditions I have experienced in my entire life, we lost 1-0 at the neutral ground of Rob Roy in Kirkintilloch. I won't go into too many details of the game except to say the field that day could have been a scene from the movie *Ice Station Zebra*.

There was a gale force wind blowing down from the Campsie Fells and cold sleet flew almost horizontally through the air. I think the only reason it went ahead was to avoid more fixture congestions. To make matters worse for us, Kenny was injured and couldn't take part, he was sitting in the stand, so I was left as our main striker.

Before the game – *Scott of the Antarctic* comes to mind, I kid you not – it was freezing so hard our team manager insisted we all take a nip of brandy to fend off the cold. Not the norm for a footballer before a game, but believe me this was needed to brave the cold. That's how bloody freezing it was!

In later years I had tried inviting Kenny to come to Hong Kong to make the draw for the Carlsberg Cup, but he told me he was not keen on long haul flights. I finally met him again by accident. I was in Britain covering the 1996 Euro Championships for *The Standard* as was Robin Parke for the *South China Morning Post*. While walking through the press room at Anfield prior to one match, Robin said, "There's your pal Kenny sitting over there."

As I walked towards Kenny he was in discussion with a chap who looked vaguely familiar. I think it was one of the tabloid journalists from England. I overheard them saying something about Terry Venables, Gascoigne and Hong Kong. I immediately said to Kenny, "Yes, when are you coming to Hong Kong to see me?"

He looked up, smiled, and said to the journalist, "He used to babysit me!"

Priceless, a brilliant answer!

I like to call Kenny a dear old friend. I'm really proud of what he has achieved through football and the extra yards he went for Liverpool fans and their families after the tragedy of Hillsborough.

When we left the Glasgow Ear, Nose and Throat hospital all those years ago, two young boys, one 18, the other 16, who would have believed that the younger one would go on to become 'King Kenny' in Liverpool and be knighted by Prince Charles, while the other would be called 'Jesus' in Hong Kong... a small miracle.

Acknowledgements

I was privileged to meet a wonderful assortment of characters on my journey, many sadly not with us any more, but I'm sure still looking down from above. I hope I have brought some of them back to life through the pages of this book. But without the acceptance of the Hong Kong people and football fans it would never have been written. They made me welcome from day one. I only hope I made them proud when I represented them on the football field. I will always feel Hong Kong is my adopted home.

I would like to thank my mum, dad and brothers who were always there for me and encouraged me to pursue my footballing dream; my wife Stella, daughter Claudia and son Philip for their patience and support over the years; and Walter and Jackie who were with me as we embarked on this incredible journey and who remained great friends.

Many thanks also to Barry Arnold, my old advertising pal, who helped in the early stages of the book, Mike Ingham for some constructive ideas and John Charlesworth for the steady hand behind me.

I am very grateful to Craig Brown, Roy Hodgson, Gavin Hastings, John Dykes, Philip Robinson and Lai Yu-ching for their kind and supportive words. And Sir Alex Ferguson for always being there as an old friend of the Currie family and for consoling me when my oldest brother Dick died.

Thanks too to Pete Spurrier at Blacksmith Books for giving me the chance to write about a special era in one of the greatest cities in the world.

And finally, a special mention for Ian Petrie; we had our differences but I owe him a big debt of gratitude for the opportunity he gave me.

EXPLORE ASIA WITH BLACKSMITH BOOKS

From booksellers around the world or from *www.blacksmithbooks.com*

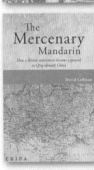

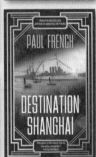